Built by the People Themselves

Built by the People Themselves

African American Community Development in Arlington, Virginia, from the Civil War through Civil Rights

LINDSEY BESTEBREURTJE

THE UNIVERSITY OF
SOUTH CAROLINA PRESS

Published by the University of South Carolina Press
Columbia, South Carolina 29208

uscpress.com

Printed in the United States of America

Library of Congress Cataloging-in-Publication Data
can be found at http://catalog.loc.gov/.

ISBN: 978-1-64336-497-1 (hardcover)
ISBN: 978-1-64336-498-8 (paperback)
ISBN: 978-1-64336-499-5 (ebook)

To my children,
without whom I could have
finished this book in half the time.

Contents

List of Illustrations

Preface

When I moved to Arlington, Virginia, in the fall of 2009 to pursue my graduate degree in history, I did not anticipate that my new home would become the topic of my research. A native of Virginia, I grew up in neighboring Fairfax County. The idea that the suburban environs around me would hold enough history and enough meaning and insight to provide for a historical deep dive had yet to occur to me. Like so many, I wrongly assumed that suburban history began in the 1960s. I thought little of the race, class, legal, and environmental dynamics at play in the residential, often homogenous, spaces of the American suburb that so many call home.

My future husband, Justin, and I chose to live in the charming condos of the Shirlington neighborhood in southern Arlington. At the time, this area was far less expensive than the more bustling, semi-urban Ballston or Clarendon neighborhoods. One day, while out on a walk with our beloved dog, a beagle mix named Roscoe, I saw a wayside along the Washington & Old Dominion trail reading "Nauck: A Neighborhood History." The sign told of free Blacks Levi and Sarah Jones, who purchased land and built a home in 1844, beginning what would become the African American suburban community. I had no idea that Arlington's suburban roots stretched so far back. More significantly, I had no idea that African American home ownership and communities were even a possibility in the antebellum South. My mind raced with questions. How did this community come to be? How did it survive the Civil War, the Jim Crow South, suburbanization, and gentrification through to today?

These questions merged with my academic interests in suburbanization, residential segregation, and the role of the built environment in people's lives. The prospect of telling a local history of an African American community who did not receive the respect and attention that they deserved in the past merged with my professional commitment to public history. I believe that historians are public servants who are responsible with the task of preserving the past and telling complicated stories for a public who may be bettered by hearing them. In this way, I hope that my research may be used by Arlington's residents—former, current, and future—to know a part of their own history. I also hope that, by using my research as a guidepost, other African Americans may be able to find their own long roots in America's suburban landscape. May this book be a spark for future conversations and learning opportunities.

Acknowledgments

I thank some of the people who contributed to the success of this book.

Thanks to the many archivists, librarians, and professionals from the Arlington Central Library's Center for Local History, Virginia Historical Society, Library of Virginia, George Mason University Special Collections and Archives, and University of Virginia Special Collections and Archives who helped me through the research and writing process. Special thanks for Ehren Foley and the entire University of South Carolina Press team.

Throughout this project I had the honor to work alongside some inspiring individuals. Thank you to all my wonderful colleagues at the Smithsonian Institution's National Museum of African American History and Culture, with special thanks to Spencer Crew, Paul Gardullo, Kevin Strait, and William Pretzer. Thank you to my academic advisors and mentors, Jennifer Ritterhouse and Zachary Schrag. Without the personal, professional, and academic support of each of you this project would not have been possible.

Thank you to some of the amazing friends in my life—Aimee, Elizabeth, Jess, Katy, and Lara. Special recognition must be reserved for Jackie Beatty, not only for her assistance with this book, but also for her steadfast friendship. The love and unyielding commitment of these women brings the world into focus, revealing the deep colors that only true friendship can lay bare.

Most important to note I give credit for the success and completion of this project to my family. To my incredible husband, Justin Rodgers, who helped to keep me both sane and motivated, a Sisyphean feat. To my children, Emma and Andrew, who bring me the kind of joy every day that was once reserved for only Christmas mornings. To my Mom, Donna Bestebreurtje, who led by example to show me the unparalleled power of hard work and dedication. To my dearly departed Dad, Anton Bestebreurtje, for sharing with me his love of history and reading. I know you would have been so proud to read this book. To my sister Katie Koentje, for always being my biggest fan, best friend, and for bringing three delightful men into my life: Erik, Ryan, and Grayson. To the family I gained through marriage—Steve, Terry, Meg, Dan, Max, Katy, Grant, and Sidney—for their love and encouragement. And to the entire Bestebreurtje, Baker, Button, Cantwell, Cash, Fitzpatrick, Jackson, Kelly, McCormick, Reitz, Rodgers, and Zirinksy clans: thank you.

I would not be who I am, or where I am, without all of you. You can take that as an insult or a compliment.

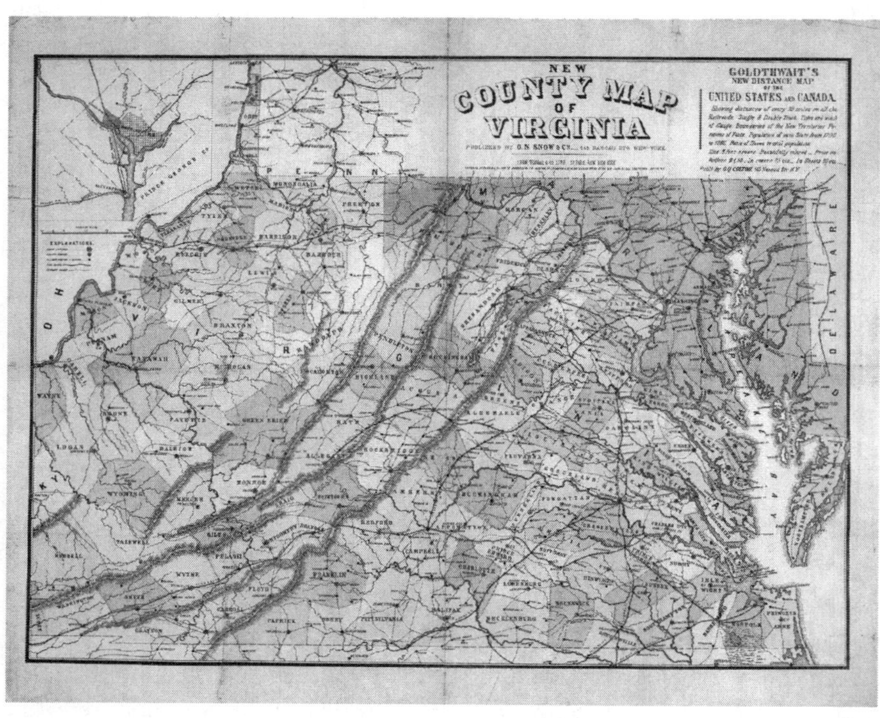

FIGURE 1. Map of Virginia counties, including Arlington, at the beginning of the Civil War. O. N. Snow & Company and Crow, Thomas & Co. *New county map of Virginia*. New York: O. N. Snow & Company, 1861. Maps Division, Library of Congress.

Introduction
Arlington's People and Communities

In the early 1860s, Hiram Fleet fled enslavement in southern Virginia for the Freedman's Village contraband camp in Arlington, Virginia. There, he and his wife, Ellen, a fellow self-emancipating slave from Virginia, began their family in freedom. At Freedman's Village, they became community leaders, helped to found Mount Zion Church, and started their family. Hiram and Ellen imparted to their children the importance of community leadership and activism. After the closure of Freedman's Village at the turn of the century, their oldest son, Edmund Fleet Sr., purchased a home in the Black middle-class Butler-Holmes neighborhood.

Edmund's leadership extended beyond his individual neighborhood as a leader with the all-Black Freemason Lodge in Green Valley, the Odd Fellows in Johnson's Hill, and at Mount Zion Church, which relocated from Freedman's Village to Green Valley. Edmund Sr.'s wife, Mary, helped to found the ladies' auxiliaries of those organizations. Their son, Edmund Fleet Jr., continued to be active in Arlington's community as an Odd Fellow, a leader within Mount Zion, and a founding member of Arlington's YMCA. A federal employee with the Navy, Edmund Jr. lived in the African American Johnson's Hill community in "a comfortable two-story brick home."[1] Edmund Jr. and his family of six moved to Johnson's Hill from Butler-Holmes in the mid-twentieth century. By this time, the Butler-Holmes neighborhood ceased to be an exclusively Black enclave.[2] The multigenerational Fleet family continued their decades-long leadership and involvement in Arlington's Black communities into the late twentieth century. Edmund Jr.'s son William H. Fleet was an active leader at Mount Zion and a federal employee. Meanwhile, in the 1960s, Alice B. Fleet returned to Arlington to teach public school after earning her master's degree from the University of Pennsylvania. Alice was an active member and frequently served in leadership positions within Arlington's Democratic Party, school board, YMCA, and League of Women Voters through the 1970s.[3]

The story of the Fleets is the story of Arlington's strong African American community. Drawn to the area by Freedman's Village, the Fleet family took advantage of federal employment opportunities and supported community institutions within and beyond the neighborhoods where they lived. They moved throughout the county as Arlington's Black neighborhoods developed and then shuttered because of federal and state changes, zoning and planning legislation, and shifts in local attitudes and realities. Despite the loss of specific neighborhoods, Arlington's strong Black parallel institutions—including churches, schools, and social, political, and fraternal organizations—endured. These institutions and the people behind them worked to ensure the continuance of Arlington's three anchor Black communities of Green Valley, Hall's Hill, and Johnson's Hill.

Built by the People Themselves tracks African American community development as the processes of suburbanization and segregation shaped lives, the built environment, and the law in the Northern Virginia county of Arlington from the 1860s to the 1970s. This book's title, *Built by the People Themselves*, comes from dual sources. In an oral history interview with community leader Terry Townsend, he lamented that Black homes had to be "built by the people themselves" in the face of a hostile county.[4] This complaint could apply to virtually any aspect of Black life in Arlington from the 1860s through the 1960s. However, this same quote also arises in an interview with African American county resident John Henderson.[5] Where Townsend is lodging a complaint, Henderson is noting a point of pride within his neighborhood. These dual ideas, of a hostile white environment and an active Black community, represent the broader goals of revealing the strategies that Black Arlingtonians used to create lasting communities that met their own needs and reflected their own preferences to the greatest extent possible within the context of white domination in a Jim Crow society.

Built by the People Themselves offers a detailed exploration of the small and little-known community of Arlington. Diverging from narratives that look at Black communities as aggregates or abstractions on the national or state level, this book examines the diverse and often interconnected forces that shaped lived experiences and, in turn, reveal universal truths. Individual stories of how families, neighborhoods, institutions, and communities interacted with their world sheds light on how common people developed strategies to survive and thrive despite systems of oppression in the Jim Crow South. By exploring how those systems were created, and maintained, on the microlevel, we are able to better understand how individuals and families built communities that reflected both their hopes for the future—with schools, churches, and fraternal orders—and contended with the realities of a restrictive present—exclusionist municipal improvements, racialized laws, and residential segregation with walls that, at times, literally boxed them in.

By 1950, Arlington County, Virginia, looked on a map like one continuous suburb of Washington, DC, but in reality, Arlington consisted of a series of distinct and diverse neighborhoods, each with divergent and often competing visions for the area's future. Some of the oldest and most enduring of these neighborhoods were the three African American communities of Hall's Hill, Johnson's Hill, and Green Valley. Their histories stretch back to antebellum Virginia and the area's influx of freed people during and after the Civil War.

It was not just these neighborhoods that endured but also their residents. Arlington's Black residents were a stable group, in contrast to many white residents of the area. They also had high rates of home ownership. In 1900, fifty-nine percent of Black families in Arlington owned their homes, above the national rate of 46.5% of home ownership for all Americans that same year.[6] These numbers continued to rise to sixty-four percent by 1920, with little turnover in home ownership for the next twenty years. This stability reflects the fact that several generations of Arlington's African American residents stayed in the homes and neighborhoods where they grew up. However, this seeming stability masks an encroaching white populace whose leaders attempted to push out Arlington's Black residents.

The 1860s and the early 1970s were bookends of major periods of transition for Arlington's Black neighborhoods and their populations. In 1863, the federal government created Freedman's Village as a contraband camp for formerly enslaved African Americans during the Civil War. Freedman's Village became Arlington's largest Black community and was the county's first entirely preplanned neighborhood. However, beginning in the 1880s, a white population that was revitalized after the destruction of the Civil War exerted social and legal pressures against Freedman's Village and Arlington's Black residents. White groups consisting of individual citizens, Arlington's social and political leaders, land developers, and the federal government, who all wanted county lands for themselves, mounted extreme pressures against Freedman's Village and its Black residents.[7] From the 1880s to 1900, all these groups worked to close Freedman's Village in an attempt to rip it from the Black families who called it home, removing what social and political power Black residents had at the same time.[8]

This closure sparked a movement of African Americans across the county, forming new communities and expanding those settlements founded before and immediately after the Civil War. With smaller periods of transition in the interim, the 1940s saw major changes in Arlington's Black living patterns as federal buildup for World War II defense industries pushed out Black communities and reshaped the makeup of the remaining African American communities through federally subsidized housing. Zoning, planning, restrictive covenants, redevelopment, and loan policies were all used to restrict and attempt to push out Arlington's Black population. Black homes and families who lived in nearly a dozen settlements in 1900 were constricted to only the three anchor communities by 1950. Despite this constriction within Arlington County's increasingly standardized suburban environment, community members remained active in neighborhood and cross-county organizations while also working to preserve their homes and communities for future generations. From 1965 to 1973, their places in the county solidified when the active organization of community residents forced the Arlington Planning Commission to include plans to preserve these neighborhoods in their Neighborhood Conservation Program.[9] *Built by the People Themselves* reveals how these neighborhoods survived and thrived, studying residents' tactics for resistance, community building, and adaptation in their struggle to stay in the homes they made for themselves and their families.

About Arlington County

Arlington is a 25.7-square-mile county in Northern Virginia, directly across the Potomac River from Washington, DC. The area that would become Arlington had notable connections to the early explorations of John Smith in 1608 and as lands owned by founding fathers George Washington and George Mason. However, the lands of the county did not become a distinct area until 1790, when Virginia donated Arlington County and Alexandria City to form a portion of Washington, DC.[10] In 1846, the District retroceded Virginia's lands back to the Old Dominion.[11]

From that time until 1870, Arlington and Alexandria functioned unofficially as separate entities. Even during the years of their formal connection, many local laws and regulations stipulated whether they were intended for the "city" or the "county" portion of what was collectively known as Alexandria. In 1870, changes to Virginia's state constitution allowed the two entities to formally split into separate municipalities. County leaders and residents alike embraced this split because the city and growing suburban county had conflicting needs and visions for their futures. They frequently competed over resources and clashed over issues of land use, but beginning in 1870, Arlington County was free to determine the trajectory of its own development without the influence of Alexandria City.

Although they functioned independently beginning in 1870, city and county were both known as "Alexandria" until 1920. County residents pushed for a new name because by the first decades of the twentieth century the county shared little with the city. Arlington had a built environment and municipal trajectory distinct from the urban development of Alexandria City. After the close of the Civil War, suburban village neighborhoods, constructed in isolation from one another, dominated the landscape. Newly minted white developers, who were often large landowners transitioning to amateur developers, laid out these villages. White county leaders used the decades around the turn of the century to create neighborhoods that fit their visions of ideal suburban environments. At the same time, they created a social and political environment that strengthened those neighborhoods. Together, the built environment and new political climate allowed county leaders to connect their neighborhoods and the visions of their founders into one dense suburban environment. Through these processes, Arlington's white community moved from one of isolated suburban villages to one contiguous suburban environment. In contrast, Alexandria continued to grow not as a suburban environment connected to the federal city but as a mixed-use urban environment.

Beyond distinctions in their preferred physical environments, county and city residents often did not see eye to eye on political matters. In 1846, county residents did not support retrocession back to Virginia from the District of Columbia as city residents did.[12] In 1860, county residents voted to remain a part of the Union, whereas city residents preferred the Confederacy. These early patterns of social divergence continued. As the county's population grew, they continued to want their own identity. By 1920, Arlington's population warranted their own seat in Virginia's General Assembly.[13] Although locals knew the difference between the areas, outsiders frequently grouped the city and county together because of their shared name, often making the county the *de facto* subordinate to the city. To distinguish themselves, Arlington white political leaders changed the county's name to Arlington after the plantation home of the county's most famous resident, Robert E. Lee, and the internationally famous Arlington National Cemetery.

Additionally, Arlingtonians wanted to create a distinct name because of bad blood between the two jurisdictions. Throughout the first decades of the twentieth century as Arlington's suburban environment expanded, Alexandria saw the true value of the lands they had lost in 1870 and began to position itself to take land from the county. In two court cases concluding in 1915 and 1929, the state's Supreme Court of Appeals deemed that "it is necessary and expedient that the corporate limits of the City of Alexandria should be extended."[14] With these new boundaries, Arlington lost three thousand acres to Alexandria.[15] These acres amounted to major losses in territory, resources, rail lines, sources of revenue, communities, and the tax base. After the 1915 decision, the county underwent a name change from Alexandria County to Arlington County in 1920. For the purpose of clarity, "Arlington" will be used throughout this book to describe the areas outside the City of Alexandria that were, nonetheless, called "Alexandria" until 1920.

Because of this informal separation of laws, lands, and people and the formal break between the two in the late nineteenth century, I deal little with Alexandria City. Then, as now, Arlington residents see themselves as largely removed from Alexandria, instead looking to D.C. in situations when community beyond the physical county is invoked. This narrative decision around scope is further supported by the historical record. Authors such as Krystyn R. Moon have shown how the trajectory of Alexandria's development and its impacts on the Black community support rather than challenge the overall narrative provided her of Arlington's Black communities. This bolstering rather than challenging of arguments further supports my decision to leave Alexandria City beyond the scope of this analysis.

About the Work

These realities of Arlington's communities, institutions, employment opportunities, and social and political makeup both reinforce and challenge elements of our contemporary understandings of African American community development. The role of community development across this timeline of more than one hundred years interacts and intersects with diverse elements of the Black lived experience. Areas of research including the built environment, political policy, education, segregation, suburbanization, parallel institutions, class, and more. This book is in conversation with the historians whose works interact with these topics, such as Andrew Weise, Kevin M. Kruse, Thomas J. Sugrue, Matthew Lassiter, Andrew Lewis, Leslie Brown, Catherine W. Bashir, Krystyn R. Moon, Eric S. Yellin, Andrew Friedman, and Thomas W. Hanchett.[16] Despite the many varied article- and book-length studies, there are holes that need to be addressed to create a more accurate historical picture. One way to address them is to explore the American South more fully. In timeline and scope, this book is similar to Thomas W. Hanchett's *Sorting Out the New South City*. However, Arlington's suburban landscape and reliance on blue- and white-collar federal employment make the patterns of residential segregation unique from the New South City of Charlotte, North Carolina. Although the cities of the Sunbelt and New South have received a great deal of attention, not enough work has been done on the American South, especially the upper-south state of Virginia. The works which do study the community development of the Old Dominion tend to focus on upper middle-class white suburban neighborhoods. Those that analyze African American community development tend to study Richmond alone. As an industrial city reliant on river and then rail travel, Richmond's development is not the same as that of Arlington, with its reliance on federal employment.

This book offers a detailed look at the relatively unknown Arlington Black communities, spotlighting the individuals and families who lived within them. In telling their stories, the work amplifies the lived experiences of the formerly anonymous, moving from the aggregate to the specific. In exploring how major historical trends shaped the lives of common citizens in Arlington, both Black and white, one can see the ways in which national changes impacted people's individual lives. By looking at the community level, one can fully understand how national changes shape lives. Experiences that seem hyperspecific or entirely personal are truly universal. This historical approach echoes both contemporary social histories and the long tradition of African American biography. As historian Kate Masur points out, African American biographies have long used deeply personal stories, like those shared here of Arlington's residents, "to explain the nuances of lives shaped not only by oppression, but also by agency and aspiration."[17]

Chapter 1, "Where They Had Lived Undisturbed for Nearly a Quarter of a Century," looks at the creation and expansion of Arlington's Black communities from 1840 to the Reconstruction Era.[18] This chapter looks at the persistent Black communities of Green Valley and Hall's Hill, with a central focus on Freedman's Village—a contraband camp unique in its focus on education, nonagrarian employment, and use of cutting-edge nineteenth century urban and suburban planning. Here, Arlington's African American residents created schools, churches, and cultural institutions that shaped the communities development for generations.

Chapter 2, "Gone Out to Do for Themselves," explores Arlington's communities in the late-nineteenth and early-twentieth centuries.[19] This includes the closure of Freedman's Village in 1900, which led to the creation or expansion of nearly a dozen African American communities in what I call the "Freedman's Village diaspora." At the same time, Arlington's white social and political leaders expanded their control while whites-only suburban villages spread. Exploring how Black and white neighborhoods interacted is key to understanding Arlington's community development.

Chapter 3, "Suburban Homes . . . in Sight of the Monument," provides a deeper look at suburban expansion in Arlington.[20] As the built environment of streetcar suburbs expanded, so too did the social and political control of white politicians, planners, and boosters, as these individuals and their institutions expanded their suburban visions of preplanned, white, middle-class communities from community-level regulation to broader attempts at control through countywide legislative changes that governed where and how communities and their people could live and grow, profoundly affecting Arlington's Black communities.

Chapter 4, "So That We May Occupy Our Rightful Place," explores continued changes for Arlington's people and built environment into the 1930s.[21] As local and state political changes limited the scope of Black rights, Arlington's Black families and communities had to adapt. Racialized zoning, planning, and municipal laws questioned the validity of Arlington's Black neighborhoods by legislating against the types of homes and environments they created in their neighborhoods. Against these mounting pressures, Black Arlingtonians used new and preexisting community institutions, a stable population, familial relations, employment, and new strategies to both adapt to and contest the countywide legal and social changes that worked against them in an attempt to maintain spaces for themselves in suburban Arlington.

Chapter 5, "Everybody Was Coming to Washington in Those Days," looks at the rapid expansion of Arlington's population and homes in the wake of the extreme expansion of the federal government during the New Deal, World War II, and the Cold War.[22] Additionally, the expansion of the federal government beyond Washington at this time had profound effects on Arlington's built environment, especially with the creation of the War Department's Pentagon building which led to the demolition of the Queen City and East Arlington Black communities. By 1950, only the three Black communities of Hall's Hill, Johnson's Hill, and Green Valley remained.

Chapter 6, "We Cannot Lose This Fight as We Lost Our Freedoms during Reconstruction Days," explores the changing political and social dynamics in Arlington.[23] The area's new residents were increasingly well-educated individuals raised beyond the South who did not embrace older political models based around small government, little spending, and racial hegemony. Because they were able to use their stable population and strong community institutions to survive to see a more socially liberal Arlington emerge, Arlington's remaining three Black communities were able to use new legislation to their own ends. In this more liberal social and political climate, Arlington's strong Black community successfully battled in court for school integration, making Arlington the first area in the state to integrate its schools in 1959. From 1965 until 1973, each of Arlington's three Black communities successfully applied for recognition as historically significant under Arlington's Neighborhood Conservation Program, revealing how collective action, parallel institutions, and neighborhood development established an African American community able and determined to carve out places for themselves in Arlington, Virginia.

Although it contains diverse elements, at its core, this is a study of African American community development, especially as it relates to suburban expansion. Previously works looked at suburbanization only through the lens of Black exclusion and white flight.[24] This great oversight began to be rectified in the 1990s and into the new millennium. With the rise of African American history in suburban studies, community building became a major focus.[25] This is especially true when looking at the neighborhood-,

community-, and state-level political battles of the long civil rights movement.[26] These works look at African American suburban development as it
relates to civil rights challenges, such as attempts of African Americans to
contest restrictive covenants to move into previously all white neighborhoods
or to challenge economic restrictions that kept Blacks from being full participants in American capitalism.[27] But other works have moved beyond a
focus on community building as it relates to civil rights to investigate African
American suburbanization in its own right.[28] Perhaps the strongest of these
works is Andrew Weise's national synthesis of African American suburbanization *Places of their Own: African American Suburbanization in the Twentieth Century*.[29] Because his subject had gone mostly unstudied to this point,
a large part of Wiese's narrative centers on showing that African Americans
lived in suburban environments where others had assumed they had been
barred.

Arlington's development offers an interesting case study in suburban
development because each of Arlington's neighborhoods developed in distinct ways. Growing in various places across the county, they each had their
own development strategies and social and class makeups. However, some
paths of community formation were consistent, as each of these neighborhoods were host to churches, schools, businesses, or social institutions.
These community institutions were not present in all of Arlington's small
Black enclaves.

For the purpose of this study, a "community" is defined as an area which
had both homes and at least one community institution, such as a church,
school, or civic organization. An area can also be defined as a community if it
was centrally planned and platted as such. In contrast, an "enclave" only featured homes that were not centrally planned and was host to no community
institutions. Although the distinction between "community" and "enclave" is
not solely defined by size, enclaves usually featured fewer families than communities, and their residents had to travel beyond the neighborhood for all
community institutions.

Arlington's Black neighborhoods were often located in some of the most
geographically desirable areas. These neighborhoods sat on hills, had access
to transportation, commanded striking views. It was unusual for African
American communities to be in such sought-after landscapes. Instead, most
African American communities elsewhere across the country took shape far
from downtowns or preferred views. The one thing that African American
settlements beyond Arlington seemed to have in common was they were seen
as undesirable in some way. Nationally, the only African American communities formed in such desirable areas were domestic service enclaves built so
domestics could live close to the elite homes they serviced. Seven percent

of Arlington's African American residents worked as domestic workers, including Hall's Hill residents Ellen Hayson, who worked as a cook, and her daughter Margaret, who worked as a live-in maid.[30] But this employment type does not seem to have impacted African American settlement patterns.[31] Meanwhile, even elite and middle-class Black communities of the New South, such as the Black Hayti neighborhood of Durham, North Carolina, were forced to take up residence in an undesirable periphery of mud flats outside the city.[32] However, these residential patterns are not present in Arlington.

Instead, the locations of Black neighborhoods in desirable areas can be linked to Arlington's Civil War and post-war realities. Federal occupation during the war and Reconstruction hurt white Arlingtonians' social and political power, and the war's destruction and lean postwar years hurt their economic power. In Arlington, the physical destruction of war and federal occupation led to the devastation and seizure of lands, crops, farm animals, and homes. After the Civil War, Arlington's existing white community was not in a position of strength to keep the best lands for themselves. Economic hardships led many white Arlingtonians to subdivide and sell their land. At the same time, rail networks expanded in the county. The possibility of easier commuting further pushed expansion in Arlington. In the immediate postwar years white Arlingtonians took a less active role in shaping the county and their own communities into a unified suburban environment.

Community institutions grew from and continued to perpetuate strong African American communities, and they helped to create some communities which were much more entrenched than other communities, Black or white. However, institutions alone were not enough to secure a neighborhood's continuation, as the case of Arlington's Queen City reveals. Queen City began in the early 1900s and was host to three churches and several businesses before being unceremoniously condemned and torn down in 1942 to make way for the road network of the War Department's Pentagon building. Clearly, the presence of African American parallel institutions was not enough to explain the continued presence of Arlington's three persistent communities.

Putting African American development patterns at the center of the narrative is an important contribution to the history of Black community development. Additionally, *Built by the People Themselves* has a strong focus on the understudied history of the Black built environment. This is especially true in suburban environments such as Arlington, as recognition of the presence of African Americans in suburbia entered the public discussion relatively recently. A study of the built environment establishes a physical understanding of the layout of homes, churches, schools, and club houses created by Arlington's Black population as they relate to one another and to white encroachment. The built environment is a too often overlooked element of community, with studies of community development focusing on institutions and communities as theoretical abstractions rather than tangible places. An examination of Arlington's built environment shows how the broader African American community of Arlington related to their individual neighborhoods as well as their countywide institutions. Additionally, by looking at the physical spaces created by African Americans—the homes, yards, and institutions that reflected their present lives and future aspirations—we can see how, and in what instances, the built environment they created was similar to or different from that of their neighboring white communities.

What makes a study of Arlington's persistent Black neighborhoods especially interesting is to explore their relationship with the changing environment, from semirural to suburban over the course of several decades. Such a study allows an investigation of race and class divisions within the county, including competing aesthetics and ideas about what constituted desirable homes and neighborhoods. This challenges and expands common understandings of what makes a "suburb." The environments described by this word changed over time, from isolated suburban village communities dotted across the landscape, to one contiguous, dense suburban environment of interconnected communities. Historians who study suburbia and suburbanization are constantly reworking their definitions. Suburbs are both a residential planning type and a symbol of aspiration to multiple generations. Both physically built and existentially pondered, the "suburb" is thus difficult to define.[33]

Arlington's white communities and developers pushed for a vision consistent with the idealized streetcar and picture window suburbs studied by early historical studies—defined, in Kenneth Jackson's words, through "function (non-farm residential), class (middle and upper status), separation (a daily journey to work), and density (low relative to older sections)."[34] By the early 1920s, Arlington was a "thickly settled" continuous suburban community.[35] This suburban development pitted the suburban ideal pushed by Arlington's white social and political leaders and developers against African American neighborhood development and autonomy. It is imperative to explore both the African American and white communities alongside one another to fully understand the true lived experiences of the individuals who populate this book. Understanding how neighborhoods, groups, leaders, and legislation were in conversation and in opposition is the only way to understand Arlington's built environment, a physical manifestation of segregation's color line.

In Arlington, whites tried to exercise authority over and exclude their Black neighbors even when Black visions of suburban development were in line with the preplanned, streamlined, and middle-class visions of their white counterparts. Although neither Arlington's white leaders nor its Black residents got exactly what they wanted, African American planning and community creation in Arlington shows the important role that the process of suburbanization played as visions of community development between Black and white competed during the Jim Crow era.[36]

CHAPTER 1

"Where They Had Lived Undisturbed for Nearly a Quarter of a Century"

Freedman's Village and the Expansion of Black Arlington

In the second half of the nineteenth century, Arlington was a community in transition.[1] Arlington, County, Virginia, moved from rural hinterland toward suburban enclave after the Civil War. Freedman's Village was paramount to this change. The federal government established Freedman's Village as a contraband camp for the formerly enslaved. On its opening, the Village was Arlington's first successful preplanned neighborhood. The Village attracted many new African American residents to the area, mostly from other parts of Virginia and Maryland, which greatly increased the county's Black population from about one-third to just over half of the total population.[2] The War Department envisioned the Village as a social experiment, giving formerly enslaved individuals and families the social, educational, work, and domestic skills they would need to survive in freedom.[3] Residents embraced these aims and shaped the Village to improve their lives in other ways. Immediately after its founding in 1863, residents began creating churches, schools, and political and social institutions, turning the Village into a community that would greatly impact Arlington's development.

During and immediately after the Civil War, local white Arlingtonians were struggling. Federal occupation during the war and Reconstruction hurt their social and political power, and the war's destruction and lean postwar years hurt their economic power. Economic hardships led many white Arlingtonians to subdivide and sell their land, turning the former farming community into a more densely populated environment. At the same time, rail networks expanded in the county. The possibility of easier commuting further pushed suburban expansion in Arlington.

African Americans purchased much of the lands sold at this time. They were drawn to Arlington by Freedman's Village, employment opportunities, the possibility of building new communities, and a tradition of African Americans settling in the periphery of southern antebellum cities.[4]

The desire to build strong Black communities and connections in freedom made early African American residents of Arlington dedicated to community development. By contrast, as they readjusted to post-war realities, white Arlingtonians did not take as active a role in shaping the county's suburban growth as their Black counterparts immediately following the Civil War. This allowed African American communities to form and expand. Beginning in the 1880s, however, a revitalized white population exerted social and legal pressures against Freedman's Village and Arlington's Black residents. All manner of pressure from white individual citizens, land developers, county leaders, local and state officials, and the federal government, who all wanted county lands for themselves, mounted extreme pressures against Freedman's Village and its Black residents. As whites began to assert their vision for the county, it became clear that they hoped this vision would not include African Americans, but Arlington's new Black residents and their social institutions would not be pushed from the county; rather, they would be dispersed within it.

Beginning in the 1890s, the Village's people, institutions, and resources moved throughout the county, expanding other existing neighborhoods, such as Green Valley and Hall's Hill, and leading to the establishment of new communities. These new areas included Johnson's Hill, Queen City, Butler-Holmes, and many other smaller enclaves sprinkled throughout Arlington. These new and expanded Black communities had distinct goals and aesthetics representing the aims of the individuals and families who called them home. Each community represented its residents' ideas regarding what would make an area a good place to live. Because of this, their environments ranged from semirural to aspirationally urban, to suburban.

The types of homes and communities created were tied to class. Working-class neighborhoods used their homes' lands and locations to generate income. This was accomplished either by creating semirural, small-farm communities, as was the case in Hall's Hill, or by establishing themselves along main thoroughfares with easy connections to employment opportunities and customers, as in Queen City. Although working-class communities were grounded in needs and subsistence, the aesthetics and choices of middle-class communities were tied to future aspirations for themselves and their children. Communities such as Johnson's Hill attempted to create a more urban environment, mimicking the homes from the Black neighborhoods in Washington's Foggy Bottom neighborhood, whereas the middle-class Butler-Holmes subdivision had the aesthetics of a traditional streetcar suburb, with preplatted lands and more standardized single-family homes. All these communities and community types shaped Arlington's early suburban development, affecting a region in transition after the Civil War.

However, despite these differences in aesthetic, Arlington's African American communities all had unified goals of creating community institutions like churches, schools, and mutual aid societies. These institutions were very often cross-community endeavors that connected these diverse and, at times, physically isolated communities to one another to establish a connected Black Arlington. Community residents also shared the aim of home ownership across all communities and classes. These foundations would be essential in maintaining a Black Arlington against outside pressures throughout the twentieth century.

Arlington's Earliest Roots of Black Community

Green Valley was Arlington's earliest Black community. Its roots can be traced back to the 1840s. At this time, the county was predominantly made up of small farms growing staple crops, although there were a few larger plantations; including the Parke Custis family's Arlington House.[5] Arlington had a relatively small free Black population in the decades leading up to the Civil War. In 1840, the county was home to two hundred ninety enslaved and two hundred thirty-five free people of color within a total population of approximately fifteen hundred.[6] These individuals and families lived throughout the county, in small clusters or intermingled among white farms and homes.

One such African American family was the Jones family. In 1844, Sarah and Levi Jones purchased fourteen acres of land to farm and build a home.[7] Their property lay in southeastern Arlington on a hill overlooking Four Mile Run. According to the county's 1847 "Free Negro Register," Sarah was born free. She is described as having a dark complexion with a scar on her right arm.[8] Her husband, Levi Jones, was born into freedom in nearby Fairfax, Virginia. His parents, Davy and Evy, were originally enslaved on George Washington's Mount Vernon plantation.[9] In accordance with the will of the late president, all enslaved individuals who made up his estate were freed after the death of his wife, Martha Washington, in 1801.[10] This included Davy, Evy, and their two daughters, Sarah and Nancy. In the years to come, the Jones family grew to include three more children, David, Joseph, and Levi, all born free. In 1833, Levi moved to Arlington. Standing at five feet, eleven inches with a dark, nearly "black" complexion, Levi likely worked as a farmhand.[11] For eleven years, the Joneses saved their money until they had enough to purchase those fourteen acres. They acquired their land from Elizabeth Baggott at a rate of two hundred dollars down, and two hundred thirty-five dollars over the course of five years.[12] There, they grew oats and corn, had a fifty-tree peach orchard, and built a barn and dairy house for their animals.[13] The Joneses constructed "a big [two-story] house" in the log-cabin

FIGURE 2. Green Valley
formed along Four Mile
Run stream in southern
Arlington thanks to
the civic-mindedness
and commitment of the
Jones Family. Farmland,
stream, and homes are
seen in this sketch.
Alfred R. Waud, *4-Mile
Run Valley*, ca. 1861–63,
Prints and Photographs
Division, Library of
Congress.

style.[14] With this home and land, Levi and Sarah Jones set this area on a path to become one of Arlington's core African American neighborhoods.

The Jones family lived and worked in close proximity to enslaved laborers. Their property neighbored that of white landowner Anthony Fraser who relied on a combination of tenant farmers, Black and white, and enslaved African Americans to work the land.[15] In 1804, Fraser's father, William Jr., purchased forty-six acres of largely undeveloped and forested land from the Alexander family in southeastern Arlington.[16] In 1821, Anthony came to own the property and expanded it to include one thousand additional acres and the large Green Valley Manor home, the third largest plantation in Arlington.[17] In 1850, the Frasers owned twelve enslaved individuals—eight men and boys ranging in age from four to seventy years, and four women and girls ranging in age from infancy to thirty years.[18] Only two of these individuals are listed by name—Nathan Butler, age thirty, and Douglas Jones, age twenty.[19] In the 1860 census, Anthony Fraser is shown as owning nine enslaved individuals—five men and boys ranging in age from ten to fifty-

seven years, and four women and girls, ranging in age from seventeen to fifty-six years.[20]

Although free families of color were the exception in Arlington and not the rule, the free African American Syphax family lived and worked just two miles from the Jones property. In 1826, the Parke Custis family manumitted three members of the Syphax family—Maria and her two children, Elinor and William.[21] At this time, George Washington Parke Custis gifted Maria Syphax a seventeen-acre tract of land in Arlington County along what is today Shirley Highway, Interstate 395.[22] On this property, the Syphax family built a home and farm, and Maria bore eight more children into freedom. Maria's husband, Charles Syphax, joined his family in freedom upon his manumission in 1861.[23] Maria and her children all received formal educations, a rarity for African Americans at this time.[24] Through this education and their landholdings, the Syphax clan became an early prominent free Black family in Arlington. In the years to come, they supported Arlington's growing Black community.

The area around the Jones property did not attract other African American buyers in the 1840s and 1850s. Free African Americans held a precarious place in southern society during the era of slavery. Although not enslaved, they were also not entirely free because of the multitude of restrictive Black Codes limiting their rights, economic and educational opportunities, and personal choices.[25] Codes limiting the rights of free and enslaved Blacks began in colonial Virginia but were greatly expanded in strength and scope after the panic accompanied by Nat Turner's 1831 slave uprising in southeastern Virginia.[26] Black codes were enforced unilaterally in the 1840s, after Arlington County and Alexandria City were retroceded to Virginia.[27] The Virginia General Assembly required that county clerks note the "age, name, colour, and stature," as well as the mode of freedom and identifying marks, for all "free Negroes or mulattoes."[28]

When these restrictions lifted after the Civil War, Green Valley quickly emerged as an African American community. By 1900, Green Valley was the largest community in terms of both geography and population. The strength of Green Valley was due, in large part, to the presence of the Jones family. Levi and Sarah Jones were successful farmers, expanding their holdings with the direct intention of selling land to other African Americans.[29] The Jones family also encouraged the creation of African American institutions in Green Valley. Because of their position as landowners before the war, and their interest in both selling land to African Americans and creating community institutions immediately after the war, residents consider the Joneses' purchase of land in 1844 to be the start of the Green Valley community.

Although Arlington's free Black population was relatively small, the presence of community leaders like the Jones and Syphax families helped to shape Arlington's Black community development after the creation of Freedman's Village expanded the area's African American population.

Freedman's Village and the Expansion of Black Arlington

By the winter of 1863, the situation in the District of Columbia had become extreme. Huge numbers of African Americans poured into the capital city. War generally leads to displacement, but the American Civil War greatly amplified this displacement because enslaved African Americans took advantage of the war's upheaval to escape their bondage and flee to federal lines. This was especially true in Washington, DC, first after the abolition of slavery within the District in 1862 and, later, after the general Emancipation Proclamation in 1863. In Washington, the Black population increased from nineteen percent of the city's population in 1860, to more than 30% by midwar.[30] Many, if not most, of these individuals and families arrived in poor health, with little property or money, and with no place to live, straining the federal city's resources. In response, several camps, known as contraband camps, opened in Washington to house these individuals. Two camps were set up in southern Anacostia, and one was placed near the Capitol building. However, camps became overcrowded, with poor sanitation and hygiene. During the winter months of 1862, a smallpox outbreak swept through the Capitol Hill contraband camp. Realizing that so many people could not stay within the city alone, Colonel Elias M. Greene, chief quartermaster of the Department of Washington in charge of military construction and logistics, suggested that another camp be created, but this time beyond the city, in the "pure country air" of Arlington, Virginia.[31]

During the war, Arlington existed in an uncertain middle ground between Union and Confederate lines. Although the county—then mostly rural farmland—did not enthusiastically support secession, when Virginia seceded from the Union, Arlington did too.[32] However, Arlington's secession was never fully realized, because at the opening of the war in the summer of 1861, Arlington was occupied by federal troops. To protect Washington and its claims in Virginia, the federal government erected twenty-one forts in Arlington County.[33] This existing occupation made Arlington a natural choice when the War Department needed to expand contraband camps beyond the District. When it came to choosing a location within Arlington for the camp, government officials chose Arlington House—one of the county's few large plantations. Arlington House is located in the eastern portion of Arlington County, immediately across the Potomac River from Washington, DC, with sweeping views of the National Mall. The lands were among the most fertile and picturesque in the county, with easy access to the federal city. Arlington House belonged to the family of the area's most famous resident, Confederate General Robert E. Lee. In the spring of 1861, after Lee gave up his post in the federal army to join the Confederacy, the Custis-Lee family fled south to Richmond, Virginia. In 1862, Congress enacted land taxes on properties in rebelling states that must be paid in person. The federal government seized the plantation after Mary Custis Lee neglected to pay her tax bill of $92.07. In poor health, she sent her cousin, Philip R. Fendall, to pay the bill in her stead, but he was told that the taxes must be paid in person by Mrs. Lee alone.[34] So, the federal government seized Arlington House. The relocation of formerly enslaved individuals at Arlington House was, thus, a choice with both practical and symbolic purposes.

On December 4, 1863, Freedman's Village contraband camp opened. Contraband camps were scattered across the South, wherever the Union army held lands. Federal forces created the majority of these camps haphazardly. They functioned simply as holding grounds, "adjuncts to the plantations," or later as Union recruitment facilities for African American

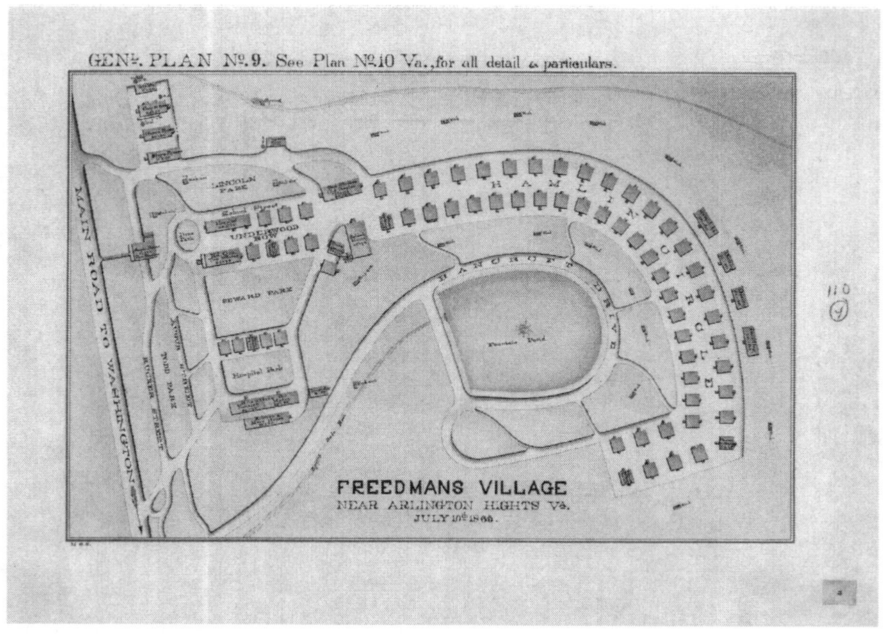

FIGURE 3. At Freedman's Village, the government created a preplanned community with houses, roads, and institutions, which was a physical representation of federal goals of moral uplift for the formerly enslaved population. US Army Corps of Engineers, "General Plan no. 9—Freedman's Village near Arlington Heights, VA" [July 10, 1865], Library of Congress.

soldiers.[35] Freedman's Village, however, was created with more thoughtful intent. The Village encompassed more than eleven hundred acres of picturesque land in the northeastern portion of the county, with sweeping views of Washington.[36] Here, the government created a preplanned community with houses, roads, and institutions. Freedman's Village "became a showplace to which government officials directed foreign visitors and other dignitaries eager to witness the progress of former slaves."[37] Indeed, the Village was opened with a bit of fanfare as an invitation-only dedication with speakers from the government and music.[38] The preplanned community built by the War Department was a physical representation of federal goals of moral uplift for the formerly enslaved population. To this end, the government erected a "neat and extensive collection of frame houses."[39]

One-hundred whitewashed, duplex-style homes "in size about 28 by 24 feet; one and a half stories in height, with 8 rooms each," lined a quarter-mile-long thoroughfare through the Village.[40] The clapboard houses used a pared-down version of the Classical Revival style. Popular in the late nineteenth century, in its grand representations, Classical Revivalism used symmetry and columns to allude to Greek temples, symbolically connecting America to the ancient democracy and its ideals through architectural style. In its vernacular execution at Freedman's Village, the Classical Revival architecture used color and symmetry to convey the ideals of the movement. The external symmetry of the home was meant to lead to social harmony and stability. The white color of the homes was meant to encourage cleanliness, godliness, and order. Initially chosen by the War Department, Black Arlingtonians embraced this housing type. They took great care in the maintenance and upkeep of these homes. When building their own homes later, residents often recreated this style.

The War Department did more than just build houses in Freedman's Village. In partnership with northern religious and aid societies, they established institutions to help educate the former slaves in practical skills and the ways of wage labor. Women were taught domestic housekeeping skills, and vocational schools for men taught them to become carpenters, tailors, wheelwrights, shoemakers, harness makers, and more.[41] Although these programs smacked of paternalism and encouraged assimilationist tendencies, they improved the lives of many. For example, blacksmithing was among the trades taught at the Village. Elsewhere in Virginia and across the South, it became increasingly difficult for African Americans to practice these professions. In slavery, individuals could learn and practice these trades, but in freedom, African American craftsmen found a harder time practicing such skills because of prejudices and restrictive policies.[42] Local laws in Washington, Alexandria, and Arlington prevented free Blacks from working in many trades.[43] Many professional laborers—such as William A. Rowe, who worked as a blacksmith—became leaders in the community because of the pay and prominence their education and specialized jobs provided.

With their new or improved skill sets, many within the Village came to work for the federal government. These individuals worked as soldiers, stewards, teamsters, and workers on fortifications.[44] Both Thomas Owens and his wife, Hannah, found federal work within the Village, she as a cook and he at the military's growing cemetery on the grounds.[45] The opportunity to work for the federal government highlights another benefit for African Americans living in Arlington. These employment opportunities provided a welcome alternative to farm labor, the most common employment type for African Americans at this time.[46] Others worked in the Village's hospital or home for the elderly. In 1864, hospital workers were paid forty cents per day, and teamsters and skilled laborers were paid one dollar per day plus rations.[47] These pay rates were consistent with white wages.[48] Some would

FIGURE 4. The one-hundred white-washed duplexes constructed by the War Department using a pared-down version of the Classical Revival style became a popular home style for African Americans beyond the Village. Alfred R. Waud, Freedman's Village seen from the Road and Freedman's Village, Arlington, Virginia, 1864, Prints and Photographs Division, Library of Congress.

transition between these regionally exceptional employment types—such as Village resident Harry W. Gray, who transitioned from a job as a skilled mason to become a messenger for the Department of the Interior.[49]

Although they benefited from the overall central planning of the Village's buildings, layout, and services undertaken by the War Department, it was the African American residents themselves who spearheaded the development of a truly robust community in Freedman's Village. Residents took great care in maintaining and improving their homes. Although initial construction did not include plaster or ceilings inside the government housing, residents "improved the premises by reflooring, be reroofing, by plastering or ceiling the rooms."[50] In many cases, residents also "added small outbuildings, such as stables, sheds, [and] chicken-houses."

The camp became home to African Americans of all ages and family types.[51] Some African American families escaping bondage were able to bring extended kin networks together at the Village. The Parks family was able to keep their entire thirteen-person family together. The head of their family, Lawrence Parks, was already in his mid-seventies when he attempted to create a new life for himself and his family at the Village. Mary Pollard came to the Village at the age of forty with her fifteen-year-old son James in 1865. Others came to the Village as individuals, such as fourteen-year-old Nancy Jackson, who was living at the Village by 1865. Although villagers differed in age or family connections, at the Village they were united in their goals of creating a strong community in freedom. These individuals and families took great care of maintaining their homes. An 1864 *Harper's Weekly* article hailed that the "place presents a clean and prosperous appearance at all times."[52] With the help of northern missionaries, residents directed the creation of religious and educational institutions in the Village. As early as 1864, Freedman's Village had primary and secondary schools for the children of the Village which educated from two hundred fifty to as many as nine hundred students.[53] Demand for education was so high among adults that a night school was established to meet their needs.[54] Residents stressed the importance of an education for themselves and their children. The song "Uncle Sam's School" could be heard in the Village, residents singing the chorus "come bring your books and don't be a fool, for Uncle Sam is rich enough to send us all to school."[55] With this enthusiastic embrace of education, literacy rates in the Village rose from only twenty percent in 1870 to fifty-six percent by 1890.[56]

In April of 1865, Confederate General Robert E. Lee surrendered to Union General and future President Ulysses S. Grant at Appomattox Courthouse, Virginia. That same spring, the management of Freedman's Village

FIGURE 5. Education was incredibly important to residents of Freedman's Village. As many as nine hundred students were educated at the Village school. "Freedman's Village, Arlington, Va." 1864. Library of Congress.

transitioned from the War Department to the newly formed Freedman's Bureau. Congress founded the Bureau to provide for the immediate physical needs of former slaves and help them transition into freedom through social, political, and legal aid.

In peace, victory, and freedom, with the newly minted federal agency dedicated to pursuing their rights, the inhabitants of Freedman's Village created and expanded schools, churches, institutions, and fraternal and mutual aid societies, deepening their roots in the Village.[57] Fraternal and mutual aid societies provided the men of the Village a way to exercise their new social and political rights. In this way, the Village became, even more than other contraband camps, "the first great cultural and political meeting ground" produced by and for African Americans.[58] One such organization was the Grand United Order of Odd Fellows, founded in the Village in 1870. This organization served many needs of the young Black community—hosting social functions, serving as a meeting ground for political functions, serving as a credit union, helping to establish internal community leadership, and supporting Black churches and schools. In 1888, Black Arlingtonians also founded their own Masonic Lodge No. 58 in the middle-class Green Valley community.[59]

In 1866, Village residents founded both the Little Zion Methodist Church and the Old Bell Baptist Church. Less than ten years later, in 1873,

Old Bell had so many members that it divided into two congregations—Mount Olive and Mount Zion Baptist Churches. Lucy Harris was a founding member of the Mount Zion Baptist Church. Lucy came to the Village in 1865 with her extended family. Lucy's commitment to expanding religious institutions within the Village shows how its long-term residents wanted to shape the Village into a truly robust community.

These churches were not just houses of worship; they were anchors of the community, and spiritual leaders were often community leaders. Old Bell's Reverend Robert S. Laws, also worked as an employment agent for the Village, helping his fellow Villagers find work.[60] Laws enjoyed a great deal of influence in the community, he was called "the leader of public sentiment in the Village."[61] This kind of influence of spiritual leaders in community affairs was not isolated to Laws. Henry Lomax came to the Village about 1864 with his wife, Mary, and their young son William.[62] Working as a laborer for the military at the Village, Lomax became Bishop of Zion Methodist, later renamed AME Zion. His position within the church helped Lomax to become a community leader, also taking up leadership positions within the Odd Fellows. These churches and organizations expanded and solidified Arlington's Black middle class, which had been made possible through employment and education possibilities provided the freedmen in the Village.

Although it was the county's largest, Freedman's Village was not the only Black community to emerge in Arlington in the 1860s. In 1865, the Hall's Hill community began to take shape. Located atop a hill in the western portion of the county, the community had breathtaking views. When writing his younger brother from his station at Hall's Hill, Civil War soldier John William observed that "from this hill you have a view of the country for nearly ten miles, and probably can see the country very near Vienna and Fairfax."[63] The hill for which the community was named also featured "a fine stream of water" that afforded "water for cooking and bathing" and "woodlands, which furnished fuel."[64]

These descriptions of lovely, pastoral views and natural resources show how Hall's Hill, like Freedman's Village, was built on desirable land. It was unusual for African American communities to be in such sought-after areas. Instead, most African American communities took shape far from downtowns or preferred views. The one thing that African American settlements beyond Arlington seemed to have in common was that they were seen as undesirable in some way. Nationally, the only African American communities which developed in such desirable areas were domestic service enclaves created so domestics could live close to the elite homes they serviced. Seven percent of Arlington's African American residents worked as domestic workers, including Hall's Hill residents Ellen Hayson, who worked as a cook, and her daughter, Margaret, who worked as a live-in maid.[65] However, this employment type does not seem to have affected African American settlement patterns in Arlington.[66]

Instead, the locations of Hall's Hill and Freedman's Village in desirable areas can be linked to Arlington's Civil War and postwar realities. The federal government created Freedman's Village on Lee's plantation as a form of payback in a time of increased land confiscation and reassignment. Hall's Hill's creation was the result of local circumstances in Arlington, which created a window for Black land purchase.[67] Federal occupation during the war and Reconstruction hurt white Arlingtonians' social and political power, while the war's destruction and lean post-war years hurt their economic power. In Arlington, the physical destruction of war and federal occupation led to the devastation and seizure of lands, crops, farm animals, and homes, so, after the Civil War, Arlington's existing white community was not in a position of strength to keep the best lands for themselves. Economic hardships led many white Arlingtonians to subdivide and sell their land. At the same time, rail networks expanded in the county. The possibility of easier commuting further pushed expansion in Arlington. In the immediate postwar years, white Arlingtonians took a less active role in shaping the county and their own communities into a unified suburban environment.

The hard times of the Civil War are what spurred white landowner Bazil Hall, the namesake of Hall's Hill, to sell his land to African Americans. Bazil Hall lost much during the war. He fled his house when a skirmish between Union and Confederate forces put his home in the crossfire. During his absence, his home and 327-acre farm were stripped of furniture, timber, fences, crops, and farm animals.[68] After this initial destruction, Hall's property was taken over by Union forces for an encampment. Before the war, Hall's land was valued at over ten thousand dollars, with an additional fifteen thousand dollars in personal property. After the war, however, his land was valued at only sixty-four hundred dollars, and his personal property was estimated to be worth only thirty dollars.[69] Hall was in his late fifties, with four young children still living at home. To survive, he needed to sell his land.

The white Fraser family, whose Green Valley Manor home became the namesake for the Green Valley community, also sold land to African Americans at this time. The Fraser home and property were greatly damaged during the Civil War. This was because occupying federal forces used their home and land for both Fort Barnard and a convalescents' camp for Union soldiers. These military installations greatly affected the physical environment of the Fraser's land as trees and crops were cleared, and trenches were dug for the fort. The convalescent camp led to huge changes to the property because of its scope—consisting of barracks, a hospital, officer and surgeon quarters, and more.[70] Family accounts hold that the steady thud of axes chopping down trees greatly saddened Anthony Fraser.[71] This stemmed from loss of income and property, worth an estimated thirty-four thousand dollars, but also because Anthony Fraser was known to be a Confederate sympathizer.[72] When the Union occupied his home during the war, they hung a Union military flag over his front door. In a small act of defiance, Fraser refused to use the front door and pass under the flag from that time forward, instead entering and exiting through the rear of the house.[73] Despite these prejudices, extreme economic hardships because of the destruction of property and loss of enslaved labor pushed Fraser to sell land to African Americans after the Civil War.[74]

New arrivals of African Americans seeking to make lives for themselves for the first time in freedom took advantage of this situation. Aided by the creation of Black community infrastructure by the War Department through Freedman's Village, African Americans in Arlington were more forward-looking than whites when it came to carving out communities throughout Arlington. Immediately after the war, those looking to buy land in Arlington were African Americans. Hall sold his land at a loss to African American individuals and families. Even at the depressed, postwar rate, Hall's land was still valued at more than nineteen dollars per acre. In 1865, he began selling his land for ten to fifteen dollars an acre. Needing funds and provisions desperately, Hall was willing to accept lump sums of cash, in-kind trade, or installments of sixty cents a month for his land.[75] This willingness to barter and pay off lands slowly helped African Americans who were just starting to obtain homes even though they had little savings or access to loans.

However, the willingness of white landowners to sell to African Americans should not be equated with support for Arlington's new and growing Black community. This is especially true in the case of Bazil Hall. Hall was known for his violent temper generally and for his aggression toward Blacks in particular. He was rumored to have "shot one negro simply in bravado" and was quoted by a Union soldier as having asserted that "any man of common sense will say that slavery is the very best thing for the South."[76] Although Hall had at least four slaves—Thomas Merchant and the Fair family, Alfred, Genny, and son John—between 1855 and 1860, none of the Hall's formerly enslaved workers stayed in Hall's Hill to purchase land from Hall. He was known for being demanding of his enslaved workers; an *Evening Star* article noted that he and his wife were known "as being hard on servants."[77] It is very possible that Merchant and the Fairs did not wish to continue any relationship with Hall in freedom. It is also possible that Hall was unwilling to sell to his former slaves.

Unfortunately for the neighborhoods' residents, Hall's involvement in their lives did not end with the bill of sale. Bazil Hall did not want the new residents on his land to "forget their places."[78] He discouraged them from taking employment that he believed was above their station, instead hoping that they would rely on his benevolence. This became another hurdle that early Black settlers in Arlington had to negotiate. Despite this, however, Bazil Hall and his land sales represented an opportunity for Black residents to buy land and create lives for themselves in a lovely, desirable location within the county.

Hall's Hill was the first post-Civil War Black neighborhood established beyond Freedman's Village. Like the residents from Freedman's Village, most came from rural lives on Virginia and Maryland farms and plantations. That was the case for James Washington, who came to Hall's Hill from a Maryland plantation as a single man to purchase two lots totaling three acres in 1866.[79] Another early purchaser was Archibald Upshire, who bought one lot for himself, his wife, Eliza, and their growing family.[80] These African American residents seeking a life and community for themselves and their families were mostly working class. Both Archibald and Eliza worked outside of the home, he as a laborer and she as a domestic.[81] In freedom, many Hall's Hill residents worked as laborers in Washington, DC, for fifteen cents to fifty cents a day, less than half the rate received by many of the skilled craftspeople educated at Freedman's Village.

These residents relied on the steam and rail trolley system to take them in and out of the city for work. Hall's Hill was built along the Washington and Old Dominion (W&OD) line, first chartered in 1853.[82] By 1870, many rail lines, including the W&OD line, were expanding freight and passenger service across Arlington County and nearby Alexandra City. The W&OD tracks ran from downtown Alexandria, along the path of Four Mile Run through Arlington, north to Rosslyn, and out to the towns toward Virginia's Blue Ridge Mountains. Feeding off of the growth of one another, rail lines continued to improve their service and expand their stops, increasingly focusing on commuter travel, encouraging and reacting to a rising commuter community seeking employment beyond the farm in Arlington County. Connections between Washington and Arlington continued to expand with the opening of the Aqueduct Bridge as a free bridge in 1886. Arlington moved slowly toward more concentrated communities of smaller land holdings, with Hall's Hill as an intermediary step. During the mid-nineteenth century, contemporaries called this transition the "middle landscape."[83] The choice of Hall's Hill's residents to locate in an area along a trolley line, which provided access to employment in Washington, DC while maintaining lots with space for homes, gardens, and expansion, was a part of this suburban growth.

At this time, rail travel was the most reliable way to travel in the county. Despite road improvements made during the war years, almost all of the county's road networks were still dirt or gravel. However, riding the trolley was more difficult for Hall's Hill's residents than for some of their more affluent white neighbors. A two-way trolley ticket cost five cents per day, taking up one-third of the residents' average daily income. Although employment in DC offered job opportunities, the significant cost to travel into the city for work shows that this employment choice was not without its trials. Most of Hall's Hill's working residents needed to travel beyond the community for their jobs, because the community had few businesses at the end of the nineteenth century.[84]

The residents of Hall's Hill used their farming skill sets to improve their economic situation. Shaping their environment to meet their needs, they created a semirural community that featured extensive gardens where residents kept horses and raised hogs, chickens, and turkeys. Here, African American working-class residents chose to recreate elements of their rural plantation past, making a choice about what their ideal neighborhood would look like. Residents used farming to supplement incomes. Residents focused on buying as much land as they could afford rather than creating elaborate homes, often expanded their land holdings slowly. For example, when Robert E. Ferguson first purchased land from Bazil Hall, he was only able to buy one-half of an acre, but over time, his land holdings expanded until his lot was large enough to support farming. Coming from rural Herndon, Virginia, Ferguson used his farming skill sets to grow cherry trees whose fruit was harvested for sale by his wife, Ellen Hayson, and their children.[85] Residents built simple single-family wood frame or brick homes themselves, often in a piecemeal fashion as supplies could be afforded and time could be secured to complete the work. These homes were often reminiscent of farm houses, constructed in a simple, modified four-square style.[86]

Beyond their individual attempts to create successful lives in freedom through work and home, the residents of Hall's Hill created church congregations and schools to help establish the kind of social and physical environment that they thought was desirable. Only one year after the first bills of sale, Hall's Hill residents created their first church. In 1866, Moses Pelham organized Methodist prayer services, which grew into the Calloway United Methodist Church.[87] Pelham came to the area from Culpeper, Virginia. Like the Parks family in Freedman's Village, the Pelhams migrated to Arlington with an extended kin network that was anchored by Moses and his brothers Burrell, Gipson, and Ed Pelham.[88] In 1868, the Black residents of the community organized a school for the community's growing population of children.[89] James Washington and his wife, Lucinda, raised six children in

Hall's Hill. Moses Pelham also had six children. The Upshires had two children when they purchased their home and four children as of 1870. These young, growing families pushed for a good education and a better life for their children.

Hall's Hill's school was a simple one-room school with one teacher. Although modest, this school was unique for the area. Hall's Hill was located within the Washington District, the county's westernmost voting district. In Washington District, local white residents resisted public education. Even after the county established a public school system in 1870, the region opted out of the program, waiting until 1878 to open the Carne School for white children.[90] This resistance likely had less to do with an outright rejection of public education than the fact that, at this time, many Arlingtonians sent their children to school in Washington, DC. The district provided the possibility for students to attend private school, and children of federal employees could also attend DC's public schools for free. With these options open to their children, Washington District's white residents resisted being taxed for education closer to home. The white residents near Hall's Hill did not yet view the area as a growing community. The disinvestment of white residents in community schools points to a continued lack of vision for the area's future development.

However, for Hall's Hill's residents, it was important not only that their children receive an education but also that they receive that education close to home. This could be the result of many practical factors, such as the difficulty for school-aged children to navigate the trolley cars. Trolley travel was dangerous, and taking the streetcar meant constantly living with the threat of "death or debilitating injury."[91] As early as the 1860s, states had railway safety commissions to deal with public safety concerns from riding the rails. Getting on and off of a moving trolley car was particularly perilous, because the average step up or down from a trolley car was three feet, truly a jump for a child.[92] The lack of curbs or sidewalks in the community's roads could have increased these safety fears. Or concerns about paying additional trolley fares beyond those already paid by parents traveling beyond the neighborhood for employment could have been a contributing factor.

However, this choice to create a school for and within their own community shows distinct visions from Black Arlingtonians about what makes an area a good place to live. Unlike their white neighbors, the residents of Hall's Hill felt that it was important to create their own schools within the community. A path also taken by the residents of Freedman's Village and Green Valley, the desire to have a local school shows not only the importance of education for the first generation of African Americans in freedom but also how schools were perceived to be neighborhood institutions, pillars of the community. The physical location of the Hall's Hill school in the center of the community, alongside the church, highlights this fact. Schools not only provided an education but also provided neighborhood children with a sense of community and connection. Neighborhood schools also provided insulation from negative outside influences from hostile whites which Black children would be more likely to experience if they had to travel great distances beyond their communities.

This call for isolation is also suggested in the layout of the community. Hall's Hill's church and school were clustered along Fairfax Road, the community's main connector to the District and other parts of the county. With homes fanning out from the main road and these institutions, Calloway Church and Hall's Hill school were the anchors of the community. With these institutions at the center of their community physically and socially, the environment built by Hall's Hill's residents was a physical representation of their preferences for what community life should be like. As previously mentioned, the county's road network was primitive with primarily dirt roads. On top of this, in Hall's Hill, the roads were narrow, and most did not open out to connect to other roads. Beyond the main thoroughfare of Fairfax Road through the community, few roads passed through Hall's Hill. This limited connectivity and general impassability of Hall's Hill's roads could certainly be inconvenient for residents; however, it also provided insulation from surrounding white neighbors. It is important to remember that although Hall's Hill was increasingly becoming a Black community, full residential segregation was not yet a reality. Instead, Hall's Hill's Black residences neighbored white farming families and newly emerging white neighborhoods in what Thomas Hanchett has described as a "salt and pepper" residential pattern common to post-Civil War southern residential expansion.[93] Residents were also isolated from other Black communities in east Arlington where Freedman's Village and Green Valley were located. This separation from a larger local network of Black communities could have heightened their desire to create some breathing room for their community by becoming insulated.

By the 1870s, only a few years after its founding, Hall's Hill was a thriving and growing Black community. The farms of Arlington's past were slowly moving toward more concentrated communities of smaller land holdings, with Hall's Hill's modest landholdings, small levels of farming, and commuting work population as an intermediary step. The choices made by Hall's Hill residents and the suburban-style infrastructure created in Freedman's Village point to the beginnings of a suburban existence for Arlington and its residents, a path shaped by the choices and preferences of the area's African American residents in combination with such factors as federal policies and postwar economic and social conditions.

Around this same time, Green Valley continued to expand as an African American community. The strength of Green Valley was due, in large part, to the presence of the Jones family. Levi and Sarah Jones were successful farmers before the war.[94] Their prosperity allowed them to expand their farm. Beginning with a lot of fourteen acres, Jones purchased eight additional acres of land as it became available. Five of these acres were obtained for the purpose of subdivision and sale to African Americans.[95] Where local white landowners often sold lands begrudgingly to African Americans because of extreme economic hardships, the Jones family actively sought Black buyers. After Levi passed away in July of 1886, Sarah continued this practice, subdividing and selling seven additional lots to African Americans before her death in 1915.[96] The Jones family also encouraged the creation of African American institutions in Green Valley. In the first decade after the war, they held religious services in their home until a local chapel could be erected for the growing Black population.

Problems for Freedman's Village

Despite early support from the federal government, the War Department, and the Freedman's Bureau, backing for Freedman's Village waned throughout the 1870s. Where the aims of the freedmen and the government had once been in line, they were now at odds. Nationally, support for Reconstruction programs was on the decline. Radical Reconstruction and Republican political control collapsed, as social and political reconciliation and reunion ended what public support had once existed for African American rights.[97] As a result, aid to former slave families fell from favor. Immediately after the war's end, other "forts about Washington [were] immediately dismounted" and "put upon the general retrenchment path."[98] Calls began for the "Government [to give] up the experiment of supporting the Blacks at Freedman's Village, Arlington."[99]

The kind of social experimentation undertaken in large-scale federal projects like the one at Freedman's Village were especially vulnerable for attack. Cracks began to show even among Village officials. Reverend Laws worked as a spokesperson for the community, pushing Village administrators to expand freedmen's rights. In this new climate, this behavior made Laws enemies; one camp bureaucrat called Laws an agitator for his support of Black rights and encouraged the minister to leave the Village.[100]

The freedmen who had once been celebrated for their improvements to themselves and the land were now categorized as "squatters."[101] This characterization was "untrue, libelous, . . . without foundation," and had no bearing on the actual environment created by the Villagers.[102] Lifelong Arlington House resident Selina Gray, who lived on the property first in slavery and later in freedom, knew better than most all the ways in which the environment changed. Gray, her husband, and their children transitioned from slavery to freedom on the property, moving from the house yard to Freedman's Village. But she called the lands "a most lovely place" that still "looks beautiful," singling out Village homes as contributing to "that beautiful place."[103]

Villagers continued to maintain the houses at the center of the Village originally built by the War Department, keeping their homes neat, tidy, and very comfortable.[104] Many residents improved upon these homes through additions and land beautification, some spending as much as two- to three-times their initial investments.[105] Beyond these improvements, residents of the Village also paid land rents as well as local, state, and federal poll, road, school, and personal property taxes.[106] So residents were not "squatters"; they were individuals and families who purchased land, improved that land, paid rent, built homes, and continued to expand their community institutions. This pattern of discrepancies between Black residents seeing a thriving community and outside white politicians and individuals seeing a shantytown began with Freedman's Village but would be repeated in community after community, as Black and white residents battled for space in the emerging Jim Crow society. What this characterization of "squatter" actually shows is racialized resistance toward the Villagers and outside forces fishing for an excuse to take lands they wanted for other purposes.

This push to take the land back from Villagers was a drawn-out process. In 1868, Congress debated the continued existence of the Freedman's Bureau. Although not closed, the power of the Bureau shrunk significantly until its powers were limited to only petitions and education for African Americans.[107] The government also attempted to close Freedman's Village at this time. In the frigid winter months of 1868, the military tore down the homes between the Potomac River and the grand porch of Arlington House. These homes and their residents were deemed unacceptable, because they impeded views to and from the elite mansion. Distraught at the sudden move, William Conway's mother-in-law asked one of the men issuing the evictions, Lieutenant Bergevin, where they should go. He responded by calling the woman a "damned fool" for thinking that was his responsibility.[108] The Army undertook this forced eviction with such little notice that some men returned home from work to find their wives and children gone.

However, Village residents organized against this closure of their community. As a result of this community activism, the government's early efforts to close the Village were not successful. In fact, the attempted relocation was so botched that it sparked an investigation by the Freedman's Bureau. Residents who lost their homes in the 1868 eviction relocated elsewhere on the property. To quell the discontent, the federal government announced that all Village residents could buy their homes while establishing what residents believed was a rent-to-own system for their land. Villagers beyond the central avenue constructed by the War Department built their own homes. Most were good quality painted frame houses with fenced in yards.[109] Villagers also created a surrounding farming community of five- to ten-acre plots called Arlington Tract Farms. Thomas and Hannah Owens initially lived in the central Village until moving to an Arlington Tract farm in 1868. Owens and his neighbors, including John B. Syphax, built homes for themselves and improved the lands by farming. Residents were hopeful these purchase agreements "shall best secure our property . . . to ourselves and our children."[110]

Six years after the first attempt to close the Village, in 1872, the Freedman's Bureau was abolished. Without a governmental body to lobby on behalf of the Village, in the 1880s, the War Department reinvigorated efforts to close it by calling for congressional action. The military wanted the land to expand Fort Myer and Arlington National Cemetery and to establish a parade ground. Others in the federal government wanted the land to create a new road network from Georgetown to George Washington's Mount Vernon.[111] By 1889, the Department of Agriculture joined in on the government's land grab for Freedman's Village by calling for four hundred of its acres for an experimental farm.[112]

Beyond the federal government, white Arlingtonians seeking voter reform to curb Black political power also wanted to close the Village. White Arlingtonians regrouped after the Civil War and were now ready to reassert their prominence by taking back rights from African Americans. Local whites claimed that "the presence of the Negroes on the reservation [Freeman's Village] has a peculiar effect on the politics" and that African Americans "controlled the county, electing their Board of Supervisors."[113] African Americans could legally vote in Arlington during military Reconstruction beginning in 1867. State-level constitutional changes solidified the changes required by the Reconstruction Amendments beginning in 1870. Also in 1870, countywide electoral reform increased the total number of political offices, made those offices elected rather than appointed positions, and divided the county into three geographically equal political districts: Washington District in the western portion of the county, Arlington District in the center, and Jefferson District in the eastern portion. The result of all these political changes was that some African Americans were elected to county positions, especially within Jefferson District, which contained Freedman's Village. James Pollard, who had come to the Village as a teen and worked as a specialized laborer, became justice of the peace.[114] William A. Rowe, who was trained as a blacksmith in the Village, was also a particularly successful African American politician. He served as supervisor of Jefferson District from 1871 to 1879 and even served as Board chairman from 1872 to 1883.[115]

But African American political power should not be overstated. Not all African Americans met the minimum requirements for voting. Of those who could vote, only one hundred forty taxpayers from Freedman's Village voted in the presidential election of 1888. Although there was an African American presence on the Board of Supervisors, they were never the majority, keeping whites in control of county affairs. Additionally, even though African Americans were able to vote and be elected to office, the white social and political leaders of Arlington had other strategies to keep Black elected officials from taking office. Despite the fact that Black men won elections to the posts of county clerk, treasurer, and sheriff, inexperience or an inability to pay election dues were used to keep them out of these offices during the 1870s and 1880s. Thus, despite election, no African Americans ever served in these positions. Early attempts to keep Blacks from taking office were seen as small victories, but white officials wanted more.

In seeking to limit Black voting power, one of the primary strategies for Arlington's emerging conservative Democratic political leaders was to attack the legitimacy of Freedman's Village. One member of the Board of Supervisors alleged that the Village was full of "paupers and indigent persons who infest the Arlington estate in the county"; a newspaper article called it a "hamlet of squalid want and destruction."[116] Attempting to break up the largest Black voting block in the county, Arlingtonians attacked the validity of the residents' claims to the land. An *Alexandria Gazette* article alleged that residents were "being supported entirely by the United States Government," and therefore they did not have a legitimate claim to suffrage.[117] In reality, a federal report found that only one Village resident, a twelve-year-old orphan girl, was on long-term welfare.[118] The Village's status as government land led Arlingtonians to argue that it was not truly within their jurisdiction and therefore they had no responsibility to contribute to schools or other municipal activities within Freedman's Village. This smear campaign against Arlington's Black residents had parallels throughout the South, as state and local governments attempted to reverse hard-won Black social and political rights.[119]

In addition to those in the federal government looking to use the Village's lands and those attempting to reverse Black enfranchisement, land developers also attacked Freedman's Village. In the last decades of the nineteenth century, Arlington was quickly becoming a streetcar suburb of Washington. Land developers were striking out to obtain more and more land where they could plat and build more suburban neighborhood subdivisions. At the turn of the century, it was estimated that the county's wealth had "increased tenfold [with] many pieces of property worth ten times their assessed value." In this state of land grab and economic frenzy, developers lured federal workers with "quiet and repose from the stir and bustle and noise" of the city to a county which was "law abiding and prosperous."[120] With the land and crops together, Freedman's Village was estimated to be worth $27,162.95 as early as 1864.[121] With so much wealth at stake, land developers lobbied for the eviction of residents of Freedman's Village to snatch that land for themselves. Calls that "Freedman's Village must go" intensified.[122] The developers had powerful allies in their corner. Virginia's US Senator, John W. Daniel, spoke on behalf of the developers, informing the War Department that the "people of the vicinity would like very much to open the way to improvement by having [the residents of Freedman's Village] removed." Daniel went on to argue that it was "improper that government property should be continually occupied by squatters who have no interest in it such as to stimulate improvements."[123] But of course, the Villagers improved the land through building, cultivation, and community formation for more than two decades.

All of these pressures against the community were coming to a head during a time of legal uncertainty for the entire property that once made up the Arlington House plantation. George Washington Custis Lee, one of Robert E. Lee's sons, was in a legal battle with the US government, claiming that his lands were illegally seized. His late mother had also struggled to secure the property, but her attempts were unsuccessful because she wanted the property to be converted back to a private residence—removing Fort Myer, Freedman's Village, and reinterring all the dead from Arlington Cemetery elsewhere. Lee, on the other hand, only called for just compensation for his family's lands. After a five-year legal battle, in 1882, the Supreme Court sided with him, and in 1883, the federal government purchased the Arlington estate house and grounds from Lee for one hundred fifty thousand dollars. Even though the purchase agreement did not call for the expulsion of the Village, the formalization of the land as federal property at a time of extreme hostility against African Americans generally and Village residents specifically provided a new legal context for efforts to uproot the Village.

Officers at Fort Myer and Arlington National Cemetery began complaining about the Villagers with renewed gusto. The Superintendent of the National Cemetery, John A. Commerford, alleged that "the colored people who live on the reservation" were cutting down the cemetery's trees for firewood during the night. He complained that "very few of these squatters buy any fuel and depend mostly on what they can [find] within the enclosure."[124] Despite years of superintendents noting the use of cemetery trees by a few Village residents, Commerford insisted that this was a large-scale problem and that these trees were meant to be decorative and not used for firewood.

These charges were added to new complaints that it was illegal for civilians to live on government property. Quartermaster General for the District, Brigadier General Samuel B. Holabird, stressed that "in violation of paragraph #138 Army Regulations, amended by General Order #26, Adjutant General's Office, 1883, civilians are residing upon the Military Reservation." Because of this, Holabird asserted that the Villagers "should be ordered to vacate their holdings."[125]

Residents who had once received the support of Village administration were now seen as nuisances. That was the case for Thomas Owens and his wife, Hannah. As previously mentioned, when they arrived at the Village, both Thomas and Hannah worked for the federal government within the Village. This work earned the couple enough respect among government agents that when rumors of the Village closing began in the late 1860s, a government official wrote on behalf of the Owens couple, asking that they be allowed to stay even if others were forced to go.[126] These eviction threats did not come to fruition at that time. Instead, the Owens family used their government jobs to save enough money to buy one of the farms within the Village for forty dollars in 1868.[127] For the next twenty years, Thomas was a successful farmer, and Hannah was able to retire from work.[128] But none of this success mattered. By the 1880s, all support for the freedmen was gone, and the officials who once supported his place in the Village now wanted him to leave. Eviction orders came down on December 7, 1887. Beginning in 1868, residents could purchase their homes and rent their lands. However, the federal government insisted that this was under "the direct understanding that they [the freedmen] are to acquire no title to the land, and are to move when required."[129] Residents did not see it this way. Owens said that "people ask us why we don't buy land and own our own homes," but he believed he had done just that and had the receipts to prove it.[130] Unlike some of his neighbors, Owens saved each of his rent receipts and provided them to the government to prove his claim to ownership. Despite that fact, the War Department gave the Villagers ninety days to leave, with no compensation.

With the prospect of being evicted from their homes, "where they had lived undisturbed for nearly a quarter of a century," Villagers organized and sent community leaders to plead their case to the Secretary of War. Villagers used the social and church institutions cultivated for a generation to organize in an attempt to resist the closure of their community. John B. Syphax was the representative for the community. He argued that not only the rents paid and the houses constructed, but also the community formed by the Villagers amounted to a valid claim to their land in Arlington. He highlighted the construction of the brick Mount Olive Church, around which "several houses were built" and "many began to plant trees, and make such other improvements." Here "coming from the shades of the past, these people have proven, in their new condition of self-reliance, more thrifty, and less vicious than could be reasonably anticipated."[131] Taking a cue from Lee's successful bid for his land from the Supreme Court, Syphax pushed that should residents be evicted from the Village, then they must be justly compensated for their homes and improvements. He called for each resident to receive $350 for their homes, lands, and relocation costs.

With the memory of the scandal around the mismanagement of eviction notices in 1868, the War Department surveyed and assessed the property in the winter of 1887–88 to silence this protest. Begrudgingly, the government acknowledged that residents had, indeed, invested in Freedman's Village and "in several cases such improvements have been equal to twice or thrice the original cost of the building."[132] In the end, most residents received at least some compensation for their lands, but these payments were far under market value. Nancy Jackson, who came to the Village on her own as a teenager soon after its opening, created a good life for herself in the Village. Nancy built a home and made agricultural improvements. She received $123.15 in compensation for her home, trees, and vines to help herself and her family.[133] Other neighbors received smaller funds. Martha Smith received forty dollars and thirty-four cents for her home and another three dollars for agricultural improvements. Lucy Harris was paid only thirty-five dollars for her home, which she purchased for fifty dollars nearly twenty years earlier. She was "distressed" at the idea of having to leave her home.[134]

Lucy lived within one of the central houses of the Village beginning in 1865, when she and several members of her extended family moved to the Village. The prolonged period of pressure against the Village drove many residents away before its formal closing. Although several members of the Harris family lived in the Village in 1865, by 1888, only Lucy remained. Other families, such as the Parks family, were able to remain together in the Village. Previously enslaved at Arlington House, the entire thirteen-person Parks family remained together in the Village. As of the federal survey, two generations of the Parks family had been homeowners at Freedman's Villages. James Parks lived in one of the original duplex structures created by the War Department in the core of the Village. He was given only thirteen dollars and twenty cents for his home. Of the second Parks generation, William Parks and the younger Lawrence Parks each received payments in the seventy-dollar range for their farms. Farmers generally received more money than those living in the central Village. The Owens family received one hundred thirty dollars for their home and farm. This was not always the case, however, as some farmers, like William Winston, received nothing at all—their modest homes and land improvements deemed worthless by the

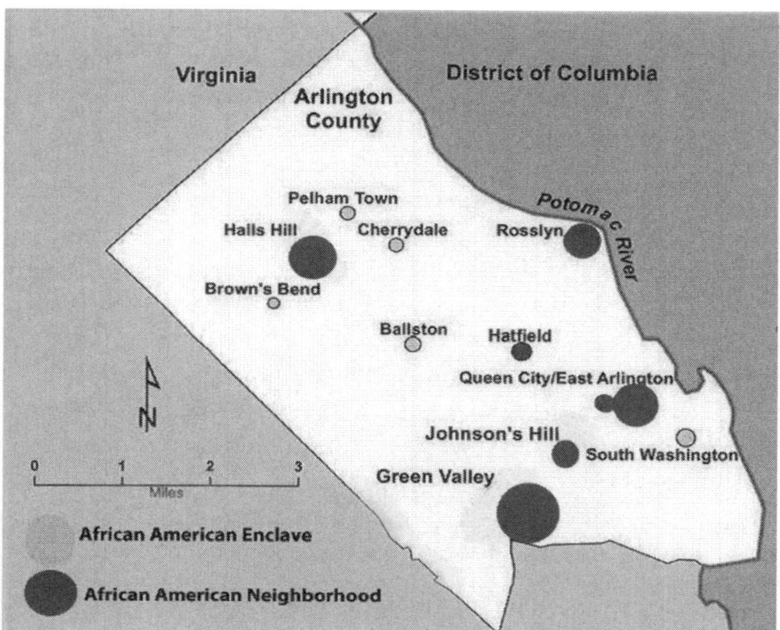

FIGURE 6. Arlington's modern borders show new and expanded Black settlements in Arlington in 1900. Original map by Nancy Perry, projection NAD 1983 UTM Zone 18N, with edits by Lindsey Bestebreurtje.

government. Ultimately, each household was paid an average of one hundred three dollars for their land and homes, less than half of what Syphax originally requested. At the same time, Congress deemed the "contraband fund tax" levied on the freedmen during the war on top of standard taxes illegal retroactively. Taxes and property valuations were reimbursed at the same time. These funds together provided each household with an average of just under five hundred seventy-six dollars with which to move, find a new home, begin improvements again, and start their lives over.[135] By 1900, the last of Freedman's Villages' residents relocated. Nearly forty years after the community's formation and thirteen years after the original eviction notice was handed down, Freedman's Village, Arlington's first entirely African American, preplanned community ceased to exist.[136]

Conclusion

The prewar Arlington of small farms gave way to an environment of suburban villages by the first decades of the twentieth century. Freedman's Village and the promise of employment with the federal government led to an expansion of Arlington's Black population.

Neighborhoods, Black and white, speckled the landscape. This expansion of Black neighborhoods across Arlington was a direct result of the closure of Freedman's Village. As the social and political power of white Arlingtonians continued to grow, white developers and politicians worked to evict African Americans from the all-white suburban county they desired. African Americans both challenged and embraced the suburban ideals of their time, creating both working-class and middle-class neighborhoods of their own. Without regard for whether Black Arlington's neighborhoods challenged or reinforced their own aesthetic visions, Arlington's white leaders steadily created legislation to push out Blacks throughout the county.

"Gone Out to Do for Themselves"

The Freedman's Village Diaspora and Arlington's Suburban Villages

The closing of Freedman's Village had profound effects on Arlington's suburban development.[1] Some Villagers left the area entirely, enticed by the "numerous applications from the North for their services," as employers knew of the Villagers' reputation for work, education, and skill.[2] Indeed, those same employers lamented that "it was almost impossible to induce any of them to migrate."[3] The majority of Freedman's Village's residents stayed local. As the Village shuttered, the government recorded that the Villagers had "gone out to do for themselves."[4] Nancy Jackson, William Green, and dozens more took the limited funds they received from the government and "set out to do for themselves" and created their own African American communities.[5]

In style and substance, former Villagers sought to create their own suburban villages in the style of their previous home. The freedmen and the first generation of African Americans born in freedom embraced the suburban land reforms from Freedman's Village.[6] From the 1840s to the 1890s, Americans came to idealize the suburban lifestyle through changing narratives around the home, nature, and domesticity.[7] Throughout this time, African Americans were affected by these same ideological pulls, if in different ways.[8] By the 1890s, through their choices of home type, neighborhood type, and travel beyond the home for work, Arlington's Black residents consciously chose suburban environments to build their homes and lives. This is evident by the fact that some migrated to the preexisting Black communities of Hall's Hill or Green Valley. Thomas and Hannah Owen and William A. Rowe relocated to Green Valley. Others formed new settlements. The closing dispersed the Village's residents, resources, churches, and institutions across the county in a diaspora. This multiplied the number and variety of Black settlements. No less than eleven small Black enclaves arose across Arlington. The majority of these new Black residential areas grew in eastern Arlington, on the outskirts of the Village's former borders.

The Freedman's Village Diaspora

Although many of these areas grew up in ways that were similar to Freedman's Village, each took its own unique path. At Freedman's Village, the War Department constructed all of the homes of the central Village at once. Lacking this type of centralized planning and building, the housing types within these new communities were more diverse. These diverse housing and neighborhood choices highlight differences within Arlington's African American population about what made an area a good place to live. These opinions were affected by class, past experiences, where one chose to build, how much land one could afford, and whether one could find someone willing to sell to African Americans in Arlington's increasingly hostile environment. These distinctions point to a lack of one central African American suburban vision for Arlington at this time. Despite these variations, social institutions linked African American communities.

Organizations were a core part of Black community formation in Arlington, but not every neighborhood could build and sustain their own institutions. This was especially true of smaller enclaves. Without institutions of their own, Arlington's African American population traveled beyond their own communities to larger nearby Black communities with these amenities. For example, when William Green built his home from land purchased from a white farmer in 1880 in the almost exclusively white Ballston neighborhood, the area had no amenities open to African Americans.[9] Instead, the family traveled more than a mile through surrounding white areas to neighboring Black communities to attend school, shop, and worship. African Americans like the Greens made the choice to live in the smaller clusters such as these because of available lands and, perhaps, because the areas were already home to relatives or friends. Additionally, by establishing themselves in small Black enclaves rather than larger Black communities, residents could slip under the radar, escaping negative white attention. It is also possible that being close to white neighborhoods allowed residents to have access to amenities such as improved roads and trolley stops, even as other amenities like churches and schools were not open to them. At this time, nearby white residents did not support these Black enclaves but, instead, benignly tolerated them and attempted to reduce their presence in their everyday lives. For example, the white neighbors who bordered Ballston's Black enclave grew their hedges high to physically obstruct their view of Ballston's Black part of town.

With the closing of Freedman's Village, areas with existing communities like Green Valley expanded. Although not as dense or centralized as the Freedman's Village, Green Valley appealed to the migrants from the Village because it was home to a church, school, and active Black community. AME (African Methodist Episcopal) Zion Church had transitioned from

Freedman's Village to Green Valley. The congregation initially met in the homes of community leaders Levi and Sarah Jones and Henson Thompson until a stand-alone chapel was completed in 1875.[10] In 1870, area residents supported their own school. As was the case in Hall's Hill, both the AME Zion Church and the Kemper School were located in the geographical center of the Green Valley Community, highlighting their importance to the local community. Initially held within the home of teacher Charity Jones, this school expanded into Kemper School in 1875.[11] This expansion was due to Green Valley's organized and active community, who energetically lobbied Arlington officials for support. In 1871, minutes for a county meeting on public schools noted that there "seemed to be quiet an interest among the colored people, as there were quite a number of the parents and friends present who seemed anxious for a Public School."[12] They attended county political meetings, where they "requested another colored school be opened in order to be accessible to those living in the southern part of the district."[13] This organization helped secure amenities for their children and community.

Residents of Green Valley were increasingly middle-class individuals who actively participated in county affairs. This distinction began with the area's first residents, Levi and Sarah Jones. Free before the Civil War, the Joneses were able to purchase fourteen acres on which they built their home in 1844 for approximately four hundred dollars.[14] Beyond the Jones family, other individuals who were free before the Civil War also chose to establish their homes in Green Valley. This included others who were free before the war, such as William Taylor, Henson Thompson, and Frank Williams.[15] These individuals were in a better position than the newly freed to purchase land, because they had more time and experience earning wages. Henson Thompson, for example, was a skilled carpenter before and after the war.[16] After the war, the area attracted individuals—whether they were enslaved or free before the war—who were able to purchase larger tracts of land. For example, Charles Coles purchased seven acres in the 1870s.[17] Nearby white landowners who were hurting after the Civil War, including the Baggott and Fraser families, sold land in Green Valley to African Americans.[18] Additionally, the Jones family actively subdivided and sold land to African Americans, as did Washington, DC, land developer John Nauck, encouraging the development of a free Black community after the Civil War.[19]

Because of the existing institutions and active, middle-class residents, relocating to Green Valley was the choice made by several of the Village's prominent community leaders. This was the choice made by Selina Gray.[20] Although she "underwent a great deal to stay at Arlington [House]" as long as she could, eventually the pressures against Freedman's Village were too great, and Selina Gray and her family had to relocate. Although she was reluctant to leave, Selina was "very happy" to create "a comfortable home of my own." Gray and her family moved into a large stucco house on ten acres bordering the Jones property.[21] Another community leader who would relocate to Green Valley was William A. Rowe. He moved to Green Valley in 1879 with his wife and three children. Rowe quickly reestablished the role he had played in the Village's Jefferson District as a local political leader. He was elected as supervisor for Arlington District, the same position he had held in Jefferson District. Rowe's daughter, Anne, also relocated to Green Valley from the Village with her new husband, Thomas H. West. West worked as a builder and general contractor. He quickly constructed middle-class homes for his fellow residents, most of which were large Colonial-style brick homes. Up to this time, Green Valley was still a mixed-race community, with white and Black families intermingled throughout the landscape.[22] However, the influx of new Black residents who had been the leaders of Freedman's Village solidified the community's path toward becoming an exclusively African American and increasingly middle-class neighborhood.

In addition to creating enclaves and expanding existing communities, the Freedman's Village diaspora also created new Black communities at this time. One of these new communities was Queen City. Unlike earlier communities like Green Valley, Hall's Hill, and Freedman's Village, Queen City was not located on particularly desirable lands. Instead, its land was flat, prone to flooding from the nearby Potomac River, and situated near several factories. Together with the adjacent community of East Arlington, Queen City was in southeastern Arlington, in the lowlands outside of what had been Freedman's Village.

Queen City was nestled in a triangle of land formed by Columbia Pike; Mount Vernon Avenue; and the Washington, Alexandria, and Mt. Vernon trolley line.[23] Despite other problems with the community's location, this placement along both roads and the rails gave residents very easy access to the cities of Alexandria and Washington. Although fare rates could prove onerous to residents, with this access, they could more easily travel to work, to shop, and to sell their wares at the larger city markets. Access to transportation infrastructure caught the attention of residential developers, who consistently sought county land for expansion and subdivision.[24] Thus, this connectivity also made residents of Queen City vulnerable to outside pressures, preventing them from developing the kind of insulation that residents of Hall's Hill cultivated.

Queen City residents built their community around their church, a church with roots in Freedman's Village. With the first rumblings about the likely closure of the Village in the late 1860s, the Old Bell Church was demolished. At that time, the church split into two congregations—Mount Zion Baptist

Church and Mount Olive Baptist Church—in what would become Queen City. In 1892, as Freedman's Village began to close, the new community of Queen City formed around their church. Despite having just been removed from Freedman's Village, residents were still hopeful about the possibility to continue their community and remain permanently in Arlington. As a representation of this desire for permanence, they constructed a large and costly brick church for Mount Olive Baptist. The two-story, red-brick, marble-front church became the geographical center of the new neighborhood, and this African American institution became the center of a new Black community.

Saving one-fourth of an acre for the church, the remaining land was parceled into forty lots to be sold to church members leaving the Village. With small plots of twenty feet by ninety-two feet, this subdivision transformed the former farmland into a denser, suburban environment. The Volins were one of the families who purchased a lot in Queen City. George Volin and his mother-in-law, Lettie Colling, took their settlements from the government and came to Queen City. The family's small lot cost thirty-five dollars, and they quickly set out building a house on the property.[25] Many of the homes constructed by former residents of Freedman's Village at this time were reminiscent of the simple clapboard houses they called home in the Village, making housing type another product of the Village's diaspora. This aesthetic choice showed the residents' continued connection to the Village and their desire to recreate some of the elements of their former community but with new choices that represented a changing Arlington. The two-story, six-room, central hallway home that the Volins constructed for themselves was still modest in size—only eighteen feet wide by thirty-two feet long—but was larger than the four-room structure of the Village. Though modest, the home cost eleven hundred dollars in building supplies from the Murphy and Ames Lumber Company.[26] This hefty price tag highlights why African American families often constructed their homes themselves and in a piecemeal fashion, putting in sweat equity wherever possible.

On their modest property, the Volins kept hogs, but they were not able to grow food on their plot. Queen City residents had to transition away from even small-scale subsistence farming because of the slight size of their lots and because their soil, so close to Arlington's brickyards and industrial district, was not ideal for farming. This inability to grow their own food was an adjustment from Freedman's Village, where the Volins' property was "full of Blackberries [and] cherry trees."[27] Without the option to grow food for subsistence or sale, Queen City resident Baldwin Gray worked multiple jobs to stay afloat. He was employed as a fisherman, selling fish in DC markets. He was also a contract employee with the federal government, mowing grass and taking care of the grounds on the National Mall around Hains Point and the

Lincoln Memorial. This was a departure from the choices previously made by working-class families in Arlington. With limited land, Gray, the Volins, and families like them had to adapt away from the older means of family subsistence that relied at least somewhat on farming. Most food was bought in DC's Black neighborhood markets, with smaller items secured within the community at the local Veney's General Store.

Beyond Queen City, other emerging Black communities in eastern Arlington grew along Columbia Pike and the newly constructed trolley car lines. The primary lines in eastern Arlington were the Washington, Arlington, and Mount Vernon line, which serviced Queen City, and the Washington, Arlington, and Falls Church Railway, which serviced nearby Black neighborhoods Johnson's Hill and Butler-Holmes, and points west beginning in 1891.[28] Queen City's proximity to the brickyards, major roads, and trolley lines made it a more industrial suburban neighborhood than some of its emerging middle-class counterparts. The new communities that grew up around these lines were increasingly smaller and more densely populated, and many residents used the lines to commute into Washington for work. The development patterns established in Black working-class neighborhoods continued the transition away from a still somewhat rural community with small farms and toward an even more densely populated, suburban existence.

More than just working-class communities emerged out of the closing of Freedman's Village. Arlington had a growing contingent of Black middle-class residents, particularly among the younger generation. The closing of Freedman's Village occurred at a time of generational shift. The first generation of African Americans raised in freedom had come of age during the Reconstruction era, when social and political rights were still relatively strong for African Americans. Men such as Edmund C. Fleet Sr., who were born in the Village, educated there, and had not personally experienced the trials of slavery, used the community institutions, education, and sense of belonging imparted to them by their parents to push for more rights through active membership in Arlington's middle-class institutions. Fleet's father, Hiram Fleet, was an active member in the community and Mount Zion Church, conveying to his son the importance of community organization. With this increase in opportunities, a new Black middle-class emerged. These families stressed "etiquette, manners, and chivalry."[29]

Arlington's Black middle-class was defined by those individuals who generally had higher levels of education, many of whom were employed by the federal government and were leaders in their communities through church leadership, mutual aid societies, and politics. Because of restrictions blocking their progress in various economic endeavors in a white-dominated society, African Americans had a slightly more malleable understanding of middle-class status that was predicated on education, community leadership, and behavior over a strictly economic definition.[30]

The Village's closing also occurred at a time of residential shift. The same changes that encouraged suburban development and movement beyond the city during the early and mid-nineteenth century intensified by the turn of the twentieth century. Suburbia continued to rise in popularity as new social and political movements continued to stress the importance of nature, space, and the single-family home over urban living.[31] Trolley networks continued to expand their lines and service to allow commuting to work from greater distances. Developers took a more active role in Arlington, platting and supporting preplanned suburban developments. Through these changes, the suburban residential type became more entrenched in Arlington. These two shifts together of a rising Black middle class and growing suburban development were reflected most fully in the creation of the new neighborhoods Johnson's Hill and Butler-Holmes.

Johnson's Hill began in 1880 when white farmer J. R. Johntson and, later, his son Richard, subdivided their farm and sold lots to African Americans leaving Freedman's Village.[32] The first rounds of purchases went to Harrison Green, Emmanus Jackson, and Harry W. Gray, son of Selina Gray. Later, other Village community leaders came to Johnson's Hill, including James Pollard.[33] Johnson's Hill sits on a hill along Columbia Pike, just outside the bounds of Freedman's Village and the expanding Fort Myer in east Arlington. The lots that Johnston sold were ten-acre plots. The larger size of these plots set the Johnson's Hill residents apart from nearby residents of Queen City, for example, who could only afford much smaller plots. The community itself had large plots but few residents and few amenities. Residents traveled beyond the borders of the community for church and school, but the community's positioning between Queen City and Green Valley meant that this travel was not arduous.

Despite lacking some other community institutions, Johnson's Hill became home to one of the most important African American middle-class institutions in Arlington: The United Order of Odd Fellows. On land purchased for two hundred dollars in 1884, along the western edge of Johnston's property, Arlington's growing Black middle class created a home for the Grand United Order of Odd Fellows. Here, Odd Fellows Steven's Lodge Number 1435 fraternal organization established Odd Fellow's Hall.[34] This hall played host to other African American institutions before they could create their own permanent places, including several churches and the Masons, further solidifying the importance of the Odd Fellows and their hall's location in Johnson's Hill. The order was originally founded in 1870 in Freedman's Village by community leaders.

FIGURE 7. Harry W. Gray (*left*) and his wife (*right*), Martha M. H. Gray, were middle-class leaders in their Johnson's Hill neighborhood after relocating from Freedman's Village. Harry Gray Gillem Collection, Arlington House: The Robert E. Lee Memorial, Arlington, Virginia.

The Odd Fellows attracted new members from the new generation of young Black men. Most joined the order in their early twenties, including James Smith at the age of twenty-two and several young men from the Parks family.[35] Although located in Johnson's Hill, this organization was "the one club which bound together Black people from all the churches and neighborhoods in Arlington."[36] Members paid dues of between twenty-five cents and $1.25 a month, depending on their ability to donate. This sliding membership scale highlights the ways in which the label of middle class was not strictly tied to income. The organization filled many needs for Black Arlingtonians. They hosted entertainment and social activities, provided burial services at their private cemetery, served as a credit union, and donated money for both the "sick and distressed" and for the general "good and welfare" of the Black community. The Odd Fellows donated to each of Arlington's Black churches and schools in turn.[37] The mutual aid and uplift of the Odd Fellows within Johnson's Hill highlights the area's growing middle-class community. The Gray family was a part of this development.

Resident Harry W. Gray was a skilled mason.[38] He also received an education and could read at a fifth-grade level. Although education was a cornerstone of the Black community and many adults worked to become literate, pre–Civil War restrictive Black Codes resulted in lower literacy rates among African Americans at this time. His vocational skills and education put Gray in high demand after the Civil War. Throughout the late 1860s, Gray

FIGURE 8. This 2003 photograph shows a modern shot of the Gray's Italianate style row home in the Johnson's Hill neighborhood. Their home demonstrated Gray's building skills, the family's middle-class status, and their aspirations about the neighborhood as becoming a more urban environment. Photo: Jennifer Hallock, "Harry W. Gray House," National Register of Historic Places, Listing date, February 11, 2004.

worked at the nearby Blick-West brickyard and as a contract laborer for Arlington House, where he improved his masonry skills.[39] In 1872, he left these jobs to become a messenger and clerk for the Department of the Interior. Six years later, he married Martha M. Hoard. Before the war, Martha had been enslaved at James Madison's Montpelier. At the age of fifteen, she moved to the District where she also began working at the Department of the Interior.[40] After marrying, the couple purchased their land in Johnson's Hill for eight hundred dollars and began constructing their home, where the couple would raise four children.[41] The six members of the Gray family lived at their Johnson's Hill residence with a live-in servant.

For their home, the Grays built a two-story, three-bay-wide, red-brick, Italianate-style row home. This style mimicked houses from DC's Foggy Bottom neighborhood, where Martha's parents lived. The row home was constructed without windows along the sides of the house. That is because when it was completed in 1882, the Grays imagined that, soon, other row homes would be built alongside theirs, predicting that Arlington would eventually become a more densely settled environment. Similar growth was occurring at the same time in other residential areas outside major cities of the South. For example, the Dilworth neighborhood outside of Charlotte, North Carolina, opened in 1887 with a semiurban grid model with diverse home types beyond the detached, single family home.[42] Gray's neighbors created Italianate- and Queen Anne-style homes for themselves, though none as ornate as the Grays'.[43] These homes highlight the type of community they hoped to create in Arlington, one that was stable and centralized, with a strong middle-class presence like the one they observed in Washington's Foggy Bottom.

Another middle-class neighborhood to emerge at this time was Butler-Holmes. Located west of Fort Myer, across Columbia Pike from Johnson's Hill, the community was named for its founders, William H. Butler and Henry Louis Holmes. Both men were African American and leaders in Arlington's Black community who began that leadership role in Freedman's Village. Butler served as commissioner of roads in 1879 and as surveyor of the roads and superintendent of the poor throughout the 1880s. Holmes served as the commissioner of revenue from 1876 to 1903 and was a leader at the neighborhood's St. John's Baptist Church.[44] Both men were active leaders in the Odd Fellows. Holmes was also a founding member of the Masonic Lodge number 58, another important African American fraternal organization established by Arlington's growing Black middle class.

In 1879, the men and their families left Freedman's Village to establish their homes in the community that would bear their names. Butler constructed a wood frame, Queen Anne-style home, and Holmes erected a bungalow house. Each of these home types, along with the Italianate-style homes of Johnson's Hill, could be seen in the growing white suburbs of Arlington and were more popular choices in newly emerging white neighborhoods than those homes being built by Black homeowners. In creating a streetcar suburb for themselves and other like-minded African Americans, Butler and Holmes highlighted how the Black middle class shared many of the same values and aesthetics as their white counterparts regarding what constituted a suburban ideal. Butler and Holmes, unlike the Grays, wanted to create a bedroom community dominated by single-family homes. Butler and Holmes helped to shape Arlington's growing suburban environment. This was achieved by creating this kind of suburban neighborhood by and for African Americans. The bedroom community model was on the rise county-wide but was not yet the dominant environment type. With this vision in mind, the two men partnered in 1882 and subdivided their lands into plats to be sold to African Americans for suburban development.

African Americans developed the Black communities of Butler-Holmes, Green Valley, and Pelham Town, subdivided in 1890. Although this was less common than purchasing land from white sellers, the option to live within a community sold by and for African Americans was an appealing choice to many. Both Sarah and Levi Jones, key land sellers in Green Valley, and brothers Burrell and Moses Pelham, former residents of Hall's Hill who founded Pelham Town, created unplanned subdivisions.[45] The Jones and Pelham families each sold lands to those who seemed to have nowhere else to go, the Pelhams mostly selling and renting land to their own family. Butler and Holmes, however, stand out for their intention to form a centralized, platted, Black community. By setting out to create a suburban neighborhood that embraced then-contemporary ideals about suburban homes and communities, they pushed their ideas from their individual homes to the community at large.

A 1900 map of Arlington shows twenty-six plats of land of between 0.5 and 0.25 acres in Butler-Holmes.[46] Families like Abraham and Julia Sommers and J. H. and Lilly Williams purchased some of the smaller plots in Butler-Holmes.[47] J. H. Williams was only twenty years old in 1900 when he purchased his land, perhaps hoping to expand his property further as he was able. Members of the growing middle class, such as Edmund C. Fleet Sr., purchased a home in Butler-Holmes. Fleet served alongside his community's founders as a leader in the Odd Fellows, Masons, and church. These individuals could have been drawn to Butler-Holmes by its founders' commitment to a suburban vision or the possibility to own land within the only Black-owned subdivision.

Most Butler-Holmes residents worked beyond the neighborhood. Men like Clarence Johnson and C. Richard worked in Arlington's brickyards, whereas other neighbors worked as laborers or sledgers at a nearby quarry. Others worked as professional laborers in Washington, DC, including teamster William West and barber George Lee.[48] Because the majority worked beyond the neighborhood in Arlington's industrial areas, Alexandria, or the District, many were also likely drawn by the community's connection to both Columbia Pike and the Fort Myer Branch of the Washington, Alexandria, and Falls Church commuter rail system. The majority of women in the community did not work beyond the home, further highlighting the area's growing middle-class status.[49]

Arlington's rising middle-class communities created spaces distinct from their working-class counterparts. Where working-class communities like Hall's Hill created more rural spaces, supplementing income with homegrown food, middle-class Butler-Holmes residents kept tidy lawns. Where other working-class communities like Queen City focused on nearby industrial work for employment, the middle-class residents of Johnson's Hill were more likely to travel by trolley for office work. This shows the diversity among Black visions of what Arlington's future should look like. These communities and their residents experienced an Arlington in transition. The area's remaining small farms were sold off into lots, and new trolley lines continued to criss-cross the county. Black Arlingtonians hoped to be a part of this transition.

Despite differences in class and aesthetics, these neighborhoods were linked by their church and social institutions, most of which had roots in Freedman's Village. At the Village, Arlington's Black residents had lived together, which helped to solidify future cross-county connections despite future difference in status and class. In addition, each community institution had ties beyond the borders of the neighborhood where it was located. For example, when life-long Village resident Edmund C. Fleet Sr., relocated to Butler-Holmes on the Village's closing, he not only continued ties with the neighbors and institutions in his new community but also became a leader at Mount Zion church and Masonic Lodge in Green Valley and the Odd Fellows in Johnson's Hill.

Beyond these core connections, something that was consistent across all neighborhoods, despite class or aesthetics, was the importance of home ownership. Despite attempts to push Black residents from suburban Arlington through efforts such as closing Freedman's Village, Arlington's Black residents were becoming an increasingly stable group. By 1900, fifty-nine percent of Black families in Arlington owned their homes.[50] This rate of homeownership was well above both the national rate of 46.5% for all Americans and 22.1% for African Americans that same year.[51] Some residents continued to rent homes. Pelham Town, platted in 1890 by the Pelham brothers, Moses and Burrel, just ten blocks from the Hall's Hill community, had high rental rates.[52] Beyond Pelham Town, which was mostly rented to Pelham relatives, those who rented were more likely to be non-native Virginians or in households headed by women, but employment type was not a deciding factor in determining who rented and who owned their home.[53] With a relatively small renting population, Arlington did not experience the speculative rental market like residents of nearby Washington, DC, where demand for cheap rental properties greatly outpaced supply.[54] African American home ownership was still quite high in the county. It was a direct result of this home ownership that new generations of Arlington's African American residents were able to stay in the homes and neighborhoods where they grew up.[55] This home ownership was made possible because of several factors. Many had received funds from the federal government when Freedman's Village was closed that helped secure down payments. Black Arlingtonians had access to loans through mutual aid societies, like the Odd Fellows, and access to the strong nearby Black community in Washington. Desperate white Arlingtonians who were looking to sell land to anyone, despite color, immediately after the Civil War provided a large supply of land. Additionally, African American residents' willingness to build their homes slowly over time as funds became available helped them to own their own homes.

Because so many of Arlington's Black residents were dispersed by the closure of Freedman's Village, it is also very likely that this negative experience with the government had shown them exactly how important home ownership was. Despite contracts with the War Department that led many residents to believe that they had purchased their homes and lands, they were removed from of their properties with the claim that they had no legal right to them in the first place. It took years of legal battles to get the federal government to admit that the residents did have a legal claim to their homes and issue minimal compensation for improvements. This highlighted the importance of home ownership for Black residents of Arlington and pushed them to own rather than rent wherever possible. Sadly, ownership and a solid legal claim to their homes and properties would not always be enough to keep encroachment from white Arlingtonians at bay.

Suburban Villages

The closure of Freedman's Village was not the only step necessary for boosters to create the kind of environment they sought. The county would need to formally excise itself from Alexandria City to allow the area's leaders to actualize their new vision for the built environment. Thanks to changes in Virginia's state constitution, in 1870, the two legally split, freeing Arlington County to determine the trajectory of their own development without the influence of Alexandria City for the first time.[56] In addition to Arlington's new autonomy, the area needed transportation infrastructure to develop. Before the Civil War, the Alexandria and Washington Railroad and the Alexandria, Loudoun, and Hampshire Railroad served the county. But both these lines were destroyed during the war.[57] From the 1880s to the first years of the new century, rail and trolley lines offering commuter service sprang up throughout the county. The Washington, Alexandria, and Mount Vernon commuter line opened in 1892, with subsequent expansions over the coming years. This line was the only Virginia trolley line offering service in Washington, DC, as well as throughout Arlington and northern Virginia. In the 1890s, several lines attempted to run tracks into Washington, but the investment that was needed to traverse the Potomac River proved too costly. Instead, rail passengers had to walk into Washington to continue on to their

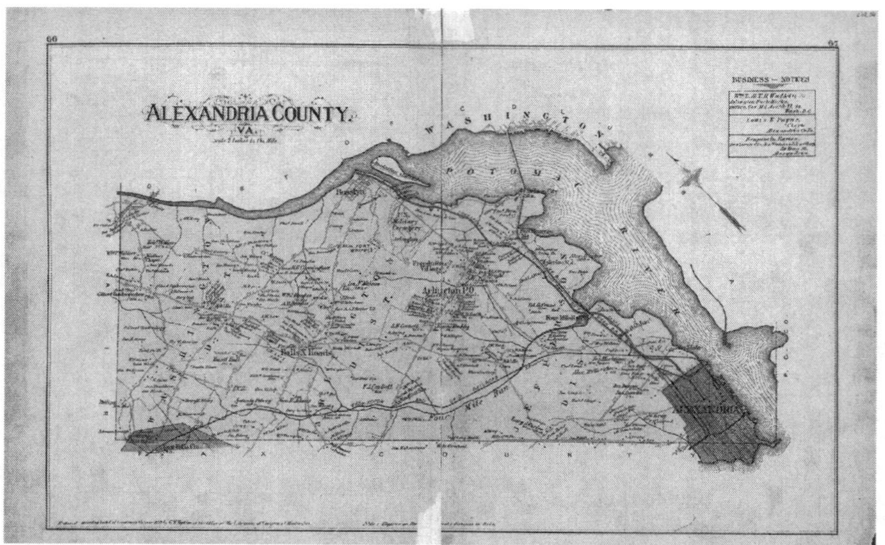

FIGURE 9. Many new communities developing across Arlington County, then called Alexandria County, as the area moved into the twentieth century are shown. Griffith Morgan Hopkins Jr., "Alexandria County, Va, 1878" [1878] Maps Division, Library of Congress.

final destinations until the completion of the Washington, Alexandria, and Mount Vernon connector line in 1906, after more than a decade under construction.[58] The Washington, Arlington, and Falls Church line also continued to expand; these lines connected at the Clarendon stop in 1907.

Suburban environments developed through the late nineteenth century as improvements in transportation via steam, omnibus, and commuter rails made it possible for people to leave city centers and still commute daily to work.[59] Arlington's rail lines were packed with commuters. Indeed, one county resident noted that you could "see more people coming home" on the trolleys in just one evening than could be seen "in ten days going around to their houses."[60] All of Arlington's early suburban development depended on the continued development of rail lines and connections to Washington, DC. For example, the Clarendon stop of the electric trolley line from Falls Church to Rosslyn helped spur substantial suburban development after it opened in 1897.[61] The Wood Harmon Real Estate Division subdivided the entire area along Wilson and Washington Boulevards, west to Clarendon Circle, and north to Key Boulevard with squared blocks on twenty-five-foot lot frontages throughout the area. Arlington saw a huge boom in growth and development, with eleven new white communities developed between 1879 and 1900 alone, and those numbers only continued to rise.[62]

Arlington needed the rail lines to encourage truly robust development, because the county's roads were in bad shape. Frank Ball, son of Ballston community leader William Ball, called the lines one of the "greatest things that occurred in Arlington County prior to 1900," because it met "the needs of the people" while also "building up the County" for future residents.[63] Developers took responsibility for roads within individual communities. As a result, some individual neighborhoods had passable roads, while the county's road networks at large remained rudimentary. In 1890, three bridges crossed from Arlington into the District, with roads fanning out from each.[64] All of these public roads remained unpaved dirt, oyster shell, or gravel roads into the 1920s.[65] Wilson Boulevard, a major thoroughfare in central Arlington, became Arlington's first fully paved public road in 1909.[66]

The rail lines provided "cheap and rapid" transportation with "the prospect for a rapid increase in the value of land."[67] The increased value of land for settlement due to the expansion of the rail lines occurred at the same time of declining farming in the area. During the decade from 1870 to 1880, Arlington's total farmland declined by almost fifty percent, from fifteen thousand two hundred sixty to eight thousand ninety-five acres.[68] The county saw similar decreases in improved lands, farm animals, and yields as the area transitioned away from small farms and toward residential development. The county began its transition away from farming. By 1900, there were only three hundred seventy-nine farms.[69] Many of which were small "truck farms," where farmers sold their modest harvest at local markets. By the mid-twentieth century, the farming lifestyle would be a thing of the past in Arlington.

Transportation was necessary but not sufficient in encouraging this early suburban growth. These transportation improvements occurred at the same time as many other changes in the American city. Immigration and population booms made city centers denser. People began to fear epidemics and crime associated with urban centers. Cities also became more industrial with the rise in larger scale factory work over smaller shops, creating more noise and pollution. At the same time, social and health opinions that pushed the importance of fresh air and space were growing in prominence. The single-family home also became a central tenet of middle-class respectability and aspiration, greatly increasing "the actual and symbolic value of the house as a physical entity," as historian Kenneth Jackson has shown.[70] Beginning in the early 1800s, and expanding after the Civil War, developers constructed suburban environments as a way to combine the city's strongest features—culture and employment—with the best aspects of the country—spacious, owner-occupied, mostly single-family homes.

At this time, Arlington's enterprising white landowners created the area's earliest white suburban communities. One such landowner who decided to make the jump from farmer to land developer was Frank Corbett. In 1864, Corbett, a transplant from New York State, purchased one hundred sixty-two acres of land along Columbia Pike, a major road between Arlington and Washington to the north and the markets of Fairfax and beyond to the south. For more than a decade, Corbett lived on and farmed this land.[71] Then, in 1885, Oscar Haring of Georgetown approached Corbett about purchasing two acres of his sizable farm.[72] In addition to its location along Columbia Pike, Corbett's land sat along the Washington and Ohio Railroad. Opened in the first years of the 1870s, the line's twice-daily trains serviced stations throughout the county, including the "Arlington Station" at Columbia Pike and Four Mile Run, along Corbett's property.[73] Haring wanted to purchase the small tract across from the Arlington Station to build a home and commute into the city. Corbett now saw an opportunity to change the trajectory of his land.

Living through these trends, Frank Corbett realized that Oscar Haring's offer to purchase two acres of land in 1885 could be the start of something much larger. By 1886, he hired a surveyor to lay out a forty-acre subdivision.[74] Corbett imagined an upper middle-class suburb, dominated by Victorian homes on large lots. He laid out a grid land-use pattern that was common at the time, with seven blocks with seven half-acre lots per block and a park.[75] This deep grid pattern mirrored the English parks of the 1820s and 1830s that became the blueprint for exclusive residential developments across the country.[76] This environment attracted upper middle-class residents to Corbett's subdivision, many of whom owned their own businesses. John Newlon moved to Arlington from the District in 1885 to open his own mill. Before relocating to the neighborhood, Newlon served as head miller of Herr and Cissel millers in Georgetown.

Another early resident, Florence T. Johnston, an independently wealthy woman, purchased three lots, totaling one-and-a-half acres. These upper middle-class residents built large, two-story single family frame houses set far back from the street.[77]

The 1880s and 1890s saw an explosion of development in Arlington. A small number of pre-Civil War communities, like Ballston, had developed slowly since the early 1800s. As farming plots became increasingly smaller, the Ballston community grew primarily around the farming plot of John Ball.[78] But most of Arlington's white communities came about during the last decades of the nineteenth century. The subdivisions of Glencarlyn, Bon Air, Fostoria, East Falls Church, Cherrydale, Clarendon, and Fort Myer Heights all emerged.[79] Unlike their earlier counterparts, these communities all grew very quickly. The rapid development of these preplanned subdivisions is easily illustrated with the establishment of county post offices in the 1880s and 1890s. As neighborhoods grew and blossomed, they needed their own amenities, like post offices. The neighborhood post offices for Arlington View (1885), Rosslyn (1888), Carlin Springs (1891), Cherrydale (1893), and Fort Myer (1895) all came about as a result of developers actively planning for Arlington's domestic-centered future.[80] Even the small grouping of homes around Ballston, growing over the course of more than eighty years, reached a critical mass in 1881, when it finally had enough residents to warrant its own post office.

Unlike their African American counterparts, these communities grew in social as well as physical isolation from one another. White neighborhoods were physically separated, scattered along the trolley stops of Arlington's growing rail lines, with expanses of still-rural lands between them.[81] Although many of Arlington's Black communities also grew in physical isolation, these communities were linked by ties of kinship, church, and social institutions. With the exceptions of Green Valley and Hall's Hill, whose roots trace back to before and the middle of the Civil War, respectively, all of Arlington's other African American enclaves and communities grew as a result of the closure of Freedman's Village. Even those two earlier communities were linked to the Village through social and political ties. Their initial interconnection at the Village meant that Arlington's Black communities were linked socially, despite their physical separation across the county. However, Arlington's white communities did not share these connections. Residents either looked beyond Arlington for social connections, feeling well served by existing accommodations in Washington and Alexandria Cities, or created amenities for their immediate residents alone, spurning broader social connections. For example, unlike Arlington's Black neighborhoods, early white churches were created exclusively by and for members of individual communities. Clarendon United Methodist in 1901, Trinity Episcopal in 1902, and several other white congregation churches formed throughout the first decades of the twentieth century. When beginning the Sunday school that would grow to become Clarendon United Methodist Church, the Overal family, for example, focused entirely on the spiritual needs of "the families of the neighborhood" but did not focus on encouraging fellowship beyond their immediate neighbors.[82] The founding for each of these churches tells the same tale of individuals within a community wanting to create a congregation within their own communities to serve those individual suburban communities alone. As new subdivisions formed, rather than join existing congregations, residents formed new churches.[83] This isolationist attitude stemmed from the fact that, unlike Black communities, white communities considered themselves to be in competition for resources. For example, as the community of Bon Air began to grow, nearby Glencarlyn did not celebrate this expansion. Glencarlyn residents worried that Bon Air's rapid growth would mean those residents would use and eventually take control of their school and community resources.[84]

Arlington's ever-expanding suburban development meant that these suburban villages were increasingly pushed together. When discussing the county's future, Crandal Mackey observed that the area's "many villages are already pressing their borders upon each other" to create "one large and prosperous" Arlington.[85] As rail lines continued to expand neighborhoods' physical isolation became a thing of the past. By 1900, trolley lines linked Clarendon, Ballston, Cherrydale, Bon Air, Glencarlyn, and Barcroft. The rail became "the cleanest and quickest way between Washington and Arlington, Fort Myer, Clarendon, Ballston, Falls Church," and beyond.[86] A swelling population also expanded the geographic boundaries between communities, bringing them in closer contact. Existing communities, such as Clarendon, expanded through additions by new developers, such as Robert W. Moore's "Moore's Addition to Clarendon" and Frank Lyon's "Lyon's Addition to Clarendon."[87] From 1900 to 1910, the county's population rose from sixty-five hundred to ten thousand.[88] New white residents were drawn to Arlington from Virginia and throughout the South for the county's suburban homes and neighborhoods with their easy access to employment in Washington.[89] As these communities became increasingly linked physically, boosters realized that if they were to have any chance at controlling the trajectory of Arlington's growth, court more buyers, and make more money, they needed to link these neighborhoods socially and politically. Mackey called for neighborhoods to be "tied together by a common interest and a common purpose"—namely, business, property development, and expansion of DC area commuters.[90] To move beyond isolated suburban villages in conflict with one another, Arlington would need a politically active group of professional developers at the helm of county affairs.

Conclusion

Freedman's Village brought many new African Americans to Arlington County at the close of the Civil War. Although the houses and physical layout of the Village were predesigned and built by the War Department, the residents themselves created and expanded the churches, schools, social, and fraternal institutions, all of which made the Village a community. These institutions and their aims reveal the kind of community Arlington's African Americans aspired to in freedom. Beginning in the 1880s and continuing into the dawn of the twentieth century, pressures from land developers, white residents, and federal forces pushed Freedman's Village to close. This closing marked the rise of white resistance to Black community formation, which would continue into the late twentieth century.

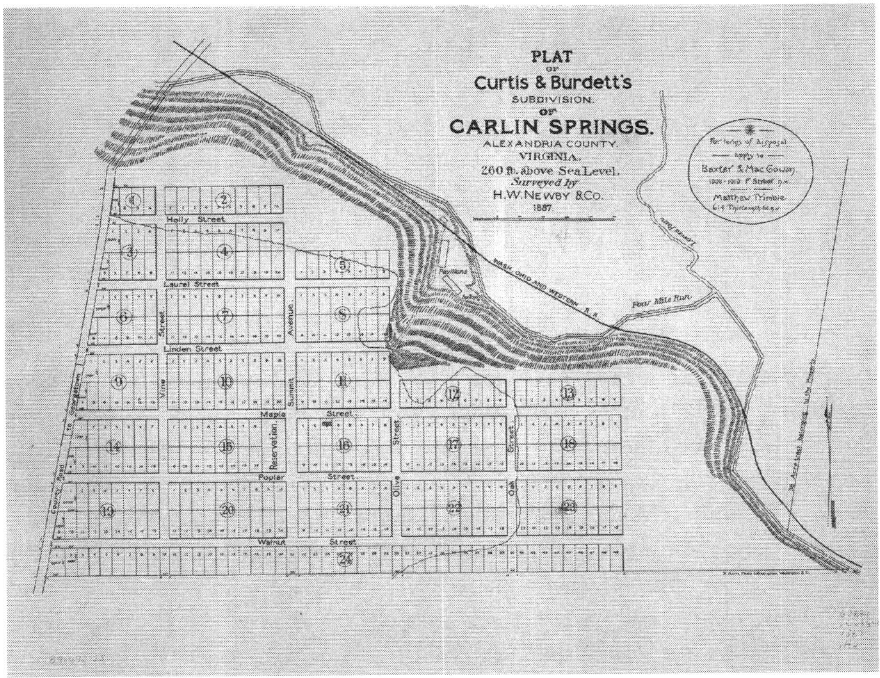

FIGURE 10. This map shows the preplanned grid plans now used by developers in Arlington's new suburban village neighborhoods. HW Newby & Co., "Plat of Curtis & Burdett's Subdivision of Carlin Springs, Alexandria County." [1887], Maps Division, Library of Congress.

On its closing, the community's residents, institutions, and ideas about community building and neighborhood aesthetics spread throughout the county. Before the Village's closing, independent African American neighborhoods began to form and expand throughout the county. Residents in the early communities of Hall's Hill and Green Valley created slightly more rural landscapes than the neighborhood model created at Freedman's Village. These landscapes merged older styles of land use seen in the county before the war with the smaller plots and more dense settlement that was a part of Arlington's postwar reality. The diaspora of Village residents shaped these early Black settlements and led to the emergence of many new African American neighborhoods and neighborhood types. In places such as Queen City, working-class residents were only able to purchase small lots—too small for the kind of semirural farming practices that earlier neighborhood residents used to supplement diets and incomes. Instead, residents used their access to trolley lines, major roadways, and Arlington's industrial center, anchored by brickyards, to support themselves and their families. Through these small lots, the residents of Queen City created a physically tight-knit and more densely populated community whose small, single-family homes were in line with the county's increasingly suburban environment.

Other new middle-class neighborhoods emerged with the closing of the Village. Former Village community leaders and the first generation of African Americans born in freedom made up the first generation of middle-class leaders in Arlington. Just as working-class visions of community development ranged from semirural and suburban, so too were middle-class ideas about what makes an area a good place to live conflicting between suburban and semiurban. The Grays in Johnson's Hill, for example, created a more urban brick row home for themselves, whereas African American land developers Butler and Holmes created a traditional streetcar suburb within their community. This shows a difference in aspirations on the part of Arlington's Black middle-class between one focused on mirroring an existing strong Black community and one that was more focused on aligning themselves with white visions. These aesthetic choices revealed aspirations for the present and the future. Each of these choices made by African Americans impacted Arlington's early development. Residents' choices of where to establish their neighborhoods, the size of their lots, how to orient themselves along new and existing transportation networks, and the houses they created all had a lasting impact on Arlington's development.

As the twentieth century dawned, white Arlingtonians regained their political power and social and civic influence. As this sway continued to grow into the Jim Crow era, Arlington's white leaders used their strength to force Black Arlington from what they increasingly envisioned as an all-white, exclusively suburban landscape. Without regard for whether Black Arlington's neighborhoods challenged or reinforced their own aesthetic visions, Arlington's white leaders steadily created zoning, planning, and covenant legislation to push out the large and diverse communities established throughout the county. Just as white residents resented Freedman's Village and lobbied for its closure, they also worked against the new African American communities that developed at the turn of the century. This resistance was the case, no matter what kind of community was created, from the working-class Queen City to the middle-class Butler-Holmes. This opposition to all Black neighborhoods, despite their class or aesthetic, highlights how new policies around zoning and planning created by white leaders that were meant to create a specific suburban vision for the county were also deeply tied to resistance to any Black presence. Although grounded in language of aesthetics of home design and neighborhood layout, the true cornerstone of white suburban desires was Black absence.

CHAPTER 3

"Suburban Homes . . . in Sight of the Monument"

Streetcar Suburbs and White Arlington's Expanding Control

Arlington's African American communities were not created in isolation.[1] Their formation was created in conversation with—and, in some cases, in opposition to—white communities. While Arlington's African American communities continued to grow and multiply after the closure of Freedman's Village, Arlington's white communities also expanded. This growth was both physical, with the formation of new neighborhoods, and ideological, with a continued solidification of social and political power. White Arlingtonians were slower than their Black counterparts to recognize the potential of the area as a suburban environment and to understand the power and influence they wielded over the built environment of Arlington. However, once whites regained social and political power after the Reconstruction Era, they took up the call of community development and expanded power with gusto. White powers-that-be continued to work against African American rights to diminish Blacks' presence. To fully understand how segregation was built into the law, one must understand not just the excluded group but also the motivations of the excluders. Only then can what historian David Delaney calls the "geopolitics of race" be understood to fully comprehend residential segregation in the Jim Crow Era.[2]

Arlington's suburban environment expanded rapidly. In addition to the African American turn-of-the-century communities already discussed, nearly a dozen new white suburban communities formed across Arlington County by 1900.[3] These communities and their homes represented something different for Arlington. Unlike Arlington's African American communities, which formed diverse neighborhoods from semirural to suburban, to aspirationally urban, Arlington's white communities created a more consistent environment across their neighborhoods. Communities followed the middle-class suburban trends of their time, transitioning from larger Victorian homes to smaller craftsman-style and bungalow models throughout the early twentieth century.

Builders constructed all these homes in centrally planned developments. Arlington was a part of a national trend away from piecemeal, individual home-building and toward large, centrally planned community developments.[4] These communities were preplanned on grid patterns primarily by developers and focused on symmetry, aesthetics, order, and the use of green space. One reason for this focus on preplanned developments was the City Beautiful Movement—an aesthetic, social, and political movement popular among the upper and middle class. Developers hoped to use aesthetics and connections to environmentalism in building to encourage order, symmetry, and harmony in life, with the aim of refashioning citizens' lives to make them engaged and well-rounded through changes in landscape design. It is not surprising that the upper and middle classes of Arlington embraced this movement so fully, as City Beautiful had a great impact on nearby Washington, DC, with the McMillan Commission's 1902 redesign of the National Mall.[5] Examples of this kind of development can be seen in the new, middle-class developments of Arlington. With these intellectual underpinnings, Arlington's developers created preplanned suburban villages consistent with suburban ideals.

White Arlingtonians' vision of their ideal suburban environment evolved over time. This vision came to be dominated by the latest trends in suburban house and land-use forms to create one contiguous suburb. However, initially individual "suburban village" neighborhoods constructed in isolation from one another dominated the landscape. These villages were laid out by newly minted developers, who were often large landowners transitioning to amateur developers. Suburban villages were secluded developments distributed across Arlington in physical and social isolation from neighboring areas. These villages created social and municipal institutions meant only for those living within their boundaries. This was unlike African American communities whose social institutions such as churches; fraternal organizations; and, in some cases, schools and stores were intended for Black residents despite the neighborhood in which they lived. This highlights a continued isolationist ideology among whites in Arlington that changed slowly over the course of the late nineteenth and early twentieth centuries.[6]

Moving beyond the suburban village model, several individual developers realized that only the ability to operate on the countywide level could allow for truly robust growth. With this ideological shift came changes in the tactics and policies of Arlington's leaders. Arlington's rising ranks of professional developers were very much connected to the political climate of the state and county. There was great overlap between Arlington's developers, boosters, politicians, and social leaders. In self-reinforcing relationships, these leaders sought to create a suburban vision for the county that used local development, politics, and policy together with state level laws to move the county in the direction of an interconnected environment that they themselves would build and control. This connectivity was supported by transportation networks that increasingly linked communities together. The decline in the suburban village model was also the result of federal expansion that brought more residents to the area, expanding white neighborhoods to make them more interconnected physically while decreasing individual neighborhood identities.

Aesthetics as well as race played into this ideal suburban vision of the county. Just as they worked to remove African Americans from political power, these leaders embarked on what they described as the "clean-up campaign" to rid the county of what they deemed less desirable Black residents. This countywide campaign sought to reform Arlington's politics and its physical landscape to create an environment more hospitable to booster control by targeting Black Arlington's rights and communities as illicit and corrupt. County leaders used the decades around the turn of the century to create neighborhoods that fit their visions of ideal suburban environments, to create a social and political environment that strengthened those neighborhoods, and finally to merge these physical and social environments to connect their neighborhoods and the visions of their founders into one, dense suburban environment as Arlington's white community moved from one of isolated suburban villages to one contiguous suburban environment.

The Good Citizens' League and Their Clean-Up Campaign

As Arlington's suburban villages began to transition to more interconnected neighborhoods through population and physical expansion, enterprising developers realized that, to control the aesthetics, class and race makeup, and wealth at stake in these communities, they would need to create a system of countywide control.[7] Arlington's boosters and developers increasingly turned their attention to state and county politics to continue their suburban vision.

One of the primary developers and leaders at this time was Frank Lyon. Like many Arlington developers, Lyon hailed from an elite Southern family. Born in Petersburg, Virginia, during the Civil War, he came from a long line of Old Dominion elites.[8] When Lyon moved to Arlington County in 1889 to attend Georgetown Law School, the county had rapidly expanded but still had large sections of rural lands open for development.[9] In this environment, Lyon saw the possibility to impact the landscape and have a hand in developing the county. This goal was impacted by his family line—Lyon's grandfather, Daniel Lyon, was one of the primary builders of the Petersburg area—and his experience working for the railroads.[10] Throughout the 1880s, Lyon traveled across the South as a clerk with the Richmond and Danville

Railroad; the Southern Railroad; and, later, with the Interstate Commerce Commission. This extensive travel influenced Lyon's land development ideas and choices. For example, while working for the Richmond and Danville line, Lyon lived in Charlotte, North Carolina. Charlotte, at this time, was a changing city, moving from a rural village to a hub of finance and trading. As Charlotte became an economic hub, the city developed streetcars and the beginnings of suburban neighborhoods.[11] Here, Lyon could see the kind of wealth and prosperity possible in the changing environments of the New South. However, in Charlotte, Lyon also learned that developments needed much more than attractive planning and access to transportation to build a successful suburb. For example, the Dilworth subdivision in Charlotte grew along the streetcar line and opened to much fanfare, but, ultimately, Dilworth was unsuccessful for nearly a decade. This was because the neighborhood lacked the appropriate social and political support.

Frank Lyon was not the only leader in Arlington who understood the necessity of creating a controlled environment where developers dominated not only neighborhood creation but also the laws and politics that governed them. Another major influencer of Arlington County affairs was Crandal Mackey. Born in Shreveport, Louisiana, in the back of a Confederate ambulance in December of 1865, Mackey came from a prominent Southern family.[12] The Mackey family is filled with generations of prominent lawmen who made their name serving as sheriffs, lawyers, and judges in South Carolina as far back as the 1770s, when Revolutionary War hero James Mackey immigrated to the United States.[13] Crandal Mackey continued this tradition of service to the law. In 1885, Mackey moved to Arlington's Rosslyn neighborhood to work for the War Department while studying law at Georgetown. There, he met Frank Lyon. The two men had similar social and political opinions. They served as co-vice presidents for the Bryan, Stevenson, and Rixey Club, a young men's club for the expanding Democratic Party.

After the end of Reconstruction, Virginia politics underwent an extended period of political shift. An initially strong interracial Republican Party lost power in Virginia in the early 1870s. In Arlington, the November election of 1872 saw strong victories for both national and local Republican candidates, with President Ulysses S. Grant and County Clerk John Syphax, the African American champion of Freedman's Village, both winning strong majorities.[14] But soon thereafter, this strength diminished. Facing stiff opposition from the increasingly powerful Democratic Party, Republicans began to move away from their commitment to rights and social progress for Blacks and the lower classes. Dissatisfied with both parties, African Americans and working-class whites seeking expansion in social reforms, like schools, as well as a meaningful voice in political participation, through government appointments and other means, joined together to create the Readjuster Party.[15] Under the unlikely direction of Confederate officer and railroad executive William Mahone, the Readjuster Party controlled Virginia politics from 1879 to 1883.[16] Although their ascendancy was brief, the Readjusters were the most successful interracial political party in the postemancipation South.[17] To counter this interracial alliance, Democrats used fear-mongering tactics centered around allegations of corruption, miscegenation, violence, and Black political control over whites. Democratic political power solidified by 1885, the same year when Mackey relocated to Arlington, with a changing of the guard in Virginia politics. In Virginia—and, indeed, across the South—a new generation of Democrats came to be dominated by a more cosmopolitan middle class of prominent businessmen, lawyers, and railroad men.[18] In pedigree and opinion, Mackey and Lyon fit in to this new political order, spearheading these kinds of political changes in Arlington County.

The two men became actively involved in Arlington County politics beginning in 1890, when they helped to establish the Good Citizens' League.[19] The League was a loosely organized social and political organization that comprised about twenty of the county's wealthiest and most prominent residents.[20] Many of their aims centered on bringing more municipal improvements to the county, recognizing a lag in public works and regulatory laws in Arlington's suburban communities as the area dramatically grew from a small farming hamlet to a more densely settled suburban environment. The League pushed for water and sewage improvements, gas and electric expansion, and road and trolley improvements.[21]

The League was a part of the Southern Progressive Movement. Late nineteenth-century and early twentieth-century Americans became active in reform programs designed to solve modern problems ranging from temperance, child labor, unchecked capitalism, and corruption in politics, all under the banner of Progressivism.[22] In the American South, these reformers took on these same issues while being greatly influenced by the region's geographical isolation, ideological mistrust of big government, and racial hierarchy.[23] Hailing from a growing suburban area, Arlington's leaders were a part of the drivers behind the Southern Progressive Movement rather than identifying with those in rural areas who sometimes resisted centralized reforms. Many contemporaries considered League member William Ball, whose family founded Ballston in the 1730s, a central leader of Arlington's Progressive Movement.[24]

While tackling real municipal needs, the League in Arlington used these improvements to expand suburban infrastructure so that League members could control the path of that development. "Those interested in developing real estate in the County" helmed the League.[25] They saw their organization as "a life-or-death struggle" without which "Arlington would [never] have grown into a fine residential community." These men knew that they could not attract buyers unless they gained political control.[26] The League members who were developers all created racially segregated communities. To shape public opinion in accordance with the League's focus on white, middle-class suburban development, Frank Lyon purchased the weekly newspaper *The Monitor*.[27] Under Lyon's leadership as owner and editor, *The Monitor* pushed League policies and opinions. Framing their social and political changes in the language of Progressive reforms, the Democrats set out curbing African Americans' social and political rights.[28] Leaguers joined many other Virginians calling for a new state constitution to limit voting rights of those opposed to their reforms to create a climate more amenable to their control.

Virginia state representatives, including those from Arlington County, sought to limit the scope of social, political, and civil rights guaranteed under the existing 1870 constitution.[29] Several League members were directly involved with the new constitution, with Lyon acting as the court reporter for the convention and Mackey serving as one of Arlington's three representatives at the event.[30] This new constitution attempted to remove the African American voice entirely from formal politics. On June 16, 1902, Virginia's Constitutional Convention presented their new constitution.[31] The Old Dominion's voting guidelines were drastically changed and required citizens to re-register to vote. The new requirements stated that anyone over twenty-one years of age could vote only if they themselves or their parents had fought in the Civil War; if they had paid a minimum property tax of one dollar, which required owning more than three hundred dollars in property; and if they could interpret a part of the state's constitution.[32] Later, a poll tax of one dollar and fifty cents was added to these requirements. Poll taxes must be paid six months before an election without the courtesy of a bill or notice.

This statewide change fit with county desires. Despite small population numbers and restricted rights for African Americans, to drum up support through racialized fear-mongering, white citizens in Arlington falsely claimed that "largely Black majorities" had to be overcome to ensure that Arlington would be a "white man's county" with "white man's rule."[33] The new voter registration requirements resulted in the disfranchisement of African Americans in Arlington and across the state. "The overall effect of the new franchise requirements was to cut the total vote in half" in Virginia, and lower voter turnout would continue to shape Virginia politics for decades.[34] Many Progressive reformers at the time believed disenfranchisement to be necessary to help African Americans, whom they saw as woefully unprepared for the responsibilities of suffrage after emancipation.[35] The aim to

FIGURE 11. The delegates of the Virginia Constitutional Convention. Frank Lyon, titled as the Clerk of the Committee, is photographed fourth from the left on the second-to-last row. Foster's Photographic Gallery, "Members and Officers of the Constitutional Convention of Virginia, Richmond—1901–2" (1901). Library of Virginia. Richmond, Virginia.

disfranchise African Americans was overt. Virginia State Senator Carter Glass of Lynchburg could not have been more explicit when he explained "Discrimination! Why that is exactly what we propose. . . . That exactly is what this convention was elected for—to discriminate to the very extremity of permissible action under the limitation of the federal Constitution, with the view to the elimination of every negro voter who can be gotten rid of."[36] This movement was not isolated to Virginia. New South progressivism led to disfranchisement of African Americans in South Carolina in 1895, Louisiana in 1898, North Carolina in 1900, and Alabama in 1901.[37]

Testing the impact of the new voting laws, the League fielded their own candidate for the first time in 1903 with the decision to nominate Crandal Mackey for the Commonwealth's attorney. This election was significant for Arlington, because it was the first election after the passage of Virginia's new constitution. Mackey faced stiff opposition from incumbent Richard Johnston.[38] Many saw Johnston as the enemy to the League not only for his relationship to what Leaguers deemed nonprogressive politics, but also because Johnston, and his father before him, sold their land to African Americans who formed the community of Johnson's Hill.[39] Mackey and Johnston engaged in a bitter race. With the virtual elimination of the African American vote, the election for Commonwealth's attorney was a testing ground to determine how much the disfranchisement of African Americans would impact the course of local elections. The contest was a dead heat. In the end, Mackey won by only two votes.[40] According to newspaper accounts of the time, "the reduction of the negro vote . . . under the new Virginia constitution, helped Mackey wonderfully."[41] This marked the beginning of the end of formal African American political participation in the county until the civil rights movement. Despite charges of corruption due to the extraordinarily small margin of victory, Mackey and the League used the election as a mandate.[42]

The decisions made at the 1902 Constitutional Convention about the voting rights of African Americans impacted both politics and suburban development in Arlington. Advertising literature for new white communities promoted Arlington's restrictive racial politics as an advantage of the area. Crandal Mackey reassured potential buyers that, although there were about "one-hundred colored" voters in the area, white registered voters outstripped them eight to one.[43] He further highlighted that, beyond this advantage in numbers, "the strictness of the election laws has improved the quality and character of the voter" by preventing these individuals from voting through the new, stringent voting laws.

The links between race and League policies about development and reform can also be seen in the League's dramatic and violent "cleanup" of Rosslyn. Beginning in the 1870s, Rosslyn's location immediately across the Aqueduct Bridge from Washington and about one mile from Fort Myer made it a hotspot for gambling and saloons.[44] But Rosslyn was also home to an African American enclave. Rather than seeing a small working-class Black community, which is how Rosslyn's Black residents would define themselves, League members characterized the enclave as "a gathering of shacks" that were "inhabited by the riff-raff" of the county.[45] The League wanted to work against Rosslyn's African American enclave "until the whole crowd was wiped out."[46] In its place, they hoped to "establish a community with a high standard of living" and "improve this area" for their own benefit.[47] With the protection of the law and political power in their corner, Mackey and the League decided to violently overthrow the less desirable elements in their county.

On Sunday, May 30, 1904, Mackey and members of the Good Citizens' League armed themselves and set out to clean up Rosslyn once and for all.

FIGURE 12. Although cartoonish in its portrayal of very real and serious violence, this watercolor by artist Rudy Wendelin demonstrates the chaos of the raid. Crandal Mackey is depicted in the doorway. Rudolph Wendelin, *Raid*, ca. 1970, Rudolph Wendelin Papers, Library and Archives, Forest History Society, Durham, NC.

Mackey and the League set out to reform Rosslyn to send a message to the county as a whole about exactly what their rule meant. Mackey sent letters to thirty county residents asking them to rally to his aid. In total, a posse of six embarked on the raid—Mackey, Lyon, and other League members Will Douglas, Lemuel Marcey, Luther Walter, and T. J. DeLashmutt.[48] They met in Washington, DC, and boarded the Mount Vernon Railroad into Rosslyn. Mackey deputized the men and handed out several sacks of weapons on the trolley—including sledgehammers, axes, and a sawed-off shotgun. The armed men disembarked at Rosslyn and headed to their first target, a "building in which all kinds of games were in the habit of being conducted."[49] Bursting in on the saloon resulted in chaos and violence: As patrons attempted to flee, "it did not bother [the posse] whether they left through the open doors or the closed windows."[50] Next, the raiders moved on to Eddie Heath's bar, Heath's Place. But Heath would not let Mackey and his League men enter his business without a fight, threatening the men with a shotgun from the door of his business. After a brief scuffle, Mackey disarmed Heath, and the raiding party entered Heath's Place.[51] The men used their weapons to hack up bars and slot machines, destroy alcohol, and arrest employees and patrons. "Glassware was smashed and the contents of the bottles, demijohns, and decanters was allowed to flow, giving the room the appearance of having passed through a Potomac flood."[52] During this breakup, the League's racial politics played a central role. The scene was violent, but the event saw only one shot fired. A League member fired his gun at the back of a fleeing Black man, who luckily was not struck.

Temperance and fears about political corruption from gambling interests were real concerns for League members and similar progressive reformers across the South, but their obsessions with respectability and lawlessness were not color-blind. These lawless elements were invariably tied to African American neighborhoods.[53] County residents did, indeed, hope that the League would be successful and "zealous in wiping the stain from the fair name of our community."[54] Many complained that saloons and gambling houses were not segregated. Throughout these decades, housing, recreation, and, indeed, life generally became increasingly segregated across the county, the state, and the South. But at these bawdy houses, "there are no distinctions made on account of class or color."[55] Racial fears of integrated drinking and socializing sparked antisaloon Progressive policies throughout the South. These kinds of interactions across the color line were a threat to the kind of New South order that Arlington's white leaders wanted to impose. As a result, African American neighborhoods throughout the South were attacked at this time under accusations that they were hotbeds of dangerous and illegal activities.[56]

Saloons were not only integrated zones; they provided a source of employment for local residents of Rosslyn's Black enclave. John Richard Bowen owned and operated one of the saloons in Rosslyn, the first Black-owned saloon in the county.[57] During this reform push, John Bowen lost his business. Without the saloon to sustain them, Bowen, his wife, Rachel, and their five young children left Rosslyn. They were fortunate, however, in that they were able to use the extended networks of Arlington's Black community to land on their feet. The Bowens were members of Mount Zion Baptist Church in Queen City and had extended kinship networks in the county.[58] With the support system of the church congregation and relatives, the Bowens relocated to Johnson's Hill, choosing a property across the street from their grandmother and in the same area as another relative, Sarah Thompson.

Only half a dozen arrests were made during the infamous raid of Rosslyn's saloons by Mackey and his League men. Still, they sent a clear message to the county. There was a new power structure in town, made up of an active ruling class with an eye toward suburban development. With this work, Arlington's leaders continued to move beyond suburban villages and toward a countywide fabric of interconnected communities in an attempt to push out all undesirable elements. "With the reclamation of Rosslyn, commercial and real estate development proceeded almost immediately."[59]

Suburban Boom

From 1900 to 1910, seventy new neighborhoods and communities developed in Arlington.[60] During the same decade, the county's population continued to expand from sixty-four hundred to ten thousand.[61] Boosters and planners actively courted this population by promoting the clean-up campaign and using their new civic power to push more development. Arlington's politicians and developers overlapped immensely. Once county leaders controlled Arlington's government, they used Arlington's existing suburban village model and rail networks to expand even further toward an interconnected suburban environment. In 1903, Crandal Mackey purchased nine acres to develop the new community of Maywood.[62] Mackey chose a location in western Arlington along the Great Falls and Old Dominion railroad line. Advertisements boasted that Maywood sat "only one car fare to any part of the city."[63] For a decade, Mackey worked to subdivide and sell lands in Maywood for an average price of five hundred twenty-four dollars.[64] By 1915, approximately thirty-nine smaller, late Victorian homes were constructed in Maywood. This development grew from Mackey's active cultivation of his neighborhood. In 1907, he published the book *A Brief History of Alexandria County*, which served as a propaganda piece for the strengths of living in the growing suburbs of Arlington.[65]

Mackey was not alone in taking an active role in both politics and development at this time. Attorney and Superintendent of Schools James E. Clements sold lots for two hundred dollars each, with five dollars down and five dollars a month in the area around Fort Myer.[66] A large part of his advertisement strategy revolved around the clean-up campaign alongside the white, middle-class, and Democrat-leaning hegemony of the area.[67] League member Charles I. Simms developed several properties within the Glencarlyn neighborhood where he also resided.[68] A lawyer by trade, Simms overtly linked his suburban ambitions to the rise of political and economic control of the county by League members like himself when advertising his neighborhoods. He boasted that, on his arrival to the county in 1894, "he immediately exerted an active interest in the political and economic affairs of the County, being particularly active in the crusade against gambling." Simms said, that because of this involvement, he was able to create some of "the choicest suburban properties," instrumental in "bringing to the County some of its leading citizens." Frank Lyon also used this tactic to sell his properties.

During the late 1910s and early 1920s, Frank Lyon and his Lyon & Fitch Realty Company subdivided and sold four hundred sixty-five acres in Arlington.[69] In accordance with the tenets of the City Beautiful Movement, "Lyon stressed the virtues of the family and clean living, and hoped that developing neighborhoods that stressed these values would improve this area."[70] He divided the acres between his two communities: Lyon Park and Lyon Village. Encompassing nearly three percent of all the land in the county, the large-scale, homogenous, segregated, suburban Lyon properties helped transform Arlington's built environment. After cutting his teeth on an addition to the growing subdivisions within Clarendon, Lyon set his sights on creating an entirely preplanned subdivision where he would be able to control all elements of the environment.

After years developing smaller additions to existing communities, Lyon began his creation of a standardized, middle-class environment in 1919 with the creation of Lyon Park. The larger of his two developments at three hundred acres, Lyon Park was "the largest real estate development in Virginia" on its opening.[71] From the Lyon & Fitch Realty Company offices in Clarendon, Frank Lyon and his business partners—son-in-law Charles Smith and C. W. Fitch—actively sold their preplatted community.

For his next project, Lyon Village, Lyon focused on adding an upper-middle-class neighborhood to Arlington. Although built only four years apart, these two communities came to be at the precise shift between rail and the personal automobile as the dominant form of transportation. The Park's development and advertisements focused on its connection to the Vinson railway station, whereas the Village highlighted the community's road connections to Washington, just fifteen minutes by car across the upcoming Memorial Bridge.[72] In 1923, when Lyon Village began, Lyon sought to make a name for his community in the "substantial suburban existence" that he himself had helped to create in Arlington. Like Lyon Park and many of the other suburbs of the time, Lyon Village had standardized, preplatted lots, each with fifty-foot frontages, and included a park and community center for community residents.[73]

Many of these new communities found success in seeking out members of the new middle class, including builders, bookkeepers, lawyers, and teachers.[74] However, a great portion of the success and growth of these communities relied on the growth of the federal government and the successful courting of federal workers to come to Arlington.[75] Administrations and federal staffs that first grew in Reconstruction continued to expand with World War I and remained high after the conflict, greatly expanding federal employment. As the federal government continued to expand, "the pressure of population upon area and upon subsistence in the District of Columbia [forced] her people into [Arlington] County," where "blocks of small houses within reach of . . . government clerks" were busily being constructed.[76]

Frank Corbett's "Corbett Tract," originally targeted at upper-middle-class residents able to buy large lots and Victorian homes, was rebranded as "Barcroft" to actively court federal workers with smaller lots and cottage-style homes.[77] The Carlin Springs Syndicate advertised "to all men and women of moderate means, or who receive stated salaries" for their one-thousand-dollar cottages.[78] Federal government workers accounted for the vast majority of the residents for the Maywood community. Clement's development in Fort Myer wooed potential buyers by highlighting that its location made "it especially convenient to employees of the government."[79] When the Krigbaum family decided to relocate from Southeast Washington in 1911, Samuel Krigbaum, who was born shortly before the move, recalled that his parents chose to move to "safer and less crowded suburban Virginia."[80] Like many of their neighbors, they chose a bungalow in Lyon Village near the trolley, allowing household head Orlando Krigbaum to continue to work for the Bureau of Printing and Engraving.

These new and expanding segregated communities were the result of increased attention and investment by white developers and boosters on the countywide level. This process began at the turn of the century and grew throughout the first two decades of the twentieth century. The continued development linked the county together as one suburban environment, resulting in the end of the separate and isolated suburban village model. This can be seen through the 1914 Suburban Control Ordinance, which required all new developments to get approval by the county engineer.[81] This was meant to ensure that the developments' aesthetics, amenities, and vision fit with the county's overall trajectory and could be incorporated into the fabric of the county beyond that subdivision's borders. This legislation was approved by the County Board of Supervisors Edward Duncan, Robert L. Walker, and W.C. Wibirt, with the influence of county politicians Crandal Mackey, Treasurer E. Wade Ball of the Ball family, and Clerk George H. Rucker, a builder and frequent contractor on Lyon's developments.[82]

At the same time that these boosters were actively creating neighborhoods, the residents of their communities began to embrace their aims of active involvement in countywide politics. As Arlington's suburban neighborhoods expanded, their residents began creating community organizations. Contemporary observers boasted that "the county abounds in . . . subdivisions each having its association of citizens who exercise a decided influence upon county affairs."[83] Alcova Heights neighborhood advertisements encouraged future residents to "participate in the development of a civic community, to share your responsibility in the maintenance of our government, to be a citizen and a voter" through participation in these organizations.[84] Between 1910 and 1914, community associations came into being in Cherrydale, Fort Myer, Rosemont, Ballston, Court House, and Clarendon. In two years, the association in Clarendon grew from forty members to three hundred fifty, making it the largest citizens' association in the State of Virginia.[85]

At this time, many other white community organizations developed. Before this time, white Arlingtonians were generally slower than their African American counterparts in creating schools, churches, fraternal organizations, and businesses within their own communities. Perhaps they considered themselves well served by options open to them in the nearby metropolitan areas of Washington and Alexandria, or perhaps their trajectory from suburban village to cohesive suburban community evolved more slowly than their Black counterparts, who had once lived together in Freedman's Village. But much like their creation of suburban communities, once white Arlingtonians began this kind of social growth in the first decades of the twentieth century, their development moved exceptionally quickly. White residents established branches of the Mason and Patron's League fraternal organization, as well as the Eastern Star Ladies' Auxiliary. Community stores developed alongside these new social institutions. Expanding beyond community stores, by 1920, Clarendon even featured two large chain stores, a host of smaller stores, including a barber shop and auto supply store, five grocers, five physicians, one dentist, and several businesses linked to the housing market, including building contractors and realtors.[86] These social and economic links helped create an interconnected suburban environment among residents, reinforcing the work undertaken by Arlington's politicians and developers toward that end.

Throughout these periods of growth and centralization of county affairs, the county's odd relationship to Alexandria City continued to loom. After the county separated from the city in 1870, Arlington's wealth and growth boomed. Throughout the early 1910s, as Arlington's suburban environment expanded, Alexandria saw the true value of the lands they had lost and began to position themselves to take land from the county.[87] In two court cases concluding in 1915 and 1929, the state's Supreme Court of Appeals deemed that "it is necessary and expedient that the corporate limits of the City of Alexandria should be extended."[88] With these new boundaries Arlington lost 3,000 acres to Alexandria. This significant loss of territory, resources, rail-lines, sources of revenues, communities, and tax base shook Arlington's boosters. They realized that an even more powerful county government with even more cross-community control must be created if they were to control the county's development and suburban vision.

Impacts on Black Arlington

Beyond the impacts on Black Rosslyn, all of these political, physical, and ideological changes in the white community had substantial impacts on all of Arlington's Black communities. The physical growth of so many white communities meant that new neighborhoods encroached on existing Black communities. That was the case in Queen City. In the early 1900s, the Arlington-based Barbor Williams and Company Real Estate and Insurance group began subdividing lots for the white Highland Park neighborhood.[89] Developers realized that the land around Queen City, "three and one-half miles from and 450 feet higher than Washington City . . . situated on both steam and electric roads" created an ideal location for a "beautiful suburban subdivision."[90] Arlington's Black community's unique existence in desirable areas meant that, according to Highland Park's advertisements, these Black families had access to the views and "cool air" that helped "make life worth living," but it also meant that white land developers sought out these same areas, putting Arlington's Black communities at risk of white encroachment.

Beyond encroaching physically on lands previously designated as African American, these communities also established housing types distinct from Black Arlington. The distinct aesthetic choices made by Black and white residents established racial inconsistencies that were visible across neighborhoods. These conflicting visions of preferred suburban environments provided whites with allegedly nonracial grounds to attack Black suburban communities as undesirable. In Arlington's African American communities, homes were predominately constructed by individual builders. This resulted in more diversity in type and a slower development for a community generally, but in Arlington's new and expanding white communities, entire neighborhoods were subdivided, and homes were built at once. Frank Lyon's developments, for example, went beyond just a centralized community design to create a streamlined environment with homogenous houses. "Ready-cut houses" provided residents with a few choices of styles to be built by professional builders with relationships to Lyon.[91] Many Lyon Park homes were constructed as somewhat modest wood-frame Queen Anne and bungalow.[92] Later builders used suburbanized iterations of the Craftsman, Colonial Revival, and Tudor Revival styles. Similarly, the homes developed in Lyon Village were professionally built, single family, large, brick homes restricted to the Classic, Colonial, Mission, or Tudor revival styles.[93] This standardization was not unique to Lyon's subdivisions. In Highland Park, for example, the Barbor Williams and Company Real Estate and Insurance not only subdivided lands for the entire neighborhood at once but also constructed all the homes for their purchasers.[94] Arlington's subdivisions were becoming increasingly standardized at this time. This standardization existed within subdivision borders, with uniform lots, layouts, and home choices, and across communities, creating an increasingly uniform environment across Arlington's new neighborhoods. This similarity was true across communities, because many were constructed and designed by the same developers and builders. For example, Merton E. Church, a pharmacist by trade, developed homes in Clarendon, Ballston, Livingstone Heights, and Falls Church.[95]

These homes fit with national trends in suburban homes, more so than those homes created in Arlington's Black communities. This can be seen most clearly with Arlington's Sears and Roebuck houses. Sears mail-order houses were extremely popular in the white community. Some of the most popular models in Arlington were the large eight-room Vallonia model, the Crescent and Westley bungalow models, and the Hathaway cottage model.[96] The popularity of these houses for white Arlington began almost immediately upon Sears offering their homes for sale. In 1908, the year when Sears began marketing their homes, the Newman family of Cherrydale purchased the blueprint and materials for their four-square-style Sears home for one thousand dollars.[97] Like George Robert Jackson, Newman worked as an engineer in the District. Before moving the family to Arlington to build their own home, the family lived in southwest Washington. The Newman family chose to modify their Sears four-square model to meet their needs as a family by turning the downstairs bedroom into the kitchen and making the kitchen an additional room to the rear of the house.

Delivery of large-scale building materials required access to rail lines to obtain a Sears house, making Arlington's ready access to rail lines throughout the county helpful to their endeavors. The neighborhoods of Rosslyn, Cherrydale, Barcroft, Glencarlyn, Fort Myer Heights, Clarendon, Lyon Park, and Lyon Village, among others, were all serviced by the area's expansive rail service, including the Washington and Old Dominion line in north Arlington. In addition to access, Sears houses may have been so popular in Arlington because of the county's close proximity to the Sears sales offices in Washington, DC, where residents could get more information about houses and styles beyond the catalog. Sears houses were so popular that, in 1927, Sears featured county resident John L. White of Clarendon in a national advertisement announcing how pleased he was with his Hamilton model Sears home.

Although Black and white Arlingtonians alike had access to these services, there is no evidence that African Americans in Arlington purchased Sears houses in a manner similar to that of their white neighbors. Perhaps Arlington's African American residents did not enjoy the style of mail-order homes. But from 1908 until 1940, through their mail-order catalog, Sears and Roebuck sold four hundred different styles of homes.[98] With so many models to account for varying tastes, this seems unlikely. Additionally, individuals could modify the Sears homes they purchased, as Newmans did, allowing for further personalization of these diverse designs. Perhaps price served as a barrier to entry for some of Arlington's African American purchasers. Materials for White's Hamilton model cost between one thousand twenty-three dollars and twenty-three hundred eighty-five dollars, depending on additions and style choices.[99] However, the Volins paid eleven hundred dollars in building supplies alone for their Queen City home.[100] Also, African Americans in Arlington had access to loans through African American fraternal organizations, like the Odd Fellows, in the county, as well as from nearby Washington's strong Black community. Additionally, the diversity of models also meant diversity in price point, making a purely economic explanation unlikely. Despite the possible reasons ranging from personal tastes to access to funds, the fact remains that the mail-order house played a major part in Arlington's expanding white suburban landscape, while it remained almost absent from Arlington's Black communities. This difference in aesthetic choices meant that, moving forward, as white Arlingtonians sought to further a streamlined and consistent vision for their county, they would see Arlington's Black homes as different not only because of their residents but also because of their styles, providing an allegedly color-blind critique that Black suburbanization did not fit with the county's residential aesthetics.

As each of these communities grew and expanded, they also created themselves in opposition to Arlington's preestablished African American communities by ensuring that they were whites-only zones. Nearly all of Arlington's new communities contained racially *restrictive covenants*—contractual agreements that prohibit purchase, lease, or occupation of a piece of property by a particular group of people, usually African Americans. Lyon Park's restrictive covenant stated that "neither said property nor any part thereof nor any interest therein shall be sold or leased to any one not of the Caucasian race."[101] Alcova Heights covenants stated that "no portion of said land shall be sold or leased to anyone of African descent."[102] Racially restrictive covenants were also agreements enforced through the cooperation of real estate boards and neighborhood associations. For example, Barcroft did not feature restrictive covenants in their community's home sales.[103] Instead, African Americans were kept out through unofficial channels of mutual understanding. Bylaws for the Barcroft School and Civic League formally articulated this exclusion, stating that membership be limited to residents "who are members of the Caucasian race."[104]

This racial makeup was a big selling point for Arlington's white neighborhoods. A Clarendon advertisement from 1915 advertised not only the community's access to transportation, views, and suburban homes but also that there was "not a colored resident within the borders."[105] When establishing the Town of Potomac in 1908, a company town for Potomac Yard railway workers in southeastern Arlington, town promoters advertised it as the first exclusively white neighborhood in the state.[106] A 1907 advertisement for the Livingstone Heights community assured that residents "would be surrounded by the refining influence of an exclusive neighborhood."[107] Lyon Village's advertisements ensured potential buyers that their beautiful suburban community was "destined to become a community of particular people," as it was "reserved for the white race alone."[108] This assertion comes on the heels of stating that the community is "restricted against objectionable structures from the standpoint of architectural harmony." This highlights how community planners saw standardization in the built environment and racial homogeneity as two parts of one greater whole for improving and controlling the future growth of Arlington to create exactly the kinds of environment they thought ideal. Once these two elements were mastered, they could "provide ample assurance of the integrity and permanence of land values" for themselves and Arlington's new residents into the future.

Conclusion

White Arlingtonians began creating suburban neighborhoods at the close of the Reconstruction era. Although they were slower than their African American counterparts to develop communities and move on from Arlington's rural past, once whites in Arlington County realized the potential of the area for suburban homes and development to fulfill the need of Washington workers, they developed dozens of new communities. Rail line expansion aided this development throughout the county. With "electric railways at almost every door and costly villas on every hill," Arlington County moved into the future.[109] Suburban villages, centrally planned within their borders but isolated socially and physically from one another, scattered throughout the county.

However, more than just commuter connections were needed to spark suburban development in Arlington. Arlington's boosters and developers became actively involved in state and county politics. They understood that being able to create a lucrative investment required control of county affairs through political control. Leaders such as Crandal Mackey, Frank Lyon, and the other businessmen-boosters of the Good Citizens' League undertook political reform movements designed to put themselves in control of Arlington's growth and development. This increased control allowed boosters to move on from isolated suburban villages to begin the creation of one contiguous suburban environment. These aims were increasingly embraced by Arlington's white citizens who also moved from seeing their communities in competition with neighboring areas to being a part of a countywide whole with shared laws, institutions, and aims. In 1914, the first steps toward this level of control became a reality with the Suburban Control Ordinance, the first piece of legislation controlling suburban development on the countywide level. Now planners and boosters were ready to expand their vision for the county even further as they moved into the first decades of the twentieth century.

Their particular vision for the county was one based on a centralized, standardized, preplanned environment filled with the latest styles of middle-class homes. A large part of this developmental vision relied on an environment dominated by all-white communities. To obtain the political control necessary to shape county politics, Arlington and Virginia politicians worked together to remove African Americans from formal politics with Virginia's 1902 Constitution. With this new racially restrictive constitution removing African Americans from formal political participation, Arlington's Good Citizens' League reform candidates such as Crandal Mackey began to "clean up" the county by attacking saloons and gambling houses that served integrated clientele, served as one source of Black business, and existed in Rosslyn along with an African American enclave. Once they controlled county politics and undertook their clean-up campaign, these men as well as other enterprising developers took an active role in building and advertising streamlined, centralized, and preplanned suburban communities. These ever-expanding communities were increasingly linked physically and socially to the neighborhoods around them, moving beyond the suburban village model. In advertising these new communities Arlington's strict racialized control of county politics and whites-only buying policies were featured selling points. Because whites in Arlington were slower to create these suburban communities, they were forced to develop around preexisting African American communities that often existed in locations that developers thought of as ideal. This led to conflicts moving forward.

The kinds of environments created within these whites-only zones were distinct from their Black counterparts. White Arlingtonians were more likely to live in communities platted, planned, and built at once by a central developer. This made them more standardized than their Black counterparts. The homes constructed in these communities were also more likely to be built by professional builders and fit with national trends, such as Sears mail-order houses which were very popular for white Arlingtonians but are virtually unseen in the neighborhoods of Black Arlington. This meant that, as Arlington continued to develop, differences in aesthetic between Black and white became increasingly acute, giving white developers something beyond race to point to as they sought to take Blacks' lands for themselves, just as they had done with the closing of Freedman's Village. These same trends continued and amplified moving forward, as Arlington's leaders continued to push the county toward a densely settled, white, streamlined vision whose development and profits they controlled. These trends had profound effects on Black Arlingtonians.

CHAPTER 4

"So That We May Occupy Our Rightful Place"

Population Boom and Changing Realities for Black Arlingtonians

Realizing the potential of the county as a suburban residential environment, Arlington's white leaders created multiple suburban communities.[1] Disconnected by physical space and developed by individual boosters without one central vision, these white communities created distinct suburban villages. Throughout the first thirty years of the twentieth century, Arlington's white boosters, planners, and politicians expanded their suburban visions of preplanned, white, middle-class communities. Their visions moved from community-level regulation to broader attempts at control through county-wide legislative changes that governed where and how communities and their people could live and grow. The physical expansion of new and existing white communities, and the laws governing them, continued to increase until Arlington was a "thickly settled," continuous suburban environment.[2]

As these realities changed, Arlington's Black families and communities had to continually adapt. As Arlington's white leaders entrenched their social and political power, and white communities transitioned from suburban villages to a densely settled suburban environment, local Black communities took a path that was similar but distinct. The suburban village model of Arlington's white communities never fit with the realities of Black communities in Arlington. Although neighborhoods sometimes grew up in physical isolation from one another, such as Hall's Hill in northwestern Arlington or enclaves scattered across the county, they were never socially isolated the way white suburban village communities were. A result of the Freedman's Village diaspora, Arlington's Black churches and other community institutions were all cross-community organizations that were built for, supported by, and in support of Black Arlingtonians.[3] Even community institutions such as small stores and schools, which provided services on a narrower community level, also provided links across communities by serving those beyond their borders.

Arlington's changing realities toward a more densely settled environment with more racially motivated legislation joined local and state-level legal changes to establish residential segregation laws that were policed by increasingly hostile white Arlingtonians. With these new realities, Black Arlingtonians used new and preexisting community institutions, familial relations, employment, and new strategies to preserve communities in an attempt to maintain a space for themselves in suburban Arlington. This occurred during a time when community numbers declined as a result of outside pressures and Arlington's Black population remained stable. In 1900 Arlington's African American population represented thirty-eight percent of the total population at twenty-four hundred sixty-seven out of a total population of sixty-four hundred thirty. By 1930, the county's total population rose to twenty-six thousand six hundred fifteen, and the African American population remained consistent at thirty-three hundred thirty-seven, now only accounting for about twelve percent of the county's population.[4]

Multiple Generations of Community Organization

Arlington County lost over three thousand acres in the annexations to Alexandria City in 1915 and 1929, sixty-five percent of Jefferson District's total land and tax base.[5] Despite this loss of land, more and more white communities continued to grow and push against Arlington's Black communities and enclaves. But after these significant losses of land, Arlington leaders realized that they needed to expand their control over the county's growth beyond the community level if they were going to be able to remain in control of their county. In response, Arlington's white boosters, developers, and politicians sought to create a unified suburban environment through increased zoning, planning, and municipal improvement laws. These laws were created in opposition to Black communities to attempt to take those lands for themselves. At this time in Virginia, all local, county-level legal powers must be specifically granted by the Virginia General Assembly, so these leaders also vigorously pursued state-level changes to provide the county more influence to govern itself and its people.

As white Arlington communities grew and expanded their social and political power over the region, the Black communities that had been created or expanded after the closure of Freedman's Village continued to solidify their place within the county as strong, Black neighborhoods. The strengthening of these communities was due in large part to Arlington's Black community institutions and their stable population.

New churches were formed while existing church buildings and congregations grew. These churches were pillars of the community, providing religious, social, and community support. Although they grew up within specific communities, churches provided cross-community links. When Saint John's Baptist Church was founded in the Butler-Holmes neighborhood in 1903, for example, it was "formed to provide for the people within the [Green Valley], Johnson's Hill," and Butler-Holmes communities, pointing to the more inclusive and broader reaching social institutions of Arlington's Black communities compared with their white counterparts.[6]

Neighborhood founder Henry Holmes and his children were founding members of St. John's Baptist Church.[7] Church institutions were family affairs, allowing entire families to participate together. At Green Valley's African Methodist Episcopal (AME) Zion Methodist Church, three generations of the Rowe family worshiped together. Community leader William A. Rowe, who relocated to that community after Freedman's Village's closure, worshiped there with his entire family. Rowe's son-in-law, Thomas Henry West, who married Anne Rowe in the late 1880s, was also an early supporter of the church. In 1922, when the church's original 1876 structure needed improvements, the Rowes and other community leaders, including Solomon H. Thompson, each donated five hundred dollars for the church's construction. Rowe's son, George K. Rowe; his wife, Martha Ellen Burke; and their nine children were also congregation members.[8] George Rowe served as a deacon at AME Zion. The church was often the first place where Arlington's Black leaders began to serve the community. Edmund Fleet Jr. was the third generation of Fleets in Arlington—his grandfather Hiram had migrated to Freedman's Village in 1865, where his father, Edmund, was born. Like his grandfather and father before him, the younger Fleet was particularly active in the community, beginning his life of participation and leadership at the Mount Zion Baptist Church.

Young Arlingtonians coming of age in the first decades of the twentieth century also gained community connections through schools. Black schools were created or expanded in Green Valley, Rosslyn, Johnson's Hill, and Hall's Hill.[9] Kemper School in Green Valley grew in 1903 from a simple one-room, wood-frame building to a much larger four room, two-story brick building. Local Green Valley resident Noble N. Thomas built this new school, making Kemper School the first public building in Arlington designed and constructed by an African American. Schools acted as inter- and intracommunity institutions. They fostered cross-county connections by hosting community social functions. This became a necessity, because new laws and practices made all recreation in Arlington County segregated during the early twentieth century.[10] Whites-only recreation zones included Luna Park amusement park, Arlington's bathing beach on the Potomac, and the Carlin Springs picnic ground. In response to a lack of services provided by public and private entities in Arlington, Arlington's Black institutions provided youth and family activities.

These schools were not without their problems. Most Black schools had poorer accommodations, larger class sizes, and fewer grade levels than their white counterparts. Arlington's parents and leaders continued to push for more and better schools for the children of their community. Many from Arlington's second generation of middle-class families contributed to this development as teachers. For example, all three of Harry W. Gray's daughters, Julia, Sara, and Martha, served as teachers in the county. Henry Holmes's son, Sumner, and his daughter, Marie, were both community leaders, working as teachers at Kemper School beginning in 1904.[11] These teachers joined parents to lobby Arlington for improved schools, attempting to match the opportunities provided to white children. Since the creation of their first communities, Arlington's Black population had sought neighborhood schools as part of their community development and to create a protected space for their children to grow and learn. This lack of in-county education impacted the generation that came of age in Arlington in the early 1900s, shaping how they felt about the importance of local education for their own children. In 1913, Kemper Principal Ella Boston petitioned Arlington County Superintendent for the creation of an eighth grade. Before that time, Black students who completed the seventh grade had to either travel into the District to attend one of Washington's Black junior and senior high schools or, as was the case for many students, leave school and join the workforce. Boston's petition was successful, and she was able to open an eighth grade, the same level of education then provided to white students in the county. Kemper's first eighth-grade class included Henson Thompson, a fourth-generation Green Valley resident and son of community leader Solomon H. Thompson. Each school was also connected to Arlington's Black middle class through the scholarship programs of countywide fraternal organizations. Despite disparities in accommodations, by the 1910s, each of Arlington's three magisterial districts had at least one school to provide for the education of African Americans.[12] This was significant because Arlington's population was very young, filled primarily with young families and their children. In Queen City in 1910, children between the ages of eight and fifteen made up half of the total community population.[13]

Like the churches and the schools, the Odd Fellows and the Masons continued to grow. Other organizations, such as the Improved Benevolent and Protective Order of Elks of the World Lodge in 1911, were established and expanded in Arlington. It was not uncommon for individuals to be involved with several or all of these organizations, helping to foster a tight-knit community, as Edmund C. Fleet Jr. was, as a member or officer in Arlington's Odd Fellows, Elks, and Masons. The new members of these organizations drew from the new generation of Black Arlingtonians. Many membership rolls feature several generations of families. Father and son Edmund C. Fleet Sr. and Jr. and extended kin Henry, Ammon, and Ammon Holmes Jr. served

FIGURE 13. Arlington's fraternal organizations provided social and cultural support to Arlington's Black community. Scurlock Studios, *Arlington Lodge #58*, July 9, 1958. Scurlock Studio Records, Archives Center, National Museum of American History. Smithsonian Institution.

together as Elks.[14] This was also true for the women's auxiliaries, the Daughters of the Elks and Household of Ruth lodges, which formed for the first time during these decades. For example, Edmund Sr.'s wife, Mary E. Fleet, was an officer and founding member of the Daughters of the Elks.[15]

The new generation of Arlington leaders were educated in local schools and grew in an interconnected community filled with family and institutions supporting their confidence and leadership. The core values of Arlington's Black families and community "emphasized academic education and church membership, as well as civic knowledge and personal competence."[16] George and Esther Cooper of Green Valley valued education so dearly that they saved to purchase a set of encyclopedias for their three daughters before the family had either electricity or indoor plumbing in their home.[17] Under their leadership, Arlington's Black institutions provided for the diverse needs of their community and became increasingly political. With changes to Virginia's state constitution in 1902, which limited Black voting rights, Arlington's community organizations took on more political issues. These organizations took active stances on questions of Black civil rights. In their annual "Proclamation," the Elks announced that "we demand more civil rights for which we must fight so that we may occupy our rightful place as citizens of our great country."[18] In June of 1918, the first rural branch of the National Association for the Advancement of Colored People (NAACP) formed in Falls Church with the express goals of working against discrimination and segregation.[19] The Town of Falls Church straddled the line between Arlington and neighboring Fairfax counties from its founding in 1875 until 1936, at which point the area of East Falls Church, which fell within Arlington, was ceded to the county. Falls Church was thought of as "the largest incorporated community within" the county.[20] Piggybacking off the formation of this local NAACP, in 1920, Green Valley community leaders, including Noble N. Thomas, spearheaded the creation of the Arlington County Colored Citizens' organization.[21] This association was another early cross-county organization for African Americans with the express purpose of increasing social, political, and civil rights for Arlington's Black residents. So, even though few Black Arlingtonians were active in formal politics, they remained civic minded.

The institutions, connections, and familial ties first forged at Freedman's Village continued to grow and expand even as a new generation of residents who never experienced living together in one, central community came of age. Arlington's new generations of African American residents continued cross-community connections because they were raised in a socially tight-knit community, even though they lived in geographically separated suburban communities. The continued development and interconnectivity of Black Arlington's community institutions was due in large part to the stability of their residents. Residential stability and support for institutions were self-reinforcing. The children of the freedmen who came to Arlington, many of whom were born in the county, continued to live in the communities where they were raised. Rosia Washington Lewis, the daughter of one of Hall's Hill's earliest purchasers, James Washington, continued to live in her childhood home after marrying Richard Lewis.[22] When the children of their Hall's Hill neighbors, the Robinsons, set out on their own, Benjamin "Benny" Robinson and one of his sisters also chose to stay within the Hall's Hill community where they were raised.[23] Both established homes of their own just a few blocks from their childhood home.[24] Edmund C. Fleet Jr. continued to live in the Butler-Holmes community where he was raised, as did Solomon H. Thompson in Green Valley. These examples are representative and not unique, creating a stable Black population with deep roots, as opposed to the new white migrants coming into Arlington's white communities from across the state.

Federal Employment and Land Boom

As the area became a contiguously settled suburban environment during this period, more than just institutions expanded in Arlington's Black communities. The area's increased development impacted and was impacted by changes in employment.[25] In 1900, the county continued to be home to small farms, continually subdivided for sale to real estate developers. Dairy farming expanded in Arlington, where many of the three hundred seventy-nine farms in 1900 were dairy farms.[26] Dairy farming requires very few acres, allowing even small farms to provide fresh milk to Washington's urban markets in a time when such a perishable product was safest when purchased locally. As the twentieth century progressed, small farms also increasingly became "truck farms," where farmers grew modest crops, usually vegetables, for sale at local markets, primarily in the District.[27] Residents beyond farms continued to garden and keep some animals. Noble N. Thomas, for example, continued to keep hogs on his Green Valley property.[28] Even though farms were on the decline, they still provided employment opportunities and a rural lifestyle for a declining number of Arlington's residents.

Some commerce began to grow in each of Arlington's Black communities. Unlike other Black communities in the South, Arlington never created a distinct Black business district or "Black downtown."[29] However, Black Arlingtonians continued to establish small shops within their communities, supporting one undertaker in Johnson's Hill and small Black-owned industrial shops along the rail lines in Queen City.[30] Most of Black Arlington's commerce was made up of small stores. Such stores included Vance Green's barber shop in Hall's Hill, as well as the Community Beauty shop and Friendly Lunch restaurant, both operated in Green Valley by the Collins family.[31] For the first time, each of Arlington's Black communities had at least one Black-owned general store or grocer; Johnson's Hill supported two such stores. George Johnson ran the community general store in Green Valley. Johnson's mother, Agnes, lived and worked in Freedman's Village before relocating the family to Green Valley after that community's closure. She continued to work late into her life as a cook for a local white family. Living his life in freedom in Arlington's stable Black community, George was able to own his own business and serve the community as a member of the Odd Fellows.[32] These community stores were often small endeavors, run by families out of their private homes. Green Valley resident Thomas H. West ran his contracting and construction business from his home in Green Valley and took the opportunity to teach his children about business. All eight of the West children, male and female, were taught "the intricacies of carpentry and business," providing them not only with a craft but also skills easily applicable in other fields "such as . . . delivering a finished product, customer relations, pricing work, and planning ahead."[33] Many of the stores provided delivery services which helped expand a store's reach beyond neighborhood borders to help the Black community more broadly.[34] These new businesses provided employment options closer to home. They also provided Arlington's Black residents some insulation from outside sources of discrimination by staying within their community to do business.

The ability to run stores from one's home was also important, because it provided new ways for families to supplement incomes as subsistence farming, such as that undertaken in Hall's Hill when the community began in 1865, became less of a possibility in an increasingly densely settled suburban environment. When further work outside of the home was needed, domestic labor was the most common employment type open to African American women and girls. However, working outside of the home generally and in domestic labor as a maid, nanny, or cook, specifically, could put African American women and girls in precarious situations. Such close personal interactions and the system of living-in left women open to all kinds of vulnerabilities, including little to no free time, as well as emotional, physical, and sexual violence.[35] In Johnson's Hill, Savannah and Maud Chase worked as domestics to help their parents, John and Susan, support their ten-person household. Their contribution, as well as that of their brother Garfield, who worked as a farmhand, helped their younger siblings attend school. The Chase girls seem to have lived at home, but other domestics lived with their employers.[36] Hall's Hill residents Eleanor V. Hayson and at least one of her daughters, Margaret Evelyn Wright, worked as domestics.[37] Eleanor worked as a cook for a local family, and her daughter Margaret first began working as a live-in maid at the age of thirteen. As a live-in domestic, she only had one day off a week. When her free Sunday finally came, she tried to return to her family's home for visits, but extenuating circumstances or bad weather meant that visits were not always possible. On her fourteenth birthday, heavy rains prevented Wright from traveling home for her day off. The next Sunday when she was able to make the journey home after nearly two weeks away from her family, a neighbor asked Wright, "How do you like your little brother?" to which she cheekily replied, "I reckon same as I always liked him." The neighbor explained that her mother had given birth the week before. A stunned Wright then replied "I didn't know I had a baby brother."[38] Her youngest sibling had, in fact, been born on her birthday, but living and working in isolation from her family, she was disconnected from family events. This was one of the reasons why Black families avoided this type of labor if possible and, instead, preferred to take control of their economic situation by opening stores within their homes that benefited themselves and their neighbors.

Beyond these small stores and domestic labor, Arlington's Black residents worked for local gas, oil, fertilizer, water, and lighting companies located throughout the county and into Alexandria City. Rosslyn was a primary business district, with a packing house, storage lots, and a wholesale coal business. These industries employed both white and Black workers. The area's largest industrial business was brickmaking. Skilled craftsmen and laborers alike were drawn to the area by Arlington's eight brickyards.[39] Although the brickyards employed Black and white laborers, they were a major employer of African Americans. Josephine Pollard Mitchell, daughter of community leader and politician James Pollard, remembered that when she was growing up in Johnson's Hill, most of the local men worked at the nearby brickyards.[40] Wilson Gray, who lived in Johnson's Hill along with the growing Gray family, worked as a brickyard worker. Charles Johnson, resident of the Butler-Holmes community, worked as a brick burner for the Blick-West brick company.[41] The Blick-West brick company in Arlington had an expansive business. This business continued to grow, because they provided bricks for Arlington's growing suburban home development as well as many federal building projects.

Some of these federal building projects reached into Arlington County. New federal installations grew on the periphery of the existing federal projects Fort Myer, Arlington National Cemetery, and the Department of Agriculture's Experimental Farms. This area also had the highest concentration of Arlington's Black neighborhoods, because neighborhoods formed just beyond the boundary of Freedman's Village after government foreclosure. As a result, Johnson's Hill, Butler-Holmes, and Queen City all called this area home. Thus, new federal expansion projects in the first decades of the twentieth century especially impacted Arlington's Black neighborhoods and people, often negatively, especially in the case of the "three sisters." In 1913, the Navy erected three huge radio towers between the Johnson's Hill and Butler-Holmes neighborhoods. These radio towers, nicknamed the "three sisters," were marvels of modern communications technology and engineering in their time. They were among the tallest man-made structures in the world on their completion in 1913, smaller only than the Eiffel Tower in Paris and towering over local pillar the Washington Monument.[42] This military experiment was likely upsetting to locals because of unknown health risks with the new radio wave technology, the constant humming noise associated with towers of this size, and the blight on their viewscape.[43]

The government's expansion into Arlington was part of federal expansion more broadly. Administrations and federal staffs that first grew in Reconstruction continued to expand with World War I and remained high after the conflict, greatly expanding federal employment. Federal work was the

FIGURE 14. The scale of the Navy's "three sisters" radio towers made them an unprecedented addition to Arlington's built environment. National Photo Company, *Wireless Tower, Arlington [Virginia]*, 1916–17, National Photo Company Collection, Prints and Photographs Division, Library of Congress.

largest and most desirable employment type in the area. In the first decade of the twentieth century, twenty-five percent of all local Washington, DC, jobs were federal jobs.[44] New residents came to the area from across the country for federal employment, and many set up homes in Arlington's thriving Black neighborhoods. In 1913, Esther Irving moved to Arlington from

Cleveland, Ohio, to become a stenographer with the Forest Services within the Department of Agriculture. George Cooper relocated from Tennessee for the opportunity to work as a technical sergeant in the Quartermaster Corps at Fort Myer.[45] Both Irving and Cooper set up lives in Green Valley, and the pair quickly married.[46] New residents were drawn to the area for federal work, but a great portion of this workforce was made up of long-term residents. Seventy-five percent of all federal positions were filled by local residents of the District, Maryland, and Virginia.[47] Federal employment was, therefore, a major career opportunity for Arlington's residents. Black Arlingtonians had a long tradition of federal employment stretching back to Freedman's Village. This pattern of employment and the possibility of advancement in federal positions was expanded and solidified through the creation of the US Federal Civil Service and the Pendleton Civil Service Reform Act in the 1870s and 1880s. Through these reforms, federal positions were secured by merit, creating possibilities for all races.[48] Additionally, African Americans took advantage of the same mechanisms of patronage available through the Republican Party system.[49]

Federal employment offered opportunities for blue- and white-collar laborers. Leonard L. Gray, a descendent of the Gray family living in Green Valley, worked as a carpenter's helper at the Experimental Farm.[50] Solomon H. Thompson worked as a laborer for the government.[51] Thompson's grandfather, Henson Thompson, moved the family from Freedman's Village to Green Valley in the 1880s. There Thompson's father, Solomon Sr., and mother, Elizabeth, raised Solomon, his three sisters, and his cousin. Other Green Valley neighbors also worked in lower level positions for the government, including a laborer for the Navy Yard, a government watchman, a janitor, and a chauffeur.[52] Lower level positions in federal employment did not always lead to significant social advancements. Postal worker Wilson Masterson's salary, for example, was not enough to provide for himself and his wife Fanny. To get by, he took a second job as a handyman, performing odd jobs including chopping wood and even cleaning kitchens.[53] Before 1910, eighty-three percent of Black federal workers made less than a messenger's salary of eight hundred forty dollars per year.[54] However, employment for the federal government, even at these low levels, was still seen as desirable because of its stability. Beginning in the 1890s, the federal government adopted many labor reforms before the private sector did, establishing eight-hour workdays and provisions that dismissal required demonstrable and just cause. Because of this, Arlington's Black residents aimed to move from general labor to government labor.

But the true appeal of federal employment was white-collar work. Beyond federal employment, white-collar jobs in Arlington were rare, with a few notable exceptions. Sumner Holmes continued to work as a teacher in Arlington. He did this to pay his way through medical school at Howard University. On graduation, he continued to live and work in Arlington as a well-known and respected physician until his death in 1930. Sumner Holmes's services as a doctor were crucial for the county, as Arlington did not have many Black professionals. Beyond Holmes, there were few other medical professionals in Arlington in the first decades of the twentieth century.[55] Thorton Gray, Henry W. Gray's only son, became an attorney.[56] But there were few Black doctors, lawyers, or other professionals in the county in the early twentieth century.[57] Federal employment was, therefore, a distinct opportunity. Solomon H. Thompson worked to move up from a laborer for the government in 1910, to a printing assistant with the U.S. Printing Office by 1930.[58] Harry W. Gray also worked his way up within the government. He began his service to the federal government, for more than forty years, as a messenger but finished his career as a clerk for the US Patent Office.[59]

Clerk was the primary white-collar federal job type for African Americans from the 1870s to the 1910s. In Washington, clerks were known as the "back bone of the city."[60] The position was a broad titled used to describe "copyists, stenographers, typewriters, transcribers, indexers, cataloguers, assistant librarians, certain kinds of attendants, translators, statisticians, section chiefs, abstracters, assistant chiefs of divisions, and a large number of miscellaneous employees."[61] Green Valley native Noble N. Thomas, architect of Kemper School, also worked as a stenographer in the district. Several other Green Valley residents worked as clerks for federal offices, including the War Department, the US Post Office, and the US Treasury.[62] Clerks were paid up to sixteen hundred dollars per year. These clerks expanded and solidified Arlington's Black middle class.

Although African Americans continued to find work in the nation's service in blue- and white-collar jobs, the nature of this employment changed throughout the early 1900s. During the Roosevelt and Taft administrations, the commitment to Black employment that created unique opportunities for Black Arlingtonians began to backslide.[63] These reversals of rights continued during Woodrow Wilson's time in the White House. The Wilson Administration marked the first time that a Southern Democrat held the White House since the Civil War. Wilson, his administration, and congressional representatives from throughout the South brought intensified racism and sectionalism with them to Washington. Civil service reforms were reversed, offices became physically segregated, and Blacks were barred from jobs and promotion opportunities had been previously available to them. "With the arrival of Southern Democrats, Washington was becoming more like other southern cities," rather than a place of Black opportunity.[64] With this decline in pull factors, fewer new African Americans were drawn to Arlington, and the multiple generations of families now living in Arlington since the opening of Freedman's Village continued a stable Black population, made up of those who came to the area before the 1910s. As new generations of Black Arlingtonians came of age, they continued to live in the county and communities where they had grown up.

As federal jobs were less of a draw for Black residents, Arlington's white population boomed. White residents from across Virginia were pulled to the area for federal employment. In the first decades of the twentieth century, Arlington's population soared. Doubling from 1870 to 1900 and continuing with massive growth in each decade of the twentieth century, this population increase was made up primarily of white residents. As Arlington's white population expanded its Black population instead stayed consistent. This stability, however, provided Black Arlingtonians with the benefit of deep running social and familial ties.

Countywide Legal Changes

The changing racial climate in Washington employment represented a broader change in race relations, which became increasingly hostile during the Wilson Administration and continued after World War I. These same changes were seen in Arlington. Laws and customs segregated accommodations in the twentieth century, forcing Black schools, churches, and fraternal organizations to provide their own social activities. County- and statewide legal changes expanded segregation to many other areas of life, including amenities, transportation, and housing, adversely impacting Black Arlingtonians. These changes profoundly shaped the physical development and built environment of Arlington's Black communities.

Municipal Changes, Zoning, and Planning

In 1912, the Virginia General Assembly passed two laws that greatly influenced Arlington. First, the "Act of Assembly of 1912" gave all "counties with a population of three hundred or more to the square mile" the right to the same legal powers as a city.[65] This law gave Arlington County, the only county that met the criteria at that time, the same legal status as a city for all acts passed by the Virginia Legislature. Lobbied for heavily by county developers and boosters, this allowed the county to create developmental control ordinances and growth regulations.[66] Second, in 1912, the Virginia Legislature passed "An Act to Provide for Designation by Cities and Towns of Segregation Districts for Residences of White and Colored Persons, for the Adoption of This Act by Such Cities and Towns, and for Providing Penalties for Violation of its Terms."[67] This law gave towns and cities, which now legally included Arlington, the legal right to segregate residential areas. As a result, Arlington was able to use these laws to legally segregate their expanding residential suburban environment. Individual neighborhoods in Arlington already used community-level restrictive covenants to block African Americans from living within their borders. For example, Lyon Park's restrictive covenants stated that "neither said property nor any part thereof nor any interest therein shall be sold or leased to any one not of the Caucasian race."[68] As subdivision creation and control of that development began to boom, Arlington had the legal right to segregate on the countywide level. For the next five years, segregation in Arlington was undertaken formally through this law. Then, in 1917, the US Supreme Court deemed such legislation unconstitutional in *Buchanan v. Waverly*.[69] But the damage had been done. This was not the end to residential segregation; rather, it was just an end to this particular brand of legal discrimination.[70]

These state and local laws regarding development were impacted by federal changes. For the first time in the 1920s, the federal government became interested in zoning and planning legislation on the state level.[71] Under Calvin Coolidge's administration, the Standard State Zoning Enabling Act and the Standard City Planning Enabling Act were created in 1924 and 1928 respectively to support state-level master planning procedures for development.[72] With this federal sanction on controlled development, Arlington lobbied the Virginia assembly for more special zoning and regulatory permissions. In 1927, a Special Act was adopted that permitted Arlington to adopt countywide zoning ordinances.[73]

These federal-, state-, and county-level reforms were a part of the housing reform movement of the 1920s. They had roots in the Progressive ideals of the City Beautiful Movement and the Garden Movement. With overcrowding becoming a real problem in American cities in the 1910s, reformers realized that it would take more than piecemeal, private investment to solve the housing crisis. The City Beautiful Movement focused on cultural improvement, environmentalism, aesthetics, order and symmetry.[74] City Beautiful reformers played a large role in reshaping Washington, the National Mall in particular, through the Senate Parks Commission's McMillan Plan in 1902. Similar academic ideas created the Garden Movement. A central tenet of the Garden Movement was the importance of government involvement in city planning to create walkable, orderly, and clean middle-class housing developments. With this ideological base, Arlington's housing reform advocates wanted to create one continuous, controlled, centrally planned environment with standardized, visually appealing housing for the upper and middle classes. It was believed that, through their ordered and centrally planned aesthetics, these new development principles would create a cohesive democratic society while also meeting market demands for housing.[75]

Through the Special Act of 1927, Arlington created a zoning commission and sought technical assistance from the contracting firm of Allen J. Saville. Saville, a city planner based out of Richmond, was committed to the principles of the Garden Movement. He helped to plan the Windsor Farms community in Richmond, one of the state's earliest entirely preplanned white neighborhoods.[76] Saville created a plan for Arlington County, known as the "Saville Plan," that shaped county zoning laws and practices for the next decade. This direction and leadership supported land use and building restrictions "for the purpose of promoting the general welfare of the community."[77] It was believed that zoning and planning laws were necessary to shape the county in ways "deemed best suited to carry out" the purpose of promoting "health, safety, morals, comfort, prosperity, [and the] general welfare of the public."[78] With the backing of federal law, a new planning movement, and professional city planners, Arlington's leaders had new support for their racialized land use and design principles. These countywide planning impulses represented an expansion of earlier ideas. Regulations that previously only applied to individual subdivisions were now used to regulate the county as a whole. Under these control principles Arlington fully moved on from the suburban village model. The continuously settled suburban environment was now made up of interconnected white communities with one central, countywide planning vision.

Impacts on Arlington's Black Community

These new laws significantly limited housing choices for African Americans in Arlington. In 1908, Abraham Syphax, nephew of Freedman's Village community leader John B. Syphax, purchased land for subdivision. He set out actively subdividing and selling lots to African Americans until 1920, but, this kind of development in Arlington was becoming increasingly rare.[79] Although many new Black communities developed throughout the last decades of the nineteenth century, by the 1910s, racialized restrictions and segregation laws established by Arlington's white leaders meant that new expansion was not open to African Americans. Previously restrictive covenants and communitywide segregation practices were executed on the individual homeowner and community level. With the 1912 segregation act, these practices were expanded to *all* new developments. The ability to restrict where and how Black communities developed became especially important to white Arlingtonians a few years later, after initial annexation by Alexandria in 1915. With less land to expand, white Arlingtonians sought to keep the best lands for themselves and took measures to prevent Black expansion into those lands. Where possible, whites also sought to take back the space currently occupied by African Americans.

The smallest Black areas were most susceptible to these attacks. White communities used these laws to root out existing small Black enclaves as they pushed against African Americans living in the county.[80] In the 1910s, a few of Arlington's Black families continued to live in small enclaves on the fringes of white settlements. Increasingly, however, Black enclaves across the county were purchased and cleared for white settlement. Not only did Black enclaves disappear from white communities, but white homes also disappeared from Black areas, a change from the intermingling of white and Black neighbors seen previously. Even the Black families who established their homes in the predominately white neighborhoods where they served as domestics were not immune to this removal process. The African American Low and Lee families lived on the outskirts of twenty white families in the Barcroft neighborhood. Both were domestics in Barcroft's white households; Billy Low was a longtime servant for Dr. John W. Barcroft, the community's namesake. But even working for local whites was not enough to save Black enclaves. The few Black residents of Barcroft before 1910 were gone from the community by 1920.[81] The quickening decline of Arlington's small Black enclaves greatly limited where and how African Americans could live in the county. They had no choice but to relocate to the existing Black communities or leave Arlington entirely. But many stayed local. Arlington saw neither the extreme swell nor the exodus of people during the Great Migration experienced elsewhere across the country at this time.[82] Individuals and families wanted to stay close to the strong roots already connecting them to Arlington's other communities through church and institutions, and existing Black communities worked to make room for them.

Because of segregation laws and discriminatory real estate practices from the 1910s forward, the physical boundaries of Arlington's Black communities did not grow. Existing Black communities became more densely subdivided. That was the case in Johnson's Hill. In 1913, after Harry W. Gray's passing at the age of forty-eight, the Gray family subdivided their land to create Gray's Subdivision within Johnson's Hill.[83] The community began as just four plots in 1880, but by 1913, that same land contained seventy plots and homes. This increased subdivision was also the case in Green Valley. Longtime Green Valley resident Thomas H. West subdivided his land into six parcels. Here, he constructed five new homes for five of his eight children.[84] Beyond just familial divisions, Green Valley saw a huge surge in population and subdivision. The neighborhood grew by seventy families during World War I alone.[85] This subdivision was made up of arrivals from rooted-out Black enclaves and new generations of Black Arlingtonians setting up households within their childhood neighborhoods.

These new families created smaller and more simplistic homes that could be erected quickly and easily on their small lots. In Hall's Hill during the 1920s, modified shotgun shacks were increasingly built in the community. These simple, one-and-a-half-story structures were smaller and more simplistic than the modified Four Square farmhouses created in the community even ten years earlier.[86] As available lands decreased, prices increased: By 1920, the average price of a lot in Hall's Hill, for example, was two hundred fifty dollars.[87] Early Black residents, the Gray family in Johnson's Hill embraced multifamily housing and more urban visions for Arlington's future more than their peers did when building their Italianate-style row home. These trends continued as Arlington's Black communities suffered restrictions. Without the opportunity to expand into new lands, several of Arlington's Black communities began looking to multifamily developments to shelter their growing population in the 1920s.[88] Although only small portions of homes countywide were multifamily units, there was an increase in duplexes, row homes, and apartments in Arlington's Black areas, including Green Valley and Rosslyn. Many whites saw these changes as threatening to the kind of ideal single-family suburb envisioned in Arlington's planning legislation as far back as 1900. "All sections of Arlington County are threatened" by row houses, warned a flyer generated by the Civic Federation organization within the elite, white Lyon Park community.[89] The people of the Federation felt that row homes would threaten the segregated, middle-class suburban ideal they sought.

In addition to these restrictions, the lives of African Americans in Arlington were impacted by zoning and planning laws that dictated how they could live. The Supreme Court decision in *Buchannan v. Waverly* in 1917, nullified Arlington's formal residential segregation law from 1912. To fill the void, municipalities turned to racially restrictive zoning and planning laws.[90] For the first time in 1930, Arlington passed a comprehensive zoning ordinance.[91] The 1930 Zoning Ordinance was partially written by Edward Duncan, a county politician who served on the Board of Supervisors beginning in 1908. As such, he played a hand in developing 1914's Suburban Control Ordinance and was well versed in Arlington's racialized building and planning practices.[92] The new Zoning Ordinance introduced the idea of different residential types, each type having their own standards. These types were "'A' Residence Districts, 'B' Residence Districts, 'C' Local Business Districts, 'D' General Business Districts, 'E' Light Industrial Districts, and 'F' Heavy Industrial Districts."[93]

The Arlington Courier

Northern Virginia's Largest Newspaper

Vol. III—No. 17   Arlington, Va., Thursday, August 11, 1938   Price 5c Per Copy

ROW HOUSES CONDEMNED

CIVIC FEDERATION MASS MEETING DEMANDS THAT THEY BE STOPPED

Colonel Garnett's Broadside Is Applauded By Monarchs, Lions, Rotarians, Kiwanians

FIGURE 15. This headline helps to highlight the resistance some local Arlingtonians felt toward row houses and other non-single-family housing in the county. "Row Houses Condemned," *The Arlington Courier*, August 11, 1938.

This legislation had significant impacts on Arlington's Black communities. For example, Green Valley, like almost the entire county, was zoned mostly "A Residence." Zone "A" was exclusively for single-family homes. Zone "B" was for multifamily homes such as apartments and duplexes. But Green Valley, like many other Black areas, had both single-family and multifamily homes. By zoning most of Arlington's Black areas as "A," the 1930 Zoning Ordinance effectively limited African Americans from building new multifamily homes, preventing Arlington's Black population from growing too large. This was one of the ways in which Arlington leaders sidestepped the decision of *Buchanan v. Waverly* and continued to create racially restrictive zoning and planning laws designed to limit the Black community. Although this law did not have overtly segregationist language, it certainly had racist undertones and implications. Because this development type was only prominent in Arlington's Black communities, it shows how zoning and planning laws set out to attack Black development patterns specifically.

Being zoned in the "A" category also meant that residents had the strongest regulations. These stipulations pushed the kinds of sleek, streamlined, standardized homes that were already a reality in places like Lyon Park. In contrast, homes in Green Valley were described as "non-descript, obsolete, . . . poorly built, and unattractive."[94] Black Arlingtonians continued to live in

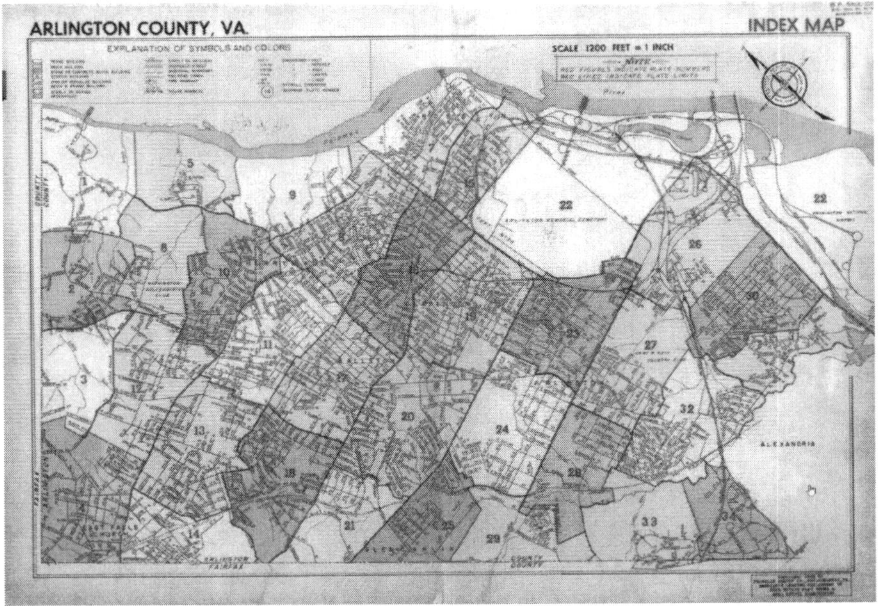

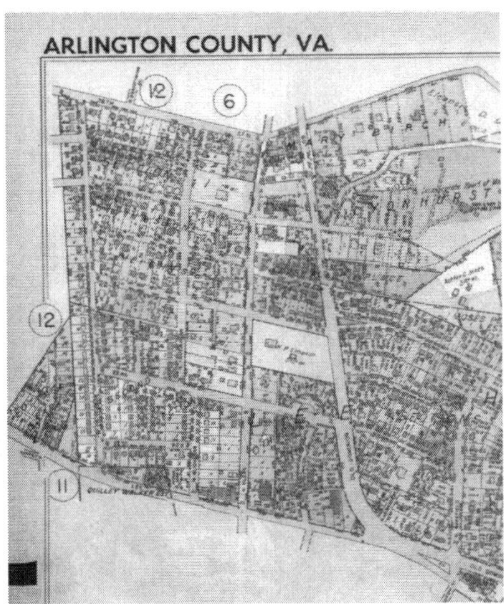

FIGURE 16. This map shows the community divisions used in the 1930 Zoning and Planning Laws. These divisions were based on the Saville Plan. Arlington's Black communities can be found in Sections 32–34 (Green Valley, Johnson's Hill), Sections 19–23 (Butler-Holmes, East Arlington/Queen City), and Sections 10–13 (Hall's Hill). Plate 10 includes the homemade wall constructed along the right edge of Cottage Park which hemmed in the Black Hall's Hill community. Franklin Survey Co., "Atlas of Arlington County, Virginia" [1935, Corrected 1941], Map Division, Library of Congress.

older homes, and new homes were constructed in older styles; hence, the charge that they were "obsolete." Although they were well maintained by residents, many homes in Arlington's Black areas did not meet the new standards within the zoning laws.

The law required that all home construction use professional contractors and be approved by the directing engineer. These stipulations added

FIGURE 17. African American row homes in the Rosslyn neighborhood of Arlington. These kinds of multifamily building patterns were not supported by the new zoning laws. John Vachon, *Backyards. Rosslyn, Virginia*, September 1937, Farm Security Administration Collection, Prints and Photographs Division, Library of Congress.

additional red tape and raised costs for Black homeowners, who predominately built their own homes. This cost hike was difficult for any working-class homeowner, but the regulation that professional contractors must be used rather than individuals was particularly hard on Black neighborhoods. Many professional contractors were not willing to work for African American families.[95] Some enterprising Black Arlingtonians saw a demand with little to no supply and created a Black housing industry in Arlington.[96] Green Valley's Solomon H. Thompson left his job with the federal government to become a realtor, and Johnson's Hill resident Tommy Crawford became a contractor.[97] Leonard L. Gray took the skills he learned as a carpenter's helper with the federal government at the Experimental Farm to work as a contractor. He built many homes in his Green Valley neighborhood.[98] In this way, Black Arlingtonians remained active in crafting Arlington's suburban environment, even as many local whites attempted to remove them through regulation. However, even with these resourceful efforts, the new zoning laws put extreme pressure on Arlington's Black communities and growth stagnated.

Arlington's 1930 Zoning Ordinance had other racial implications. Section 14 of the law specifically allowed for "the construction of a rear fence or wall to a height not exceeding seven feet."[99] In the context of the Ordinance's many other restrictions, this allowance stands out. When dealing with garages, porches, yards, and even gardening plots, the Zoning Ordinance is centered on restrictions and not allowances. This addition to allow for rear property walls and fences made way for racialized building practices. Along the rear property line of the white homes bordering Hall's Hill, including the neighborhoods of Fostoria and Waycroft, residents constructed a seven-foot-tall cinderblock wall.[100] This tactic of "out of sight, out of mind" when dealing with neighboring Black areas was a long-standing practice in Arlington's white communities. In previous decades, white neighbors of Ballston's Black enclave built tall hedges to prevent being confronted with their Black neighbors. This wall construction was executed on an individual homeowner level; however, it was planned out enough that, within a decade of this legislation, the entirety of Hall's Hill was quartered off.[101] Since its founding, Hall's Hill's residents had used strategies of isolation to insulate themselves from hostile white neighbors. Early roads and institutions faced into the community and had few external access points. However, this new more pronounced division by local white residents created a physical barrier to punctuate Hall's Hill's segregated status in an area otherwise considered the domain of white suburban development. Arlington's other Black communities were concentrated in eastern Arlington along the outskirts of what had been Freedman's Village. The wall meant that the community could not expand and that their streets did not connect to streets in the surrounding white communities, restricting access to the community to just a few points.[102] This special provision written into Arlington's first comprehensive, countywide zoning code highlights the desire for Arlington's white leaders to allow this kind of separation to endure as they continued to push against the presence of African Americans in Arlington.

Residential segregation laws and communitywide restrictive covenants that limited *where* African Americans could live and zoning and planning laws that dictated *how* they could live severely hindered continued Black neighborhood creation and expansion in Arlington. Although they caused many issues, the restrictions imposed by Arlington's government spurred by the expansion of white suburban neighborhoods increased Black neighborhood identity, as they had to fortify themselves in opposition to local white areas. With a decline in the availability of new homes and new regulations against multifamily developments, Black Arlingtonians found new solutions. Because of the reality of limited room for growth, more and more Black households took in boarders to help accommodate those who were unable to find homes of their own. Solomon H. Thompson took in a boarder in Green Valley, as did Butler-Holmes residents Claude Richard and H. Hanson.[103] There was also a rise in renting in some of Arlington's working-class Black communities. In Queen City in 1910, seven out of fifteen households in one area of the community rented rather than owned their property, a drastic change from previous decades.[104] Rents in the 1910s averaged between twenty and thirty dollars a month.[105] Despite issues with a decrease in lands available to African Americans and a sharp rise in renting in some of Arlington's working-class Black neighborhoods, home ownership rates remained high across most of the county's Black communities.[106]

Concurrent with new zoning and planning laws, during the first decades of the twentieth century, Arlington undertook many new municipal improvement programs. After five years of work, the county had a centralized public water supply system beginning in 1927.[107] Throughout the 1910s and 1920s, the county created a centralized sewer system. Arlington also undertook significant road-paving campaigns, sidewalk and curb construction, and additions of street lamps and telephone lines.[108] White neighborhoods easily secured these municipal improvements, but white Arlington officials cared little about the lack of amenities in Black parts of town. When speaking about the county's water and sewage systems, county officials assured white residents that, with the new water system, families never had to worry about sewage making its way into ground water. This contamination was a serious worry when the county relied solely on wells for potable water, but now the county had made significant improvements in every "neighborhood where there are a number of respectable white people residing."[109] No such assurances were made for Black neighborhoods.

Politicians were very interested in securing these amenities for white voters. But beyond this interest, white Arlingtonians also saw success because they created a slew of citizens' organizations to petition on their behalf. Almost every white community had a citizens' association that lobbied county officials for amenities as the county became increasingly focused on linking communities through these provisions. The Good Roads Association, created by the county to undertake road improvement, held frequent meetings with representatives from white community citizens' associations.[110] For all of their community organizations, Black Arlington had no similar institution. Most of their community organizations focused on internal Black community needs, or, in the case of the NAACP and the Colored Citizen's Association, in more rights-based rather than municipal needs. In an attempt to secure resources, Green Valley residents created the Nauck's Citizens' Association in 1926.[111] Arlington's leadership passed to a younger generation raised in Arlington's increasingly suburban environment. This impacted how they could respond to pressures against the Black community. After watching Arlington's white communities successfully use these suburban community organizations for their rights, Arlington's Black community mirrored these types of suburban organizations. Nauck's Citizens' Association was created for the express purpose of gaining access to the county's new water system. However, their petitions for county help were unsuccessful, and Green Valley remained reliant on wells with potentially contaminated ground water.

Similarly, other county municipal improvements were not extended to Black Arlingtonians. After a decade of road improvements, the Black neighborhoods of Green Valley, Queen City, and Hall's Hill all had unfinished roads and unsurfaced streets.[112] Without access to paved streets, residents continued to rely on older forms of rail travel. But connections to the rail lines could also lead to problems. William H. "Willie" Pelham, son of community founder Moses Pelham, lived in the Pelham Town community with his family. When he was a boy, he was responsible for watching the tracks during the summer when "the broom sage [grass] would grow tall."[113] White rail workers would "take a shovelful of hot coals and throw it over in that brush" when passing through Pelham Town. With homes lining the tracks, local children "would have to get out there with pine brushes and all that kind of business to smother the fire out before it got to our homes." Pelham believed that "they did it deliberately" when passing through the Black community.

Although the county provided white communities with improvements, Black communities had to take their municipal needs into their own hands. In addition to unsurfaced streets, Green Valley, Queen City, and Hall's Hill also had no street lights. Without street lights in Hall's Hill, each resident put lanterns in their front windows as a way to light their streets. The use of lanterns was consistent enough across each household that residents used this lantern light to give directions. Resident Robert Nickerson recalled that residents would "tell a friend how to come to your place [by] counting off so many lanterns to here and turn, and so many lanterns to there and turn, and so many lanterns to my house."[114] Hall's Hill also created the county's first dedicated fire station, Fire Station Number Eight, to benefit their community. Community residents in Queen City undertook so many municipal initiatives for the community that the *Washington Star* noted that "a spirit closely akin to communism reigns in the regulations governing" the neighborhood.[115] Despite their best efforts, with "every man in the town [acting as] as self-appointed supervisor of the streets," Arlington's Black communities lacked the large municipal programs they could not afford on their own.

FIGURE 18. Creating institutions such as fire companies for their neighborhoods was an important aspect of community building in Arlington. Scurlock Studios, *East Arlington Fire Company*, ca. 1933–35. Scurlock Studio Records, Archives Center, National Museum of American History. Smithsonian Institution.

In response to the inability to secure any municipal improvements and as a result of the zoning and planning laws attacking their neighborhoods, Black Arlingtonians staged a political protest. Because state voter reforms limited Black rights in 1902, Black Arlingtonians were not very active participants in the formal political process. They relied instead on their social and fraternal organizations to act as their informal political voices. In 1930, for the first time since 1903, Black candidates ran in the November 1931 County elections. George Volin Jr. of Queen City ran for the position of county sheriff. Volin was a lifelong county resident, his family relocating from Freedman's Village to Queen City before he was born.[116] Three other African American candidates ran for County Board: Mary B. Harris of Green Valley, Dr. Edward T. Morton of Hall's Hill, and C. H. Mosley of Hall's Hill.[117]

Despite assertions that "these [colored candidates] are not conceded any chance at all" of victory, the presence of Black candidates on the ballot disturbed many whites in Arlington. They worried the county's cohesive Black community could lead to large voter turnout and possible victories for the Black nominees.[118] In response, Arlington's representatives in the State Legislature, Senator Frank L. Ball and Delegate Hugh Reid, along with county social and political leaders, lobbied the Virginia General Assembly for a change in Arlington's electoral system. They sought a new system that could thwart this political challenge from the Black community. State leaders supported white Arlingtonians aims to limit Black voting power, and so state and local politicians together passed the 1930 Acts of Assembly.[119] This voter legislation gave Arlington the right to call a special election to change the county's form of government.

With this provision secured, Arlington's white political leaders immediately began to lobby support for a new form of government. Many of those leading the charge were the same leaders who spearheaded Arlington's "Good Government" reforms at the turn of the century.[120] Uniting under a banner of "Better Government," the Arlington Chamber of Commerce, the Arlington Civic Federation, and the County Bar Association used their power and influence to push for voter reform. These organizations and their zealous supporters campaigned hard, undertaking one of the most rigorous campaigns the county had ever seen. They lobbied through newspapers, by courting civic federations, and by distributing a sixteen-page pamphlet about the benefits of reform. Through their efforts, they secured one thousand twenty-seven voter signatures, far exceeding the two hundred needed, and called for a special election in 1930.[121]

With racially discriminatory overtones, this special election did away with voter districts in favor of countywide elections.[122] At-large voting gave individual communities less control. Arlington now had a homogenous form of government to mirror its contiguous, standardized suburban environment. Doing away with voting districts, the county board was replaced with a county manager form of government, the first of its kind nationwide for a county. With this change the county became governed by a five-member county board. The board then appointed a county manager to serve as the chief executive officer with direct control of the county government's executive branches.

Now running on the countywide level, none of Arlington's Black candidates won in November of 1931. Instead, Arlington's leaders, concentrated in the new, affluent suburban communities of northern and western Arlington, all but handpicked the new board. The seventy-seven-member Better Government Committee—later, the Better Government League—supported four of the five elected candidates in the 1931 elections.[123] A significant feat in itself, this was especially significant because the board saw little turnover.

In forty years, the county had only four county managers.[124] These changes were undertaken with the purpose of decreasing African American voting clout and discouraging them from running for office. The tactic worked. It would be fifty years before another African American candidate ran for office in Arlington. With Black voting rights diluted, white Arlingtonians could continue to push racist planning laws.

Racial Conflict

These legal, zoning, planning, and municipal attacks on Arlington's Black neighborhoods were not the only shifts that represent more aggressive attitudes toward African Americans in Arlington. Arlington also saw an increase in racial violence. This was a part of larger regional and national trends. Beginning at the close of the nineteenth century, and continuing into the early decades of the twentieth, overt violence against African Americans was on the rise across the South. Violence and lynching grew as a tool for regulating Black behavior and policing the boundaries of racial propriety.[125] Although not without its problems, Arlington did not see any reported lynchings in the early 1900s, a fact touted by local whites.[126] Local white resident George W. Keys for example, boasted that this made Arlington County much more civilized than their contemporaries.[127] White Arlingtonians turned to a more ordered form of racial control through restrictive laws rather than the outright violence consistent with Progressive Era ideals of the time.[128] Still, racial tensions, aggression, and new segregation laws led to conflict as white Arlingtonians enforced the new reality of segregation through violence and threats of violence.

One of the earliest segregation laws to lead to overt racial conflict in Arlington was the segregation of the trolley lines. Rail segregation had long been a hot-button issue in the county. In February of 1868, Kate Brown, a Black woman and federal employee at the Senate, was physically ejected from a rail car in Arlington's "Alexandria Junction" on the Alexandria and Washington Railroad's line.[129] Brown was assaulted and physically ejected from the ladies' car. According to the *Chicago Daily Tribune*, this "brutal violence . . . on account of her color" left her "a cripple."[130] This assault prompted a Senate investigation, which ruled in the victim's favor and was a Black eye on Arlington's reputation.[131]

Arlington's 1902 Virginia Act Concerning Public Transportation passed, "allowing but not requiring segregation on streetcars" and giving conductors police powers of enforcement.[132] One white editorialist observed that "no act since the close of the Civil War has tended to arouse a more bitter feeling of racial antagonism" than the segregation of the trolley cars.[133] Rail transportation was especially important in Arlington, owing to the fact that the county relied on it so heavily for its suburban expansion. Because of this, residents felt that "if you said anything about that railroad you said it about the whole community."[134] In 1904, a white man severely beat an African American man, throwing him head first through a trolley car window after he and two female traveling companions got into a verbal altercation with the white man over seating on a trolley. The injured Black man was fined five dollars for swearing, but the white man who beat him was not prosecuted.[135]

Rail lines were a flashpoint for racial tensions. In 1908, African American residents Sandy James and Lee Gaskins traveled home on the streetcar. Accusing them of rowdiness, the conductor attempted to remove the men in Rosslyn. Rosslyn was the first stop in the county after crossing from Washington, DC, putting them a good distance from their Falls Church stop, the last stop in the western portion of the county. Far from their destination, the men declined to leave. When they refused, the "whole carload" of white passengers began to beat them, including Ernest Putnam, a local blacksmith, who "hit them with a batch of horseshoes."[136] Fleeing this attack, James and Gaskins left the trolley car and waited at the Rosslyn stop for the next car to arrive to take them the rest of the way home. When the next car arrived, Jack Bolden, a local white resident, refused to let the bloodied men board. Weighing in at nearly three hundred pounds, Bolden blocked the men from boarding the second trolley by kicking them "as hard as he could" until the trolley pulled out.

Later that night, someone was accused of throwing rocks at a trolley car in Falls Church and then attempting to derail the car by piling stones on the track. Rumors of the violence on the trolley car, the attempted derailing in Falls Church, and James's and Gaskins's involvement spread through the county. A white mob formed in Ballston. The gang went door to door, searching twenty-five Black homes, with "shotguns, pistols, rifles, and axes" as they hunted the men.[137] Gaskins was found, tried, and sentenced to ten years in jail despite flimsy evidence.[138] Still, his fate is likely better than that of James. After that night, Sandy James was never seen again. Some speculate that he was murdered by longtime Arlington Sheriff Howard Fields. In the years after the incident on the trolley, Fields boasted that "he hit Sandy James with a Blackjack with lead in it twenty-five times just as hard as he could hit him in the head."[139] The trolley was not the only zone of racial conflict in Arlington.

With so many social and legal changes in the first decades of the twentieth century, Black Arlingtonians lost some physical and ideological space in the county, but they were determined to police those new lines carved out for them within the system of segregated accommodations. Because of this, racial tensions arose on the bus lines, not over the existence of segregation but when white patrons attempted to take space designated as Black. The white-owned bus lines provided segregated service when those services began in the 1920s. Hall's Hill had a Black-owned bus line, the Hicks Bus Line, for a brief period in the 1920s and '30s in an attempt to prevent racial conflict on the white bus lines. But the Hicks line was not able to compete with ever-expanding white bus services.[140] When white passengers entered the areas of the bus reserved for African Americans, Black riders had the option to either sit in the front of the bus or to take a stand against the white passengers. Both options had potential risks. Lifelong Hall's Hill resident Benny Robinson reflected that, if you sat in designated white seats, it was likely that the police would be called, and they might "take you off the bus and lock you up for disorderly."[141] Although this had its risks, taking a more defiant stand against white passengers was more dangerous, because, as Benny and his fellow Black residents knew, this tactic meant "the Klan was goin' to say something" to you.

The Ku Klux Klan (KKK) was active in Arlington. The years after World War I saw a huge surge in the political power and membership of the KKK nationally. Changing realities after the war came together to create the perfect storm of social anxiety among the Klan's primarily middle-class, Protestant, white, male members. Some of these changes included the presence of Black servicemen from a new generation that was increasingly assertive about their rights, the rise of labor movements, economic recession, the rise of women's rights movements, an uptick in immigration, and general fears of anti-Americanism.[142] The Klan's national offices lay just miles away in downtown DC, and a Klan propaganda radio station broadcast two miles from Green Valley. "Klan Klavern Number Six," operating out of Ballston, had more than one hundred members. Klansmen terrorized local Black residents through violence and threats of violence.[143] Robert Nickerson of Hall's Hill described Klan intimidation tactics. Klansmen marched through Hall's Hill from nearby white Cherrydale.[144] They also burned crosses in areas of Black recreation, including Peyton Field in Green Valley, and carried out their ceremonies in public, in neighborhoods such as Ballston and Rosslyn.[145] Klan threats and violence often centered on voter intimidation, sometimes running motor convoys through Arlington's Black neighborhoods on election day to deter voter turnout.[146] They used these tactics as a form of general intimidation and racial policing to remind Black residents that Klansmen were always present should they step out of line.

The same issues that led to the rise of the Klan and racial violence in Arlington were connected to changing realities in Washington, DC. In the years after World War I, strains over Black servicemen, postwar recession, and the hostile and segregated environment under the Wilson administra-

FIGURE 19. Ku Klux Klan members march in a funeral parade in the Bon Air neighborhood, March 18, 1922. *Parade of the Klu [sic] Klux Klan through counties in Virginia bordering on the District of Columbia last night*, March 18, 1922, Prints and Photographs Division, Library of Congress.

tion all created an extreme amount of racial tension in Washington, which had one of the largest urban Black populations in the country.[147] Despite the decline in upward mobility in federal service previously discussed, federal employment for Blacks was still a major source of tension. One white Southerner who relocated to the District explained that he "deeply resented the idea that colored people should have any government positions."[148] These tensions came to a head in the summer of 1919.[149] Known as the "Red Summer," 1919 saw race riots in Chicago, Knoxville, Omaha, and several other US cities and towns, including Washington, DC.

During the spring and summer of 1919, Washington's white press played up a string of alleged sexual assaults carried out against white women by Black men.[150] Washington's NAACP warned the press they were "sowing the seeds of race riot" with their salacious and irresponsible reporting. On Friday, July 18, 1919, while walking home from her job at the Bureau of Engraving and Printing, Elsie Stephnick, a white woman, was allegedly accosted by two Black men, ultimately escaping unharmed. Washington police questioned African American Charles Ralls about the attack but let him go because of insufficient evidence. Hearing about the attack and Ralls's release, a mob largely made up of servicemen formed. With tensions particularly high between Black and white servicemen, local enlisted, retired, and civilian employees for the armed forces took up the cause of policing the color line enthusiastically. Creating a "mob in uniform," the crowd of more than one hundred marched, with pipes, clubs, and pistols, the half mile across the National Mall toward Ralls's home, beating Black passersby as they went.[151] Ralls's African American friends and neighbors rallied to his defense, protecting their neighborhood through return fire while hunkering down into their homes, preparing for a fight.

Although the police effectively dispersed this initial mob, the violence that had been unleashed did not stop with this event. Every night from July 19 until July 24, violence swept through Washington. White mobs, made up largely of servicemen, attacked Black communities while Black retaliatory mobs formed to defend themselves and their communities. In the end, fifteen people lost their lives, and more than one hundred fifty were injured. During the riot, much of the violence centered on streetcars, as Black passengers were pulled from the trolley cars and beaten. On July 19, a mob formed at the trolley depot at Pennsylvania Avenue, a connection site for Arlington's Washington, Alexandria, and Mount Vernon line. Some of Arlington's Black residents, commuting between work or social activities were undoubtedly affected by this violence.

Some African American residents relocated from the District to Arlington after the race riot of 1919. Arlington provided many draws for those looking to relocate. First, the county was very nearby, allowing for easy commuting. Within the county, there were several Black communities to choose from. Although these communities lacked some of the amenities of living in the District, Arlington had a stable Black population of longtime residents, with strong institutions. And perhaps most appealing at the time, Arlington experienced comparatively peaceful race relations. Although the initial violence erupted at Ninth and D Streets Southwest, just two miles from Arlington's Queen City neighborhood, Arlington did not see similar violence. Arlington was not without its violence, but its race relations were still more stable than those seen in Washington or elsewhere in the South. Although the Klan was active in Arlington, their tactics were based largely on threats and intimidation. Even in situations where mob violence did arise, such as when the white mob formed to search for James and Gaskins, they restrained their violence for those men alone. When searching Black communities for the men, violence and destruction did not sweep through these areas widely. Even some political leaders took the time to give lip service to local Black Arlingtonians. Sheriff Howard Fields stated that "County Negroes are as good as any that can be found anywhere," and Commonwealth Attorney Crandal Mackey praised Queen City for its "almost unblemished reputation."[152] This is not meant to excuse or downplay Arlington's racial violence, threats, and intimidation but rather to show the county's somewhat restrained levels of racial violence when compared with the realities of their time.

One such family to relocate after the riot was the Drew family.[153] Richard Drew was a skilled carpenter. He was one of the few Black members of the secretary of the Local 85 Carpet, Linoleum, and Soft Tile Layers Union. Drew even served as secretary of the union. His wife, Nora, was college educated. After attending Howard University, she became a stay-at-home mother to the family's four children. Educated, skilled, and active in community institutions, this family relocated to Arlington. Like so many other Americans, Black and white, the Drews saw success in the suburbs.[154] A fifth child was born in Arlington, and the five Drew children—Charles, Joseph, Elsie, Nora, and Eva—were brought up in a household that emphasized education, church membership, and civic knowledge and responsibility. In Arlington, they found a community that shared these values. The Drew's oldest son, Charles Drew, went on to attend Amherst College and Howard Medical School. Charles had an exceptional career in medicine. He became the first African American surgeon selected to serve as an examiner on the American Board of Surgery and pioneered blood transfusions for the military during World War II.[155] As Charles's career took him beyond Arlington, his siblings remained attached to their adopted home. Joseph, Elsie, Nora, and Eva all continued to live in Arlington, where they each served as leaders in the community through church and civic service.

When the Drews came to Arlington, they relocated from the Foggy Bottom neighborhood of Washington. In Arlington, the family chose to establish their home in Johnson's Hill. The Drews' pull to Johnson's Hill makes sense because of that neighborhood's middle-class status and its connections to their former neighborhood of Foggy Bottom. The Gray family's connections to relatives in Foggy Botton influenced the architecture of their home. In Johnson's Hill, the Drew family purchased a large four-bedroom Queen Anne-style home. By 1920, the style was no longer popular amongst area whites. Homes in middle-class neighborhoods like Butler-Holmes and Johnson's Hill continued to be constructed in the Queen Anne style. White neighborhoods had moved on to more modern home styles, including the bungalow and mail-order-kit houses. With a decline in economic upward mobility, particularly within the federal government, a lack of new styles in Black neighborhoods could reflect their inability to afford these new homes. Perhaps family size affected home preference. Nationally, the average home had 4.5 residents in the first thirty years of the twentieth century.[156] In comparison, Arlington's African American households were often large. James

Pollard and his wife, Elizabeth, had nine children, including Josephine, in their Johnson's Hill home.[157] In Butler-Holmes, the Chase family had ten members. Many households also included extended kin networks and borders, such as the Thompsons' nephew who lived with the family in Green Valley.[158] In Butler-Holmes, the Holmes household comprised ten people, including two cousins and a boarder.[159] Or perhaps, older home styles remained popular because they were constructed within existing communities where these styles already existed, unlike the communities of white Arlingtonians who were able to expand into new areas. However, this divergence of trends in middle-class tastes between Black and white, which had previously been consistent, could reflect African American families continuing to prefer styles from a time when their full participation in Arlington's suburban vision was still a reality. In an increasingly hostile environment that used segregation, violence, zoning and planning laws, and political changes to end Black enclaves and push against Black neighborhoods, Black Arlingtonians made new choices in an attempt to maintain the homes and communities they had been building for nearly seventy years.

Conclusion

Racialized zoning, planning, and municipal laws challenged the validity of Arlington's Black community by legislating against the types of homes and environments they created in their neighborhoods. Against these mounting pressures, Black Arlington used their strong community institutions and stable population to adapt to the countywide legal and social changes that worked against them. Where possible, they provided their own municipal amenities. Fraternal, school, and church organizations provided community-wide social and recreational activities. Individual communities took minor municipal improvements into their own hands, improvising solutions to missing services such as streetlights. As for larger projects such as paving and water systems, Black communities could not undertake these large and expensive projects on their own. In response, they attempted an unsuccessful bid into formal politics to secure these changes. They also formed Arlington's first Black citizens' associations, including the Nauck Citizens Association in Green Valley, mirroring the citizens' associations of white Arlington communities.[160] Although unsuccessful in getting improvements from the county at this time, many more Black community organizations were formed after the 1920s to lobby the county for municipal aid. These organizations added to Black Arlingtonians' lineup of organizations designed to fight for their communities and rights.

Discriminatory laws and practices prevented local Black communities from expanding physically, but they adapted so that more families could create their homes in Arlington. They increasingly subdivided land within their preexisting communities, created multifamily homes where possible, and took in boarders to allow more African American families to establish homes in Arlington. These families were primarily second- and even third-generation county residents. Despite these adaptations, Black enclaves, including those in Rosslyn and Ballston, were largely lost from the county, and other homes were threatened because of their inability to meet new building codes. In an attempt to prevent this loss, Black-owned real estate and construction companies were established. During the first decades of the twentieth century, Black Arlingtonians carved out a foothold for themselves. Although they lost ground with the inability to expand their communities and the loss of smaller enclaves throughout the county, their communities were able to resist mounting pressures from white Arlingtonians in an increasingly hostile environment.

Beyond impacting Arlington's Black communities and people, these changes in planning and zoning laws revealed a changing county. Whereas the suburban village model of small dispersed communities interested in only their own development reigned at the opening of the twentieth century, by 1930, these communities were interconnected through countywide municipal improvements and zoning and planning legislation which moved from the community level to the county level. Arlington was now a "thickly settled" continuous suburban community.[161] This dense environment was due in large part to Arlington's population boom. The county's population jumped from sixty-four hundred thirty in 1900 to 26,615 in 1930, making it "the fastest growing county in America."[162] This growth was dominated by white in-migration from Virginia and other southern states.[163]

In the first decades after the Civil War, Arlington's Black population had greatly expanded from a small, prewar enslaved and free Black population. These individuals and families were drawn to the area by Freedman's Village, employment opportunities (especially in the District), political rights, and because of available lands sold by a struggling white population. However, in the first thirty years of the new century, these draws began to stagnate and disappear. Federal employment opportunities shrank, legal rights backtracked, and physical community development stopped and even reversed as enclaves were engulfed by expanding white communities. As a result of these factors, Arlington was not a major destination for the early phase of the Southern Diaspora. Only about three percent of the county's Black population came from states south of Virginia.[164] Whereas new white residents came to the area in droves with suburban land booms and the expansion of federal employment, Arlington's Black population stayed consistent. The decrease in Arlington's Black population in proportion to total population numbers did not represent an exodus of African Americans but a consistent population where other new whites were entering. Although these changes put Arlington's Black population at a disadvantage, it also meant that this relatively small Black population was connected by countywide social and communal institutions across multiple generations. This made an organized and strong community prepared to make their voices heard as the county continued to see significant changes in the second half of the twentieth century.

During the next two decades, Arlington's population, environment, and realities would change rapidly. The white population would undergo a huge transformation as New Deal and World War II federal workers came streaming into Arlington from around the country. These individuals were not the native Virginians of Arlington's past. They brought with them new, moderate, and sometimes progressive, ideas about race relations. The extreme population boom, along with more urban sensibilities from these new residents, also changed Arlington's built environment into a far more densely settled suburban environment than Arlington's early twentieth-century developers imagined or desired.

"Everybody Was Coming to Washington in Those Days"

The Arrival of War Workers and Arlington's Suburban Explosion

Arlington experienced a population and building boom during the first two decades of the twentieth century that changed the area from an environment of suburban villages to a landscape characterized by contiguous suburban developments.[1] This environment was filled with a swelling white population made up primarily of Virginians and southerners. At the same time, Arlington's Black population largely remained steady. However, this early twentieth century growth pales in comparison with the extremes of suburban boom that hit the county in the decades to come.

Beginning in the 1930s and continuing through the 1950s, federal expansion during the New Deal, World War II, and continuing into the early years of the Cold War created a huge number of new federal jobs. This expansion of the government necessitated the relocation of federal facilities beyond Washington. Many of these facilities, including the War Department building, were built in Arlington County. Newly arrived federal workers from around the country chose to settle in Arlington County, long considered a premier bedroom community of Washington, in record numbers for these expanding federal jobs. Arlington had a population of 26,615 in 1930 and 57,040 in 1940.[2] Those numbers continued to rise. In 1950, Arlington's population was 135,449, growing to 162,401 by the close of that decade.[3] Suburban development throughout the county exploded in response to this rise in population and corresponding demand. Before addressing the social impacts of these changes, one must understand the physical changes brought about by this new population boom. A 1948 magazine article observed that all "separate communities are now merging," making it "hard to distinguish between the various separate parts of Arlington . . . through the maze of wartime and postwar . . . new houses."[4] Existing communities expanded their borders and became increasingly subdivided, while more than half a dozen new neighborhoods formed.

These new residents and the built environments they created in some ways were a continuation of the suburban trajectory that Arlington's leaders worked hard to establish at the turn of the century. However, in other significant ways, this was a departure from the visions of developers, planners, and politicians like Crandal Mackey, Frank Lyon, and the Good Citizens' League. To accommodate such an influx of population, these neighborhoods increasingly used higher density duplex, garden apartment, and apartment developments. These building types joined Arlington's almost exclusively single-family neighborhoods. New federal building programs funded many of these developments, with the Federal Housing Authority and Public Housing Administration assisting in the building of apartment village complexes across the county. This marked a change in Arlington's built environment that many existing leaders and residents did not plan for or agree with. These developments were often pushed through despite protest because of wartime housing necessities and increased federal involvement. New residents and the development patterns they ushered in led to conflicts between new arrivals and existing residents, who resisted the changes they saw in their county and greeted new residents with skepticism, if not hostility.[5]

All of these changes impacted Arlington's Black communities. Expansion of federal jobs had both positive and negative components. More federal work opened up more jobs to existing Black residents and attracted new arrivals from elsewhere in the United States. Although Blacks were drawn to Arlington for federal jobs, Arlington's African American population grew only slightly. Black populations largely continued existing patterns of relative stability, comprising only seven thousand residents of the population of just over one hundred thirty-five thousand in 1950.[6] Throughout this boom, Arlington's African American communities continued to be squeezed into an increasingly dwindling number of areas available to them. Civilian and federal home loans discriminated against African Americans, and individual neighborhoods restricted Black residents from purchasing homes through strategies such as restrictive covenants. Expansion of segregated all-white neighborhoods for federal workers pressed against Arlington's Black neighborhoods. Developers bought land that had previously been Black owned, boxing in and shrinking Black communities and leading to the end of others. This expansion of neighborhoods combined with the expansion of the federal government's facilities beyond Washington for the first time. The government used a combination of eminent domain and payment to seize lands that once belonged to African Americans for their construction projects. The government took over land in east Arlington, dominated by Black communities since the closure of Freedman's Village, for the construction of the War Department's Pentagon building, the Navy Annex, and the federal airport.[7] These forces combined until only three anchor communities remained—Hall's Hill, Johnson's Hill, and Green Valley.

Like the generations before them, Arlington's African American population used strong social and cultural institutions to resist these outside pressures, relocating many institutions and families to the precious few remaining communities, just as they had done after the closure of Freedman's Village. Arlington's stable Black population was well organized and solidified after generations of organization and shared community development. Although they were not able to resist all closures or constrictions to their borders, Arlington's African American people and institutions were able to hold those final three communities.

The Arrival of New Federal Employees

A large influx of federal employees and their families flowed into the area as part of President Franklin Roosevelt's expanded New Deal government. In 1940, Washington, DC, led all states in growth with an increase in population to about six hundred ninety thousand, up from about four hundred eighty-eight thousand dollars.[8] Throughout the 1930s, Arlington continued to grow and expand as a suburban community. From 1920 to 1940, Arlington County's population more than tripled—from about sixteen thousand to fifty-seven thousand.[9] More than half of the county's employed adult residents worked for the federal government. In many ways, the New Deal's federal programs can be seen as a continuation of the reform politics that came before, especially Progressivism. Unlike those earlier reform movements, however, the New Deal's primary focus was to recover a society rocked by the complete economic collapse of the international Great Depression. New Deal policies of reform were, thus, broader in scope and more overtly economic.[10] This system of reform was impacted not only by powerful political players in the federal city but also by the civically minded citizens and professionals, businessmen, and lawyers who settled in Arlington. In Arlington, these political actors comprised the men and women who used their diverse talents to power the reform machine of the New Deal, shaping policies in their areas as lower level federal employees.[11]

Federal expansion only continued into the 1940s with the militarization of the United States in the years before and during World War II. From 1941 to 1945, the county's permanent population rose from fifty-seven thousand to 120,000, and would reach one hundred thirty-five thousand by 1950.[12] These new arrivals were transplants relocating from across the nation to serve their country. Washington, DC, can be a dispassionate and transient city. Instead, many of these individuals and their families chose to make their homes in Arlington.

Although most new federal positions went to white workers, changes on the federal level impacted African American employment as well. The federal government had long provided a unique job opportunity for African Americans living in Washington. Even with declines in job availability and advancement opportunities after the Wilson administration, the spike in federal job opportunities greatly expanded the possibilities for African American employment beginning in the 1930s. Many existing Arlington residents transitioned into federal employment during this time as opportunities rose. In 1910, twenty-year-old Arlington native Edward Moorman worked as a live-in domestic servant. By 1940, thanks to expanded positions within the federal government, he was able to transition into working as a laborer with the US Printing Office.[13] More than ninety percent of federal jobs open to minorities were blue-collar and subprofessional posts like the one held by Moorman.[14] The remaining posts were clerical. Although Moorman was still performing manual labor, his new position provided him with more flexibility in his schedule, better pay, and job security. Many other Arlington natives came to work for the federal government at this time. Life-long Hall's Hill resident Mary Gardner was still a teenager when she was first hired as a messenger with the War Department, eventually working her way up to the post of file clerk.[15]

Despite these limitations, federal jobs open to African Americans increased by fifty-six percent throughout the 1930s and 40s, helped by the Ramspeck Act of 1940. The Ramspeck Act prohibited discriminatory hiring in federal employment, giving Washington one of the best hiring rates for African Americans.[16] Many African Americans were drawn from farther south to Washington, DC, by these war-time industries, making up the second wave of the Great Migration in the 1930s. James N. Gregory tracks the Great Migration in two phases: Phase One from 1900 to the 1920s, and Phase Two from the 1940s to the 1970s.[17] The Washington area's regional pull for the Great Migration began earlier in the 1930s because of the unique reality of New Deal-era federal job expansion, while the rest of the nation experienced an interlude from migration during the Great Depression. The majority of these new arrivals settled in Washington proper, but a portion came to Arlington.[18] Twelve percent of Arlington's African American residents in 1940 arrived during the Great Migration.[19] This growth was dwarfed compared with the surge of white arrivals. Although the ratio of whites to Blacks in Washington was two to one in 1950, that rate was twelve to one in surrounding suburbs.[20] On the whole, Arlington's African American population continued to be dominated by a stable population of families present for generations.

In 1938, 12.8% of Arlington's African Americans worked in civil service jobs.[21] That number continued to rise during the 1940s. The majority of these federal positions were low-level, subprofessional jobs, ninety percent of which were custodial.[22] The War Department alone employed a custodial staff of seven hundred in 1942.[23] Pay rates, even for low-level employees making less than sixteen hundred dollars per year, were still better rates than those of their peers in the private sector.[24] To match her federal salary as a custodian at the War Department when she left federal service, Mary Gardner had to work two jobs, cooking in the Langston School cafeteria by day and at Peoples Drug Store at night.[25] Esther Irving Cooper found herself in a similar situation. As previously mentioned, Cooper moved to Green Valley from Ohio in 1913 to work as a stenographer for the Department of Agriculture. She left federal services in the mid-1920s to work part time teaching stenography while her three daughters were young. After her departure, the family still had the benefit of a federal salary, because her husband, George, continued to work in federal service at Fort Myer. However, when George passed away in 1937, the family was in a tough financial position. Esther attempted unsuccessfully to regain federal employment. To supplement a federal paycheck, she had to work several teaching jobs.[26] Despite the technically low level of these federal positions, federal employees took great pride in their positions with the government.

This pride in federal employment was not simply wedded to income. When Celestine Dole came to Arlington in 1936 from Southern Virginia, she settled into "a little white house" in Queen City and found work as a domestic in Clarendon.[27] But in 1942, she transitioned to domestic work for the government, "doing custodial work." Although this transition increased her salary, it also gave Dole other, less quantifiable advantages. Despite the inherent limitations on advancement, Dole felt that in a government office, "everybody was treated equal." Although Dole noted that "it was hard work," she enjoyed working in an environment where her race didn't guarantee harsh treatment. "I'd never worked in a place like that," she observed. "It felt good." A local priest working with the African American community saw many others experiencing the pride Dole described. He noted that these men and women treated their federal employment as "a prized possession."[28] Federal positions allowed employees to insist that whites treat them with respect, not "the way [they] would treat Southern Negros." With this professional respect in the workplace, African Americans saw themselves as "a new element: the government elite."

This expansion of jobs and reputation for minimal discrimination attracted new Black residents to the area. In August of 1933, nineteen-year-old Lula Mae Graham arrived in Arlington from her family's farm in North Carolina in the hopes of finding better pay and more opportunities.[29] She had worked as a domestic in North Carolina for fifteen dollars a month, but "it was thirty dollars a month" in Arlington, which was "a whole lot of money" to her. This relocation was, undoubtedly, a daunting prospect, but she was not entirely on her own. Lula Mae's older brother, Johnny, and his wife, Mae, had recently migrated from North Carolina. Johnny found government work, and Mae worked as a domestic for a white family.[30] Lula Mae quickly made contacts beyond her brother, as she joined a church congregation, connected with fellow domestics, and met her future husband, Linton Graham.[31] Much like Lula Mae, Linton was a native North Carolinian. He was pulled to the area generally by work opportunities, finding a position as a laborer at the Peoples Chemical Plant associated with the regional drug store chain. Linton came to Arlington specifically because of familial ties—his aunt, uncle, and cousin lived in Hall's Hill.[32] Many of Arlington's new arrivals were drawn not only by employment but also by friends and family who had come before them. Kinship networks of African Americans were very influential in drawing people to specific suburban areas from specific regions of the country, with entire families migrating in a stepwise fashion.[33]

Suburban Sprawl

Beyond the federal government, local African Americans found employment in aspects of the area's booming construction economy. Despite discrimination in these firms, local building supply company, Murphy and Ames Lumber, expanded rapidly because of the boom in Arlington's housing production. Founded in 1908, by Thomas B. Murphy and N. T. Ames in Rosslyn, by 1939, Murphy and Ames Lumber had two locations in Arlington, with Rosslyn and Falls Church lumberyards, and an additional yard in neighboring Fairfax County.[34] The lumberyard was a major supplier of Arlington's suburban boom; as one newspaper reported, "Murphy and Ames . . . have provided many millions of dollars' worth of the building material that has gone into the tremendous growth of the Northern Virginia suburban area" during the 1930s and 1940s.[35] Arlington's construction projects relied heavily on local sources of labor for their employees.[36] Beyond lumber, brickyards were still present in south Arlington near Queen City.[37] Local bricks were in high demand to create the suburban homes of Arlington, a great majority of which were one- or two-story red brick houses almost as a rule.[38] Establishments like the brickyards and lumberyards provided local employment opportunities beyond the federal government to laborers and craftspeople.

Although they provided a source of employment, unfortunately, many of these jobs were day laborer positions that did not provide stability. Black men looking for jobs in the sprawling construction sites across Arlington and Northern Virginia waited in Arlington at what became known as the "Hard Corner" to be picked up as laborers.[39] They worked for only two dollars per hour, doing hard labor, clearing land, and grading roads.[40] One of these men was Tommy Crawford from Hall's Hill. Crawford was trained as a contractor, but despite that training, Crawford's stepson James Taylor remembered the unreliability of the work.[41] According to Taylor, Crawford "would build something" whenever he "got a chance." Between construction jobs, he made and sold food for construction workers from a "chuck wagon" that he moved between different construction sites. These men worked building the suburban homes that did not welcome them as residents.

America's Fastest Growing County

From 1930 to 1950, Arlington was the fastest growing county in the United States, and the changes in the built environment associated with this boom seemed as sharp and they were sudden. A local builder noted, "Arlington County awoke one day to the fact that it was busting out at the seams [with] people from all over America, coming to our nation's capital to help our government grow even greater."[42] These people looked for homes within Arlington's suburban developments. Each of Arlington's existing neighborhoods expanded, subdividing land and removing green space to allow for more residents. In addition to the expansion of existing neighborhoods, seven new communities were constructed—Arlington Forest, Dominion Hills, Fairlington, Madison Manor, Tara Leeway, Williamsburg, and Westover. One reason why these neighborhoods were able to grow so quickly and completely was because of Arlington's comprehensive Zoning Ordinance of 1930.[43] That law classified almost the entire county, including then-unsettled land as "A Residential." So, when demand suddenly rose for housing, Arlington's existing neighborhoods and unsettled land alike were ready to become residential housing.[44]

This housing expansion required serious development of Arlington's road networks. Although Arlington's suburbs initially developed along rail lines, local community advertisements highlighted road over rail access beginning in the early 1920s. By the 1930s, the personal car dominated the suburban landscape.[45] Builders of individual suburban developments were responsible for creating internal roads for those communities. Thus, a major part of Arlington's construction business centered on clearing and grading for roads.[46] However, more than internal community roads were needed to accommodate the boom of new residents and their commuting needs.

With their population boom, local Arlington residents recognized that "Arlington has a lot to do," and among the most pressing was that "highways will have to be improved."[47] Highway creation was a major part of the process of suburbanization, providing easy access between home and businesses.[48] So much expansion was needed because of "low density residential development [spreading] throughout the area" and because of federal employment expansion within and beyond the boundaries of the District.[49] Local and Virginia state officials joined with regional representatives from Maryland and DC, as well as federal representatives from the National Capital Planning Commission and the military, to create Arlington's road networks.[50] This meant that local Arlington officials lost some of their power in controlling the area's development to state and federal authorities.[51] Jefferson Davis Highway, Henry G. Shirley Memorial Highway, Columbia Pike, Lee-Jackson Highway, Lee Highway, the Falls Church Bypass and Fairfax Drive, the George Washington Memorial Parkway, Glebe Road, and Arlington Mill Drive all required expansion to meet demand.[52] The largest of these highways, Shirley Highway, expanded to six lanes of traffic at a cost of $4.6 million dollars and saw as many as fifteen hundred sixty-five cars per lane, per hour by 1962.[53] Of these roads, only Columbia Pike, expanded to four lanes, was a cross-county road whose construction would benefit county residents exclusively.[54] All others aided commuters within the county and suburban developments that were farther out in Fairfax County who were traveling to businesses within Arlington, mostly federal installations, or into Washington.[55] Even with this preference for commuter needs over local needs, Arlington's road system was largely modernized and complete by the mid-1950s.[56] The meetings on highway expansion were limited to officials, meaning that the voices of common citizens were left out of the discussion of road expansions that would greatly impact their lives and communities.[57]

Despite the citizens' lack of representation in road decisions, Arlington's expanded road network greatly aided the expansion of suburban communities. Although distinct in some ways, these neighborhoods shared many similarities. These communities were all segregated. Existing communities, such as Lyon Village, continued to state that their homes were for "whites only" in their advertisements, and new communities such as Dominion Hills and Tara Leeway (whose name was inspired by the Tara Plantation in *Gone with the Wind*) had the same racially restrictive policies.[58] They were also primarily for middle-class residents. A newly built two-story, three-bedroom, brick single-family home in the emerging Arlington Forest community located in western central Arlington cost $5,990 in 1939.[59] By contrast, a much larger existing home in the older Lyon Park community in central Arlington went for the same rate around the same time.[60] This shows a preference for the new buildings of Arlington's rapidly expanding suburbs. Architect Robert O. Scholz and builder Meadowbrook, Incorporated construed all of Arlington Forest's eight hundred fifty homes.[61] These homes were entirely standardized eleven-hundred-square-foot houses. These houses were constructed in one building boom beginning immediately after their purchase of the land in 1938.[62] At these price points, both new and existing neighborhoods provided single-family housing for middle-class residents. Other new neighbor-hoods, such as Bellevue Forest, used larger houses, irregularly shaped lots, and the inclusion of natural landscaping to attract more upper middle-class residents.[63]

This building boom was enough to make "older real estate men dizzy" from the unbelievably soaring land and home price points, according to *Evening Star* writer George Kennedy.[64] With so much rapidly expanding development, the handful of Arlington leaders who acted as builders and developers in the suburban expansion of the previous decades were replaced with a new generation of builders. Rather than a small elite group, Arling-ton now had a hugely expanded number of professional architects, builders, developers, and landscapers leading the charge of development in the county. The rapidly expanded demand in housing and increasingly available financ-ing to whites for building also encouraged individuals with little experience as developers to break into the housing development market. Lou Pomponio founded the A&H Plumbing Supply Company in Arlington as a family busi-ness in the 1930s.[65] When Arlington's land values and building demands began to boom, the Pomponio family decided to turn their small plumbing business into a construction firm, building on the family's land holdings in Rosslyn.[66] Pomponio's son, Lou Jr., "took charge of construction," his brother Peter "handled design," and another brother, Paul, handled finance. Other families joined this pattern. After seeing the success of centrally planned community developments in Arlington, the DeLashumutt family decided to create their own housing development within the Barcroft community.[67] Brothers Thomas, Charles, John, and Basil DeLashumutt were all trained as engineers. Seeing the economic prosperity associated with Arlington's con-struction boom, they formed the DeLashmutt Brothers Construction and Engineering Company. The DeLashumutt family had moved to Arlington in the early twentieth century. Their father, T. J. DeLashmutt, was involved in county politics with Mackey's Clean-Up campaign, participating in the violent raid of Rosslyn in 1904. Basil followed in his father's footsteps, par-ticipating in county politics as a member of the Arlington County Planning Commission and Arlington County Board.[68]

Despite the building boom, however, single-family housing alone was not sufficient to meet Arlington's growing housing needs. Multifamily hous-ing was common in the Black community but was still rare in Arlington's white neighborhoods. Some of Arlington's white neighborhoods introduced garden-style apartments for the first time. Arlington's African American neighborhoods had previously embraced multifamily housing types to accommodate expanding populations in the face of consistent or shrinking lands in their communities as populations grew. But until the 1930s, white

GREATEST U. S. BOOM TOWN
IS THE NATION'S CAPITAL

is now bringing workers to Washington at a rate of 850 a week. The city has not yet come to the point of building barracks for clerks beside the Union Station as it did in War I days, but it may soon.

Washington's growth is not merely a defense phenomenon. Defense has only given an extra fillip to something which has been going on steadily since the first days of the New Deal. In 1933, for instance, Washington had 471 beauty parlors doing a business of $1,500,000 a year. In 1940 it had 690 beauty parlors turning over $3,500,000 a year. When the 1940 census was taken last spring, Washington showed by far the greatest growth of any major U. S. city, having jumped since 1930 from 14th to eleventh largest with an increase of 176,284 (36.2%) to a population of 663,153. Since the census began eleven months ago, an estimated 85,000 people have migrated to live in Washington, and it has almost certainly passed Pittsburgh to become the tenth city of the land.

Today Washington stands as visible evidence of the peaceful revolution which has been going on in American life since 1933. This social and economic revolt is, by general agreement, permanent. Even if Willkie had been elected last year, the Federal Government would unquestionably have gone on being far bigger and playing a far bigger part in U. S. lives than ever before. Today the citizen who goes to Washington sees the future in action.

CONTINUED ON NEXT PAGE

FIGURE 20. In their March 10, 1941, "Washington Worker" issue, *LIFE* magazine featured Arlington Forest as representative of the new ideal for suburban housing in the Washington, DC, area. Cast in sharp contrast with the snow from above, the standardized size and shape of the homes within the community is evident. Once forest land, during their construction blitz to create the neighborhood trees were clear cut, making the "Arlington Forest" name ironic. "Greatest US Boom Town is the Nation's Capital," *LIFE*, March 10, 1941.

neighborhoods in Arlington hardly ever offered multifamily housing as an option. In the 1930s, Arlingtonians joined the ranks of builders and developers across the United States looking toward European models of housing and planning to find solutions for the shortage in housing that plagued the country during and after the Great Depression.[69] These multifamily units were centrally planned to help decrease waste and sprawl while providing the most amenities at the best cost.

Federal Involvement in Arlington's Suburban Growth

The first large-scale garden apartment complex built in Arlington—indeed, one of the first complexes of its kind in the nation—was 1935's Colonial Villages by Gustave Ring.[70] Professional developer Gustave Ring was a pioneering force in the garden apartment style with his work in Washington during the early 1930s.[71] Born in West Virginia in 1910, Ring grew up in the District and attended George Washington University before establishing Ring Construction Company in 1928.[72] Despite his successes in Washington, Ring struggled to get funding for his ambitious building project in Arlington. Banks were hesitant to invest in apartments, whose foreclosure rates were particularly high during the national housing crisis of the Great Depression.[73] They were also hesitant because Arlington had so few apartment units before this time that investors were not sure how popular they would be in a county dominated by single-family homes. "People kept telling me I was crazy to build over there," Ring recollected.[74] Lacking private investment in his project, Ring decided to turn to the newly formed Federal Housing Administration (FHA) for support. The National Housing Act of 1934 created the FHA to stimulate housing growth for lower and middle-income white Americans by supplying federally sponsored loans for construction.[75] Ring changed his intentions for the development, lowering rents to twelve dollars and fifty cents per room for the one- and two-bedroom units to qualify for funding. Using Section 207 of the National Housing Act, which focused on rental housing and suburban development, Ring secured funding for his whites-only Colonial Village project.[76]

The first stage of construction began with two hundred seventy-six units on twenty-five acres of land off Wilson Boulevard between Rosslyn and Court House. From October 1935 to July of 1937, construction continued until two hundred thirty-three two- and three-story Colonial Revival red-brick buildings, containing just under one thousand total apartments, were complete.[77] Despite the huge number of buildings, structures only made up about eighteen percent of the total land in the Colonial Village complex. Landscaping and comprehensive design was an important element of the garden apartment movement and the design of Colonial Village. Buildings were nestled in low-density, nonstandardized formations called "super blocks," with interior green spaces and courtyards professionally landscaped by designer James K. Wright. This stands in sharp contrast to the clear cutting of trees and absolute abandonment of landscaping that occurred to construct communities such as Arlington Forest. Called "one of the outstanding developments of its kind in America" by *Architectural Forum* magazine in August 1939, Colonial Village apartments were hugely popular among Arlington's white renters.[78] The national attention on the project, with Colonial Village alone garnering twenty articles in various architectural magazines and journals from 1935 to 1940, the complex's desirable aesthetics, and the need for moderately priced housing in Arlington where demand for housing from newly arrived white federal workers far outpaced supply, are all reflected in the fifteen thousand applicants Colonial Village received for the first two hundred seventy-six units made available.[79]

Ring secured FHA loans to make Colonial Village possible. Meanwhile, the FHA participated in discriminatory lending practices, known as redlining. These policies broke down an area's worthiness for receiving loans on the basis of eight criteria.[80] These were: relative economic stability; protection from "adverse influences"; freedom from special hazards; adequacy of civil, social, and commercial centers; adequacy of transportation; sufficiency of utilities and conveniences; level of taxes and special assessments; and appeal.[81] These criteria allowed personal biases of an area's desirability to influence an individual's ability to get a federally insured loan. The FHA's 1938 underwriting manual asserted that "if a neighborhood is to retain stability, it is necessary that properties shall continue to be occupied by the same social and racial classes."[82]

Gustave Ring played a role in shaping the trajectory of discriminatory lending within the FHA. The racist lending practices of the FHA have long and complicated roots. They were certainly shaped by earlier race-based policies within federal bodies dealing with housing.[83] But scholars like Louis Lee Woods and Paige Glotzer outline how these federal institutions relied heavily on local building professionals.[84] Federal institutions were not looking to reinvent the wheel when it came to crafting federal housing policies. James Taylor, associate director of the FHA's Division of Economic Statistics, highlighted the power of local leaders on national policy when he said that "mortgage lenders and real estate men can aid" federal officials by directing them in existing lending practices so that "we can all ride to town together" and be prosperous.[85] This power on the part of local bankers, realtors, and developers allowed Ring to shape early FHA policies.

Colonial Village was among the very first FHA-insured projects, serving as a prototype for similar installations across the country.[86] Ring worked with members of the FHA's large-scale housing division to shape their policies for future developments.[87] Before working with the FHA, Ring created apartment complexes throughout the Washington area. In these developments, Ring instituted a selection process for applicants that sought out exclusively white, middle-class residents.[88] With this existing commitment to single-race and single-class communities, Ring's Colonial Village FHA application included racially based restrictive covenants. *Architectural Forum* noted Ring's influence with the FHA, stating that "All big businesses have their big men, and one of these usually stands head and shoulders above the rest. In the FHA-insured rental housing business this man, first, last and always, is Gustave Ring."[89] Indeed, by 1939, Ring controlled thirty-seven million dollars of the FHA's one hundred million dollars worth of mortgage insurance.[90] Although certainly not the only factor leading to the creation of the FHA's discriminatory loan policies, as one of their premier builders, Ring played a hand in their creation through his work in Arlington. These policies, in turn, applied "ethnic and racial worth to real estate appraising on an unprecedented scale."[91]

Although it was the earliest, Colonial Village was far from the only development of its kind in Arlington. Other FHA-sponsored apartment complexes included the DeLashmutts' Barcroft Apartments, the Commons of Arlington, and the Ring-helmed Arlington Village in south Arlington.[92] These projects, as well as other large-scale apartment communities, such as Buckingham in central Arlington near Lyon Park, were whites only.[93] Other similar housing units quickly followed. From the late 1930s to the early 1950s, the core years of Arlington's suburban boom, garden and low-rise apartment complexes became a dominant home and architectural type in Arlington until a total of one hundred seventy-six individual apartment buildings existed throughout the county.[94]

Despite their need, popularity, architectural praise, and racial policies that fit local customs, many local Arlingtonians resisted garden apartment communities. This was especially the case when apartment complexes neighbored or fell within existing single-family home communities. The Citizens' Association of Lyon Village took an active role in resisting apartments. Despite their resistance, Lyon Village Apartments opened during the boom of apartment housing in the 1930s. For decades after its construction, residents continued to encourage other residents to work to "[keep] out apartment houses" and other "encroachment."[95] Although the apartment buildings of Lyon Village Apartments were within the boundaries of their community, Lyon Village residents were told to "man the ramparts" by community organizers working to keep the people living within these apartments from participating in community organizations.[96]

Resistance from Arlington's existing populations to new arrivals was not restricted to apartment dwellers. When Dr. B. T. and Lillian Simms relocated their family in 1945, it was for his new position as the chief of the Bureau of Animal Industry.[97] The Simms family settled into the Aurora Hills neighborhood in south Arlington, where they purchased a newly constructed home.[98] Aurora Hills was first established in 1915 in eastern Arlington.[99] Initially, bungalow homes dominated the community, which featured a fire station and library branch by the mid-1920s. But the neighborhood became increasingly subdivided as more contemporary, World War II-era, 1.5-story, brick box homes were added to the mix. The Simmses' house was actually constructed for a different federal family, but, according to Lillian, "just six months before we bought the house, the people were transferred to Ames, Iowa."[100] Rapid turnover of federal positions kept the area and its people changing. This was a source of contention between longtime residents and new arrivals. The Simms family did not feel welcomed by their new neighbors, who "wanted regular people who were intending to stay there." Indeed, this characterization of not being "regular" because they were drawn to the area for federal employment was a sentiment commonly expressed to outsiders. Existing white Arlingtonians saw both the new homes and the people living within them, mostly newly arrived war workers from across the country, as something entirely different from Arlington's pre-1930s single family homes filled with native Virginians.[101] These Arlingtonians did not feel that federal employees were true members of their community; therefore, they bitterly resented the new opinions, political leanings, attitudes, cultures, and building styles brought with these individuals.

In their new neighborhood, the Simmses were one of many federal families. "There were a lot of people from the Department of Agriculture living in Aurora Hills," and B. T. participated in a neighborhood car pool.[102] The prevalence of federal workers was a reality across all of Arlington's existing neighborhoods. In Lyon Park, federal work became the dominant type of employment by the late 1930s.[103] Professionals from clerks to engineers, to lawyers, physicians, architects, and chemists all were categorized under the umbrella of "federal employee." Entire households often worked in federal service. Black women working outside of the home was common in Arlington from the late-nineteenth century onward, but this pattern of employment was newer among Arlington's white families. Patrick and Saidee Byrne of Lyon Park both worked for the federal government as clerks. This pattern of employment was true, despite family size. Couples with children, such as the Byrnes who had one son, Patrick Jr., as well as couples without children, such as federal clerks Norman and Dorothy DeNeale, were frequently dual-income families with both spouses working in federal service. Not just couples contributed to the predominance of federal employees within households. For extra money and to accommodate the population swell, more and more of Arlington's white residents took in boarders. Harry Hay, an auditor with the Department of Revenue, and his family rented a room in their Lyon Park bungalow home to a fellow federal employee, a young man named Edwin who worked as a clerk.[104]

For the first time, white women moving on their own came to the area for federal employment. Nationally during WWII, almost four hundred thousand women served in the armed forces, with millions of American women going into civilian service toward the war effort.[105] Some older white women, such as War Department Clerk Kate Ricker who was in her mid-60s at the outbreak of the war.[106] Some were married with husbands serving overseas, but the vast majority were young, single women just out of high school or college.[107] Most of these unmarried, young white women worked as clerks, including Bessie M. Blincot of New York and Emma Brown of Georgia.[108] These women often stretched their incomes, which ranged from about twelve hundred dollars to sixteen hundred dollars, by living with roommates.[109] Ricker lived intermittently alone or with a lodger in her Lyon Park home.[110] When moving to the area from New York to work as clerks, sisters Maretta and Nellastine Hartshorn shared the cost of their small, brick single-family home in Lyon Park.[111] Marjorie Downey came to Arlington from Iowa in May of 1942 at the age of twenty-two to work as a typist for the Social Security Office.[112] She rented a room in a house near Virginia Square. But there were so many workers, and accommodations so limited, that she shared that one room with "six of us girls who worked for the government." This situation was not unique, as many newly arrived federal employees found themselves sleeping in shifts in rooms rented out by impromptu landlords.[113]

Black women also came to Arlington at this time, but their in-migration did not match that of their white counterparts. For example, Arlington Hal Station, a wartime cryptography center created from a junior college off of Route 50, only approximately fifteen hundred of the ten thousand female employees were African American.[114] Ethel Just, for example, came to Arlington from Ohio. An African American woman with a bachelor of arts from Ohio State University and a master's degree from Boston University, She worked as a part of an all-Black code-breaking unit and earned a leadership role in the unit as an expert translator.[115] Her education likely helped her secure this role, but many African Americans with advanced degrees were relegated to menial positions.[116] Unit head William "Bill" Coffee, an African American transplant from Knoxville, Virginia, studied English at Knoxville College. Despite this, he was hired as a janitor with the Army in 1942, eventually working his way up to "Assistant Civilian in Charge" with

FIGURE 21. African American women worked as code breakers with the Army at Arlington Hall. "Code Girls," NSA Archives, HIST-026–013.

nineteen subordinates by November of 1944.[117] This was "the only professional unit" of African Americans at Arlington Hall with "a large number of Black Americans working in . . . custodial type jobs."[118]

Federal Building Projects

Many younger women who migrated to Arlington found housing in emergency wartime federal housing. Beginning in 1940, in anticipation of the arrival of even more federal employees, the government began constructing temporary wartime housing throughout the greater Washington area. The largest were the dormitories built on the recently vacated Arlington Experimental Farm grounds.[119] Commonly called "Girl Town," the twenty-eight-acre complex dotted with gray, concrete dormitories housed up to forty-two hundred seventy-five female federal employees. One such resident was Mary Olena Adams, a former schoolteacher from Missouri.[120] Residents included service women, primarily from the Naval Reserve's Women Accepted for Volunteer Emergency Services (WAVES), but largely consisted of white federal civilian employees.[121] Like the FHA-funded projects, this dormitory was racially segregated. African American women in federal service like

Ethel Just were housed at Langston Hall in Northeast DC. Others had to find housing in Arlington's existing Black neighborhoods, such as nearby Johnson's Hill.[122]

These whites-only dormitories were one of many federal civilian emergency wartime building projects in Arlington at the time. Despite the rapid building of suburban homes and apartment housing with both private investment and federal funding assistance, there were still not nearly enough homes to match the sharp increase of federal employees looking to settle in Arlington. This was especially true after federal expansion ballooned further with the United States' entrance into World War II in 1941. A 1942 survey found that six hundred fifty family housing units received forty-three hundred applicants.[123] The Public Housing Administration stepped in to fund building programs in 1943. The largest and most ambitious of these projects was the Fairlington community.

The construction of Fairlington, which was located in south Arlington, across the small Four Mile Run creek from Green Valley, was undertaken from 1942 until 1944.[124] In those two years, thirty-four hundred forty-nine one-, two-, and three-bedroom Colonial Revival apartment and townhouse units were built along curving, landscaped streets, consistent with contemporary building ideals.[125] The project was publicly financed through the Defense Housing Corporation (DHC). A part of the National Housing Agency, the DHC focused on building housing for defense workers and their families. Fairlington was their largest project, accounting for sixty-one percent of the organization's total apartments built and thirty-one percent of all dwellings built. Unlike many of the World War II-era emergency housing projects created for war workers, Fairlington was always meant to remain a permanent part of the county after the war's end. This was reflected in the community's detailed architectural care, landscaping, and the inclusion of parks, a community center, and a school.

In 1941, the DHC also authorized the construction of the Columbia Forest neighborhood. Columbia Forest was intended to provide housing for "young married officers and ranking government officials."[126] With this federal backing and focus on housing federal civilian and military personnel, the Army Corp of Engineers designed houses and supervised construction of the community. Unlike its neighboring community of Fairlington, Columbia Forest had far less design integrity, filled with simple, brick, two-story box homes and less landscape and community planning. Although more simplistic, these homes still conformed to suburban ideals of the time. Demand was so high that construction was undertaken hastily, and the community's development hit many snags. County, state, and federal forces all came together to push major highway projects in the 1940s and 1950s, but roads in individual communities were still the responsibility of developers. Although bordering several major county roads, including Columbia Pike, the neighborhood's internal road networks were not linked to the county's road networks, creating problems for residents' commutes. Columbia Forest's roads were inconvenient, but other issues were dire. In March of 1943, Arlington County officials had to evict several families from the neighborhood after it was discovered that they had been living for two months "without sewer services on a street pitted with yawning holes filled six feet or more deep with water."[127]

Columbia Forest had design issues, but subsidized barracks-style homes were created even more quickly and with even less consideration for design integrity and municipal needs. One such barracks project was the George Pickett Homes development, built within the Columbia Heights neighborhood in east Arlington. Emergency overflow housing for newly arrived war workers, homes were utilitarian in look and feel, constructed quickly on concrete slabs. Unlike their counterparts, these projects were undertaken without regard for Arlington's existing zoning or planning laws. In addition to George Pickett, other emergency wartime housing projects included Shirley, J. E. B. Stuart, and Jubal Early homes. These whites only developments were named after Confederate officers, highlighting the racial underpinnings behind their construction as well as the degree to which this racialized thinking was normalized within the framework of Virginia's Civil War "heritage."

These federal housing projects were undertaken as a part of a broader trend of federal building in the county. During the 1940s, as existing institutions and the alphabet soup of federal projects created under the New Deal continued to expand in response to increased federal needs during World War II, federal departments in Washington began to outgrow their offices and moved beyond the boundaries of the federal city. Virginia politicians like Senator Carter Glass, the chairman of the Senate Appropriations Committee, pushed hard to ensure war-time spending pork came to Virginia.[128] Arlington had a long tradition of federal installations within the county borders, with Arlington National Cemetery, the Experimental Farm, and Fort Myer. With this tradition of building in Arlington and active courting from Virginia politicians, federal building projects looked to Arlington. With its existing federal sites and new additions, eighteen percent of Arlington's total land became federally controlled.[129]

The largest of these developments came with the War Department's new headquarters, commonly called the Pentagon. In 1941, the War Department opened a new headquarters in the Foggy Bottom neighborhood of

Washington. However, the institution found that it had outgrown the location of its new headquarters immediately upon its opening. Its ever-growing staff was scattered across more than seventeen buildings. The lack of centralization led to delays and inefficiencies that went from inconvenient to potentially catastrophic with the arrival of war. Ground was broken for the Pentagon in September 1941, and seventeen months later, on February 15, 1942, the War Department's comprehensive headquarters was complete.[130] The site contained 3.6 million square feet of office space, making it the largest office building in the world on its opening. As a child living in Lyon Village, Larry Palmer would go to the Pentagon site with his friends to watch the dizzying pace of construction.[131] A fourth grader when World War II began, Palmer, along with his friends, found Arlington's construction boom thrilling—watching construction at the Pentagon, playing in the dirt and bricks of building sites, and daring one another to race across the tar of newly paved streets. Local Black residents who were directly affected by the new installation's construction had a different perspective about the building's erection.

When choosing a location for the Pentagon building, the Army Corps of Engineers, Department of Interior, National Capital Park and Planning Commission, congressional committees, and other affected parties originally looked to lands nestled between existing federal projects.[132] This plan to fit yet another federal building into the federal corridor between Arlington National Cemetery, Fort Myer, and the newly expanded airport is what led designers to propose the unique pentagonal shape for which the building gets its nickname. However, those who were interested in maintaining views from Arlington National Cemetery and continuing Pierre L'Enfant's original plans for the federal city strongly resisted such a large federal project in that area. Therefore, another site was scouted for the building, but its unique shape remained.

Arlington politicians fully supported the government's move into the county. Indeed, before the final site for construction was even chosen, County Board Chairman Freeland Chew told the Senate committee investigating locations "we are 100% behind anything that the government wishes to do."[133] This kind of blanket support without requirements for preserving existing neighborhoods put Arlington's Black populations at great risk. Federal authorities were exploring locations almost exclusively in southern Arlington. With the exception of Pelham Town and Hall's Hill in northern central Arlington, all of Arlington's remaining Black communities, including Green Valley, Queen City, Johnson's Hill, and Butler-Holmes, were in southern Arlington. Local Black residents, like Vivian Bullock of Hall's Hill, called South Side Arlington "the Black side."[134]

Impacts on Arlington's Black Communities

Although the expansion of the federal government offered employment opportunities, it resulted in increased housing discrimination. The majority of federally built and subsidized projects were segregated as "whites only," and federal building projects targeted Black neighborhoods for removal in order to build new government instillations. This destroyed neighborhoods. It also limited the size and availability of existing Black neighborhoods where the displaced could relocate. Politicians and planners were preoccupied with aesthetics; they cared little about the existing African American neighborhoods directly impacted by the construction. Indeed, as planners paid "special attention" to maintain the "aesthetic values . . . [of] the Pentagon," they were conscious that such provisions were not made for "adjacent properties."[135] This included the neighborhood Queen City and the bordering area of East Arlington.[136]

In Queen City, more than two hundred working-class families lived in modest but well-kept frame houses.[137] Generations of families grew in Queen City after the community was founded after the closure of Freedman's Village. Native Queen City resident William Volin, grandson of George Volin, was one of the community's earliest residents who relocated to Queen City from Freedman's Village.[138] Two generations later, the Volins again found their home and community threatened. William Volin described his neighborhood as a "real happy, solid community."[139] Volin saw a strong working-class community, but federal authorities surveying the area for a location for the War Department saw something else entirely. Just as was the case in Freedman's Village, where residents saw a thriving community, outsiders saw the Black neighborhood as a ghetto. The neighborhood was described as an "industrial slum" by developers.[140] One highway consultant constructing road networks for the Pentagon went so far as to call the homes within Queen City "darkey slave cabins" that must be removed in order to "clean up that strip" of land.[141] When President Roosevelt came to Arlington to view the site of the future Pentagon building, it was pointed out that, although they were not within the grounds of the building itself, the houses of Queen City would "mar the environment of the new building."[142] On the basis of this observation, "the President said they ought to be acquired" and torn down.

That is exactly what happened. In January of 1942, construction began for the Pentagon's road networks in the path of the communities. Plans moved forward for construction without anyone informing occupants. According to Queen City resident Gertrude Jeffress, after authorities told her that their home had been condemned and they must relocate, "they only gave you a short length of time, and next thing the bulldozers were there."[143] Indeed, it was not until February of 1942 that residents received word that,

FIGURE 22. Aerial photograph showing Shirley Highway snaking through Arlington County. This area was once home to the African American neighborhoods of East Arlington and Queen City. Arlington saw a huge uptick in federally funded highway construction during the 1940s and '50s because of the expansion of the federal government, especially within the boundaries of Arlington County through installations such as the Navy Annex (*left*) and the Pentagon (*center*). Regional Highway Planning Committee, *Washington Metropolitan Area Transportation Study* (Washington, DC: Department of Highways, 1952), GMU Special Collections.

on March 1 of that year, they would have to move.[144] Property was seized through a combination of eminent domain laws and modest payments.[145] Residents who owned their homes were paid two thousand fifty-two dollars.[146] These funds were not enough to buy or build homes in other communities. Even the least expensive homes in the county sold for more than double that price, and the average home price was exponentially higher.[147] Still, this was preferable to the case for renters, like Celestine Dole, who were not eligible to receive relocation funds.[148] Despite these modest payments, residents like Ruth Shanklin and their neighbors were distraught.[149] This was justifiable, after all, as Shanklin asked, "If somebody took your home, wouldn't you be upset?"

With the push of wartime urgency, residents of East Arlington and Queen City were not able to delay eviction notices as residents of Freedman's Village had two generations before. Despite comments from federal

FIGURE 23. Queen City with the Pentagon in the background in early spring of 1942. Mount Olive Church, in the left-hand corner of the shot, as well as brick and wood-frame homes are visible. Although modest, they are a far cry from the "shacks" that many federal builders alleged made up Queen City. Within days, the community was demolished. US Army, *Pentagon*, April 1942.

authorities such as construction supervisor Lieutenant Bob Furman, who said the area was only "really, really rough shacks," Queen City residents such as Jeffress pushed back against this categorization of her neighborhood.[150] She insisted, "whoever said it was nothing but shacks, well that ain't true. This was a nice little neighborhood."[151] Almost all of those who lost their homes were Black. Queen City and the neighboring East Arlington were demolished to make way for the Pentagon, Navy Annex, and their road networks—but the nearby white neighborhood of Columbia Heights, which also bordered the projects, was left largely untouched.[152]

But more than homes were lost. Churches, community institutions, and businesses were also demolished. Like Queen City, Arlington's brickyards bordered the Pentagon's construction site. These yards had long provided Arlington's Black men an option for masons and other skilled labor employment beyond the federal government. They were shuttered because of the Pentagon construction. Like many of her neighbors, Jeffress was employed at the Pentagon. That job gave her the opportunity to leave the world of domestic service for the stability and better pay of a federal job. This reality for Jeffress and her federally employed neighbors highlights the contested relationship that African Americans had with federal explosion at this time. Expansion provided good jobs, but it greatly restricted housing through demolition and the support of housing segregation through federal building and lending processes. While Jeffress worked for the government, her mother and grandmother ran a catering business out of their home, selling food to local brickyard and construction workers.[153] As a result, when their home was taken, the Jeffress family lost both home and business.

The loss extended to the loss of community institutions and neighborhood networks. Even Mount Olive Church was demolished. Mount Olive was first established in Freedman's Village. Its lands became the basis for the community when its parish members were cast out from Freedman's Village by the government in 1900. The church had been renovated and expanded just three years before. In 1939, the Mount Olive congregation pooled their modest resources to expand and remodel their church, building a beautiful brick structure at the center of the Queen City community many of the members called home.[154] The church provided more than just worship for members: It provided recreation, education, and fellowship for the entire community.[155] In July of 1942, residents held their last service in their community church—now "a roofless, partly demolished church, void of furniture."[156] The loss of their church on top of the loss of their individual homes and neighborhood was especially distressing for Queen City residents. A member of the church, Dole pointed out that "the church looked out for the people," so when that institution also found itself without a place to call home, "it was kind of rough."[157]

These residents were not sure where to go. Lieutenant Furman admitted that he and his men did not "think . . . much about their welfare" when removing residents from their homes.[158] One resident, Eunice, who was only twelve years old when the communities closed, reflected that "it was just such a sad story because so many people had nowhere to go . . . no idea what to do."[159] Relocation was especially onerous, because there were so few homes. Consistent with national trends, Arlington was experiencing a housing crisis in general.[160] This crisis was especially acute in the Black community, as was the case regionally and throughout the country; residential segregation and restrictive covenants barred Arlington's African Americans from living in the majority of Arlington's new suburban community and apartment complexes.[161] In this kind of housing market, "Where in the world [can] we find a place?" Celestine Dole reasonably asked.[162]

After losing their homes with little notice, few funds, and little supply, many people left the area entirely. Friends and families who had lived together in a community for a generation never saw each other again. John Henderson remembered, "everyone who lived there was really separated," as previously tight-knit residents were pushed apart.[163] But many families who were affected did stay local. One of the primary options for these individuals was the federal government's emergency housing. To help with displaced residents in need of immediate assistance to avoid homelessness, the federal government created a trailer camp on mud flats on the outskirts of Green Valley. Like Freedman's Village, these trailer camps were constructed to serve only as temporary housing. However, their construction was far inferior to the emergency wartime housing the government provided in 1863 for the formerly enslaved. Entire families, no matter their size, squeezed into trailers equipped with stoves for heat and cooking, convertible couch-beds meant to sleep four people, and no running water. The tight quarters, lack of proper sanitation, and muddy environment led to rats so large that Henderson viscerally remembered them shaking the boards of the walkways that residents used to traverse the mud-soaked landscape.

Trailers were technically illegal in Arlington County, and officials were anxious to remove the camp.[164] Gertrude Jeffress and her sister Mary got a trailer when they were relocated from Queen City.[165] They lived in that trailer until "the government put up temporary housing for us." The government created barracks-style wartime emergency housing. Whereas whites had George Pickett, Shirley, J. E. B. Stuart, and Jubal Early emergency wartime housing projects, Arlington's African American residents in need of emergency housing could live in the George Washington Carver Homes in Johnson's Hill or Paul Dunbar Homes in Green Valley.[166]

Many residents relocated to federally sponsored housing, but some residents from Arlington's closing Black neighborhoods were able to tap into extended family networks within Arlington to find housing. Eunice and her family moved to her grandmother's home with the closing of Queen City.[167] However, her family of ten was too large for her grandmother's small house. After leaving their home in Queen City, they were forced to move into a wooden shed with a dirt floor in her grandmother's backyard.

Beyond just family, residents from Arlington's former Black communities were able to tap into the strong social, church, and fraternal networks that linked them across neighborhoods and, with such a stable African American population, across generations. John Henderson reflected that "it was quite a trying time," but "I think the love and association of people is what kept people together."[168] Arlington's African American population worked in cross-community organizations, such as the Odd Fellows. In 1946, local African American columnist Maggie B. Speller detailed a "day in the life" of an average African American resident in the area.[169] Whereas many new arrivals see the area as a dispassionate city full of transplants, Arlington's Black residents had the benefit of extended connections. The individual was anchored by a strong Black community built around church, recreation, sharing meals, and attending community organization meetings. Church congregations also reached beyond their borders. Mount Olive Church relocated to nearby Johnson's Hill after being demolished in Queen City.[170]

Through this tradition of community organizations working across all of Arlington's Black communities, individuals living beyond the affected Black communities also did what they could to help. James Gaskins Sr. relocated with his family from Yonkers, New York, in the 1940s.[171] Gaskins saw that Arlington's Black neighborhoods were congested and in need of more housing after community closures. After graduating from Virginia State University, Gaskins began a lifelong career with the US Postal Service. In his spare time, he began building, selling, renting, and remodeling houses across south Arlington. Through his efforts, Gaskins created forty affordable housing options for African Americans in the area. Lifelong Green Valley resident Leonard L. Gray, descendent of Freedman's Village transplant Selina Gray, also worked as a contractor in his spare time, constructing homes for African Americans in Green Valley when he was not working as a carpenter for the federal government. By 1950, there were twenty Black construction companies and three Black realtors in Arlington.[172]

Whether individuals and families moved in with family, moved into federal housing, or found their own housing, if staying local, residents had limited choices of where to move. Formalization of building, planning, zoning, and segregation laws had restricted Arlington's African American populations to only a few neighborhoods, closing smaller enclaves. At the same time the extreme expansion of white neighborhoods across every portion of the county physically pinned in the remaining communities and worked against them. With more and more encroachment from white suburban sprawl, Black and white neighborhoods were pushed even closer together. This brought the two into sharp contrast. In Green Valley, *Washington Post* reporter Isolde Weinberg noted that "homes ranging from little more than shacks . . . comprise a ghetto" in Green Valley, whereas just across the street a white neighborhood forms "[uniform] middle-class . . . housing."[173]

However, more was at stake than just aesthetics by this proximity. White neighborhoods created physical barriers to keep existing Black communities from growing. Expansion also led to land speculation, sharp increases in taxes while Black incomes held steady, and a desire among communities to buy these lands.[174] In 1943, even the National Capital Housing authority reported that while "the white population is very conscious of Negro expansion into areas formerly occupied by whites" in the Washington area, they were "scarcely aware of white expansion into areas formerly occupied by Negroes. The net result is loss of territory by Negroes."[175]

Beyond areas cited for federal expansion projects, the most at-risk neighborhoods were Hall's Hill and Pelham Town in northern Arlington, isolated from the other Black communities in southern Arlington. In the 1930s and 1940s, the land on the outskirts of Pelham Town was purchased for a white housing development.[176] When developers built new roads for this development, they boxed Pelham Town in by not connecting to the community's existing streets. William Pelham Jr., grandson of Pelham Town founder

Moses Pelham, noted that, despite "traveling back and forth through [that area] since my father was born," residents could no longer use these routes to enter and exit their neighborhood. This pressure really "put the screws" to the Pelham family and the others who lived in their small neighborhood. This physical isolation, coupled with rising costs and the fact that the new white community's developer was willing to buy their property, led to the end of Pelham Town.

Other communities faced similar fates. The Butler-Holmes community slowly ceased to exist as an exclusively African American community in a similar way, though the neighborhood kept a sizeable Black presence.[177] Members of the Hall's Hill community observed simply and tragically that "the land left us."[178] After years of permit denials and rejections of home improvement loans, many Black homes did, indeed, need to be torn down. This excuse allowed developers and planners who wanted the land for themselves as an excuse to seize Black real estate. Shrinking Black communities and expanding white communities meant that by 1950, Arlington's Black population made up only five percent of the county's overall population, down from thirty-eight percent in 1900.[179] But this was a population of nearly seven thousand who all needed to be housed within an ever-shrinking geography.[180]

Where eleven Black communities started at the turn of the century, by the 1950s, only three remained: Hall's Hill, Johnson's Hill, and Green Valley. These communities were almost one hundred percent African American.[181] New residents, as well as those relocating from Queen City, Pelham Town, and Butler-Holmes, had to relocate to one of these three neighborhoods. These communities became incredibly overcrowded. In Hall's Hill, for example, as the community absorbed the residents from Pelham Town in addition to other new arrivals, the boundaries of the community shrank. Although Hall's Hill was "two-fifths of its original size," only spanning six blocks by five blocks, it "increased seven times in its population density"— hosting two hundred sixty-three families, totaling twelve hundred fifty-one people by 1950.[182] Hall's Hill's active community organizations—especially the politically minded John M. Langston Community Organization, which was founded to keep the community abreast of changing zoning and planning laws—attempted to keep the community intact against such outside threats. However, without countywide support beyond the Black community, they were no match for the slow push of white expansion against their borders. Johnson's Hill and Green Valley found themselves similarly squeezed.[183] Green Valley grew by more than seventeen percent from 1950 to 1960.[184] Residents did what they could to make room for new arrivals, renting out spare rooms, further subdividing lots, and creating more multi-family housing units where possible.

The federally created George Washington Carver and Paul Dunbar homes were an important addition of multifamily housing units in Arlington's Black communities. Like the trailer camps, these barracks housing units did not comply with county zoning and planning laws. Because of this, at the war's end, Arlington County government pushed to have the buildings condemned and closed. The white housing developments, almost exclusively populated with recent arrivals of war workers, quickly folded to such pressures, and the white housing complexes, George Pickett, Shirley, J. E. B. Stuart, and Jubal Early, closed shortly after the war. However, the Carver and Dunbar homes were populated with a more diverse mix of residents. Some were newly arrived war workers, but the majority were individuals with long roots in the county who had been displaced by closing Black communities. African Americans in Virginia's Tidewater region also created cooperatives to successfully save wartime housing after World War I.[185] Joining this tradition, both created cooperatives to help residents stay in their homes. At Dunbar Homes, within six years of its completion the eleven-acre complex was home to eighty-six Black households.[186] Facing yet another potential closure, residents Robert McGregor, Frances W. Burgess, William H. Horton, James M. Smith, and others banded together to form the Dunbar Mutual Homes Association. The Association pooled resident resources and enlisted the help of supporting lawyers and real estate men, Black and white, until they had enough money for a down payment. They purchased their homes from the federal government for two hundred sixty-four thousand dollars with a cash down payment of thirty thousand dollars and two hundred thirty-four thousand dollars in mortgages.[187] Even with these and other types of building projects, there was a finite amount that could be done, and Arlington's Black neighborhoods had reached their outer limits by the end of the 1950s.

The population density also meant that Arlington's Black neighborhoods could support new and diverse kinds of all-Black businesses and professions. Arlington never had a large enough population to support a "Black downtown" like those seen in other areas of the New South. Instead, only small stores existed to serve a community, with larger specialty items secured in Alexandria or Washington. This lack of local amenities put Arlington's Black communities in sharp contrast with the growing commercial zones dedicated to white shoppers developing in tandem with Arlington's sprawling segregated suburban neighborhoods.

White Arlingtonians saw an expansion of their commercial districts. Clarendon established itself as a major shopping destination for locals during the 1920s, but by the 1940s, "Clarendon glittered as the shopping center of northern Virginia."[188] Between 1940 and 1951, the area became home to JC Penney, Sears, GC Murphy, Kann's, and Hecht's department stores.[189] In addition to the expansion of Clarendon's shopping district, which gave that area a "downtown atmosphere," Arlington also experienced the rise of the strip mall shopping center.[190] The spread-out nature of new suburban homes and the mass consumer culture of World War II-era America saw its physical representation in the shopping center.[191] The inclusion of shopping centers in new community developments was a common practice in Arlington. For example, Colonial Villages included a multiphased business complex, and Arlington Forrest, Williamsburg, and Westover communities each created community shopping centers.[192]

These commercial zones were convenient for local white residents, but they served residents within these communities almost exclusively and thus did not provide benefits for Arlingtonians writ large. Because each of these new communities was racially segregated, the location of commerce in shopping centers within white, middle-class suburbs meant that African Americans did not have equal access to these new, attractive economic spaces. African Americans were able to use some of these facilities, but accommodations were still segregated. Completed in 1945, the Fairlington Shopping Center located near Green Valley brought the county's first lunch counters.[193] Here, Black customers could shop but were not served at the segregated lunch counters.[194]

As a result of this restriction from expanding white commerce and increased population density in Arlington's existing Black neighborhoods there was more demand for various goods and services that Arlington's previously smaller Black community could not sustain. More and more of Arlington's residents established new community businesses.[195] Pharmacist Dr. Leonard "Doc" Muse opened the Green Valley pharmacy and lunch counter in 1952. Many of these new businesses were helmed by women. Decorator Grace Scipio of Hall's Hill and designer Ann Walker of Green Valley joined the ranks of many local Black women advertising services such as tailoring, dressmaking, and calligraphy to their ever-expanding array of neighbors.[196] "Mamie" Mell Mackley Brown used the cosmetology degree she earned from Storer College in West Virginia to open Friendly Beauty Salon and cosmetology school in Green Valley in the 1930s.[197] Her institution graduated more than one hundred Black female students in cosmetology, providing them with the education to improve the lives of themselves and their families.

Restaurants were another major source of employment within Black communities. Evelyn B. Simms and her family owned the restaurant in Hall's Hill, where she worked as the cook.[198] Although Arlington's white restaurants served Black customers beginning in the late 1950s, Black patrons did not feel welcome here.[199] Simms's husband, Princeton, remembered that

FIGURE 24. Dr. Leonard "Doc" Muse opened Green Valley Pharmacy in 1952.
The drugstore also featured a lunch counter and served as a neighborhood hub.
© Lloyd Wolf / Arlington Photographic Documentary Project.

despite being allowed to eat at these restaurants, proprietors would destroy
any plates used by Black patrons. "Anything we ate out of they broke it up . . .
Right in front of you, right on the counter. After you finished eating, they'd
pick up the plate and throw it in the trash because they wasn't going to serve
any white person out of that plate." Because of this kind of outward hostility, Black customers continued to prefer to patronize their own restaurants despite integration. Green Valley featured the Shady Dale Restaurant,
owned by the Oliver family. Hattie Berger Oliver spearheaded the enter-
prise, working as head chef, buyer, manager, and even dishwasher, and her
husband worked two custodial jobs to keep their family of five afloat.[200] The
County's property yard, which houses county equipment such as buses and
snowplows, borders the Green Valley community on South Arlington Mill
Drive. Into the 1950s, Shady Dale Restaurant was the only local establishment within walking distance where these drivers and county workers could
purchase their lunch. Because of this, the county made a special arrangement
with the Olivers so that they could serve Black and white patrons. Although
Shady Dale actually served an integrated clientele, it remained primarily an
African American restaurant. Residents used the opportunities available to
them within the realities of midcentury Arlington to create businesses and

opportunities within the three anchor communities that were still open after Arlington's suburban boom and federal expansion.

Conclusion

Federal expansion greatly shaped Arlington. New arrivals of war workers resulted in an explosion of suburban development. This development created more single-family housing communities while also adding multi-family housing options to Arlington's built environment, changing the character of the county's residential landscape. The expansion of housing for federal employees significantly impacted Arlington's Black communities. All of these new communities were segregated whites-only spaces that prevented Black Arlington from expanding. White neighborhoods and developers used existing zoning, planning, and buyout tactics to take land they wanted for themselves. Federal building projects, including FHA-funded communities, added new tools to this land grab from African Americans. Through these tactics, communities like Pelham Town and Butler-Holmes ceased to exist as Black neighborhoods, and areas such as Hall's Hill shrank geographically, despite increasing in population density. The expansion of government buildings into Arlington, most significantly with the War Department's Pentagon building, led to the closure of additional Black communities in Arlington.

Arlington's remaining anchor communities—Hall's Hill, Johnson's Hill, and Green Valley—worked to absorb people from these lost neighborhoods as well as new arrivals. They used the people, churches, community organizations, and social institutions that worked within and across all of Arlington's Black neighborhoods as their support system when their immediate community was lost. Arlington's stable Black population was well organized and solidified after generations of organization and shared community development.

Although the expansion of Arlington's suburban growth and the area's federal expansion put pressure on African American communities, both realities provided opportunities as well. Arlington's built environment was not all that changed as a result of the sharp rise of new federal employees. The residents themselves also marked a break from Arlington's previous growth. Like the previous generation of new residents, these new arrivals were predominately white. But unlike those who came before them, these residents came from across the country and not just from elsewhere in Virginia or the South. Mostly college educated, this new batch of residents brought with them more socially liberal ideas about race, education, and the proper role of government. These new opinions had profound impacts on Arlington's social and residential policies.

CHAPTER 6

"We Cannot Lose This Fight as We Lost Our Freedoms during Reconstruction Days"

Politics, School Integration, and Neighborhood Preservation

Individuals and families drawn to the area as a result of the federal expansion of the 1930s through 1950s dramatically changed the county's built environment.[1] This physical change had a marked impact on Arlington's African American communities. A drastically expanded white population led to an unparalleled housing and construction boom that resulted in the closing of Black enclaves and communities and the shrinking of the three remaining communities—Hall's Hill, Johnson's Hill, and Green Valley.

It was not just the numbers of new residents but the residents themselves who also marked a break from Arlington's previous growth. Like the previous generation of new residents, these new arrivals were predominately white, but unlike those who came before them, these residents came from across the country and not just from elsewhere in Virginia or the South. This group was highly educated, with the majority having attended college.[2] This new batch of residents brought with them more socially liberal ideas about race, education, and the proper role of government that had profound impacts on Arlington's social and residential policies.

In many ways, the county was finally the community that early white planners had sought for the past half-century: The county was squarely suburban, with communities interconnected by large-scale social programs and municipal services, which made it a premier residential community for Washington's federal employees. However, the influx of so many federal employees changed the character of the county. The skyrocketing population caused a housing shortage that changed the character of housing to a mixture of town homes, multifamily homes, and single-family residences. Before World War II, Arlington's housing was seventy-three percent single-family homes.[3] These homes were seventy-five percent owner occupied, but by 1950, that number had shrunk to fifty-one percent single-family homes. This had a "marked effect upon the living patterns of Arlington residents and their identification with the community." This broke with the picture-window, exclusively single-family ideal of early developers. Additionally, the people living within these new home types did not care as much about stamping out the African American presence in Arlington. Some new residents had very progressive views on race, which called for inclusion and equality, but most were white moderates who wanted what was best for themselves and their families, including good schools and increased spending on municipal needs, regardless of potential ramifications on race. The fact that Arlington's Black population was small—making up only five percent of the county as of 1940—and contained within the three Black communities also helped many embrace this moderate attitude.[4]

With the breathing room created by an increasingly moderate social and political attitude from the white majority, Arlington's African American communities, which had long been organizing and carving out a place for themselves, were able to secure more rights and social, political, and physical space within the county. Long-tested African American institutions, such as churches and fraternal organizations, were helped by new institutions and an increasingly active, young African American population pushing for more and more rights. The majority continued to work in federal service. One federal report noted that these positions within the professional class helped Arlington's Black population, "some of them whose families have been in Virginia for generations," in "leadership and community spirit" to ensure the continuation of their communities.[5]

New Arlingtonians and Changing Political Realities

The new residents of Arlington greatly changed the social and political makeup of the county from the political realities in place since the early 1900s. In the first decades of the twentieth century, men such as Frank Lyon and Crandal Mackey dominated Arlington politics. These politicians, businessmen, and developers used local and state politics to bolster a vision of Arlington dominated by white residents in single-family homes. Arlington's leaders and residents were also predominantly Virginians and Southerners committed to the Democratic Party. Although economically and socially more diverse and urban than their counterparts farther south, "politically," as one midcentury commentator put it, the county had "traditionally been one party (Democratic), poll-tax, Southern."[6]

In the twentieth century, the Virginia Democratic Party was dominated by the Byrd political machine. Named for Harry F. Byrd, who served as a state senator, governor, and U.S. senator during his tenure in public office, the Byrd Organization began in the 1920s. Byrd took an already tightly run Democratic Party in Virginia and turned it into a formidable political machine. The Byrd Organization controlled Virginia almost completely and was defined by a commitment to racial hegemony, small government, and fiscal conservatism.[7] This push for small government and little spending meant that funds were not spent, even for needed social and municipal improvements, creating an environment that could hurt the very individuals who supported the organization. Although not as engrained in machine politics as, for example, their counterparts in south-side Virginia, Arlington's political and social leaders before and during the 1930s very much agreed with and worked within the polices of the Byrd Organization. These old-guard Arlingtonians stood in opposition to newly arriving residents, whom they referred to as "outlanders" and "foreigners."[8] When the Simms family relocated to Arlington for federal employment, they did not feel welcomed by their new neighbors in their Aurora Hills neighborhood. Lillian Simms said that her "neighbors were very awful to [federal workers]." Unless you had lived in the area for "eight years or so," you could expect Arlington's pre-World War II population to be "aloof," if not downright hostile.[9] The experiences of the Simms family were far from unique.

Federal families cuttingly felt this sense of othering, but this resistance to their presence in the county was especially pronounced for African Americans who came to the area to work for the federal government. First Lieutenant James Franklin McCall was the first African American officer assigned to the Army's Third Infantry at Fort Myer in Arlington.[10] There, his tasks included the honor of guarding the Tomb of the Unknown Soldier at Arlington National Cemetery. A native of Philadelphia, McCall served in Kentucky and abroad in Europe before being assigned to Fort Myer.[11] Despite their experience at other military installations within and beyond the South, the McCalls had a difficult time penetrating the "clique" they found in Arlington.[12] McCall felt that, as the only Black family at the base, he and his wife, Yvonne Jackson McCall, had to act as role models for the entire race. Yvonne, in particular, worked hard to charm the officers and their wives at social events, and over time, the pair found acceptance. At military social functions held beyond the base, an integrated military clashed with segregated society. In these situations, an advance team from the military had to go to restaurants to warn the facilities managers that the party would be integrated. At these facilities, the service staffs were frequently Black. However, over time on Fort Myer, the McCalls found more tolerant families who went above and beyond to make them feel welcome. James felt that "there was a desire to say 'we're not like those people you may have heard about.'"

This story of gradual acceptance helps to highlight the ways in which Arlington's newly arrived majority of federal employees stood in contrast to the old-guard Arlingtonians on issues of race. Although Arlington's new residents did not universally push for overt equality or civil rights, neither was this new majority willing to shun the McCalls and people like them. This reality fits with narratives that challenge the idea of a "solid South" and with those of scholars such as Matthew Lassiter, Andrew B. Lewis, and James H. Hershman Jr., who have explored the political and social strengths and limitations of moderates in Virginia. In some ways, the progressive shift seen in Arlington challenges narratives such as those of Thomas J. Sugrue, Andrew Wiese, and Jeanne Theoharis, who argue that racism and segregation were national, not southern, problems. Although these issues were unquestionably national problems, Arlington shows how a significant shift in a population to people who are college educated, white-collar, and not exclusively Southern in an area with a small Black population can allow for the embrace of racially progressive policies.[13]

Federal families were more likely to be well educated, to have been born or raised in states beyond the South, to express more moderate social and racial views, and to work as white-collar professionals. By 1950, Arlington County's adult education level was twice the national average.[14] When people like Lillian Simms came to Arlington with their families, they brought with them a distinct worldview that was not consistent with Arlington's existing political environment. Before coming to the area for an assignment with the Department of Agriculture, the Simms family spent nearly twenty-five years in Oregon. There, she and her husband, B. T., worked for Oregon State University, he as a researcher and professor and she as a secretary.[15] Lillian was born in Minnesota and raised throughout the western United States and Canada. Highly educated and raised beyond the South, Lillian was also active in social and political institutions, such as the League of Women Voters and the Parent-Teacher Association (PTA), on her arrival in Washington. The Simms family represented a new kind of Arlington resident.

Disagreements on social issues and the proper role of the government in people's daily lives was also a major source of contention. Arlington's new residents were not committed to the political austerity of the Byrd regime. Societies beyond the South where this worldview did not reign supreme shaped many, and, as federal employees, many believed in a more actively involved government. Beyond this theoretical disagreement with a lack of county organizations, the arrival of huge numbers of new people greatly strained Arlington's existing resources. By the late 1940s, all municipal and recreational services needed expansion. New residents wanted and needed more services, and they were prepared to pay for them. "Why assume the sidewalks, additional garbage collections, and additional recreation facilities can be provided without additional taxes?" asked Arlington County Board Member Florence Cannon.[16]

FIGURE 25. When attending social events such as the one above with other military families, the McCalls (center) were often the only people of color present outside of the wait staff. Because Virginia was segregated, the Army sent advance teams to make sure that facilities managers knew the party would be integrated. The McCalls felt that these African American men and women were very excited to see them there as guests, giving Yvonne Jackson McCall special accommodations as a way of saying, "We're with you." *Black and White digital print of sing-along social of officers of the 3rd Infantry, Fort Myer, Virginia, ca.* 1950, James Franklin McCall Collection (AFC/2001/001/29772), Veterans History Project, American Folklife Center, Library of Congress.

Part of the reason for a lack in responsiveness had to do with Arlington's local form of government. In 1930, Arlingtonians called a special election to establish a county manager form of government.[17] Supported by Arlington's existing white residents and those in power before the influx of new arrivals, this government rejected district voting for an at-large voting system that elected five county board members for four-year terms.[18] These members, in turn, appointed an individual from their ranks to serve as county manager who, in turn, appointed county department heads.[19] Instead of coming from a cross-section of the county, new board members most frequently hailed from the wealthier and less diverse northern section of the county. Because local districts no longer voted for their own representatives, this at-large system made the county government less responsive to individual community needs. And because county politicians generally subscribed to the Byrd Organization political theory of small government and little spending, they were disinclined to spend money on regional improvements. The change to the county manager form of government also had racially discriminatory overtones.[20] The change of government representation came after four African American residents ran for office in 1930 stood a chance of winning, because of residential segregation that isolated the Black vote to South Arlington's Jefferson District.[21] The switch to an at-large system all but guaranteed that African American candidates could not win a countywide election.

As a result of a less responsive county government, beginning in the 1940s and 1950s, local residents looking to fill the gap between needs and government provisions created new county political organizations. One such organization was the Better Government League, a nonpartisan group with overtly political aims. They sponsored events with local and state officials to discuss local issues, such as public utilities and recreation, as well as governmental reforms, such as improvements to the state's financial and tax systems.[22] The Better Government League was joined by organizations such as Arlingtonians for a Better County (ABC) and the Arlington Independence Movement (AIM) by the mid-1950s.[23] These organizations were nicknamed "Agitators By Choice" and "Arlington Is Mine" by their detractors from Arlington's old-guard residents. Together, new residents hoped that "these [groups] will mark a turning point in the drive of Arlington's civic-minded groups and individuals for a more democratic, more enlightened local government."[24] One of the major organizations in this swell of new participatory groups was the Arlington Civic Federation. The Federation combined thirty-nine civic groups into one body that could work to shape municipal and governmental policies in the county and state. A large part of their reform aims had to do with attempting to remove the Byrd Organization from local politics. As one Lyon Park community member wrote, "it is more important that the voice of the people should prevail in Arlington election matters at the nominating level."[25] They pushed for nonpartisan primaries for local officials.

These organizations were nonpartisan and pushed for the removal of party politics from many local elections because of the status of many Arlingtonians as federal employees. Federal employees were limited in their political participation by the 1939 Hatch Act.[26] Named for Senator Carl Hatch of New Mexico, the Hatch Act prevented federal employees from "any active part" of campaigning in any federal, state, or local elections with candidates from national political parties.[27] Additionally, controlled primaries were an important tool of the Byrd Democratic machine. Because of the power of the political machine, primaries all but decided who would come out victorious in the general elections.[28] And only small numbers of the population participated in primaries. From 1925 to 1941, only 11.5% of eligible voters in Virginia voted in the Democratic primaries.

One reason for such low turnout was confusion over Virginia's voting system for new residents. The amendments to the new state constitution in 1902 included a large number of voting restrictions, including poll taxes.[29] These taxes were to be paid in advance of the election without a bill being sent. Although specifically targeting African Americans, these voting restrictions also hurt Arlington's new arrivals, Black and white. With many residents arriving from beyond Virginia and the South, these taxes led to a great deal of confusion for new residents. The League of Women Voters sent out directions explaining bills and timelines to new residents. Once over twenty-one years of age, an individual must live in Virginia for one year, in Arlington for six months, and in their voting district for thirty days before being eligible to vote.[30] This meant that the newest arrivals could not vote in Arlington. After that first year, "in order to vote you must have paid, six months before the November election, any poll taxes due for the three years preceding the year in which you wish to vote." Taxes of one dollar and fifty cents were levied annually, regardless of voting intention, without bills being sent. The Lyon Village Citizen's Association reminded existing residents to help their new neighbors understand the system. They encouraged members to look out for "any new residents in your immediate section tell them that poll taxes must be paid . . . if they wish to vote either in the primary or the general election this year," providing reminders about due dates and details about how to identify your poll tax receipts—"it's pink in color."[31]

Delays in voting eligibility, combined with complicated poll tax billing systems that saddled voters with debts they were not aware of, led to decreases in voter participation. As a result, some new residents were discouraged from voting in Arlington.[32] In 1955, Arlington's PTA organized a "voter drive to qualify more voters in Arlington by encouraging payment of poll taxes."[33] Citizens' groups lamented that "in Arlington, Federal employees . . . constitute the largest segment of the population" but, because of restrictions on voting, "their lack of an adequate role in local elections . . . has been the reason for the inadequate services and poor community facilities provided by the county government."[34] New arrivals strained resources and were incapable of voting for municipal expansions that Byrd Democrats refused to finance.

Although these restrictions hurt new arrivals, they targeted African Americans specifically, and their impacts were most felt within that community. The level of activism in Arlington's Black community would suggest a high level of political participation, but all but a small number of

Arlington's Black residents were blocked from voting into the mid-twentieth century. For example, despite an active local community, only sixteen percent of Arlington's Black female population attempted to register to vote in 1941.[35] That same year, nearly thirty percent of Arlington's white female population attempted to register to vote. As people, Black and white, ran into issues registering to vote, nearly half of all of Arlington's Black population were blocked through poll tax laws. Additionally, white women were registering to vote as recent arrivals to the county. In comparison, the majority of Arlington's Black female voters who were thwarted from registration were lifelong residents seeking to vote for the first time, not just for the first time in a new place of residence. Women like Alice Fleet, Lula Pelham, and Selina Syphax, who had lived in Arlington all their lives and whose families had lived in Arlington for generations, could not register to vote because of voting discrimination.

Beyond formal political organizations, Arlington's new and increasingly active residents also used social and cultural organizations to tackle the lag between community needs and provisions. They created new organizations to deal with these problems. That was the case in the Rock Spring community. Here, new arrivals found older residents to be extremely hostile to their presence and ideas. Like many of Arlington's neighborhoods, Rock Spring began as a small clustering of homes around the time of the Civil War and grew into a streetcar community with the expansion of the Great Falls and Old Dominion railroad in the area.[36] This growth continued as one hundred fifty additional acres within the community were subdivided and sold beginning in 1946. At that time, Marvin T. Broyhill and Sons' construction erected three-bedroom brick ramblers *en masse* in the North Arlington community. The people who occupied these homes were active and engaged World War II federal employees, including notables such as Major General Charles "C. G." Helmick, who helped lead US troops into Paris when liberating France.[37] Helmick joined with other socially active neighbors Elizabeth and Edmund Campbell, Virginia Stitzenberger, Anna Barber, and Dudley Babcock to form the Rock Spring Civic Association (RSCA) in 1950.[38] The RSCA sought "to promote the mutual interests and general welfare of the community." Group leaders felt that this was necessary because they observed an extreme lag between Arlington's growing needs and its realities, and many of their neighbors agreed. The group began with five hundred members in 1950 and continued to grow in membership into the 1960s. The group became very active in community and county affairs, working toward school improvement, helping found the Rock Spring Cooperative Nursery, creating a county homeless shelter, working with at-risk teens, and much more. These activities put the RSCA in a state of constant conflict with older members of the community who resisted all social programs that might raise taxes.

In addition to the creation of new organizations, residents reimagined existing social and community organizations to reflect their ideals and visions for the county. This can be seen with the Lyon Park Women's Organization. Founded in 1924, in the 1940s, the functions of this organization shifted from community social and local campaigns, such as improvements for pedestrians, to a group interested in international and governmental affairs. Educational programs on the United Nations, the state of relations with Russia and China, and the Greek economy all show up on meeting minutes. The Organization sent provisions to Germany and the Philippines. Although local issues remained on the docket, this shift reveals the changing attitudes of the county's new residents, whose numbers and connection to the federal government through their spouses and their own employment shaped what they hoped their community organization would bring to them. Other organizations were similarly affected. Lillian Simms was active in politics on the West Coast and brought those sentiments with her to Arlington, becoming a member of the League of Women Voters of Arlington. Founded in 1921, the League of Women Voters was active in political and social issues, primarily on the local or state level.[39] Member Sue Renfro recalled a real conflict within the organization, beginning during World War II, between women who wanted to be active participants in politics and those she dubbed "the tea party group."[40]

In the late 1950s, the new political groups formed by Arlington's new moderate voter base had a great deal of political power. In 1956, ABC and AIM candidates each held two seats on the county board, with the fifth seat going to a moderate Democrat.[41] Although new residents increasingly influenced county politics, this was not the case across the board. The county was still at the mercy of hardline Byrd Democrats in Richmond. "Is the voice of Arlington fairly heard in Richmond? Decidedly not," complained residents of Lyon Village.[42] Because local areas must be awarded specific rights by the state before they could govern their own affairs, Arlington's citizens still had an uphill battle against state politicians and the older powers that be to create effective reforms in Arlington County.

Arlington's Rising Civil Rights Movement

Much of the conflict in Arlington emerged in response to the growing civil rights movement. In the 1940s, Arlington's Black population became even more active in pushing for social and political rights through their longstanding social and civic organizations. Recall that the area had the earliest nonurban branch of the National Association for the Advancement of

Colored People (NAACP) with the nearby Falls Church chapter, founded in 1918.[43] Support for the NAACP and its causes continued to expand until Arlington County could support a separate dedicated branch in 1940 with seventy-one members.[44] The branch continued to grow and soon became one of the largest branches in the state.[45] This long civil rights movement fit with national trends during the 1940s, as African American middle- and working-class individuals were no longer willing to accept the slow moving strategies of uplift often used by elite Blacks.[46] In Arlington, this shift toward more pronounced organization for social and political equality was reflective of national trends that saw returning veterans of color from World War II push for increased rights and was also influenced by county realities that saw the arrival of increasingly liberal and active federal workers, Black and white.

The first African American in the State of Virginia to challenge the poll tax in court was Arlington's Jessie Butler.[47] Butler was a resident of Green Valley who was active in her church congregation and Arlington's chapter of the NAACP.[48] Like many women of color throughout the South, Arlington's Black female population played an important role in challenging poll taxes and voting restrictions in the county.[49] Butler's case made it to a three-judge district panel but was dismissed in February of 1951 under the argument that, because poll taxes applied to both Black and white voters, this "plaintiff [cannot] maintain that she personally has been discriminated against by virtue of her race."[50] Although unsuccessful, this court battle highlights the growing activism of Black Arlingtonians in the strengthening civil rights movement and its legal challenges.

Arlington's proximity to Washington often shaped the area's connection to major national civil rights players and organizations. Princeton Simms of Hall's Hill was working as a cab driver in the early 1940s when he happened to pick up noted civil rights activist Mary McLeod Bethune on a fare.[51] Bethune's work with the National Association of Colored Women and the National Council of Negro Women on issues of education and social welfare for African American children and families propelled her to national prominence. Beginning in the 1930s, President Roosevelt consulted Bethune as an expert, and over time, she became a close friend with the Roosevelts. Simms was surprised when "this well-dressed Black woman" requested to go to the White House. After this chance encounter, Bethune took an active interest in Simms, and he became her personal chauffeur. Simms's wife, Evelyn, insisted that "everyone knew Mrs. Bethune" because of her local work. In addition to her work nationally for African American advancement, Bethune was known among many in Arlington for her efforts in securing jobs in the federal government for local African Americans, especially young people.

Under her encouragement, Simms became a civilian employee at the Pentagon in 1943.

A few years later, Simms transitioned from the Pentagon to a position with the Post Office.[52] However, the Post Office was not initially a welcoming environment for Simms. On his first day as a mail carrier, Simms's white supervisor asked him, "Boy, what do you want?" When Simms told the supervisor that he was the new hire, he was told "We don't need no help here," and was sent home. Postmaster Roy North, who had hired Simms directly, reprimanded Simms's supervisor, who eventually got in line, even calling Simms "Mr. Simms" when he later returned to work. Despite this hostility, Simms worked hard at his position with the Post Office, eventually receiving a promotion to utility carrier. "I got the job," Simms knew, "because . . . nobody in the post office knew as much about Arlington County as I did, so they couldn't pass over me." But advancement was slow. It took Simms seven years to receive a promotion, because any time a new white man was hired, Simms was "bumped off my route." When reflecting on the discrimination he experienced in his workplace, "That made me angry." Simms took that anger and transformed it into constructive change. In addition to working to improve his personal condition in the workplace through promotion, Simms became an active member of Arlington's NAACP, where he worked to end segregated accommodations in Arlington's facilities and sought fair treatment.

Arlington's Schools

Arlington's civic groups pushed changes, including abolishing the poll tax and reforming the state constitution and judicial process, but school improvement was, by far, the biggest issue for these organizations.[53] New and existing Black and white organizations focused on improving Arlington's schools, but the scale and scope of these organizations changed dramatically within the white community. The Better Government League sought members among "all those who believe . . . in better government and better schools for Arlington County."[54]

The School Improvement Movement

Although Arlington's first schools were established at the close of the Civil War, sixty years later, they remained small neighborhood institutions without rigorous curriculums. A report created by the US Bureau of Education in 1930 ranked Arlington's school system twenty-fourth out of twenty-eight comparable school districts.[55] In 1930, Arlington's white parent and teacher organizations from across the county banded together to create the County Council of PTAs. The issue of school improvement was on the rise throughout the 1930s, but the situation became even more serious for Arlington parents when Washington, DC's schools began limiting their institutions to city residents or requiring tuitions in 1946. Until these restrictions were put into place, parents who were interested in elite educations for their students, be they Black or white, sent them into Washington to be educated. The elimination of this option spurred many of Arlington's parents into action.

Local parent and federal employee Warren E. Cox warned that "the tide of younger children threatens to overwhelm the limited facilities of our Arlington Public Schools."[56] There were so few classrooms that nearly one thousand white students had to attend classes in shifts.[57] In the 1940s and early 1950s, school budgets and policies were still controlled by Byrd Democrats and old-guard Virginians who avoided spending at all costs.[58] Arlington's school board was appointed by the county manager and was either "incapable or unwilling to meet the resulting problems" from the huge population influx when "the Federal Government engulfed the area with new population."[59] This attitude is highlighted by School Superintendent Fletcher Kemp. When asked about the status of schools in the Fairlington community, Kemp replied that, because that development was built by the federal government for federal employees, those children were not his responsibility.[60] Kemp quipped that "the children can sit on the curb and shuck peanuts" until their schools were built for all he was concerned.[61]

In 1946, ABC got involved with school and with school board reform. At the same time, the County Council of PTA's membership soared. Starting with one thousand members in 1931, the group had more than twelve thousand members by 1949.[62] These members were predominately made up of Arlington's newly arrived federal workers. The Citizens Committee for School Improvement (CCSI) was formed to merge civic, professional, cultural, and PTA groups all working toward school improvement.[63] The CCSI held monthly meetings with parents and representatives from each of Arlington's school districts, as well as members from civic organizations including the Arlington Civic Federation and the Better Government League. All of these organizations came together under the umbrella of Arlington's Better School movement.[64]

The ranks of these varied organizations were filled with men such as Warren E. Cox. Born in Nebraska, Cox was educated in public schools in Florida and Georgia before studying law at Emory University in Atlanta.[65] Cox moved to Arlington in 1941 to serve as a lawyer with the Legal Division of the Federal Housing Administration. Arriving in Arlington with two school-aged children, Cox valued public education and became actively involved in school reform, serving as County Council president in 1949. New residents such as Lillian Simms also became involved in the school movement through other organizations. When Lillian relocated with her family to Arlington after her husband, Dr. B. T. Simms, became the chief of the Department of Agriculture's Bureau of Animal Industry, their children began attending Arlington's schools. Both B. T. and Lillian were highly educated. These educated people wanted a strong public school system for their children. Reformers sought not only more buildings but also improved curriculums and better teachers. Journalist Elmore M. McKee noted that "because of their special abilities and interests, government researchers and administrators were particularly alert to the mental and environmental needs of their children."[66] Longtime Arlington residents disagreed, resisting the intervention of new arrivals into their school system. One Arlington native complained, "If you know how to stick a pin in a butterfly, you can get a job in the Agriculture Department, and that's the kind of nitwits we have living here and trying to ruin our schools."

All of these organizations together successfully campaigned for bonds to support Arlington's schools.[67] Most significantly, together, these groups worked to create a quorum to call for, and then win, a special election in May of 1947 to make membership on the school Board an elected position rather than an appointed position.[68] Ten thousand Arlingtonians voted on the issue, making it the largest special election turnout to date.[69] One Arlington resident involved in the reform movement, Harley M. Williams, predicted that "these actions will make a turning point in the drive of Arlington's civic-minded groups and individuals for a more democratic, more enlightened local government."[70] When Arlington residents were finally able to vote for their own school board candidates, every individual who campaigned on platforms of school improvement won. In fact, the winning candidate with the fewest votes still earned more than twenty-three hundred more votes than the highest of the old-guard candidates supported by the Byrd Organization.[71] The first board was made up of Barnard Joy (chair), Elizabeth Campbell, Colin MacPherson, O. Glenn Stahl, and Curtis Tuthill. These individuals had a different kind of background than their predecessors. Two were federal employees, the Hatch Act allowing for participation in nonpolitical posts; one was a professor at George Washington University; and one was a teacher.[72] Most were involved in Arlington's Better Schools movement as well as other new midcentury reform organizations: Campbell, for example, was a member of the CCSI, her local PTA, and the League of Women Voters, and she was a founding member of the RSCA.[73] This group began making changes to Arlington's schools. By the mid-1950s, Arlington County schools had several new buildings; more than a half-dozen renovation projects; new special needs services for both disabled and gifted students; curriculum improvements; and the addition of music, health, and physical education classes.[74]

These school improvement organizations were not intended to help further Black education. Despite this fact and, although not distributed evenly, school improvements reached Arlington's Black schools thanks to the hard work of an engaged population. In the late 1940s, the NAACP supported ABC candidates for the school board in exchange for a promise that Black schools would also be improved.[75] Education had long been a cornerstone of African American community development in Arlington. Since the first calls for schools in Freedman's Village, Black Arlingtonians saw schools and education as important in their own right and for the future opportunities they would provide. Arlington's Black community had been involved in school improvement programs since the 1910s, when Ella Boston successfully lobbied the county for an African American eighth grade.[76] Arlington's Black parents founded PTAs in each of the Black schools. Green Valley resident Esther Cooper greatly valued education for her three daughters. The family saved to purchase a set of encyclopedias even before installing electricity or indoor plumbing into their home. Coopers' interest in improved education was not isolated to her own home and children. She herself worked as a teacher and was very active with the PTAs at her children's schools, even serving as PTA president for several years.[77] Green Valley neighbors Alice B. Fleet, also a teacher, and Edward Stother also became actively involved with the PTA in the community.[78]

Beyond individual school PTAs, Arlington's Black leaders also participated in countywide school improvement organizations. Black and white civic groups took up education and school improvement as a cornerstone of their aims. This made Arlington's school improvement movement a powerful social and political force in the 1940s and 1950s. Stother became a member of ABC. Others in the African American community created parallel institutions for school improvements, including the Arlington County Civic League. The League worked to be a unified voice for African American parents, teachers, and schools. At the start of the 1930s, Arlington's Black schools were in an even worse condition than those of their white counterparts. Although supported by community funds and bolstered by a commitment to education, Arlington's African American population had fewer schools, with larger student bodies, and no high school, and African American teachers earned lower wages. Despite these realities, many teachers were very committed to their students. Clarissa Thompson remembered that "one teacher, Miss Coles, let me know that she expected me to 'step up to the bat,'" working hard with Thompson on her academics until school felt like "my home away from home."[79] Her brother, Stephen Thompson, also felt that some teachers "took . . . interest in us and were concerned about whether or not we succeeded."[80]

Focused lobbying by Black community and parent groups resulted in the establishment of Hoffman-Boston High School in 1931 in the Johnson's Hill neighborhood. Founded six years after Arlington's first white high school, Washington and Lee, opened its doors, Hoffman-Boston served all of Arlington's Black students. Its location in southern Arlington was convenient for students from Johnson's Hill and Green Valley but required students from Hall's Hill to travel several miles, past closer white schools, to receive their education. Although they were successful in securing a Black high school, Arlington's Black parent and civic organizations were not content. Hoffman-Boston did not have a rigorous curriculum, with many of its courses focusing on vocational training. Because of its subpar facilities and curriculums, which did not prepare students for college, and the great distance that some of Arlington's Black students had to travel to school, the dropout rate was very high. In 1953, one hundred thirty-five African American students began the seventh grade, but only thirty-six graduated the twelfth grade, with the majority dropping out in ninth grade.[81]

Court Challenges, Resisting Massive Resistance, and School Integration
Education reform was a focus of African American communities, not just in Arlington but also throughout the South and the nation.[82] Because of this, some of the earliest civil rights challenges took aim at school segregation.[83] Arlington's NAACP chapter was especially rigorous in pushing for reforms to Arlington's schools through the courts. In addition to her work with school organizations, Esther Cooper served as the first president of Arlington's NAACP branch, further solidifying the joint aims of racial and school improvement. In 1947, the NAACP helped Hoffman-Boston student Constance Carter go to court over unequal facilities and coursework when she could not take Civics II, Spanish, typewriting, or physical education.[84] Rather than resulting in integration, this court battle brought improvements to Hoffman-Boston. In June 1950, the Fourth Circuit Court of Appeals ordered Arlington to provide equal facilities for its Black students. Thompson remembered coming back after summer break to find "a new gymnasium, auditorium, cafeteria, and chemistry lab."[85] However, the improvements were only skin deep: "The lab had no equipment," Thompson complained, yet "the purpose of this renovation was to show that we were getting an 'equal' education."

After this initial court case, Arlington's Black community continued to work through the court system with several other court challenges. Arlington's active NAACP was aided in their court battles by national opinions from civil rights organizations at the time about how best to combat segregation. In the 1950s, the NAACP's legal defense saw areas such as Arlington

FIGURE 26. This 1948 photo of Hoffman-Boston's library highlights the lacking provisions at Arlington's Black high school, as most of the shelves are empty of books. *Library of Hoffman-Boston*, 1948, Records of the US District Court for the Easter District of Virginia, National Archives and Records Administration, Washington, DC.

with smaller African American populations as the key places to challenge school segregation.[86] These court cases were predominately filed by African American families on behalf of their children, but sometimes featured white plaintiffs as well. Although school reform was important to a majority of Arlington's white parents, especially new arrivals, for them, school improvement did not necessarily mean integration. However, some of Arlington's white parents also supported full integration. White parents like Barbara Marx joined the cause for integration by adding her children Claire and Ann to the court cases challenging Arlington's segregated schools.[87] Others joined Arlington's NAACP, which featured both Black and white members who worked with other like-minded parents to push for full integration.[88]

These integration cases are part of a larger story of similar challenges to segregation taking place across the country. Eventually, these challenges made it to the Supreme Court in the landmark 1954 *Brown v. Board of Education of Topeka* case. With *Brown*, the highest court in the land reversed the *Plessy v. Ferguson* (1896) case that created the precedent of "separate but equal" to deem school segregation on the basis of race unconstitutional.[89]

After the *Brown* decision, the Virginia General Assembly created a board to study the process of integration. The statewide commission was known as the Gray Commission for State Senator Garland Gray, who headed the group. The Gray Commission, which comprised thirty-two white members, met for an entire year before releasing their segregationist plan, veiled in conciliatory language, in November of 1955, a few months after the 1955 *Brown II* ruling, which called for "good faith compliance" as quickly as possible.[90] Because Arlington was the only county in the state with their own school board, Arlington held a parallel commission to explore the process of integration in their county and present their findings. School board member Elizabeth Campbell read Arlington's findings, which recommended the continuation of public education and compulsory attendance laws, that state officials give local schools latitude to decide for themselves how to integrate, and that the state comply with all federal mandates.[91] Alongside this proposal, Arlington School Board Chair Dr. E. R. Draheim also made it clear that Arlington would "comply with any action taken by the State Legislature."[92] The Gray Commission created a plan for local control of student placement, assuming that locales would not allow integration, and established state ability to close any schools that did integrate.[93] This set Virginia on a path of massive resistance.

County leaders hoped to balance the demands of both the state and federal mandates. Arlington's school board created a pragmatic policy that they hoped would comply with both the Supreme Court's and the State's rulings. The county established "a plan which would permit integration in a few elementary schools in the fall, several junior high schools the following year, and one senior high school in 1958."[94] This was the minimum amount of integration that could occur to comply with federal law while also attempting to comply with Virginia's resistance to integration. Arlington's plan for integration was a moderate, stepwise plan that would have affected a maximum of sixty students. Arlington's 1958 school integration plan affected few students because of the realities of Arlington's extremely segregated residential environment. Only the Black Hall's Hill community was located among white communities in northern Arlington. Johnson's Hill and Green Valley were located near one another in southern Arlington, allowing county officials to argue that the school segregation of those communities was the result of *de facto* residential factors.

Despite this moderation, the General Assembly patently rejected the plan. Those who supported massive resistance refused to allow Arlington to make its own plan to integrate, fearing that if "you ever let them integrate anywhere, the whole state will be integrated in a short time."[95] Virginia's General Assembly threatened the state with school closures should any schools integrate despite court orders, and they threatened Arlington specifically with the loss of their elected school board. Attempting to keep their county schools open while also keeping the elected school board system they had won in 1947, the school board immediately began backtracking on their plan. In February of 1957, the Virginia State House revoked Arlington's right to its elected school board. Virginia politicians led the charge of southern states rejecting integration plans and instead chose to set out on a path of opposition. Senator Harry F. Byrd Sr. promoted the "Southern Manifesto" in 1956.[96] Signed by nineteen senators and seventy-seven representatives, the document said that they would fight integration through "all lawful means," creating a policy known as "massive resistance."[97] In September of 1958, Governor Lindsay Almond began closing Virginia's schools rather than allowing them to integrate.

While Arlington's school board took a moderate approach, many of its citizens agreed with Almond and the massive resistance movement. One such organization was the American Nazi Party. In 1958, the American Nazi Party was founded in Arlington County by George Lincoln Rockwell.[98] Several factors drew him to Arlington specifically to create his hate group.[99] Rockwell saw "New Deal liberals" as a great threat to America.[100] Sneering at them as "race mixers," Rockwell saw Arlington's large population of federal workers as a stain on the nation and the "white power" he hoped to encourage.[101] Rockwell was also drawn to Arlington specifically because residents provided him with support. Local sympathizer Floyd Fleming bought the group a house to use as their headquarters in the Ballston neighborhood.[102] Rockwell and his American Nazi followers supported continued segregation at all costs. The fifty to sixty members active in the organization in the late 1950s and early 1960s frequently attended school board meetings in their Nazi uniforms as a form of intimidation.

Arlington's branch of the Ku Klux Klan also reasserted itself at this time. The Klan had declined in visibility in the area after its heyday in the 1920s but reemerged in the wake of school integration. Many participants in Arlington's integration court cases had crosses burned on their front lawns. Barbara Marx, like many of her peers, received phone calls from self-identified Klan members alleging that they would "drive her out" of Arlington and bomb her house.[103] Although Marx kept her daughters' names on the court case, these threats were too much for other parents, who chose to remove their children from the proceedings.[104]

Other supporters of segregation and massive resistance worked against Arlington's plans on integration through new social and political organizations. One Arlington mother told a newspaper that she would rather the schools close than integrate, stating that "a year or two years without any schools is a cheap price to pay if it staves off integration."[105] Arlingto-nians founded a chapter of the Defenders of State Sovereignty and Indi-vidual Liberty. Virginia's equivalent of the White Citizens Councils that emerged throughout the Deep South, this group supported massive resis-tance and preventing integration at all costs.[106] Arlingtonians like founder Jack Rathbone came together to create the Tenth District Education Cor-poration. This group raised money, filed anti-integration court cases, and founded an alternate school system in Arlington. Rathbone and his sup-porters opened the private George Mason Grammar and Academic High School in a four-square-style, single-family home in Arlington to accommo-date white families who did not want their students to suffer forced integra-tion. Likening the school to a "bomb shelter" put in place in case integration "strikes" Virginia, Rathbone told a reporter from CBS News that "the South will never accept integration."[107] Despite assuring a solid education, the group misspelled grammar as "Grammer" on their sign, thus belittling their own cause. Groups like the Defenders of State Sovereignty and Individual Liberty and the Tenth District Education Corporation provided a more law-abiding and measured response to the threat of integration than those in the Klan and American Nazi Party. These organizations together show the continuation of the social and political attitudes of old-guard Arlingtonians, despite changes made in the area.

While Virginia set out on a path of massive resistance, Arlington's NAACP continued to challenge segregation in court. In May of 1956, Clarissa Thompson and three other Arlington families filed suit against Arlington's school board.[108] The African American students on this case were all from Hall's Hill. This was because of the community's position as the only Black neighborhood in northern Arlington, where the other two anchor Black communities existed in southern Arlington. Because of this isolation from other Black communities, when creating Arlington's Black high school district, county officials dubbed Hall's Hill as the "Hoffman-Boston 'north'" district. This school district circled the adjacent Green Valley and Johnson's Hill communities and then ran in a thin line up Glebe Road for about four miles, until it reached Hall's Hill. This location of Hoffman-Boston, far from Hall's Hill, provided Black Arlingtonians a strong foothold to challenge the county's segregated school system by showing that the segre-gation was, indeed, based on *de jure* legal changes and not *de facto* neighbor-hood segregation.

Clarissa Thompson was nervous at the prospect of leaving Hoffman-Boston, but that hesitation mattered little. "How you felt was not something you talked about," Thompson reflected. "I looked in my mother's face. I knew what she expected of me."[109] Clarissa's mother, Ethel Mozelle Jordan, came to Arlington from North Carolina ca. 1934, leaving her rural farm to find work as a messenger for the federal government.[110] After settling in Arlington she married Clarence Thompson, whose family had long roots in the county. In the late 1940s, Ethel joined Arlington's branch of the NAACP. Although her daughter felt that "she was quite a passive-seeming woman," Ethel held a deep commitment to African American rights and education. This commitment stemmed from her own difficulties securing an education in the face of adverse poverty and the tragic, unprosecuted lynching of her older brother, Council, when he was twelve.

The Thompsons and the other committed families pushed for integration. In 1957, Judge Albert V. Bryan, an Alexandria native, called for the admission of seven African American students into white schools. Judge Bryan defended his decision, stating that, in Arlington, integration would change little. Judge Bryan noted "into a white population of 21,345, only seven colored children will enter."[111] Despite the limited scope of the ruling, it was still challenged in court. This resistance was because people of the time saw changes in places like Arlington as significant on the national stage. One Louisville, Kentucky, newspaper observed that "what happens in Arlington is vital to the Deep South. It could mean school chaos. Or it could mean that a new pattern is beginning to emerge."[112] As supporters of segregation worried about a breakdown of massive resistance, segregation, and the theoretical solid south, continued appeals prevented Arlington's schools from integrating. Students like Clarissa Thompson graduated and moved on to college without school integration.[113] However, Arlington's parents and the NAACP continued to push new challenges to segregation with more and new students, such as Thompson's sister Gloria, who joined the court cases.

In September of 1958, Arlington's school board, again made up of appointed members, met with thirty students who applied for transfer to white schools through the state's Pupil Placement Act.[114] One tool created by Virginia to prevent integration, the 1956 Pupil Placement Act, made it so that any student transferring from their current school must be approved by a state board that evaluated the academic, physical, and emotional preparedness of the child.[115] The panel denied twenty-five of these students on the grounds of either attendance area, overcrowding at white schools, academic accomplishment, or psychological problems.[116] The final five students were denied admission to white schools on the vague grounds of lack of adaptability. This adaptability stemmed from the argument from Arlington's school superintendent that the students would be harmed when going from Black schools where they were leaders to white schools where they would be average pupils; this, despite the fact that all had tested "just above the achievement median" of their prospective schools. Judge Bryan upheld the rejection of twenty-six Black students to white schools but ruled that Arlington must admit four students to its all-white schools come the winter semester of 1959.[117]

Throughout the rise of massive resistance and the ongoing court battles, Arlington's moderate white majority, already active in school reform, pivoted from reform in general to the specific task of keeping Arlington's school open. Arlington's white moderates feared a reversal of all the progress they had made in reform organizations should Virginia continue on the path of massive resistance. Beyond the loss of their school board, Arlingtonians greatly feared the reversal of school spending bonds to improve school structures, raise teacher salaries, and purchase new textbooks. They also feared the end of a more responsive county government, which they had been creating for a decade.[118] Parents and education groups created the Arlington Committee to Preserve Public Schools (ACCPS) and the Save Our Schools movement. Many of the members and leaders within this group were recent arrivals brought to the area by federal employment, such as Theda Henle. Henle was born and raised in California and attended Swarthmore College in Pennsylvania before coming to Arlington in 1949 when her husband, Peter, took a position with the federal government.[119] Henle was active in social and political organizations in her new home county and, as a mother of three school-age children, took an active role in ensuring that schools stayed open in Arlington.[120] ACCPS stated that "we are here concerned neither with perpetuating segregation schools nor hastening integration."[121] Instead, they wanted to pursue any avenue to keep the improved public schools they had helped create over the previous decade open. This stance highlights the limits of white Arlington's progressivism. They were not interested in integration or racial equality but rather wanted to keep their own schools open while working within the legal system.

Beyond parents, business leaders also came to reject massive resistance. They recognized that the end of public education would hurt business development because, without a school system, new arrivals would cease to see Arlington as a viable place to raise their families. One realtor complained of "a big drop off in the number of families moving here in the past month or so—they don't want to come to a town whose schools might close down."[122] Were this to continue, Arlington would see a downturn in home building, buying, and selling. Real estate was Arlington's largest employer beyond the federal government. Real estate developers and politicians with stakes in Arlington County did not want to see this decline. Congressman Joel T. Broyhill, who represented Arlington as a part of Virginia's Eighth Congressional District, initially resisted integration, even signing his support to the "Southern Manifesto."[123] However, when massive resistance became the policy of the day, he worked hard to prevent closures in Arlington. This change in positions was partly because of potential economic consequences for the county. Broyhill was a major real estate developer in the county. Before entering Congress in 1952, Broyhill was the general manager of the Broyhill and Sons real estate firm, which built new housing in the expanding Rock Spring community. As a congressman, Broyhill continued to hold a one-third interest in the firm, amounting to $2.83 million in real estate holdings in the county.[124] This support from liberal and moderate whites, who were motivated by fears that massive resistance would hurt their own lives and interests, bolstered the cause of integration. Coinciding with Judge Bryan's decision on Arlington's schools, the massive resistance policies of Governor Lindsay Almond, Virginia, and the Byrd Machine were found unconstitutional.[125]

On February 2, 1959, four African American students in Arlington were the first to integrate Virginia's public schools. These students were Hall's Hill residents Ronald Deskins, Michael Jones, Lance Newman, and Gloria Thompson.[126] Together, they integrated Stratford Junior High School. The four students were selected for their academic excellence but also under the hope that beginning at a new school as seventh graders, a time when all Arlington students were moving from elementary to middle school, would help ease their transition into integrated environments.

Although it was deemed "The Day that Nothing Happened" by contemporaries, integration was a tense process for these four students, their parents, and their communities.[127] Ronald's mother said that though she hoped there would be no violence, that she "didn't know what to expect."[128] Ronald feared that he would be spit on and that his father's car would be stoned.[129] Newman became so nervous that on the way to school he got sick and "lost his breakfast." The Arlington chapter of the Defenders of State Sovereignty and Individual Liberties announced plans to picket the school and passed out signs to children reading "2-4-6-8 We Don't Want to Integrate."[130] As a preventative measure, one hundred uniformed police officers, twenty-five per African American student, ringed the school in anticipation of violence. Stratford School Counselor Joseph Macekura knew that "a lot of the teachers were World War II vets" and overheard them "saying it was like a war zone out there."[131] Some locals and newspapers began calling the event "D Day" for "desegregation day,"[132] and although Rathbone frequently spoke out against "violence of any kind" as the spokesman for his organization, he also made clear that, should violence begin, he and his supporters were "ready and willing."[133]

Some local white allies stepped in to help the parents of the four students. Theda Henle lived near Stratford. Henle was a member of ACCPS, working to keep schools open through massive resistance. She was also an active member of Arlington's Democratic Committee, the League of Women Voters, and Arlingtonians for a Better County. Her husband, Peter, worked with CCSI for county school improvement.[134] They lived in the increasingly progressive Rock Spring community, which neighbored Stratford. At the time, one of the three Henle children was a student at Stratford. Henle "became worried about what that first day would be like for them and their parents."[135] She invited the parents of Stratford's newest students to wait in her home during the day "so they could be closer to their children." On the morning of school integration, Arlington police escorted four mothers and two grandmothers to Henle's home. Stratford could be seen from the house's bedroom window. Throughout the day, parents took turns looking out at the school, confirming that all was well. "Every once in a while, one of the mothers would get up and walk back to the bedroom to make sure the school hadn't been bombed, then she would come back and nod to the others," Henle recalled. A bomb threat was, indeed, called in to the school. No one was told of the threat while the building was searched, because "school authorities, convinced the call was a hoax, decided against evacuating the school."[136]

Thankfully, no violence occurred, but these students still faced trying times ahead. Twelve-year-old Gloria Thompson thought that "at first all the attention was fun."[137] However, this quickly wore off and soon "it wasn't fun . . . it was very isolating." She felt that "our Blackness, the thing that had always made us so visible, now made us disappear." The four Black students were escorted between classes. They were prevented from "milling around in the school hall or grounds," making socialization difficult.[138] Additionally, they were discouraged from participating in social functions and activities.[139] Although overt threats were officially not tolerated, with students reportedly being sent home for using racial slurs, policy and reality were not always in sync.[140] Gloria recalled threats and the taunts of "nigger."[141] Some of the prejudice came from teachers. Thompson lamented that "you could tell which teacher was prejudiced" by the way they "were trying to say 'there was no room for us inside their white schools'" with their actions. For Thompson, however, "the abuse was just to be taken for granted . . . it wasn't something you came home and told your parents about."

The four students continued, and in the coming years, more African American students integrated Arlington's elementary, middle, and high schools, thanks to the pioneering efforts of Arlington's organized community and institutions. Tammy Sligh, Hall's Hill resident and daughter of Clarissa Thompson, knew well the wall around her community that divided the Black residents of Hall's Hill from their white neighbors for decades.

FIGURE 27. Stratford Junior High School was turned into a fortress with the presence of one hundred uniformed officers and several undercover plain-clothes officers. Arlingtonians feared integration would lead to violence after what they had seen in places like Little Rock, Arkansas, and because many of those families who challenged segregation had received threats. (*Top*) officers block the entrance to the school while a line of uniformed officers line a path in the distance (J. R., *African American Integration Schools VA 1959*, February 2, 1959, Associated Press Photographer). (*Bottom*) Deskins, Jones, Newman, Thompson, and a few white students walk toward school (Anonymous, *African American Integration Schools VA 1959*, February 2, 1959, Associated Press).

Although the wall around Hall's Hill remained in place, it could no longer keep Black and white apart. As an elementary schooler, Tammy and her classmates "went through the opening in the wall to school."[142] With integration over time, Arlington's retention rate of Black students improved. In 1950, the average Hall's Hill resident had only an elementary education, but that average rose slowly to a middle school education in 1960 and a partial high school education in 1964.[143] From 1950 to 1960, the number of high school graduates rose by twenty percent, and from 1950 to 1964, the number of college graduates more than doubled.[144] Increasingly more residents completed high school, and many went on to college.

Fighting for Preservation

At the same time school integration unfolded in Arlington, Black residents pushed for neighborhood improvements. Arlington's school integration story played out in a time of nearly complete residential segregation in the county. By 1950, Arlington's small Black population was isolated to the three anchor communities of Hall's Hill, Johnson's Hill, and Green Valley. While pushing for integration in schools to improve the lives of future generations of African Americans in the county, Arlington's Black residents took a different route when it came to community improvements. Home ownership was thought of as crucial to racial justice and civil rights improvements during the mid-twentieth century as African Americans sought to gain rights as property owners.[145] In addition to homeownership generally, African Americans wanted to maintain their presence in Arlington's suburbs, lest they be forced to relocate to the only other property open to them in the declining inner city.[146]

These three communities were filled with generations of Arlington's Black families, many of whom came from lost neighborhoods such as Butler-Holmes, Pelham Town, and Queen City. Thus, they were particularly motivated to work to save their new homes and communities. Residents used the people, churches, community organizations, and social institutions that worked within and across all of Arlington's Black neighborhoods to gain recognition and improvements for their existing communities to maintain them as Black spaces, lest planning legislation and continued threats by white expansion again be used to push them from the county entirely. Additionally, Arlington's Black residents had particularly strong ties to their homes and communities because they had literally been built by the residents themselves. Second-generation Green Valley resident Alfred O. Taylor Jr., lived in a home that his father constructed. He recalled his father telling him, "I built on this land for us. It should stay with us."[147] Contrasted with the newness of many of Arlington's white residents, Arlington's small but stable

Black population spent generations building homes, neighborhoods, and community institutions that they wanted to preserve. They sought assistance in the continuation of these neighborhoods through calls for improvements and services from the county. For the first time, these calls were met with a new level of responsiveness in the wake of changing social, political, and community preservation realities.

During the 1950s and 1960s, these realities were largely shaped by Arlington's more socially liberal white majority, who took on many reform initiatives. Beyond the political and school reforms discussed, they improved streets, undertook public health initiatives and the opening of Arlington's first hospital, improving countywide sewer and water systems, and forming more community planning initiatives. Many of these improvements continued with well-known existing patterns, where improvements would make it only to the outskirts of Arlington's Black neighborhoods without actually providing these improvements to its African American residents. Individual neighborhoods pushed for improvements, seeking funds to develop community features and to direct any potential redevelopment. For example, Lyon Village residents used their civic association to lobby for neighborhood improvements, calling out the "need for additional curbs, gutters, [and] sidewalks."[148] These improvements and other various "zoning problems" were addressed almost immediately by the county board. Board Chairman Leo Urbanski even attended the Lyon Village meetings as a show of support from government officials.

Residents of Hall's Hill also lobbied county officials for these same changes. In 1956, Leslie Hamm, who would join Arlington's integration lawsuits, wrote to the Arlington County Board requesting sidewalk, curb, and gutter work for Hall's Hill.[149] Unlike the experience of the Lyon Villagers, county officials were not responsive to Hamm's request for the community. This was despite the fact that the needs of Hall's Hill were arguably much more pressing than those of Lyon Village. Where the Village sought improvements to existing systems, Hill residents "lacked curb and gutters" entirely. For the next five years, Hamm continued to write the board to request these minimal municipal needs. Although they were seemingly aesthetic complaints, these lacking amenities resulted in serious "traffic and pedestrian hazards," led to frequent flooding, and meant that children walking to and from school had to walk in the street.[150]

These problems were not isolated to Hall's Hill; they were present in all of Arlington's three anchor Black communities, as many of the county's general road, sidewalk, and municipal improvements were not extended into their communities. Green Valley also did not have sidewalks, curbs, or gutters. The community remained physically isolated, with no direct bus lines to Washington, the Pentagon, Crystal City, Rosslyn, or Arlington Court House. Green Valley was also isolated because of several dead-end streets, including where the neighborhood's Sixteenth Street should have connected with the major county thoroughfare Walter Reed.[151] The county's water, sewer, and trash pickup theoretically extended into Arlington's anchor Black neighborhoods, but service was infrequent and repairs were slow.[152] Hamm also pushed for many other improvements to Hall's Hill roads, trash and municipal services, and recreation facilities, arguing that they were "so badly needed to help bring this community up to the desired standards of our county."

With the sharp rise of suburban development in the 1940s and 1950s, Arlington's leaders realized that they needed to create new community planning laws and procedures to harness Arlington's growth. County officials played a large role in the 1950 long-range capital improvement planning; in 1954, the county created the Arlington Committee of 100, designed to use leaders from Arlington's communities to solve planning problems, and in 1957, Arlington joined with other regional governments in the Metropolitan Area's Council of Governments, all to help expand planning and neighborhood improvement initiatives.[153] Arlington Planning Director and county resident Tom Moore observed that "Arlington is a planner's paradise."[154] Builders welcomed these changes. One builder observed that "Arlington County had been consistently re-zoning the . . . area, giving builders a fair shake and getting results. Money flowed into the area. Buildings mushroomed."[155] In 1961, the county adopted a new Master Plan for development.[156] Arlington's Master Plan had three broad goals: the preservation of open space, the improvement of roads, and redevelopment of declining areas.[157]

With their requests for improvements so often ignored, residents of Arlington's three anchor Black communities were apprehensive about the final aim of the 1961 Master Plan, the "redevelopment of old and obsolete areas."[158] Residents worried that these zoning and planning laws would be used to push them from their homes as had been the case with Freedman's Village, Butler-Holmes, Pelham Town, and Queen City, among others. In addition to suffering these same municipal shortfalls, in Johnson's Hill, residents worried about how the new laws would impact the area because of changes in zoning designations that came out of the 1961 plan.[159] Although the community was predominantly zoned as residential, with forty-three of the community's sixty-two acres occupied by homes, four acres bordering the community were ominously zoned "undetermined" in the 1961 Land Use Plan.[160] Residents feared that this would "encourage detrimental speculative activity within the neighborhood."[161] This, in turn, could threaten the racial and residential makeup of the three anchor Black communities as residents sought to improve their neighborhoods while ensuring that they were not lost.

But only two years after the creation of the Master Plan, the county's planning policy shifted yet again. In 1963, the county created a special planning commission to "conserve values found in neighborhoods" and "establish a program of neighborhood conservation."[162] Nine county residents who were meant to be a cross-section of the community staffed the commission. However, the majority of these individuals lived in the more affluent north Arlington, all but one lived in single-family homes, and all were white living in segregated communities.[163] This additional zoning and planning work was the result of the dual forces of a national trend toward preservation and a local push for changes in the greater Washington area's transportation network. Throughout the early 1960s, local communities around the country responded to two major national developments to increase interest in historic and neighborhood preservation.[164] These national changes were urban renewal programs of the 1940s and 1950s and Eisenhower's National Interstate and Defense Highways Act of 1956, which, together, resulted in the destruction of historic sites, homes, and communities to make room for new road and housing construction projects.[165]

Calls for renewal and redevelopment concerned Black Arlingtonians.[166] Although they worked to keep their houses in order, dilapidated homes and facilities in need of repair were almost entirely restricted to the county's three Black neighborhoods. A minister serving the Green Valley community noted that you could almost see "the invisible dividing line between racially separated neighborhoods" because of the presence of rundown homes within Black communities.[167] This was despite the fact that residents worked to ensure that the area "is a neat, well cared for neighborhood."[168] Even in Johnson's Hill, which remained a solidly middle-class community—home to eleven community, civic, and social organizations with a large number of newly constructed single family homes—the neighborhood still struggled with dilapidated and vacant homes.[169] Of the community's two hundred thirty-three residences, sixty-five were newly built single-family homes, but thirty-one were deteriorating, three were dilapidated, and three were vacant, meaning that nearly sixteen percent of Johnson's Hill's homes were in some state of disrepair. In comparison, of the two hundred fifty-six homes in the white Maywood community, only twelve were described as deteriorating, and none were either dilapidated or vacant.[170] This reality was due, in part, to the age of Arlington's Black communities compared with many new and expanding white neighborhoods that sprang up during World War II.[171] It was also due to the lack of available funds for home improvements, a lack of contractors willing to work with African Americans, and the increased regulation on construction created under Arlington's zoning and planning laws of the 1930s. The state of individual houses was compounded in Arlington's Black neighborhoods by the fact that officials refused to extend county improvements, amenities, or resources into these communities, creating the appearance of dilapidation despite the presence of active citizens and groups.[172] One Hall's Hill resident lamented that county neglect makes the community "seem unattractive and presents the appearance of many county and state neglected communities of the Deep South."[173] Because of these conditions, Arlington's political leaders asserted that the county's Black neighborhoods had "all the classic elements [that] created the center city urban slum" and thus should be considered for renewal and redevelopment.[174] This pattern of outside white politicians and individuals seeing a slum where Black residents saw a strong community in need of some municipal improvements first began with Freedman's Village and clearly continued into the civil rights era, as Black and white residents continued to battle for space.

Although redevelopment concerned Arlington's Black residents, both Black and white county residents worried even more about road creation disturbing their county through the expansions of the existing road networks and the threat of new roads, most notably Interstate 66. This was especially true, as areas beyond Arlington in Fairfax, Loudoun, and Prince William Counties "began to attract more and more of the families pouring into the . . . area" in the 1960s.[175] In the early 1960s, the Washington metro area's planners transitioned from a focus on roads to a focus on rail development.[176] In 1962, a plan was launched for a greatly expanded rapid transit plan linking suburbs such as Arlington to downtown Washington, DC.[177] The development of the Washington Metrorail system had the capacity to greatly impact Arlington through construction of the lines themselves and to change the nature of the county's growth by encouraging urban development patterns.[178] With these local and national trends both serving as potential threats to Arlington's existing neighborhoods, Black and white, Arlington's various neighborhood and community groups, which first began in the 1920s, came together to lobby the county for a new governmental organization to help create changes to zoning and planning policies that would ensure neighborhood preservation. When the Arlington Planning Commission established the Neighborhood Conservation Program, Black Arlingtonians knew that they muse harness this program to secure improvements and preservation for their neighborhoods to prevent it from becoming yet another tool used to shutter their areas.

The Neighborhood Conservation Program was a countywide program designed to provide development guidelines for individual neighborhoods.

Created in 1963, the overall goals were to improve street conditions, update traffic and transportation management, and encourage business development. The program provided neighborhoods with funding to support municipal, recreational, building, and planning improvements on a scale that was larger than the typical, smaller scale "one-and-done" county projects. All of this was so that the character of Arlington's neighborhoods could be maintained. This "character" was determined by the people living within the community, as access to funds and support from the county required a minimum of seventy-five percent participation from community residents. Requiring widescale community participation in the effort was an attempt to ensure that residents, not developers, decided what the character of the community would be in the years to come. The idea was to improve Arlington's neighborhoods so that they might be better maintained. This would put them at lower risk of being razed, as building trends with highways and rail encouraged both the development of higher density development and the destruction of existing neighborhoods to make way for this kind of expansion. In making their pitch for municipal improvement funds, neighborhood residents needed to successfully make the argument that their community was historically significant to Arlington County and thus deserved to continue into the future.

The program's requirement of strong participation from residents within the neighborhoods helped Black Arlingtonians. After decades of community activism and participation, Arlington's three remaining African American neighborhoods were in a unique position to rally support from residents already primed for these programs. For example, Hall's Hill residents who had lobbied the county for improvements for a decade, to no avail, immediately sprang into action. In the early 1960s, Hall's Hill continued to battle Arlington County for their place. In 1964, the county board proposed zoning changes to build high-end apartments in the neighborhood. By 1967, Arlington Hospital sought to tear down the community twice to expand their hospital system—first for a resident's hall for the Arlington Hospital's doctors and nurses and then for a nursing home.[179] However, the Hall's Hill John M. Langston Civic Association saw the Neighborhood Conservation Program as a chance to secure their neighborhood's place once and for all.

Established in the fall of 1937, the Civic Association was active in all matters concerning the welfare of the community. It tackled issues such as equal access to employment, as well as zoning and development issues. The Association understood what was at risk if they did not solidify their community through the new program. On July 15, 1964, the Association held a mass meeting so that Mr. Hall Gibson, chairman of the Committee on

Conservation of Residential Areas, and others from Arlington's Planning Staff could explain the details of the new neighborhood provisions. The Association created the Neighborhood Conservation Committee specifically to tackle this project. It was headed by community residents Birdie Alston, Captain George S. Burke, Leslie Hamm, and Alonzo Spriggs.[180] With such an active neighborhood, committee members easily obtained the necessary seventy-five percent participation of residents and gave presentations to the county board calling for change, including a "Look-See" neighborhood tour for county officials. The residents proposed rezoning; land acquisitions; improvements to playgrounds; creating curbs, gutters, streetlights, and sidewalks; street improvements (including providing more outlets out of the neighborhood to major roads); and creating a community recreation center.

However, unlike earlier zoning and planning changes that had led to the end or shrinking of Black communities, these changes occurred in a different social and political climate in Arlington. As evidenced by the eventual rejection of massive resistance in favor of public schools remaining open even in the face of some school integration, Arlington's new white arrivals were unwilling to continue on the trajectory established by previous leaders and residents. Instead of denying Black rights while attempting to squeeze them out of the county, they shifted to an unwillingness to hurt Black causes if it would damage their own positions, as had been the case when the Byrd political machine blocked all spending no matter how needed. This resulted in tacit support of Black aims. After the civil rights victories of the 1950s, and after generations of community building, Arlington's Black population was ready to move to call for more rights with the emergence of this more inclusive attitude, taking the opportunity to cement civic organizations, call for neighborhood betterment, and secure better housing.

In February 1965, Arlington announced the three initial neighborhoods that would be a part of the first round of neighborhood conservation. Among them were Johnson's Hill and Hall's Hill.[181] The fact that two of the three communities were African American is significant. After decades of creating civic, social, church, and political organizations to push for their rights, Black Arlington was uniquely poised to secure the high rates of community participation needed to get county funds through the Neighborhood Conservation Program. Additionally, the intense residential segregation imposed upon Arlington's African American communities meant that they each had well-defined boundaries that helped them easily articulate existing community conditions and future needs in their reports. Although the residents of Green Valley also initiated their studies in neighborhood conservation in 1965, along with the residents of Hall's Hill and Johnson's Hill, their neighborhood conservation plan was accepted during the second round of conservation plans in 1973.[182] Each neighborhood's age also helped in their argument for historical significance. Many of Arlington's white communities were created in the World War II era, but Green Valley dated back to 1844, Hall's Hill to 1865, and Johnson's Hill to the 1870s. Each was also home to institutions dating back to Freedman's Village, providing strong bids for historical significance.

In Arlington's first round of preservation funding Hall's Hill and Johnson's Hill were joined by the white Maywood community. Maywood was platted in 1903 by Crandal Mackey. First developing along the Great Falls and Old Dominion Railroad, the community now lay along Lee Highway (Route 29). Residents feared that planned construction of Interstate 66 could lead to the destruction of their neighborhood, which consisted of a combination of styles from late Victorian of the 1910s to ranch-style homes of the 1960s.[183] However, residents were not particularly organized, and they were not aware of the county's preservation program, which could help them resist potential changes threatened by highway construction. Maywood's residents did not even know about the program until they heard about Johnson's Hill's participation in the project, which "aroused our interest in preserving Maywood."[184]

The ability for Arlington's African American communities to use a planning program to their advantage during the late 1960s and early 1970s, when the preservation movement became powerful, is distinctive. Nationally, many African American communities were singled out for redevelopment and destroyed under similar improvement programs because of the same kinds of problems experienced within Hall's Hill, Johnson's Hill, and Green Valley.[185] This same pattern was also repeated locally.[186] The preservation movement led to the destruction of the African American communities Fort and Macedonia/Seminary in neighboring Alexandria City and the loss of Navy Hill and Fulton in Richmond, Virginia.[187]

Although these programs offered an unmatched possibility for Arlington's African American communities to use county planning changes to their benefit, the recognition from the county came with an odd stipulation: Each of Arlington's anchor African American communities changed their name in their forms for county finances. Hall's Hill became High View Park, Johnson's Hill became Arlington View, and Green Valley became Nauck. High View Park was a subdivision platted in 1892 by Dr. John Pickering Lewis. Lewis purposefully purchased land immediately adjacent to the growing Hall's Hill community, advertising his property to African Americans who were eager to become a part of the Hall's Hill community.[188] Arlington View was the name of a subdivision created near the existing Johnson's Hill community, as was Nauck, a subdivision named for the land platted by John Nauck within the Green Valley community in the 1880s.[189] This pattern of renaming existing African American communities after subdivisions created by white developers was the standard choice in the renaming of Arlington's African American communities. Although these new names had historic roots and connections to their communities, before their presence on preservation documentation, they were never the names used for these communities. The strongest connection to the new name came from Green Valley. Residents always called the community itself Green Valley, but they named many community institutions, such as their civic association and revitalization organization, after the early Nauck subdivision.[190] Residents did not embrace these formal name changes and, instead, many continue to use the original names into the present. Hall's Hill resident Amanda Lewis stated, "I been calling it Hall's Hill all my life. . . . I didn't really pay attention that they was trying to change it."[191]

There is no formal record of why these name changes occurred. The fact that residents of these communities continued to use the original names for their communities and not the new designations and the fact that no white communities experienced similar name changes suggest a white-led, top-down insistence on change. Perhaps county officials found it more palatable to provide formal recognition to Arlington's African American neighborhoods if they had new names which were not associated with Black communities by local white residents. It is also possible Arlington's politicians wanted to focus on builders and developers in their name changes, privileging the role of white developers over Black community builders and members.

These plans showed how far each of the neighborhoods had come in successfully organizing their residents so that they could fight against the kinds of racialized legislation that had been used for decades in an attempt to push them from their homes. According to Hall's Hill community activist Dorothy Hamm "we had a dream that our community could be 'The Model Community,' and that dream was becoming a reality because the County Board approved our plan."[192]

The neighborhoods' desires for improvements and to maintain their environments in a way that was in line with broader county goals, suggests that by the late twentieth century, African American ideals of the built environment could be reconciled with white visions. Beyond the single-family homes that all communities Black and white shared, Arlington's Black communities were also aided in their applications by changes in Arlington's built environment during the 1940s and 1950s. Since the 1930s Arlington's Black communities included multifamily housing types. At that time, however, multifamily housing was not embraced by white Arlingtonians and their communities. However, in the 1940s and 1950s, the extreme population boom in Arlington led to the establishment of many row houses, garden apartments, and apartment buildings in white communities that had previously been all single-family homes. This diversification of white communities brought them closer to Arlington's Black communities in the style of their built environment. Therefore, when making the case for community funds and preservation, the diversity of housing type to include both single-family and multifamily homes in Arlington's Black communities was no longer an issue on which they could be ostracized as "other."

Additionally, the creation of the Neighborhood Conservation Plan provided hope. Unlike earlier legal changes that were used to push against Black Arlington, this new law happened after two fundamental changes in the county. The first was the demographic shift away from native Virginians and toward a more socially and racially progressive populace who wanted to improve conditions in the county but did not dwell on the racial politics of these changes. Increasingly, college-educated individuals who had been born, raised, and educated and who had lived in diverse locations around the country brought with them different ideas about the proper functions of government, planning, and race that were often more progressive than those of their earlier counterparts, if not necessarily egalitarian. Arlington's new white residents were no longer willing to sacrifice their own standards just to prevent African Americans from meaningful improvements, in a political philosophy articulated in the school battles that showed that, although racial equality was not an aim, programs would not be abandoned just because it could be a by-product. Additionally, emerging in the 1960s, these legal changes occurred at the same time as a strengthening and spreading of local, state, and national civil rights challenges.

Because of the implementation of these plans, Arlington County finally provided the improvements and municipal needs that the three anchor Black communities needed. Hall's Hill resident Lula Mae Graham recalled that once the plans were approved, the county "had to keep the streets clean and pick up our trash" and put in new "sewage and running water" lines.[193] One Green Valley resident and business owner noted that "Once this place [was] cleaned up, you [could] even feel it in the air. . . . Pride."[194] With these community-generated plans, the improvements they secured, and the county's approval of them, the place of Arlington's three Black anchor communities seemed to finally be secure. Green Valley resident and community leader Alfred O. Taylor Jr., hoped that, through these improvements, he could ensure that "the land doesn't leave us."[195]

Conclusion

From the 1940s into the 1970s, Arlington underwent many changes. It saw a huge population boom in response to federal expansions under the New Deal, World War II, and the Cold War, which brought huge numbers of new residents to the area. These new residents were primarily white, educated individuals and families from across the United States, standing in contrast to Arlington's previous generations of residents who were primarily native Virginians. The increasingly progressive social attitudes that these individuals brought with them manifested themselves in Arlington through increased governmental spending and involvement in municipal affairs. These people wanted to secure improvements to communities, roads, and schools, and unlike those in previous generations, they were not willing to compromise on improvements because of potential ramifications to racial politics and improvements within the Black community.

After one hundred years of community formation and institution building dating back to Freedman's Village, Arlington's stable but small Black population used new and existing community associations and a strong organizing tradition to push for the changes and support they had long worked for—now with more room to make real progress because of the new social and political climate. One of the most significant battles fought and won by these communities was the battle for school integration. Their strong organizing tradition and small Black population, which made court challenges more likely to succeed than those in the Black belt of the Deep South, helped Arlington County to become the first municipality in the State of Virginia to integrate in February of 1959. The location of Hall's Hill within the otherwise white communities of northern Arlington aided these segregation contests by challenging the idea of the allegedly *de jure* segregated community school. Although school integration continued to be negotiated into the 1970s with battles over busing, the more progressive stance taken by Arlington's politicians, educators, parents, and students after years of activism and calls for change from Arlington's Black community was a significant turning point for the county, highlighting the ways in which the social and political realities of the white populace shifted since the re-emergence of an active white Arlington at the dawn of the twentieth century.[196]

Unfortunately, of the many varied Black communities at the turn of the twentieth century, only three remained to see these changes. During the Jim Crow era of residential segregation, zoning and planning laws coupled with pressures from white builders and buyers pushed against Arlington's Black communities. From the nearly dozen communities established in the years surrounding the Civil War and the close of Freedman's Village, by 1950, only Arlington's three anchor Black communities of Hall's Hill, Johnson's Hill, and Green Valley continued as majority-Black neighborhoods. Each of these communities had active church, school, social, civil rights, and community groups that helped them survive. That was also the case for ghost communities such as Queen City. Both Johnson's Hill and Green Valley were more middle-class in their makeup, providing them with more resources to challenge closure. However, the same class status could be said for other neighborhoods, like Butler-Holmes, which ceased to exist. The strong institutions, active individuals, and stable population of Arlington's Black communities helped them endure the forces working against them throughout the first half of the twentieth century. By chance, luck, and hard work, these three communities survived into the modern era.

But because residents had saved these communities, they were poised to take the increasingly socially liberal attitudes of Arlington's government and turn them toward their own aims of neighborhood preservation. Whereas planning legislation had previously challenged and led to the end of Black neighborhoods in Arlington, the 1963 Neighborhood Conservation Program that emerged from the 1961 Master Plan resulted in the preservation of Arlington's three remaining Black communities. Black residents ensured that this was the case through their active citizens and community institutions that were ready to take advantage of county improvement and planning funds once changing social and political realities afforded them a place of their own within the county's social system and physical environment.

Conclusion
An End to Residential Segregation

Arlington's African American communities continued to thrive into the late twentieth century, thanks in part to their ability to secure preservation and improvement funds through Arlington's Neighborhood Conservation program. By midcentury, Arlington was very residentially segregated, with nearly all of its Black residents living in the three communities of Hall's Hill, Johnson's Hill, and Green Valley.[1] Although they sought to preserve their neighborhoods, this did not exclude Arlington's Black population from also seeking homes beyond their communities. Although improvements had been made, Lyle Bryant, a member of the Committee of 100 and the Arlington County Planning Commission, felt that the statement "'no Blacks wanted here' . . . would be the most succinct statement" that summarized the policies of Arlington's white neighborhoods and the attitudes of many of their residents.[2] Since the 1930s, Arlington's African American neighborhoods were prevented from growing by segregation, zoning, and planning laws that restricted their borders. Lots were increasingly subdivided, and multifamily housing options were added throughout these communities in an attempt to deal with the housing demands.

This practice had its limits, however, and in the improved social and political climate of 1960s Arlington, Black Arlingtonians pushed for more space. In the late 1960s, a now-familiar pattern emerged in which Arlington's Black community organized through existing organizations and created new organizations to help aid their community and demand increased rights. Local citizens, church groups, the League of Women Voters, the Northern Virginia Fair Housing Alliance, the Coalition for Open Occupancy Legislation (COOL), and the American Association of University Women all worked together to lobby Arlington County's government for access to fair housing.[3]

These efforts became the center of federal attention in Arlington in the late 1960s. Because of the large number of military installations in the county in the form of the Pentagon, Fort Myer, and Navy Annex, the Department of Defense (DOD) became involved with housing and discrimination issues in Arlington. In 1967, the DOD found that only then percent of Arlington's available housing units had open, nondiscrimination policies. The military decreed that servicemen could only live within complexes and communities with open housing. Although this policy was only for military families, it opened up more housing options for both military and civilian home-seekers by forcing changes in individual housing unit policies. The next year, federal changes targeted residential segregation nationally. In 1968, the Civil Rights Act and Fair Housing Act made *de jure* segregation in housing illegal.

The effects of these local and federal changes were not immediate. One federal report on Arlington's housing segregation found that many Black residents were hesitant to make "such a pioneering step" by moving into previously all-white neighborhoods.[4] In June of 1968, Arlington became the first county in the South to pass a local ordinance against housing discrimination on the basis of race and created the Fair Housing Board. Within a year, twelve formal and six informal complaints were lodged against various individuals and apartment complexes that sold and rented single-family homes and apartment units. Although none of these initial cases resulted in action, residents such as Bryant said that they trusted the five-person board and its decisions, partly because Arlington's only Black realtor, Harold Mann, served as a member. Slowly over the course of the 1970s and 1980s, Arlington's formerly segregated communities, Black and white, began to integrate.[5] This process of residential desegregation took place not only in Arlington but also across the nation, providing increased opportunities for the next generation of Black Arlingtonians to move beyond the three anchor Black communities and beyond the county, state, and region.

The decline in residential segregation provided existing and new residents with more housing options, but it also threatened the continuation of Arlington's anchor Black communities as historically Black neighborhoods. Lifelong Hall's Hill resident James Taylor felt that "once they had integration . . . it seemed like they took away something from the Black man" because of the deterioration of Black neighborhoods and businesses.[6] With more opportunities opening to African Americans, fewer young people stayed within their childhood communities to make their homes in adulthood.[7] For example, after three generations of living in Hall's Hill, three of Lula Mae Graham's four children moved beyond Arlington after graduating from Hoffman-Boston.[8]

Although many from the next generation of Hall's Hill, Johnson's Hill, and Green Valley residents moved on, new residents were increasingly non-Black. Hall's Hill resident Saundra Green saw that "Hall's Hill is really changing. One time it was all African American, you cannot say that anymore. It's really diverse and becoming more and more so every year."[9] By 1990, Green Valley's Asian and Latino population doubled, whereas the white population rose by twenty-one percent and the Black population declined by sixteen percent.[10]

FIGURE 28. A group of children and their caregiver smile on the stoop of her Green Valley home, 1980. © Lloyd Wolf / Arlington Photographic Documentary Project.

Changes in Arlington

Beyond the beginnings of community integration, Arlington saw many changes in the late twentieth century. The county's Black communities began to struggle with new issues of violence and drugs.[11] Hall's Hill resident Lillian Ambers felt a shift in Hall's Hill, with increasingly more "teenagers—children—[getting] into trouble and drugs on the corner."[12] Her Hall's Hill neighbor, Amanda Lewis, also lamented the effects of drugs on Arlington's Black neighborhoods: "It was bad around here, is them drugs and them drugs would tear you down, tear you down, that is what it was."[13] Ambers knew that, because of these changes, her neighbors became "scared to leave their homes."[14]

Arlington also saw demographic shifts. For the first time since before the Civil War, Arlington's population began to stagnate in the 1960s, as many chose to make their homes in outer-ring suburbs.[15] The development of more highways and interstates, as well as the Washington's Metro public transit system, helped support this shift.[16] This population decline was partly the result of white flight because of Arlington's school integration.[17] The loss of population led to school closures throughout Arlington.[18] According to an economic survey of the county, "by late 1960s Arlington began to experience declines—in population, number of families, school enrollment, and importance as a retail center."[19]

Beyond changes in rates of growth, Arlington's population was changing in other ways. Residents were increasingly younger individuals without families. A 1978 economic analysis of the county found that "concurrent with these losses were gains in the number of households, young adult segment of the population, labor force and at-place employment." Many of these young individuals were renters and not homeowners. Additionally, for the first time, Arlington was not defined racially by only Black and white.[20] In 1940, Arlington's population was ninety-five percent white and five percent Black, with statistically inconsequential numbers of other races tracked by the census.[21] This reality changed after the 1960s, partly as the result of changes to national immigration policies. The Immigration and Naturalization Act of 1965 eliminated the quota system for immigrants and focused on relocating entire families. These shifts had particularly dramatic impacts on the number of Latino and Asian immigrants.[22] In the 1970s, Arlington became home to a small but distinct and active Vietnamese population. These individuals and families were primarily refugees who had served American forces in Vietnam in various capacities. They were drawn to Arlington because of its proximity to the nation's capital and the county's military installations.[23] This group changed the face of some of Arlington's neighborhoods. For example, the Barcroft community expanded to include the Blessed Vietnamese Martyrs Church in the 1970s to accommodate a growing Vietnamese popu-

FIGURE 29. Despite many changes in the 1970s and '80s, Arlington's Black neighborhoods continued to create programs and events to foster a sense of community. Here, a group of teens pose at a Drew School event focused on Dr. Martin Luther King Jr. Lloyd Wolf, "Teens at Program for MLK," ca. 1980. © Lloyd Wolf.

lation.[24] A distinct Vietnamese business district known as "Little Saigon" also emerged in Clarendon.[25] Beyond the Vietnamese population, Arlington saw a rise in other Asian nationalities as well as the Hispanic population. By 1980, the county was eighty-three percent white, nine percent Black, and five percent Asian and Hispanic.[26]

These demographic changes, along with continued changes in work patterns, combined to alter Arlington's built environment. One journalist noted that "the decentralization policy of Washington [businesses] is forcing Arlington out of its pattern of a residential suburb."[27] Because of the rise of businesses and federal installations in Arlington, increasingly more people worked in the county. This meant that individuals either commuted to Arlington or stayed in the county to live and work. As early as 1960, 11,678 workers commuted into Arlington from neighboring Fairfax County alone.[28] The rise of more businesses and the commuters that they brought with them led to many transportation changes in Arlington, as roads were expanded and mass transit developed in the county. These changes all moved Arlington away from a suburban environment, primarily defined by commuters from preplanned homes and neighborhoods, and toward an edge-city environment made up of road networks and businesses that made Arlington a commuting destination in its own right.[29] Arlington's transition toward an increasingly more urban environment was aided by the creation of the Washington-area Metro rapid-transit subway system and the evolution of communities in Rosslyn and the Jefferson Davis corridor in eastern Arlington into business districts.[30]

Because of these changes, Arlington became the wealthiest county in the Washington metropolitan area, with the highest pay rates and property values.[31] Indeed, Arlington had one of the highest per-capita incomes in the nation, with an average annual income of around eleven thousand dollars in 1965 and twenty-two thousand dollars in 1976.[32] However, this wealth was not divided equally across the county. Pay rates within Arlington's Black community stagnated during these same years.[33] A 1971 study found that in Arlington's Black community, the majority of people had salaries between three thousand dollars and sixty-nine hundred dollars, with many having salaries below three thousand dollars and only a handful with salaries reaching up to twelve thousand dollars.[34] These trends continued through the 1980s and 1990s. The rise of Arlington's average income raised rents, mortgages, and land values, leading to increased poverty in Arlington's three anchor Black communities. Although prices in Hall's Hill, Johnson's Hill, and Green Valley rose more slowly than the rest of the county, home rates still rose at a rate that made it difficult for existing residents to remain in their homes.[35] Despite having ensured funds for municipal programs and neighborhood improvements through the Neighborhood Conservation Program, by the 1990s these areas were in need of revitalization funds. Thus, these three Black communities were some of the only areas of somewhat more affordable housing in the county. Because of this financial reality combined with the end of legal residential segregation, for the first time, the communities became destinations for non-Black residents looking to live in Arlington beginning in the 1970s.

Areas of Hope for Arlington's Black Neighborhoods

Arlington's Black communities did not experience hardships alone. Despite some of the problems encountered in the late twentieth century and the decline of Black businesses and neighborhoods after integration, the successes of creating a more egalitarian and integrated society should not be forgotten. Lula Mae Graham remembered that, after the political changes of the 1960s, "now we [were] considered as humans, too." After working for her children to have a better life than she herself had, she felt that "we have anything anybody else have . . . it's much better."[36]

Although there were breakdowns in certain traditional elements of Arlington's African American communities, other areas of Black life in Arlington stayed stable. African American community institutions continued to grow and thrive. The Hall's Hill civic association continued to work to improve the community. Resident Saundra Green said that these efforts were undertaken "to always retain the history, to celebrate the culture, and to retain those things that are important to the community."[37] New institutions were also added to the ranks. In response to the growing drug epidemic, Arlington's Black communities used the skills they had deployed for generations to organize against this new threat. Edmund C. Fleet Jr., continued to be active in the community. Fleet came from a family of activists: His grandfather, Hiram Fleet, helped to found Mount Zion Church in Freedman's Village; his father, Edmund C. Fleet Sr., was an active member of the Butler-Holmes community; and his wife, Alice E. Fleet, worked to challenge political discrimination in Arlington. In addition to being active in church, social, and fraternal organizations, Fleet was a prominent fundraiser for Arlington's African American branch of the YMCA, founded in Green Valley in 1949. Fleet worked throughout the 1970s to expand and improve the YMCA to help Black youths have activities beyond drugs. The Fleet family continued its involvement in Arlington's Black communities. Son William H. Fleet worked for the Department of the Navy and was an active leader in Green Valley's Mount Zion Baptist Church. Meanwhile, their daughter, Alice B. Fleet, returned to Arlington to teach public school after earning her master's degree from the University of Pennsylvania. She was a member and leader with the county's Democratic Party, school board, YMCA, and League of Women Voters.[38] Individuals from the Hall's Hill and Green Valley communities who were already serving on neighborhood watch organizations came together to create the Family Support Group to organize community patrol efforts and help residents feel safe.[39] Green Valley residents also created the Intensive Drug Treatment Component Advisory Committee and the Substance Abuse Advisory Board to help rehabilitate and guide affected residents.

To combat the area's growing need for child care, various day care centers; resources for working mothers; and early education, preschool, and kindergarten programs were all formed.[40] In 1965, President Lyndon B. Johnson established the Head Start program for lower income children as a part of his Great Society social programs. Two years later, Arlington's Green Valley community lobbied the government to create a Head Start program in their community. The program was a great success. It educated one hundred thirty-five children, both Black and white, in a year-round program.[41]

Additionally, whereas the decline of a stable Black population—with children increasingly leaving the area in adulthood and a decline in solidly

FIGURE 30. First Lady Claudia Alta "Lady Bird" Johnson reads to children at a Head Start program in Arlington's Green Valley community. Local parents, Black and white, took advantage of the social and educational resources secured by Black Arlingtonians through President Johnson's Great Society programs. Robert L. Knudsen, White House Photograph Office, *Photograph of Lady Bird Johnson Visiting a Classroom for Project Head Start*, March 19, 1968, Collection LBJ-WHPO (1963–69), Series: Johnson White House Photographer (11/22/1963—1/20/1969), NARA.

Black community demographics—was, in some respects, a negative shift, the growing diversity of Arlington's Black communities was also a positive change for these areas. Lillian Ambers of Hall's Hill remembered lots of new kinds of people moving into the neighborhood. She recalled, "At first it kind of bothered [me]," but "not no more it don't."[42] Ultimately, Ambers decided that "that's the way it is supposed to be, I guess. Everyone seem[s] to get along all right . . . people are just people." Beyond just welcoming a more diverse populace into the neighborhoods, other residents actively worked to make these new residents a part of their area's organizing tradition. Green Valley Community Organizer John Robinson Jr., worked to integrate this new population into the neighborhood's existing organizations and traditions so that both the new residents and the existing institutions could thrive through his work at Green Valley's community center.[43]

Furthermore, although staying within Arlington's three anchor Black communities was no longer the norm, many with long family roots in Arlington still chose to continue to make Arlington their home. Mary Gardner lived in Hall's Hill her entire life, along with several members of her extended family.[44] Of Mary's five children, three returned to Hall's Hill to establish their own homes after college. She felt that her children and their peers "got their education and came back to the community to give back to the community. And I really think that's what has held the community together, the young people who got their educations and came back to Hall's Hill." That was the case for Clinton N. "Skeeter" West. Great-grandson of community leader and Freedman's Village and Green Valley resident William A. Rowe, West grew up in Green Valley and remained local, founding his medical diagnostics laboratory in Washington, DC, after graduating from Howard University.[45] Through their efforts, Mary Gardner found the young people who returned "have stuck together, so they could keep it—so they can keep Hall's Hill 'Hall's Hill.'"[46]

Beginning in the 1970s and 1980s, Green Valley actively worked to keep young families within the community. The Nauck Civic Association worked with the Arlington Housing Corporation to renovate twenty-four older townhomes within Green Valley, with preference given to young couples and families who had previously lived in the neighborhood. Nauck Civic Association President Jennie T. Davis helped to create the program because "what I found was we had young people get married who wanted to stay, but there was no housing for them."[47] This was the case for Cecilia Braveboy. A fourth-generation Green Valley resident, she and her husband wanted to return to her childhood neighborhood to be near family and live within a stable community environment, but they found that they could not afford to live there without the affordable housing secured through this program. Through the program, Braveboy could live "two blocks from where I grew up," where "people know you and watch out for your kids." Second-generation Green Valley resident Alfred O. Taylor Jr. always remembered his father telling him, "never sell the family land."[48] Taylor worked to keep this promise himself and helped to ensure that other Black families could keep their homes.

Struggles of Gentrification

This promise became increasingly difficult over time. The cost of homes continued to skyrocket as Black incomes remained stagnant, making it difficult for new residents to purchase homes and for existing residents to continue to afford rising property taxes. This issue of income inequality that pushed out all but the most elite became a problem throughout the country.[49] Although some success was made in keeping younger generations within Arlington's three anchor Black communities, in the 1990s and 2000s, the housing bubble, new building preferences that favored new and large homes, and residential patterns that encouraged residents to move back into the inner-ring suburbs they had abandoned in previous decades all combined to dramatically change the neighborhoods' built environments and threaten the stability of these communities once more through gentrification.

Arlington's anchor Black communities began to see the purchase and demolition of existing homes to make way for larger and more expensive housing. In Green Valley, the cooperative Dunbar Homes was tapped for potential redevelopment in 2005.[50] Many older residents of the community had relocated to Dunbar Homes after the demolition of Queen City to make way for the Pentagon. One such occupant was Gertrude Jeffress, a Pentagon employee who had moved with her family from Queen City first to the temporary trailer camp and, eventually, to Dunbar Homes after the destruction of their home. Within the Green Valley neighborhood that became her new home, Jeffress became involved in community activities as the president of the Mount Zion Church's Ladies' Auxiliary Trustee Board in the 1960s.[51] Now eighty-eight years old and retired from federal service, Jeffress argued, "I am against selling," both because Dunbar Homes had been her home for sixty years and also because "they haven't given us actual figures" of what residents would be paid.[52] After receiving far less than market value for her Queen City home, Jeffress and other older residents were wary. Neighbor Samuel C. Buress complained, "we're getting robbed. They're going to make a windfall profit on this land." Michael Leventhal, Arlington's historic preservation program coordinator at the time, "didn't think [demolition] would ever happen to those buildings" because "it's a nice neighborhood, and they are well kept up."

After much debate, the Dunbar Mutual Homes Association cooperative agreed to sell the development to a Reston construction company for thirty-seven million dollars. The amount received by individual residents is unknown, but with eighty-six units, the settlement provided a maximum of approximately four hundred thirty thousand dollars per unit. In June of 2006, the average price of an existing single-family home in Northern Virginia was five hundred twenty thousand dollars. This means that residents could not afford homes in Arlington after this settlement, even if they received this seemingly large amount per unit, and it is doubtful that residents received this full amount.[53] As was the case with the closing of previous historically Black communities, some residents stayed local, but many were priced out of the county's real estate market and left the area. Jeffress relocated to a senior citizens home. In the end, Dunbar Homes was replaced with a complex of large, luxury townhomes.

Increasingly, new residents were not interested in existing homes but rather wanted to build new, large homes on the lots. A *Washington Post* report noted that "the trappings of modern Arlington now fill swaths of land once dominated by two-story brick houses and wood-frame bungalows that once characterized" Green Valley and Arlington's other historically Black neighborhoods.[54] The home of Hall's Hill resident Lillian Ambers, where she had lived since the late 1920s, was demolished around 2014. "No, the house I grew up in is no longer there," she lamented, "the old house was torn down and the new house was put up there."[55] These building patterns were common throughout Arlington and not merely its Black neighborhoods. The majority-white Barcroft community began seeing these kinds of building changes as early as the 1970s, as older homes, especially multifamily housing units, were torn down to make room for new, larger, single-family homes. In-fill housing between existing homes was also a major trend. This building technique squeezes homes onto increasingly smaller lots, cutting down on green space and sometimes leading to disparities among homes that are not aesthetically pleasing.

Although these patterns were not isolated to Arlington's Black neighborhoods, the realities of what this construction looked like in Black compared with white neighborhoods were divergent. For example, although both Barcroft and Hall's Hill experienced the loss of older homes and in-fill housing, in Barcroft, builders attempted to surround existing homes with housing that was architecturally compatible. Near older homes, brick buildings with mansard roofs were constructed, blending modern and traditional aesthetics. In contrast, in Hall's Hill, little to no effort was made to merge new homes into the existing nature of the neighborhood. Additionally, these homes had ever-rising price tags. Previously, planners protested architectural inconsistencies in Arlington's Black communities as a way to undermine their stability and continued presence using the allegedly color-blind critiques of zoning and planning legislation. Complaints were absent, however, once the price points of the homes rose and the builders and buyers of the homes ceased to be exclusively African American. Residents from within the communities protested these changes to the built environment. Green Valley resident and community activist John Robinson Jr., complained, "some of these corners don't even look like they're part of the community anymore."[56] Robinson argued that "we need to find a way of making sure this new development doesn't overrun the old."

In the 1990s, Green Valley attempted to resist and counteract these changes by participating in a county revitalization plan that targeted the community's social and physical needs to prevent the kind of deterioration that makes communities vulnerable to gentrification.[57] At one meeting about potential community changes, "dozens of [Green Valley] residents showed up to discuss their concerns about the development."[58] A County Board official noted that it was "the most highly attended meeting" in months. The Hall's Hill community called out these new buildings and building types as a potential threat to the neighborhood they would like to combat in their updated Neighborhood Conservation Plan in 1990.[59] Similarly, Green Valley's updated Neighborhood Conservation Plan targeted not only communitywide needs but also the need to set aside funds to help maintain individual properties so that older homes would not be lost.[60] Although not always successful, this program has helped residents improve and maintain their homes.

Arlington's Future

It is not yet certain whether Arlington's three anchor Black communities will be able to resist the tides of gentrification as successfully as they resisted similar threats in the past. In 2016, the Carver Homes cooperative that was constructed in Johnson's Hill during World War II suffered the same fate as the Dunbar Homes. The development was razed to make way for luxury town homes. Indeed, where the county had approximately twenty thousand affordable housing units in 2000, by 2016, that number had fallen to only twenty-seven hundred eighty.[61] Fears of gentrification only rose after Amazon announced in November of 2018 that Arlington would be home to the corporation's "HQ2" headquarters. Fears of rising home prices were joined by concerns that Arlington's neighborhoods would lose their individuality and character. This fear only intensified pushes to rename three South Arlington communities that house their office sites. The areas of Pentagon City, Crystal City, and Potomac Yard have now been rebranded "National Landing" in Amazon's publications.[62]

Despite these losses, there is an increasing urge to recognize Arlington's Black community. In 2015, the Virginia Department of Transportation (VDOT) worked to add recognition of Freedman's Village back into the landscape of suburban Arlington by naming a bridge in honor of the Black community.[63] VDOT Project Manager Christiana Briganti-Dunn explained that "we wanted to pay respect to the local significance of Freedman's Village. Four pylons will show the name and there will be medallions on the bridge replicating scenery in the village, taken from a Harper's Weekly story from 1864." This kind of work is important. Saundra Green of Hall's Hill recognized that "there's always a danger. You don't want to lose your history."[64]

The role of naming and memorialization took on increasing importance in the late 2010s. In Arlington, the conversation over the continued presence of Confederate memorialization resulted in the renaming of Robert E. Lee Memorial Highway. After winning the right to rename roads on the county level without the need for approval from the state legislature, Lee Highway became Langston Boulevard, named after Hall's Hill African American community organizer John M. Langston.[65] In 2019, Green Valley began to reclaim their historic name and renamed the Nauck Citizen's Association as the Green Valley Citizen's Association. In 2020, Arlington voted to remove the six-columned Arlington House, the historic mansion once belonging to Robert E. Lee and his family, from the county logo.[66]

The next generation of African American residents of Arlington's three anchor Black communities continues to work to make their communities vibrant places to live. Local school teacher Jacqueline Coachman grew up in Green Valley and returned to the community in adulthood in the early 2000s. To her, the neighborhood's history was a significant draw. "The fact that I live in a community settled by freedmen is really important to me," she said.[67] Not just the historical roots of the community but also her personal ties to the area drew Coachman back to Green Valley. "It's been important for me to come back here," she stated, "largely because of my love for what my grandparents did to get and hold onto this land."[68] Coachman returned to the same shotgun-style home her family has occupied since the early twentieth century. Green Valley native Charles P. Monroe became an Arlington County board member in 2003, continuing his family's legacy of service.[69] In 2002, N'Dri Sligh entered public school in Arlington, County. N'Dri was the great-grandson of Ethel Thompson, grandson of Clarissa Thompson, and son of Tammy Sligh. When learning about Arlington's school integration story, he was proud to see "a picture of Aunt Gloria . . . on a poster that had been put up for 'Black History' month."[70] Clarissa wondered "What would Ethel think?" of this historic moment. She had passed away two years before, in 2000. These efforts were helped by national conversations about race, racism, and institutional racism during the 2020 COVID-19 pandemic and social justice demonstrations. In Arlington, residents Black and white turned out to have conversations about the role of segregation and racism in their communities.[71] This exposure and recognition by residents may prove beneficial to preservation efforts. With luck, determination, and continued use of evolving community institutions, the next generation of residents will continue to work to keep Hall's Hill, Johnson's Hill, and Green Valley from losing their identities and help them continue to be an important part of Arlington County.

Arlington's proximity to Washington, DC, profoundly affected its suburban development and residential segregation patterns. The federal city provided blue- and white-collar employment for African Americans, creating a unique employment type that was not available to most southern Blacks. This helped Arlington's Black community to create a strong middle-class core. However, Arlington's proximity to federal employment also resulted in huge influxes of white workers. The communities created by and for these individuals physically encroached on and sometimes pushed out Arlington's Black neighborhoods. At the same time, large portions of Arlington were physically occupied and controlled by the federal government. This occupation led to the destruction of several Black neighborhoods, including Freedman's Village, Queen City, and East Arlington. Of course, Arlington is also affected by those federal policies that affected the entire country during this time, such as Federal Housing Administration (FHA) lending policies. In the county, the FHA worked closely with developer Gustave Ring to create the Colonial Village garden apartments that served as a "model for subsequent FHA-insured projects."[72] The proximity of the federal city, the government's physical occupation of the county, as well as the federal policies that created suburban subsidies, loans, and tax policies not only for Arlington but nationwide, meant that Arlington's development had an exceptional relationship to federal authority.

Throughout the establishment of Arlington's suburban environment, the rise of Jim Crow society meant that Arlington's development played out at a time of evolving racial segregation. Local, state, and federal laws; developer practices; and lending policies all came together to create increasingly restrictive residential segregation. These developments prevented Arlington's Black neighborhoods from expanding, led to the end of Black enclaves and the loss of several Black communities, and severely restricted residential choice for African Americans. As a result of these trends, only the three African American communities of Hall's Hill, Johnson's Hill, and Green Valley were able to survive into the mid-twentieth century. These Black neighborhoods became increasingly dense with increased subdivision and the rise of multifamily housing. Paradoxically, however, residential segregation also helped to strengthen community institutions and create well-defined neighborhoods, and it spurred an active populace to demand the community improvements to which they were entitled.

Whether these neighborhoods are able to continue, the ways in which Arlington's African American communities developed expands historical understandings of what constitutes a suburb. As we have seen, Arlington's suburban environment not only included African Americans but also was profoundly shaped by their presence. Green Valley and Hall's Hill both existed as transitional communities as Arlington emerged from rural hinterland to suburban enclave. Additionally, Arlington's first entirely preplanned community built to adhere to then-contemporary suburban standards was the all-Black Freedman's Village community. Looking at Arlington's long development during the nineteenth and twentieth centuries together shows how suburban visions changed over time. As Arlington transitioned from suburban villages to a contiguous suburban environment, Arlington's Black communities of all kinds shaped this development, from working-class communities such as Queen City to middle-class communities, such as Butler-Holmes and Johnson's Hill. In response to these varying visions, the built environment changed to reflect variations in building trends, current realities, and future aspirations.

Notes

Introduction: Arlington's People and Communities

1. *The Virginia Arrow*, ca. 1950, RG 11, Box 4, File 5, Arlington Central Library, Center for Local History, Arlington, Virginia (hereinafter abbreviated as CLH).
2. Edmund Fleet Jr.'s first wife, Gertrude Sparrow, passed away, and Fleet remarried Alice West in 1937. The family relocated between 1940 and 1950 from 1809 South Ninth Street in Butler-Holmes to 1710 South 14th Road in Johnson's Hill. *US Census, 1940* (Washington, DC: Government Printing Office); "Arlingtonian Elected DST Region Director," RG 11, Box 4, File 5, CLH.
3. Mount Zion Baptist Church, *Mt. Zion Centennial, 1866–1976* (Arlington: 1976) RG 6: Arlington Churches, Box 3, CLH.
4. Terry Townsend, interview by Sara Collins, February 13, 1976. Zonta Oral History Program, CLH.
5. John Henderson, interview by Jessica Wallach. Jessica Wallach, "Stories from Queen City: The Loss of a Neighborhood, the Cost of Progress," *Patch*, October 14, 2011.
6. Perry, Crew, and Waters, "'We Didn't Have Any Other Place to Live'": Residential Patterns in Segregated Arlington County, Virginia"; *United States Census, 1900* (Washington, DC: Government Printing Office). http://www.census.gov/.
7. Fort Myer was originally opened as Fort Whipple. Named for Brevet Major General Amiel Weeks Whipple in 1863, the installation was renamed for Brigadier General Albert J. Myer in 1881. For the purposes of this project, it will be called Fort Myer throughout.
8. The process of closing Freedman's Village began in the late 1860s, took on new life in the late 1880s, and was completed by 1900. RG 103: Freedman's Village Collection, CLH.
9. First established as a county program in 1963, conservation plans were approved for Hall's Hill and Johnson's Hill in 1965 and Green Valley in 1973.
10. Office of the County Manager, Arlington, "A History of the Boundaries of Arlington County, Virginia" (Virginia: 1955, 2011), 14.
11. President James K. Polk signed the lands of Arlington County and Alexandria City back to Virginia on February 3, 1846, after lobbying from Virginia businessmen, resistant to competition with Georgetown, and supporters of slavery, worried about restrictions on slavery and the slave trade in the federal city.
12. Reese, George H., ed. *Proceedings of the Virginia State Convention of 1861, February 13-May 1* (Richmond: Virginia State Library, 1965) through *Secession: Virginia and the Crisis of Union*. https://secession.richmond.edu/.
13. Virginia General Assembly, *Acts of Assembly*, 1920, chapter 241.
14. Alexandria County, Deed Book 146, p. 378; Acts of Assembly, 1930, Chapter 167. See also Office of the County Manager, Arlington, "A History of the Boundaries of Arlington County, Virginia" (Virginia: 1955, 2011).
15. For more information on the impact of annexation on African American communities within the lands transferred to Alexandria City, see Moon,

"The African American Housing Crisis in Alexandria, Virginia, 1930s-1960s," 28–68.

16. Hanchett, Sorting out the New South City; Brown, Upbuilding Black Durham; Yellin, Racism in the Nation's Service; Kruse and Sugrue, The New Suburban History; Wiese, Places of Their Own; Lassiter and Lewis, eds., The Moderate's Dilemma; Bashir, "Looking at North Carolina's History Through Architecture," 297–311; Moon, "The African American Housing Crisis in Alexandria, Virginia, 1930s-1960s," 28–68; Taylor, Embattled Freedom: Journeys through the Civil War's Slave Refugee Camps.

17. Masur, "Patronage and Protest in Kate Brown's Washington," 1049.

18. John B. Syphax to William C. Endicott, January 18, 1888, RG 92, File: Office of the Quarter Master General, NARA.

19. "From Washington," *Alexandria Gazette* (Alexandria, D.C.), 6 Dec. 1887. *Chronicling America: Historic American Newspapers*. Library of Congress. https://chroniclingamerica.loc.gov.

20. Barbor, Williams & Company Real Estate Insurance, "Falls Church Virginia" (advertisement), ca. 1910; Netherton, *Arlington County in Virginia* (1987).

21. Elks, *Proclamation*, 1927, RG 11: Papers of Edmund C. Fleet, Box 3, File 7: Minutes and Resolutions 1924–25, CLH.

22. Marjorie Downey, interview by Steve Vogel, February 11, 2004.

23. James Lee School, "Meeting Flyer" (Falls Church, VA: 1955); Morris "A Chink in the Armor," 329.

24. Kruse, White Flight: Atlanta and the Making of Modern Conservatism.

25. Gregory, The Southern Diaspora.

26. Chafe, *Civilities and Civil Rights*; Sugrue, *Sweet Land of Liberty*. By far, the most popular topic on Arlington's African American community development has been its relationship to the civil rights movement generally, and school integration specifically; Campbell, "The Road to Integration: Arlington Public Schools 1959–1971," 27–42; Morris, "A Chink in the Armor," 329–66.

27. Connerly, *The Most Segregated City in America*; Korstad, *Civil Rights Unionism*.

28. Lassiter and Crespino, "The End of Southern History"; Sides, *LA City Limits*; Self, *American Babylon*; Johnson, "From Romantic Suburb to Racial Enclave," 264–70; Orser, "Secondhand Suburbs," 226–62; Little, "The Other Side of the Tracks," 268–80; Hanchett, *Sorting out the New South City*.

29. Wiese, *Places of Their Own*.

30. Margaret Evely Wright, interview by Terry Townsend, December 15, 1974, Zonta Oral History Program, CLH.

31. These suburban patterns of development challenge the Black suburban types outlined by Wiese; Wiese, *Places of Their Own*; Perry, Crew, and Waters, "'We Didn't Have Any Other Place To Live,'" 404.

32. Brown, *Upbuilding Black Durham*.

33. Jackson, *Crabgrass Frontier*.

34. Jackson, *Crabgrass Frontier*, 11.

35. In the 1920s, Clarendon attempted to become its own incorporated town. But the Virginia Supreme Court determined that they did not have the right to break away, because the county was one densely settled suburban area and not a series of separate towns. *Bennett v. Garrett*, 132 VA 397 (Opinion June 15, 1922); *Cases Decided in the Supreme Court of Appeals of Virginia*, CXXXII (Richmond, VA: David Bottom, Superintendent of Public Printing, 1922), p. 400.

36. *Chicago Manual of Style* (Seventeenth edition, section 8.38) states that "Names of ethnic and national groups are capitalized," whereas *The Diversity Style Guide* recommends the capitalization of "Black" and not "white." Rachel Kanigel, *The Diversity Style Guide* (Wiley-Blackwell, 2019).

Chapter 1: "Where They Had Lived Undisturbed for Nearly a Quarter of a Century"

1. Source for the quotation used as the chapter title is correspondence from John B. Syphax to William C. Endicott, January 18, 1888, RG 92: Records of the Office of the Quartermaster General, NARA.
2. Provine, Alexandria County, Virginia Free Negro Registers 1797–1861, 10.
3. Bestebreurtje, "Beyond the Plantation."
4. Suburban growth and communities began first in the South with African American developments on the outskirts of antebellum cities; Wiese, *Places of Their Own.*
5. Although no longer numerous by the outbreak of the Civil War, large plantations had been the dominant land type in the land that would become Arlington throughout the eighteenth century. The plantations of George Washington, George Mason, and Lord Fairfax, among others, extended into lands that would become Arlington County. Arlington House and plantation would come to be the home of Robert E. Lee and his wife, Mary Custis Lee, in 1857.
6. This designation is of African Americans living in the county outside of Alexandria City. The total population of the area was ninety-nine hundred sixty-seven, with eighty-four hundred fifty-nine residents living in the City of Alexandria. *United States Census, 1840* (Washington, DC: Government Printing Office).
7. Also listed as "Sarah Ann" and "Ann." US Southern Claims Commission, "Virginia, Alexandria, J, Jones, Levi" (ca. 1872–77). Microfilm Publication M2062, 36 Rolls; NAI 55715. Records of the Accounting Officers of the Department of the Treasury, Record Group 217, National Archives, Washington, DC (hereinafter abbreviated as NARA); G. M. Hopkins, "Atlas of Fifteen Miles Around Washington: 1878," Virginia Historical Society, Richmond, Virginia.
8. Arlington County, "Free Negro Register," 1842–1847, Library of Virginia. http://rosetta.virginiamemory.com:1801/delivery/DeliveryManagerServlet?dps_pid=IE3500439.
9. Also spelled "Eby." Donald Sweig, *Registrations of Free Negroes, Book 2* (Fairfax, VA: Fairfax Historical Commission, 1977), pp. 66, 96, 98.
10. George Washington (July 9, 1799), "Last Will and Testament of George Washington," Mount Vernon Special Collections and Archives, Mount Vernon, Virginia. http://www.mountvernon.org/.
11. Arlington County, Virginia "Register of Free Negroes," 1847–1861, Library of Virginia, p. 100; Provine, *Alexandria County, Virginia Free Negro Registers 1797–1861;* G. M. Hopkins, "Atlas of Fifteen Miles Around Washington: 1878," Virginia Historical Society, Richmond, Virginia.
12. Arlington County Government, *Arlington County Deed Book, L-P,* p. 36, Vertical File: Nauck, CLH; Arlington County Government, *Arlington County Deed Book,* pp. 154–79, Vertical File: Nauck, CLH.
13. US Southern Claims Commission, "Virginia, Alexandria, J, Jones, Levi" (ca. 1872–77). Microfilm Publication M2062, 36 Rolls; NAI 55715. Records of the Accounting Officers of the Department of the Treasury, Record Group 217, National Archives, Washington, DC (NARA).

14. The Jones's home was destroyed during the Civil War. After the conflict, they successfully petition for funds that they used to build an even larger, two-story, wood-frame home. "Testimony of George Shorter" (November 22, 1873) in US Southern Claims Commission, "Virginia, Alexandria, J, Jones, Levi" (ca. 1872–77). Microfilm Publication M2062, 36 Rolls; NAI 55715. Records of the Accounting Officers of the Department of the Treasury, Record Group 217, NARA.

15. White farmers John Casey, age sixty, and Edward Clements, age thirty, worked the land as tenants. *United States Census, 1850* (Washington, DC: Government Printing Office) database with images, FamilySearch (https://familysearch.org), Anthony N. Frazier, Alexandria county, part of, Alexandria, Virginia, United States; citing family 1545, NARA microfilm publication M432 (Washington, DC: National Archives and Records Administration, n.d.).

16. Also spelled "Frazer." Daniel Fraser first emigrated from Scotland in the early 1700s. Daniel's son William settled in Arlington in 1758 as a tenant farmer on the Alexander family's Abingdon plantation. Arlington County Courthouse Microfilm for Deeds: A4–348, 531, 561–2. B4–319. C4- 146–8, 174, 565–6. D4–6, 7. E4-l76–8, 0,58–60, 563–4. F4–76–7, 165–8. G4–124–5, 164, 488–9. H4–373–5, 378, 380–1, 486. 14–137. 14–192–3. M4–426–7. N2-U2–220–5, 268–9, 253–4, 309, 334–5, 350–2. Y2–466–7. X3-Z3–96–7. S4–51, 164, P467, 175, 332–3. C4–78–82; Templeman, *Arlington Heritage: Vignettes of a Virginia County*, 60.

17. Arlington County, Deed Book 9 X-Z, p. 17 1–3.; Rose, Arlington County, Virginia; Templeman, Arlington Heritage, 60; Arlington County Government, Arlington Ridge Neighborhood Conservation Plan, 21.

18. *US Census, 1850: Slave Schedule* (Washington, DC: Government Printing Office) database with images, *FamilySearch* (https://familysearch.org/ark:/61903 /1:1:MV8K-H9G: 7 November 2014), Anthony Frazier, Alexandria County, Alexandria, Virginia, United States; citing line number 12, NARA microfilm publication M432 (Washington, DC: National Archives and Records Administration, n.d.); FHL microfilm 444,973.

19. *US Census, 1850* (Washington, DC: Government Printing Office) database with images, *FamilySearch* (https://familysearch.org/ark:/61903/1:1:M88L-D4T: 9 November 2014), Anthony N. Frazier, Alexandria county, part of, Alexandria, Virginia, United States; citing family 1545, NARA microfilm publication M432 (Washington, DC: National Archives and Records Administration, n.d.).

20. US Census, 1860: Slave Schedule, Anthony Frazier, Alexandria County, Alexandria, Virginia (Washington, DC: Government Printing Office).

21. "From Washington," *Alexandria Gazette* (Alexandria, D.C.), 14 July 1886. Chronicling America: Historic American Newspapers. Library of Congress. https://chroniclingamerica.loc.gov/.

22. Maria Cater Syphax is believed to be the unrecognized daughter of George Washington Park Custis and his enslaved house servant Arie Anna Carter. This is one explanation for his decisions to educate, free, and gift land to Maria. Dr. Evelyn Syphax, interview by Anonymous, n.d., RG 103: Freedman's Village, Box 2, Folder 30, CLH; US Army Quarter Master Department, "Map of Reservation: Arlington Va Fort Myer and Nat. Cemetery," [1883], NARA; Arlington County Archivist, "An Annotated Guide to Selected Maps of Arlington County 1600–1900," 56–65.

23. Robert E. Lee freed Syphax in 1861 in accordance with the terms and conditions of George Washington Park Custis's last will and testament. Alexandria, *Will Book #7*, p. 267; Dorothea E. Abbott, "The Land of Maria Syphax and the Abbey Mausoleum," 64–80.

24. Maria was educated alongside her probable half-sister Mary Ann Randolph Custis at Arlington House, while her children were educated in Alexandria and Washington. It is not known whether Charles was formally educated, but it is possible that he also received some informal education, because he served as a "house slave" and because his father, William Syphax, was a free man of color who served as a preacher in Alexandria. Alexandria, *Will Book #7*, p. 267; Abbott, "The Land of Maria Syphax and the Abbey Mausoleum," 1984.

25. *Free Black Registers*, no. 1–3, Arlington County Courthouse, Arlington, Virginia.

26. Ford, *Deliver Us From Evil: The Slavery Question in the Old South*; O'Brien, "Factory, Church, and Community," 509–36; Kaye, *Joining Places*, 1–50.

27. For example, although Arlington required the registration of free Blacks in accordance with Virginia's Black codes, this practice was far from comprehensive. However, in the years immediately after retrocession to Virginia, the numbers of free Black registrants rose sharply without a corresponding in-migration of people. So these individuals were required to register for the first time under the new social and political climate. *Free Black Registers*, no. 1–3, Arlington County Courthouse, Arlington, Virginia.

28. Arlington County, "Free Negro Register," 1842–1847, Library of Virginia. http://rosetta.virginiamemory.com.

29. Lands and improvements were valued twenty-five hundred eighty dollars for fifteen acres, about one hundred sixty-six dollars per acre, before 1865. In comparison, local white landowner Bazil Hall's land was valued at only thirty per acre, although his property was substantially larger, resulting in greater personal wealth overall. US Southern Claims Commission, "Virginia, Alexandria, J, Jones, Levi" (ca. 1872–77). Microfilm Publication M2062, 36 Rolls; NAI 55715. Records of the Accounting Officers of the Department of the Treasury, Record Group 217, NARA.

30. US Census Bureau, "Table 23: District of Columbia—Race and Hispanic Origin, 1800–1990," https://web.archive.org/; Masur, *An Example for All the Land*, 33, 56.

31. Colonel Elias M. Green(e), "Letter to Major Gen. S.P. Heintzelman," May 5, 1863, RG 92—Arlington, Virginia. Box 7, NM-81, Entry 576, NARA; Laurie McClellan, "Land of the Free," *Arlington Magazine* (November–December 2013), p. 55.

32. In the elections leading up to the Civil War, Arlingtonians supported Constitutional Unionists, who ran on platforms of maintaining both the Union and slavery. In contrast, residents of nearby Alexandria City supported secession; Richards, "The Debates Over the Retrocession of the District of Columbia, 1801–2004."

33. Robert Knox Sneden, *Contours of Union Forts on South Side of Potomac.* [S.I., 1864-1865] Map, LOC, https://www.loc.gov/item/gvhs01.vhs00242/; Rose Jr., "Civil War Forts in Arlington."

34. Robert Desty, ed. (1883). "United States v. Lee; Kaufman and another v. Same. December 4, 1882 (106 US 196)," Supreme Court Reporter. Cases Argued and Determined in the United States Supreme Court, October Term, 1882:

October, 1882-February 1883. Saint Paul, MN: West Publishing Company. 1: 240–86.

35. Alexandria City Government, *Finding The Fort*; Walker, "Corinth: The Story of a Contraband Camp," 5–22; Ira Berlin, "The Wartime Genesis of Free Labor," 132.

36. General Services Administration, Records of the Superintendent of Education for the District of Columbia, Bureau of Refugees, Freedmen, and Abandoned Lands 1865–1872, Washington, DC, 1978, p. 1.

37. Berlin, "The Wartime Genesis of Free Labor," 133.

38. "Dedication of Freedman's Village, Arlington," *The Evening Star* (December 2, 1863), LOC. https://chroniclingamerica.loc.gov.

39. "Freedman's Village, Arlington, Village," *Harper's Weekly*, May 7, 1864. Vertical File: Freedman's Village, CLH.

40. "Military Reservation of Fort Myer and Arlington, VA," 1888, NARA.

41. Leech, *Reveille In Washington 1860–1865*, 251–252; Schildt, "Aladdin's Lamp: Education in Freedman's Village."

42. Ross discusses her father's 1880s blacksmithing business in Arlington and his inability to work as a blacksmith in Lynchburg, Virginia. Katherine Mosley Ross, interview by Annon, 1995, RG 103: Freedman's Village, Box 2, File 30, CLH.

43. Provine, "The Economic Position of the Free Blacks in the District of Columbia," 58.

44. Records of the Field Offices for the District of Columbia, Bureau of Refugees, Freedmen, and Abandoned Lands, 1865–1870, Subordinate Field Offices, Local Superintendent for Washington and Georgetown, Records Relating to Employment of Freedmen, Labor Contracts, M1902, Roll 18, NARA; "Labor Contracts: William Tucker, William Henry, William Morgan, LA Bartlett" (4 April 1866), Records of the field offices for the District of Columbia, Bureau of Refugees, Freedmen, and Abandoned Lands, 1863–1872, M1902, Roll 18, NARA.

45. Dickinson et al., *Montgomery C. Meigs and the Building of the Nation's Capital.*

46. Schildt. "Freedman's Village: Arlington Virginia 1863–1900," 11–22.

47. John P. Sherburne, Assistant Inspector General of the Military District of Washington, to Brigadier General J. H. Matrindales, Military Governor of the District of Columbia, July 9, 1863, RG 103: Freedman's Village, Box 2, Folder 17, CLH.

48. Reidy, "'Coming from the Shadow of the Past." See also Berlin, Reidy, and Rowland, eds., "The Black Military Experience."

49. US Department of Commerce, Bureau of the Census, 1910. Special Collections, Alexandria City Library.; National Register of Historic Places, *Harry W. Gray House*, by Jennifer Bunting Hallock, by May 2003.

50. "Military Reservation of Fort Myer and Arlington, VA," 1888, NARA.

51. Field Office—District of Columbia, Subordinate Field Offices, Freedman's Village, "Register of People Arriving at Freedmen's Village, 1863–1865," Records of the field offices for the District of Columbia, Bureau of Refugees, Freedmen, and Abandoned Lands, 1863–1872, M1902, NARA.

52. "Removal of the Contrabands," *Soldiers' Journal* (Rendezvous if Distribution, VA), July 20, 1864.

53. "The Eviction of the Squatters from Freedman's Village," 1887.

54. Edwin M. Stanton to Major General Heintzelman, W 43, Letters Received, Series 5382, Department of Washington, RG 393 [4557]; Felix James, "Freedman's Village, Arlington, Virginia: A History," 1967.
55. "Pennsylvania Adopted Children," *Juniata Sentinel* (Mifflintown, PA) March 28, 1866; Morris, "The Freedman Record, Vol. 1," 160; James, "Freedman's Village, Arlington, Virginia," 1967.
56. Schildt, "Aladdin's Lamp."
57. For similar social institutions created by and for freedmen in the South, see Hunter, *To 'Joy My Freedom*, 21–43.
58. On the political realities of contraband camps, see Hahn, *A National Under Our Feet*, 73.
59. Stanford, *Suburban Black Elderly*, 1978.
60. "Henry Lomax," Records of the field offices for the state of Virginia, Bureau of Refugees, Freedmen, and Abandoned Lands, M1913, Roll 39, NARA.
61. C. S. Potter, "Letter to E. P. Smith," January 26, 1867, American Missionary Association Archives, 1828–1969, Box 181: Virginia, 1866 October 16, 1867 March, HI-9626, Amistad Research Center, New Orleans, Louisiana.
62. Sara Collins et al., *Freedman's Village*.
63. John William, "Letter to Henry William," January 1, 1862.; Scott S. Taylor, "The View from Hall's Hill: Civil War Letters from Hall's Hill Virginia," 49–60.
64. Parker, "Letter to Robert G. Cater;" Wise, "Bazil Hall of Hall's Hill," 23.
65. Margaret Evely Wright, interview by Terry Townsend, December 15, 1974, Zonta Oral History Program, CLH.
66. These suburban patterns of development challenge the Black suburban types outlined by Wiese. Wiese, *Places of Their Own*; Perry, Crew, and Waters, "'We Didn't Have Any Other Place To Live,'" 404.
67. Hall's home was first constructed in 1866. Until its destruction in 1999, the home was located at 1700 North George Mason Drive in Arlington. Southern Claims Commission Records, no. 2422, Bazil Hall, 1871–1880. NARA; Bestebreurtje, "A View from Hall's Hill," 19–34; Alexandria City Government, *Finding The Fort*.
68. "Oral History Interview with Basil Hall and Robert S. Lacey," CLH; Wilson, "Regimental History of the Twenty-Second Massachusetts Infantry," 1979; US Southern Claims Commission, "Bazil Hall no. 2422," NARA.
69. US Southern Claims Commission, "Bazil Hall no. 2422," NARA.
70. Arlington County Land Records; Arlington County Probate Records; Arlington County Government, *Nauck: A Community Rich in History*, 24.
71. *Nauck*, 6.
72. A total of $34,342 for the estate's damage. US Southern Claims Commission, "Virginia, Alexandria, Anthony Fraser, no. 8738" Records of the Accounting Officers of the Department of the Treasury, Record Group 217, NARA
73. US Southern Claims Commission, "Virginia, Alexandria, J, Jones, Levi" (ca. 1872–1877). Microfilm Publication M2062, 36 Rolls; NAI 55715. Records of the Accounting Officers of the Department of the Treasury, Record Group 217, NARA.
74. Anthony Fraser passed away in 1881, leaving his estate to his youngest daughter, Antonia, and her husband, J. E. Sickles. Sickles, a native of New York City and a major in the Union Army, did not support the institution of slavery before the

war. The Sickles family continued the tradition of land sales to African Americans in Green Valley. *US Census, 1860* (Washington, DC: Government Printing Office) database with images, *FamilySearch* (https://familysearch.org/), Anthony Frazier, 1860; "District of Columbia Births and Christenings, 1830–1955," database, *FamilySearch* (https://familysearch.org/), J. E. Sickels in entry for Sickels, 16 August 1878, Washington, District of Columbia, FHL microfilm 2,114,648; Taylor, *Bridge Builders of Nauck/Green Valley: Past and Present*; Research Committee, "Some Black History in Arlington County," 11–17.

75. The price of land quickly rose from this early rate from 1865, when sales began, to 1888, when Hall passed away; "A Shocking Murder," *Alexandria Gazette*, December 15, 1857 (Alexandria, D.C.); Wise, "Bazil Hall of Hall's Hill"; Arlington County Government, *Neighborhood History Preservation Study of Hall's Hill Highview Park*, 1987.

76. Arlington County Government, Neighborhood History Preservation Study of Hall's Hill Highview Park; Cooling, Symbol, Sword, and Shield, 95.

77. "A Shocking Murder," *Alexandria Gazette*, December 15, 1857 (Alexandria, D.C.).

78. Stanford, *Suburban Black Elderly*, 24–25.

79. Arlington County Government, *Arlington County Deed Book XZ*, 309; Wise, "Bazil Hall of Hall's Hill," 24; Arlington County Government, *Arlington County Deed Book C*, no. 4, p. 1.

80. Variously spelled Upshire, Upshur, and Upsher. The family had two children when they purchased their home, and four children as of 1870. Arlington County Government, *Arlington County Deed Book A*, no. 4, pp. 333–35; Wise, "Bazil Hall of Hall's Hill," 24; *US Census, 1870* (Washington, DC: Government Printing Office) index and images, Virginia, United States, NARA.

81. *US Census, 1860* (Washington, DC: Government Printing Office) and *US Census, 1870* (Washington, DC: Government Printing Office) index and images, Virginia, United States; citing p. 50, family 356, NARA microfilm publication M593 (Washington, DC: National Archives and Records Administration, n.d.); FHL microfilm 553,138.

82. Chartered as the Alexandria, Loudon, and Hampshire Railroad, the line changed names several times throughout the late nineteenth century until the name became Washington and Old Dominion in 1911. To avoid confusion, Washington and Old Dominion is used as the name of this line throughout.

83. Clark Jr., *The American Family Home, 1800–1960*, 29–30.

84. Advertisement for "Public Sale of Valuable Personal Property" issued by A. D. Torreyson in 1915. Vertical Files: Hall's Hill, CLH; Arlington County Government, *High View Park Neighborhood Conservation Plan*.

85. Arlington County Government, *Arlington County Deed Book E*, no. 4, 284; Wise, "Bazil Hall of Hall's Hill," 24; Arlington County Government, *Neighborhood History Preservation Study of Hall's Hill Highview Park*; Margaret Evely Wright, interview by Terry Townsend, December 15, 1974, Zonta Oral History Program, CLH; "Virginia, Marriages, 1785–1940," Robert E. Ferguson and Eleanor "Ellen" D. V. Hayson (also spelled Hyson), 23 October 1878; citing Falls Church, Alexandria, Virginia, reference 141; FHL microfilm 30,497.

86. Arlington County Government, Neighborhood History Preservation Study of Hall's Hill Highview Park.

87. Arlington County Government, *Arlington County Deed Book O*, no. 4, p 319, Arlington County Office of Land Records, Arlington, Virginia.

88. William H. Pelham Sr., interview by Edmund D. Campbell and Cas Cocklin, November 21, 1986, Arlington County Libraries Oral History Program, CLH, p. 2.

89. David Best, Vivian Bullock, Phyllis Costley, Mignon Johnson, "Addendum to the Summary of Oral History Transcripts for High View Park (Hall's Hill)," August 9, 1995.

90. Arlington County School Board, "Minute Book" (1870–1905), CLH.

91. Welke, *Recasting American Liberty*, 33.

92. This is the average height for trolley cars in the 1880s. Welke, *Recasting American Liberty*.

93. Hanchett, *Sorting Out the New South City*.

94. Lands and improvements were valued at twenty-five hundred eighty dollars for fifteen acres, about one hundred sixty-six dollars per acre, before 1865. In comparison, local white landowner Bazil Hall's land was valued at only thirty dollars per acre, although his property was substantially larger, resulting in greater personal wealth overall. US Southern Claims Commission, "Virginia, Alexandria, J, Jones, Levi" (ca. 1872–77). Microfilm Publication M2062, 36 Rolls; NAI 55715. Records of the Accounting Officers of the Department of the Treasury, Record Group 217, NARA.

95. Purchased five additional acres from the Elizabeth Baggott estate in the 1870s. In 1878, Jones owned seventeen acres of land after sales. Arlington County Land Records; Arlington County Probate Records; Arlington County Government, *Nauck: A Community Rich in History*; G. M. Hopkins, "Atlas of Fifteen Miles Around Washington: 1878," Virginia Historical Society, Richmond, Virginia.

96. Department of Community Planning, Housing and Development, *A Guide to the African American Heritage of Arlington County*.

97. On racial implications of reconciliation, see Blight, *Race and Reunion*.

98. *Evening Star* (Washington, DC), 8 May 1865. *Chronicling America: Historic American Newspapers*. Library of Congress. https://chroniclingamerica.loc.gov/.

99. *Evening Star*, 8 May 1865.

100. Captain Ezra B. Gates, Arlington National Cemetery, Fourth Annual Report of the Assistant Commissioner, Bureau, Refugees, Freedmen, and Abandoned Lands, for the District of Columbia, West Virginia, Maryland and Delaware, October 10, 1868, Bureau, Refugees, Freedmen, and Abandoned Lands, MSS, Record Group 105.; James, "Freedman's Village, Arlington, Virginia."

101. This characterization of Freedman's Village residents as squatters could be seen in military correspondents and amongst civilians. J. A. Commerford, Superintendent of National Cemetery, to Major and Quarter Master G. B. Dandy, November 12, 1878, RG 103: Freedman's Village, Box 1 Folder 1, CLH; The Freedman's Village, *Alexandria Gazette*, December 7, 1887. Vertical File: Freedman's Village, CLH.

102. Board of Supervisors, Minute Book, February 13, 1884, RG 103: Freedman's Village, CLH.

103. Selina Gray to Mrs. Mary (Custis) Lee, 1872, Mary Custis Lee Papers, 1694–1917, Virginia Historical Society, Richmond, Virginia (hereinafter abbreviated as VHS).

104. H. E. Simmons to Elias M. Greene, January 23, 1864, RG 92, CQMGF, MSS, NARA; James "Freedman's Village, Arlington, Virginia" (1967).

105. Most purchased their homes for thirty-five to fifty dollars. L. H. Carbenter to Richard C Drum, December 7, 1887, Vertical File: Freedman's Village, CLH; James "Freedman's Village, Arlington, Virginia," 59.

106. US Government, Valuation of Property in the Village, 1888, RG 92, CQMGF, MSS, NARA; James "Freedman's Village, Arlington, Virginia" (1967).

107. 15 Stat. 83 (July 6, 1868) and 15 Stat. 193 (July 25, 1868), M1869: Records of the Assistant Commissioner and Subordinate Field Offices for the Bureau of Refugees, Freedmen, and Abandoned Lands, 1865–1872, NARA.

108. Sergeant S. N. Clark, "Bureau Refugees Freedmen and Abandoned Lands Headquarters Assistant Commissioner, District of Columbia, Washington, to Colonel," December 29, 1866, RG 103: Freedman's Village, Box 1 Folder 10, CLH.

109. Records of the Assistant Commissioner for the District of Columbia, Bureau of Refugees, Freedmen, and Abandoned Lands, 1865–1869, M1055, NARA accessed through the National Museum of African American History and Culture, "Freedmen's Bureau Digital Collection, 1865–1872"; James, "Freedman's Village, Arlington, Virginia," 59.

110. J. H. Laws et al. to O. O. Howard, 20 July 1868, Freedmen's Village, Washington, DC, Agent, RG 105. [A-9911]; Reidy, "'Coming from the Shadow of the Past,'" 20.

111. *The Soldiers' Journal* (Rendezvous of Distribution, Va.), 20 July 1864. *Chronicling America: Historic American Newspapers*. Library of Congress. https://chroniclingamerica.loc.gov/; "Closing the Village," RG 103: Freedman's Village, Box 1, Folder 1, CLH.

112. 31 Stat., 135; Blueprints, Arlington Reservation Files, Records of the Judge Advocate General, War Department; Tasmussen and Wiser, "Arlington—An Agricultural Experiment Farm in a Changing Era," 24–30.

113. Article, *Alexandria Gazette*, September 2, 1872. Vertical File: Freedman's Village, CLH.

114. Records of the field offices for the state of Virginia, Bureau of Refugees, Freedmen, and Abandoned Lands, M1913, Roll 38, NARA. Sara Collins et al., *Freedman's Village*.

115. Research and Records Committee, Arlington Historical Society, "County Officials in Arlington, 1870–1960."

116. Board of Supervisors, Minute Book, December 6, 1875; Rose, *Arlington County, Virginia* (1976); "Washington," *Richmond Dispatch*, June 25, 1886.

117. The Freedman's Village, *Alexandria Gazette*, December 7, 1887, Vertical File: Freedman's Village, CLH.

118. US Government, Valuation of Property in the Village, 1888, RG 92, CQMGF, MSS, NARA.

119. For discussions of reversal of African American political rights, see Hahn, *A National Under Our Feet*; Blight, *Race and Reunion*; Neff, *Honoring the Civil War Dead*; Gillette, *Retreat from Reconstruction, 1869–1879*.

120. "From Washington," October 30, 1903, *The Alexandria Gazette*, p 2.; Alexandria Co., Va. Board Of Supervisors. *A brief history of Alexandria County, Virginia*. [Falls Church, Va., The Newell printing co, 1907] Pdf. https://www.loc.gov/item/07038327/.

121. Letter to General Edwin M. Stanton, Secretary of War, August 15, 1864, RG 103: Freedman's Village, Box 1, Folder 9, CLH.

122. *Alexandria Gazette*, (Alexandria, D.C.), 06 Dec. 1887. *Chronicling America: Historic American Newspapers*. Library of Congress. https://chroniclingamerica.loc .gov.

123. John W. Daniel to Redfield Proctor, December 18, 1890, RG 93, File Arlington Reservation, Consolidated Correspondence, Y-123, NARA

124. J. A. Commerford, Superintendent of National Cemetery, to Major and Quarter Master G.B. Dandy, November 12, 1878, RG 103: Freedman's Village, Box 1, Folder 1, CLH.

125. Brigadier General Samuel B. Holabird to William C. Endicott, November 17, 1887, RG 93: Office of the Quartermaster General, NARA.

126. Captain VRG Supt. To Bvt. Brigadier General C. H. Howard, Department Commissioner of Washington, DC, November 9, 1866, RG 103: Freedman's Village, Box 1, File 1, CLH.

127. US Government, Valuation of Property in the Village, 1888, RG 92, CQMGF, MSS, NARA.

128. Hannah Owens' employment is listed as "keeping house" beginning in 1880. *US Census, 1880* (Washington, DC: Government Printing Office).

129. Arlington Estate, Memorandum, RG 92, File: Arlington Estate, DNA, Y-122, NARA.

130. "Eviction of the Squatters from Freedman's Village," December 8, 1887, *New York Herald*.

131. John B. Syphax to William C. Endicott, January 18, 1888, RG 92, File: Office of the Quarter Master General, NARA.

132. "Military Reservation of Fort Myer and Arlington, VA," 1888, NARA.

133. She had a child in 1867. "Hospital Records" (October 1867), District of Columbia Field Offices, Freedmen's Village, Register of People Arriving at Freedmen's Village, 84, January 1867; US Government, Valuation of Property in the Village, 1888, RG 92, CQMGF, MSS, NARA.

134. *US Census, 1870* (Washington, DC: Government Printing Office), National Archives, microfilm publication M593 (Washington, DC: National Archives and Records Administration, n.d.); US Government, Valuation of Property in the Village, 1888, RG 92, CQMGF, MSS, NARA; James "Freedman's Village, Arlington, Virginia," 1967; Collins et al., *Freedman's Village*; "Local Intelligence," December 7, 1887, *Washington Post*; James "Freedman's Village, Arlington, Virginia," 62.

135. There were one hundred thirty households within the Village in 1888. US Government, Valuation of Property in the Village, 1888, RG 92, CQMGF, MSS, NARA. As of 2023, the Arlington County Department of Real Estate Assessments values homes of this type in the areas that border Freedman's Village at just over half a million dollars.

136. US Government, Valuation of Property in the Village, 1888, RG 92, CQMGF, MSS, NARA.

Chapter 2: "Gone Out to Do for Themselves"

1. Source of quotation used in the chapter title is description used by the Federal Government for those leaving federal lands. See District of Columbia Field Offices, Freedmen's Village, Register of People, M1902, Roll 18, NARA.

2. "Important Order," *Evening Star* [No. 3,801] (Washington, DC), 8 May 1865. *Chronicling America: Historic American Newspapers.* Library of Congress. https://lccn.loc.gov/sn83045462.

3. "Important Order," *Evening Star.*

4. See District of Columbia Field Offices, Freedmen's Village, Register of People, M1902, Roll 18, NARA.

5. District of Columbia Field Offices, Freedmen's Village, Register of People at Freedmen's Village, NARA.

6. Historian Andrew Wiese has shown how African Americans specifically were impacted by these same ideological pulls, if in different ways. Wiese, *Places of Their Own,* 67–93.

7. Jackson, *Crabgrass Frontier: The Suburbanization of the United States,* 45–72.

8. Wiese, *Places of Their Own,* 67–93.

9. Deed Book F4, p. 293, Arlington County Office of Land Records; District of Columbia Field Offices, Freedmen's Village, Register of People at Freedmen's Village, NARA; Perry et al., "'We Didn't Have Any Other Place to Live.'"

10. O'Brien, "Historic Survey of Nauck Neighborhood, Arlington County, Virginia" (unpublished paper, December 1987), CLH; Arlington County Cultural Affairs; Arlington Department of Community Planning, Housing and Development; Virginian Foundation for the Humanities. "Community Voices: The Nauck Community Heritage Project" (Arlington, Virginia: August 2008).

11. Arlington's First Negro Teacher Dies, *The Sun,* April 11, 1941, Vertical File: Nauck, CLH; Rose Jr., "Public Schools in Arlington District of Alexandria County Virginia, 1870–1905," 17–39.

12. Meeting Minutes, January 11, 1871, *Minute Book of Arlington District, 1870–1905,* CLH; Vogel, "The Integration of Reed Elementary School," 33–42.

13. Meeting Minutes, October 4, 1875, *Minute Book of Arlington District, 1870–1905.* CLH.

14. Levi Jones moved to Arlington from nearby Fairfax in 1833. He likely worked as a farm hand based on his upbringing in the rural Fairfax County and his listed profession of farmer from the 1840s until his death in 1886. The Jones family purchased eleven acres from local white landowner Elizabeth Baggott at a rate of two hundred dollars down and two hundred thirty-five dollars over five years. Provine, *Alexandria County, Virginia Free Negro Registers 1797–1861*; Hopkins, "Atlas of Fifteen Miles Around Washington: 1878," Virginia Historical Society, Richmond, Virginia; Arlington County Government, *Arlington County Deed Book, L-P,* p. 36, Vertical File: Nauck, CLH; Arlington County Government, *Arlington County Deed Book,* pp. 154–79, Vertical File: Nauck, CLH.

15. Taylor was born free, and Williams was emancipated by Charles Lewis. Registration, December 6, 1853; 3, no. 87, p. 91; Registration, August 3, 1847; 3, no. 211, p. 29; Provine, *Alexandria County, Virginia Free Negro Registers 1797–1861,* 29, 43, 237; Hopkins, "Atlas of Fifteen Miles Around Washington Including the Counties of Fairfax and Alexandria, Virginia," [1879], Map F232.A7.1878, VHS.

16. Thompson became a leader in the community through work with AME Zion Church and as Arlington District's Superintendent of the Poor from 1874 to 1879. Board of Supervisors, "Minute Book" (1975–1979), Arlington, Virginia.

17. O'Brien, "Historic Survey of Nauck Neighborhood, Arlington County, Virginia."

18. Baggotts sold land to African Americans, including the Jones family, Coles, and Wallace Boswell; O'Brien, "Historic Survey of Nauck Neighborhood, Arlington County, Virginia."

19. John Nauck purchased a total of sixty-nine acres from 1874 to 1875, which he subdivided and sold between 1880 and 1900; Research Committee, "Some Black History in Arlington County: A Preliminary Investigation," 13–14.

20. Selina Gray to Mrs. Mary (Custis) Lee, 1872, Mary Custis Lee Papers, 1694–1917, VHS.

21. Purchased ten acres in 1867. Arlington County Government, *Arlington County Deed Book, H-Z*, no. 9, p. 222. Vertical File: Nauck, CLH.

22. The Frasers continued to live in Green Valley Manor, although on a far smaller plot of land and with only two servants. In the 1880 Census, Fraser is down from nine enslaved workers in 1860 to two paid African American workers, Lucy Wardwell, age 27, and George Carter, age 25. *United States Census, 1880* (Washington, DC: Government Printing Office), database with images, *FamilySearch* (https://familysearch.org/ark:/61903/1:1:MCP6-KFM: 11 August 2016), Anthony R Fraser, Jefferson, Alexandria, Virginia, United States; citing enumeration district ED 7, sheet 443B, NARA microfilm publication T9 (Washington, DC: National Archives and Records Administration, n.d.), roll 1351; FHL microfilm 1,255,351.

23. This trolley line opened in 1892. A two-way trolley ticket cost five cents per day. Advertisement for "Public Sale of Valuable Personal Property" issued by A. D. Torreyson in 1915. Vertical Files: Hall's Hill, CLH; John E. Merriken, *Old Dominion Trolley Too: A History of the Mount Vernon Line* (Dallas, TX: Taylor Publishing Company, 1987).

24. Perry, Crew, and Waters, "'We Didn't Have Any Other Place to Live.'"

25. "Platt of Queen City," *Alexandria County Deed Book N-4*, p. 265 (9 June 1892), CLH.

26. "Lot no. 25," *Alexandria County Deed Book Y-4*, p. 210, CLH.

27. George Volin Jr., interview by Susan Gilpin (CLH); Gilpin, "Queen City" (1984), p. 4, CLH.

28. Merriken, *Old Dominion Trolley Too.*

29. "Interview with the Grandchildren of Anne Rowe West," reprinted in Taylor, *Bridge Builders of Nauck/Green Valley*, 17.

30. Gilmore, *Gender and Jim Crow.*

31. Wilson, *The City Beautiful Movement*; Jackson, *Crabgrass Frontier*; Marsh "Reconsidering the Suburbs: An Exploration of Suburban Historiography," 579–605.

32. Johnston is at times also written as "Johnson" in the record of both the man and the neighborhood in the first years of the community. Johnson's Hill: Vertical File, CLH.

33. Mr. Ernest W. Bowen and Mrs. Josephine Pollard Mitchell, interview by Elsie Smith, 1970, Hall's Hill Oral History Project, CLH.

34. William H. Duncan, Clerk, "Virginia Circuit Court Arlington County Clarendon VA," March 24, 1884. RG 11: Papers of Edmund C. Fleet, Box 2, Folder 7: Property Deed to GUOFF 1884, Carbon Copy, CLH.

35. James Smith, relative of Village resident Martha Smith, was initiated in 1875. Lawrence Parks (farmer) was initiated in 1882, and his brother, William H. F.

Parks, laborer, was initiated in 1879. US Census Records, 1900. Department of Commerce Bureau of the Census. Volume 3. Enumeration District 1, Sheet 5, Line 32. Microfilm, Alexandria Library, Special Collections.; Collins, *Freedman's Village*.

36. Gilpin, "Queen City" (1984), p. 9, CLH.

37. See Odd Fellows records in RG 11: Papers of Edmund C. Fleet, CLH.

38. Emma and Sarah Wilson (Syphax), "Personal Statements," December 6, 1929. Vertical File—Arlington House, CLH.

39. As a contract laborer for Arlington House, Gray earned forty-five dollars per month. Selina Gray "Letter to Mrs. Mary (Custis) Lee," 1872, Mary Custis Lee Papers, 1694–1917, VHS.

40. Hoard's exact position at the Department of the Interior is not known. However, she worked under Secretary of the Interior Columbus Delano, at a rate of ten dollars per month. Positions open to women at this time included stenographer, clerk, copyist, nurse, cook, and charwoman (cleaning woman). On the basis of her pay rate, it is likely that she held a lower level position, including nurse, cook, or charwoman. Columbus Delano et al., "Annual Reports of the Department of the Interior" (Washington, DC: Government Printing Office, 1875); Martha Gray Gillen, interview by Robinet, Interview Transcript, 1963. RG 103: Freedman's Village, Box 2, File 31, CLH.

41. *Alexandria County Deed Books* Liber E4, Folio 310, October 6. 1880.

42. Hanchett, Sorting Out the New South City, 47–68.

43. Manin, "Virginia's Fastest Growing County," 1; National Register of Historic Places, *Harry W. Gray House*, 15.

44. Stanford, *Suburban Black Elderly*.

45. Wiese, *Places of Their Own*; Pearl (Pelham Town resident), Interview with Nancy Perry, November 9, 2012; Perry et al., "'We Didn't Have Any Other Place to Live.'"

46. Virginia Title Company, "Map of Alexandria County Virginia," [1900], Map Division, Library of Congress, Washington, DC (hereinafter abbreviated as LOC). http://lccn.loc.gov/89692758.

47. *US Census, 1900: Virginia, Alexandria, ED 1 Arlington District* (Washington, DC: Government Printing Office), NARA, pp. 16–17.

48. US Census, 1900, Arlington District.

49. Those women who worked beyond the home were primarily employed as domestics. *US Census, 1900: Virginia, Alexandria, ED 1 Arlington District* (Washington, DC: Government Printing Office), NARA, pp. 16–17.

50. US Census, "Historic Census of Housing Tables," Home Ownership Rates, National and Virginia, 1900 http://www.census.gov; Perry et al., "'We Didn't Have Any Other Place to Live.'"

51. US Census, "Historic Census of Housing Tables," Home Ownership Rates, National and Virginia, 1900 http://www.census.gov; Maloney, "African Americans in the Twentieth Century," http://eh.net/encyclopedia. Andrew Wiese suggests that pre-World War II home ownership rates are higher among working-class and minority Americans because of their conceptualization of home as necessary for stability and a source of labor, rather than as an investment as for their white middle-class counterparts, therefore sacrificing more to own a home of their own. Wiese, *Places of Their Own*, 67–93.

52. Perry et al., "'We Didn't Have Any Other Place to Live,'" 417.

53. *United States Census, 1900*: Reel 801. Alcorn (cont'd: ED 15, sheet 22-end), Benton, Bolivar (part: EDs 1–11) Counties (Washington, DC: Government Printing Office), NARA.

54. Borchert, "Alley Landscapes of Washington, D.C.," 281–314.

55. Pearl (Pelham Town Resident), Interview with Nancy Perry, November 9, 2012; Perry et al., "'We Didn't Have Any Other Place to Live.'"

56. Richards, "The Debates over the Retrocession of the District of Columbia, 1801–2004."

57. V. P. Corbett, Sketch of the Seat of War in Alexandria and Fairfax Counties (May 1861); Stephenson, *The Cartography of Northern Virginia*, 54.

58. The connector was under construction from 1894 to 1906. Before that time, for an additional five cents, passengers could cross the Aqueduct Bridge to the Twelfth and Pennsylvania Street station without changing trains; Merriken, *Old Dominion Trolley Too*.

59. Jackson, Crabgrass Frontier; Clark Jr., The American Family Home; Stilgoe, Borderland.

60. Ball, "Electric Railways of Arlington," 33.

61. Arthur W. Trust, "Clarendon Presbyterian Church: A Partial History through 1947" (paper presented July 1, 1975), RG 6: Arlington Churches, Box 2. CLH.

62. Rose, *Arlington County, Virginia*.

63. Ball, "Electric Railways of Arlington," 31.

64. These three bridges were the Chain Bridge (1797), the Aqueduct Bridge (1843, later renamed the Key Bridge), and the Long Bridge (1808, later renamed the Fourteenth Street Bridge).

65. Rose, *Arlington County, Virginia*, 141; Harper, "Arlington County, Virginia: Transportation through 1945." (unpublished paper, March 1985). Vertical File: Transportation, CLH.

66. Kinnier, County Planning Engineer, "The Renaming of Arlington Streets"; Netherton, *Arlington County in Virginia*.

67. Griffith Morgan Hopkins Jr., "Alexandria County, Va, 1878," [1878]. Maps Division, LOC.

68. *US Census, 1870* (Washington, DC: Government Printing Office); *US Census, 1880* (Washington, DC: Government Printing Office).

69. *US Census, 1900* (Washington, DC: Government Printing Office); Howell and Taylor, "Map of Alexandria County, Virginia for the Virginia Title Co.," [1900], Map Division, LOC; Arlington County Register of Historic Places, *Reevesland, Torreyson Farm*, by Beth Bolling (Arlington, March 2002).

70. Jackson, *Crabgrass Frontier*, 85.

71. Chataigne, *Chataigne's Alexandria City Directory*, 1876–77.

72. *Arlington County Deed Books*, Deed Book F4, p. 565.

73. This line started in Rosslyn and ran through Fort Myer to Green Valley, with stops running past Court House and Falls Church.

74. *Arlington County Deed Books*, Deed Book 161, p. 380; Deed Book 167, p. 520; Deed Book 173, p. 173; Deed Book 187, p. 487–90.

75. "Map of Corbett" [ca. 1886], Arlington Deed Book C, no. 4, p 448–89. Arlington, Virginia.

76. Walter, "The Original Developers of Barcroft." 5–20; Wilson, *The City Beautiful Movement*; The Cooperative Building Plan Association, Architects, *Selected Designs from Shoppell's Modern Houses*.

77. Although on larger lots than later suburban environments, these homes were designed to exist together within Corbett's subdivisions as a part of a suburban environment rather than maintaining older agrarian models of settlement; Walter, "The Original Developers of Barcroft."

78. Templeman, "Ballston's Beginnings," 52–54

79. Community Planning, Housing, and Development, "Planning and Development History" (Virginia: Arlington County Government, 2023).

80. Trust, "Clarendon Presbyterian Church: A Partial History through 1947" (paper presented July 1, 1975), RG 6: Arlington Churches, Box 2, CLH.

81. Glencarlyn Citizens' Association, "GCA Meeting Minutes," 1922, RG 62: Glencarlyn, Box 3, File 7, CLH.

82. Dorothy Overal Hook, James F. Overal, and William J. Overall (Grandchildren of William Joseph Overal) interview by Phyllis W. Johnson. RG 6: Arlington Churches, Box 1, File: Clarendon United Methodist Church, CLH.

83. St. George's Episcopal Church, "100 Years, 1908–2008" (Arlington, Virginia: 2008). RG 6: Arlington Churches, Box 4, CLH.

84. Glencarlyn Citizens' Association, "GCA Meeting Minutes," 1922, RG 62: Glencarlyn, Box 3, File 7, CLH.

85. Mackey, *A Brief History of Alexandria County, Virginia*, 35.

86. Washington-Virginia Railway, "Railway" (advertisement), 1910, Vertical File: Transportation, CLH.

87. These additions occurred between 1904 and 1919. Alexandria County Deed Book 108, p. 563; Alexandria County Deed Book 110, p. 262; Alexandria County Deed Book 165, p. 20.

88. *US Census, 1900* (Washington, DC: Government Printing Office); *US Census, 1910* (Washington, DC: Government Printing Office).

89. O'Brien, "Historic Survey of Nauck Neighborhood, Arlington County, Virginia," CLH. For more on Southerners drawn to Washington for work, see Yellin, *Racism in the Nation's Service*.

90. Mackey, *A Brief History of Alexandria County, Virginia*, 36.

Chapter 3: "Suburban Homes . . . in Sight of the Monument"

1. Source for quotation used in chapter title: Barbor, Williams & Company Real Estate Insurance, "Falls Church Virginia" (advertisement), ca. 1910; Netherton and Netherton, *Arlington County in Virginia: A Pictorial History*.

2. Delaney, *Race, Place, and the Law, 1836–1948*.

3. Rose, *Arlington County, Virginia: A History*.

4. Wilson, *The City Beautiful Movement*.

5. Senate Committee on the District of Columbia, The Improvement of the Park System of the District of Columbia.

6. For more on isolationism in the South and turn-of-the-century attempts to change this ideology, see Link, *The Paradox of Southern Progressivism, 1880–1930*.

7. Land values in Arlington soared as neighborhoods were created, infrastructure was further solidified, and trolley lines continued to expand. *The Monitor* newspaper speculated in 1903 that lands in the early 1900s were worth ten times more than they had been just a decade before, and many contemporaries speculated that even this was an underestimation of Arlington's true wealth and potential. Rose, *Arlington County, Virginia*, 157.

8. "Frank Lyon: Biographical Sketch," 123–25.

9. Glencarlyn Citizens' Association, "GCA Meeting Minutes," 1922, RG 62: Glencarlyn, Box 3, File 7, CLH; Rose, "The Role of Frank Lyon and His Associates in the Early Development of Arlington County."

10. "Frank Lyon: Biographical Sketch," 123–25.

11. Hanchett, *Sorting Out the New South City*, 47–68.

12. Pope, *Shotgun Justice*.

13. Other family members involved in law enforcement include John Mackey (sheriff), Thomas Jefferson Mackey (lawyer), and Richard Mackey (lawyer and judge); Pope, *Shotgun Justice*, 15–25.

14. O'Leary, "The Electoral History of That Part of Alexandria County Now Known as Arlington County: 1870–1920."

15. Dailey, *Before Jim Crow*.

16. RL 00863, William Mahone Papers, 1853–1895, David M. Rubenstein Rare Book and Manuscript Library, Duke University, Durham, North Carolina.

17. Dailey, *Before Jim Crow*.

18. Link, *The Paradox of Southern Progressivism, 1880–1930*; Rose, *Arlington County Virginia*, 131; Birge et al., "Democratic Politics in the 8th District of Virginia, 1886"; Pope, *Shotgun Justice*.

19. Rose, *Arlington County Virginia*; Pope, *Shotgun Justice*.

20. Full League membership can be found within Ball, *Mt. Olivet Methodist: Arlington's Pioneer Church*, 99.

21. Lee, *A History of Arlington County, Virginia*.

22. McGerr, *A Fierce Discontent*; Woodward, *The Origins of the New South*, 235–63; Link, *The Paradox of Southern Progressivism*; Dittmer, *Black Georgia in the Progressive Era*.

23. Link, *The Paradox of Southern Progressivism*.

24. Pope, *Shotgun Justice*; Throughout its history, Ballston was also known as both Birch's Crossroads and Ball's Crossroads; Templeman, "Ballston's Beginnings."

25. Frank Ball quoted in Ball, *Mt. Olivet Methodist* (1965), 97–99.

26. Rose, *Arlington County, Virginia*, 151.

27. Lyon purchased *The Monitor* newspaper in 1901; Rose, *Arlington County Virginia*, 165.

28. Dittmer, *Black Georgia in the Progressive Era*; Link, *The Paradox of Southern Progressivism*; Dailey, *Before Jim Crow*.

29. Dailey, *Before Jim Crow*.

30. Pope, *Shotgun Justice*.

31. Virginia General Assembly, *Virginia State Constitution*, Article II, Sections 18–19 (1. http://confinder.richmond.edu/admin/docs/Virginia_1902.pdf.

32. Wythe W. Holt, "The Virginia Constitutional Convention of 1901–1902: A Reform Movement Which Lacked Substance" *The Virginia Magazine of History and Biography*, 76, no. 1 (January 1968), 67–102; Virginia General Assembly, *Virginia State Constitution*, Article II, Sections 18–19 (1902); Holt, "Virginia's Constitutional Convention of 1901–1902," 204–06.

33. "Tomorrow Will Be An Eventful Day," *Alexandria Gazette*, May 22, 1901. LOC

34. Dabney, *Virginia: The New Dominion*.

35. Link, *The Paradox of Southern Progressivism*, 79. For then-contemporary evidence of this sentiment, see the writings of Thomas Dixon's "Trilogy of Reconstruction."

36. Carter Glass, "Address" (Virginia Constitutional Convention, Richmond, Virginia, 1902).; Pope, *Shotgun Justice*, 24.

37. Woodward, *Origins of the New South, 1877–1913*, 235–63; Pope, *Shotgun Justice*.

38. Pope, *Shotgun Justice*.

39. The neighborhood was spelled both "Johnson" and "Johnston" throughout its early founding but was spelled "Johnson" by the early decades of the twentieth century; Rose Jr., "The Map of Arlington in 1878—Places and People," 17–33.

40. Crandal Mackey received three hundred twenty-three votes to Johnston's three hundred twenty-one; Frank O'Leary, "The Electoral History of That Part of Alexandria County Now Known as Arlington County: 1870–1920."

41. "Alexandria Affairs," July 24, 1903, *The Evening Star.*; Pope, *Shotgun Justice*, 35.

42. Arlington citizens Walter Varney and Richard Johnston filed suit against Mackey claiming fraud, but the suit was abruptly dropped by Johnston in December of 1903; Article about dispute between Mackey and Johnston, *Alexandria Gazette*, 1903. Chronicling America: Historic American Newspapers. LOC. http://chroniclingamerica.loc.gov.

43. Mackey, A Brief History of Alexandria County, Virginia, 25–26.

44. Arlington County Government, *A Guide for Justices of the Peace.*; Shafer, "Recreation in Arlington, 1870–1920," 63; January23, 1892, Article on Rosslyn, *The Evening Star*, p 5. Chronicling America: Historic American Newspapers. LOC. http://chroniclingamerica.loc.gov/lccn/sn83045462/1892–01–23/ed-1/seq-5/; Troxell, "80 Year Old Resident Tells of Laying First Sidewalks."

45. Ball, *Mt. Olivet Methodist*, 98–99.

46. Ball, *Mt. Olivet Methodist*, 98–99.; Link, *The Paradox of Southern Progressivism*, 58–72, 239–67.

47. Fisher, "Lyon Village," 15. Vertical File: Lyon Village, CLH.

48. Pope, *Shotgun Justice*, 66.; Lee, *A History of Arlington County, Virginia*.

49. *The Evening Star*, 1904, Article about the raid; Pope *Shotgun Justice*, 66.

50. *The Evening Star*, 1904, Eyewitness account of the raid; Pope, *Shotgun Justice*, 66.

51. Pope, *Shotgun Justice*, 66–67.

52. "Article," *The Evening Star*, 1904, Article about the raid; Vogel, *The Pentagon*, 108.

53. The false narrative that these Black communities were entirely made of criminal elements that required the League men to rehabilitate them was reiterated in histories of the area; Lee, *A History of Arlington County, Virginia*.

54. *Barcroft News*, November 9, 1903, Arlington on League politics. http://bscl.org/1903news.htm.

55. *Washington Star*, 1892, Article about Arlington saloons; Pope, *Shotgun Justice*. 45.

56. For fears on interracial socializing and drinking see Link, *The Paradox of Southern Progressivism*, 42–46, 95–123; Dittmer, *Black Georgia in the Progressive Era, 1900–1920*, 102–22. For attacks on Black neighborhoods see Hunter, *To 'Joy My Freedom*, 4–20.

57. Mr. Ernest W. Bowen and Mrs. Josephine Pollard Mitchell, interview by Elsie Smith, 1970, Hall's Hill Oral History Project, CLH.

58. Mr. Ernest W. Bowen and Mrs. Josephine Pollard Mitchell, interview by Elsie Smith, 1970, Hall's Hill Oral History Project, CLH. The Thompsons lived in the Jefferson District. It is possible that she and her family also lived in Johnson's Hill. *United States Census, 1880* (Washington, DC: Government Printing Office) database with images, *FamilySearch* (https://familysearch.org), Sarah Thompson in household of Chas Thompson, Alexandria, Alexandria, Virginia,

United States; citing enumeration district 3, sheet 329D, NARA microfilm publication T9 (Washington DC: National Archives and Records Administration, n.d.), roll 1351; FHL microfilm 1,255,351.

59. Margaret L. Bendroth, "Church Architecture and Community in 20th Century Arlington" (unpublished paper, ca. 1990), RG 6: Arlington Churches, Box 4, CLH.

60. Netherton, *Arlington County in Virginia.*

61. *US Census, 1900* (Washington, DC: Government Printing Office); *US Census, 1910* (Washington, DC: Government Printing Office).

62. Arlington County Will Books, Will Book 10, 306.

63. The line opened in 1906 but was under construction when Mackey began his subdivision; Williams, *The Washington and Old Dominion Railroad.*

64. *Arlington County Deed Books,* Deed Book 115: 184-185; Deed Book 131: 558-560.

65. Mackey, *A Brief History of Alexandria County.*

66. Rose, Arlington County, Virginia, 157; Clements, "Lots" (advertisement) ca. 1900; Mackey, A Brief History of Alexandria County, Virginia, 42.

67. O'Leary, "The Electoral History of That Part of Alexandria County Now Known as Arlington County: 1870–1920"; Porter, *County Government in Virginia, A Legislative History, 1607–1904.*

68. Charles I. Simms, "Simms Real Estate" (advertisement), ca. 1900; Mackey, *A Brief History of Alexandria County, Virginia,* 46.

69. Lyon and Fitch, Inc., "The Book of Washington: Lyon Village," 1930, Vertical File: Lyon Village, CLH.

70. Amy Ballard, "Historical Analysis of Lyon Park" (unpublished paper, May 1988), 5, Vertical File: Lyon Park, CLH.

71. Clarendon Citizens Association, *Clarendon, Virginia,* ca. 1920, brochure, Vertical File: Lyon Park, CLH.

72. Lyon and Fitch, "The Book of Washington: Lyon Village," 1930, Vertical File: Lyon Park, CLH.

73. Ballard, "Historical Analysis of Lyon Park" (1988), CLH.

74. *Nelson's Suburban Directory* (1912–1913), 213–14; (1916), 311–17; (1917), 295–301; (1918), 307–13; (1923), 423–30; *Polk's Washington Suburban Directory* (1927–28), 655–58; (1930–31), 437–39.

75. Mackey, *A Brief History of Alexandria County, Virginia,* 36.

76. Mackey, *A Brief History of Alexandria County, Virginia,* 36; Forney, "Editorial"; Green, Washington: Village and Capital, 1800–1878, 15.

77. *Arlington County Deed Books,* Deed Book U3-W3, p. 321; Walter, "The Original Developers of Barcroft."

78. Carlin Springs Syndicate, "Carlin Springs" (advertisement), 1887, RG 8: Glencarlyn, Box 1, File 1, CLH.

79. Rose, *Arlington County, Virginia,* 157; James E. Clements, "Lots" (advertisement) ca. 1900; Mackey, *A Brief History of Alexandria County, Virginia,* 42.

80. Mr. Samuel Krigbaum, interview by Mary Ellen Didion, February 25, 1988, Vertical File: Lyon Village, CLH.

81. Rose, *Arlington County Virginia,* 222.; National Register of Historic Places, *Ashton Heights Historic District,* 127.

82. Pertinent Acts of Assembly affecting Arlington's representation in the General Assembly are: Ch. 162 /1870–71; Ch. 121/1877–78 ; Ch. 674 and Ch.

567 /1901–02; Ch. 140 and Ch. 271/ 1922; Ch. 387/1942; and Ch. 17 and Ch. 18/1952. A R egister of the General Assembly of Virginia, 1776-1918, and of the Constitutional Conventions by E. G. Swem and John W. Williams (Public Printer, Richmond, 1918).

83. Mackey, *A Brief History of Alexandria County, Virginia*, 26.

84. American Realty Exchange "Alcova Heights" (advertisement), ca. 1915, Vertical File: Alcova Heights, CLH.

85. Rose, *Arlington County Virginia*, 157.; Clarendon Citizens Association, *Clarendon, Virginia*, ca. 1920, brochure, Vertical File: Lyon Park, CLH.

86. Clarendon Citizens Association, *Clarendon, Virginia*, ca. 1920, brochure, p. 36, Vertical File: Lyon Park, CLH.

87. "Record no. 773 from the Circuit Court of Alexandria County" filed with the Virginia Supreme Court of Appeals in the case of *The City Council of Alexandria v. Alexandria County, et al.*; Office of the County Manager, Arlington, "A History of the Boundaries of Arlington County, Virginia."

88. Office of the County Manager, Arlington, "A History of the Boundaries of Arlington County, Virginia." For more information on the impact of annexation on African American communities within the lands transferred to Alexandria City, see Moon, "The African American Housing Crisis in Alexandria, Virginia, 1930s-1960s," 28–68; Rose Jr., "Annexation of a Portion of Arlington County by the City of Alexandria in 1915," 22–36.

89. Advertisements for the community began ca. 1907, and construction was underway by 1910.; Mackey, *A Brief History of Alexandria County, Virginia*, 48.; Arlington County Government, *Aurora/ Virginia Highlands—Preliminary Draft of Committee, Reports Neighborhood Conservation Program*, by Aurora Highlands Civic Association, August 1969, RG 15: Neighborhood Civic Association, Box 22, CLH.

90. Mackey, *A Brief History of Alexandria County, Virginia*, 48.

91. Lewis Manufacturing Co. and George H. Rucker and Co. were Lyon's primary builders. Clarendon Citizens Association, *Clarendon, Virginia*, ca. 1920, brochure, p 47. Vertical File: Lyon Park, CLH.

92. Fisher, "Lyon Village," 15, CLH.

93. National Register of Historic Places, *Lyon Park Historic District, Arlington County, Virginia*, Section 8, p. 174.

94. Mackey, A Brief History of Alexandria County, Virginia, 48; Arlington County Government, Aurora/ Virginia Highlands—Preliminary Draft of Committee, Reports Neighborhood Conservation Program, by Aurora Highlands Civic Association, August 1969, RG 15: Neighborhood Civic Association, Box 22, CLH.

95. US Pharmacopoeia Convention, *Pharmacopeia of the United States* (Philadelphia: 1905), xxiv; Netherton, *Arlington County in Virginia*.

96. Halpin, "Sears, Roebuck's Best-kept Secret," 24–29; Murray, "Mail-Order Homes Sears Sold in 1909–37 Are Suddenly Chic"; Schwartz, "When Home Sweet Home Was Just a Mailbox Away," 90–101; Goldberger, "Mail-Order House Plans: Are You Ranch or Tudor?"; Mapes, "Sears House More Than Just a Home."

97. Originally houses were unnamed. The Newman model was likely "Model no. 52," selling for between seven hundred eighty-two dollars and nineteen hundred ninety-five dollars in 1908; Sears, Roebuck & Co. "Model Home no. 52,"

10; Newman "Eighty Years in a Sears Mail-Order House: The Newmans of Cherrydale."

98. Stephenson and Jandl, *Houses by Mail.*

99. Sears, Roebuck & Co., "Model Home no. 102—The Hamilton," 12. This home model was sold from 1908 to 1914.

100. "Lot no. 25," Alexandria County Deed Book Y-4, p. 210, Vertical File: Black History—2, CLH.

101. Alexandria County Deed Book 165, p. 20.

102. Alcova Improvement Company, "Deed," 1916, CLH.

103. Fox and Wright Co.; Map of Corbett, from Arlington County Deed Book N4, pp. 448–89; Walter, "The Original Developers of Barcroft."

104. Barcroft School and Civic League, 1908, Vertical File: Barcroft, CLH; McQuade, *History of Barcroft Community,* Vertical File: Barcroft, CLH.

105. Healey, "Clarendon Alexandria County Directory," Vertical File: Clarendon, CLH.

106. Rosslyn Civic Association, Directory and Year Book, Rosslyn; Rose, Arlington County Virginia, 159.

107. Mackey, *A Brief History of Alexandria County, Virginia,* 54

108. Lyon and Fitch, "The Book of Washington: Lyon Village," 27, Vertical File: Lyon Park, CLH.

109. *The Monitor,* 1903, Article about Arlington's suburban growth; Rose, *Arlington County, Virginia,* 157.

Chapter 4: "So That We May Occupy Our Rightful Place"

1. Source for quotation used in the chapter title: Elks, Proclamation, 1927, RG 11: Papers of Edmund C. Fleet, Box 3, File 7, CLH.

2. *Bennett v. Garrett,* 132 VA 397 (Opinion June 15, 1922); *Cases Decided in the Supreme Court of Appeals of Virginia,* CXXXII (Richmond: David Bottom, Superintendent of Public Printing, 1922), 400.

3. African Americans from nearby Fairfax County and Alexandria City also attended these churches; Alexandria City Government, *Finding The Fort.*

4. *US Census, 1930, Arlington, Virginia* (Washington, DC: Government Printing Office).

5. Office of the County Manager, Arlington, "A History of the Boundaries of Arlington County, Virginia."

6. Marcia M. Miller, *St. John's Baptist Church: Arlington, Virginia* (Virginia: St. John's Baptist Church Pamphlet, October 31, 1988), RG 6: Arlington County Churches, Box 4, CLH.

7. Marcia M. Miller, *St. John's Baptist Church.*

8. "History of the Rowe Family" (unpublished paper, n.d.), Vertical File: Black History 1, CLH.

9. Arlington School Board, "Meeting Minutes: Summary" (20 September 1922).

10. "Interview with Margaret Evelyn Wright" (15 December 1974), oral history project, Arlington County Library, CLH.

11. Arlington Deed Book B, p. 441; Arlington County School Board, "Minute Book, No. 4-6" 1905-1915.

12. *City Council of Alexandria v. Alexandria County et al.,* Record no. 773 (Virginia Supreme Court of Appeals, 1915).

13. *US Census, 1900* (Washington, DC: Government Printing Office); *US Census, 1910* (Washington, DC: Government Printing Office).

14. Henry and Ammon are brothers. Elks, "Elk Membership," 1924, RG 11: Papers of Edmund C. Fleet, Box 3, CLH.

15. N.E. Fleet to Arlington Lodge no. 384, November 27, 1923, RG 11, Box 3, File 4, CLH; *United States Census, 1910* (Washington, DC: Government Printing Office) database with images, *FamilySearch* (https://familysearch.org/ark:/61903/1:1:MPGB-NFY: accessed 28 August 2015), Edmund C. Fleet Jr. in household of Edmund C. Fleet Sr., Arlington, Alexandria, Virginia, United States; citing enumeration district (ED) 9, sheet 7B, family 153, NARA microfilm publication T624 (Washington, DC: National Archives and Records Administration, n.d.); FHL microfilm 1,375,633.

16. "Biography of Charles Drew," The Charles R. Drew Papers, Profiles in Science Series, National Library of Medicine, Bethesda, Maryland. https://profiles.nlm.nih.gov/ps/retrieve/Narrative/BG/p-nid/336.

17. Cooper recollection in Taylor, *Bridge Builders of Nauck/ Green Valley* (2015).

18. Elks, Proclamation, 1927, RG 11: Papers of Edmund C. Fleet, Box 3, File 7: Minutes and Resolutions 1924–5, CLH.

19. Bunch-Lyone and Douglas, "The Falls Church Colored Citizens Protective League and the Establishment of Virginia's First Rural Branch of the NAACP"; Office of the County Manager, Arlington, "A History of the Boundaries of Arlington County, Virginia."

20. Because of this, the development of the Falls Church branch of the NAACP is very much connected to Arlington's Black community. John F. Bethune, Mayor to Senator Frank L. Ball, January 31, 1930, RG 12: Papers of Frank L. Ball, Box 1, File 1, CLH.

21. Town of Nauck, Arlington Deed Book B, p. 441.

22. *United States Census, 1910* (Washington, DC: Government Printing Office).; Richard Lewis in household of James Washington, Washington, Alexandria, Virginia, United States, citing enumeration district (ED) 14, sheet 2B, family 41, NARA microfilm publication T624 (Washington, DC: National Archives and Records Administration, n.d.); FHL microfilm 1,375,633.

23. As of the 1870 Census, there were seven Robinson children ages three to sixteen years. In his oral history, Benjamin "Benny" Robinson, the fifth child and second boy, mentions only one sister, although he had three; Sara Collins et al. *Freedman's Village: Arlington's First Free Neighborhood; United States Census, 1870* (Washington, DC: Government Printing Office) index and images, *FamilySearch* (https://familysearch.org/ark:/61903/1:1:MFGK-VXT: accessed 18 April 2015), Benjamin H. Robinson in household of B. H. Robinson, Virginia, United States; citing p. 72, family 217, NARA microfilm publication M593 (Washington DC: National Archives and Records Administration, n.d.); FHL microfilm 553,157; Benjamin "Benny" Robinson, interview by William Moris, November 6, 2003, Hall's Hill Oral History Project, CLH.

24. His childhood home was located at Nineteenth Road and Twenty-First Street North, Arlington, Virginia. Benjamin "Benny" Robinson, interview by William Moris, November 6, 2003, Hall's Hill Oral History Project, CLH.

25. For the impacts of federal employment on Black suburban community development in the Washington area, see Bird, "Building Community: Housing for Middle-Class African Americans in Washington, DC, and Prince George's County, Maryland, 1900–1955."

26. *United States Census 1900* (Washington, DC: Government Printing Office); Howell and Taylor, "Map of Alexandria County, Virginia for the Virginia Title Co.," [1900], Map Division, LOC; Arlington County Register of Historic Places, *Reevesland, Torreyson Farm*, by Beth Bolling (Arlington, March 2002).

27. Arlington County Government, Williamsburg Neighborhood Conservation Plan, 1–41.

28. Arlington County Government, *Community Voices: The Nauck Community Heritage Project*, by Arlington Cultural Affairs.

29. Brown, *Upbuilding Black Durham*; Alexandria City Government, *Finding The Fort*; Richardson, *Built By Blacks*, 49–69.

30. Mr. Ernest W. Bowen and Mrs. Josephine Pollard Mitchell, interview by Elsie Smith, 1970, Hall's Hill Oral History Project, Center for Local History, Arlington Central Library, Arlington, Virginia.; Katherine Mosley Ross, interview by Annon, 1995, RG 103: Freedman's Village, Box 2, File 30, CLH.

31. Arlington County Government, *High View Park Neighborhood Conservation Plan*, by Evelyn Bell, Darnell Carpenter, Daphine Ruffner, Inez Waynes, Frank Wilson, and Sherri Young (Virginia, January 1992).

32. O'Brien "Historic Survey of Nauck Neighborhood, Arlington County, Virginia" (unpublished paper, December 1987), CLH.; Mr. Ernest W. Bowen and Mrs. Josephine Pollard Mitchell, interview by Elsie Smith, 1970, Hall's Hill Oral History Project, CLH.

33. Taylor, Bridge Builders of Nauck/Green Valley, 17.

34. Ernest Bowen worked as a delivery boy for the community store in Johnson's Hill. Mr. Ernest W. Bowen and Mrs. Josephine Pollard Mitchell, interview by Elsie Smith, 1970, Hall's Hill Oral History Project, CLH.

35. Sharpless, *Cooking in Other Women's Kitchens*.

36. *United States Census, 1900* (Washington, DC: Government Printing Office) database with images, *FamilySearch* (https://familysearch.org/ark:/61903/1:1:MMF6 -ZQ7: accessed 19 September 2015), John Chase, Arlington District, Alexandria, Virginia, United States; citing sheet 8B, family 173, NARA microfilm publication T623 (Washington, DC: National Archives and Records Administration, n.d.); FHL microfilm 1,241,698.

37. Margaret Evelyn Wright, interview by Terry Townsend, Zonta Oral History Project Program, December 15, 1974, CLH.

38. Wright, interview by Townsend.

39. New Washington, Hydraulic Press, West Brothers, Walker Sons, Potomac, Virginia, Rosslyn, and Jackson-Phillips Brick Companies. Mackey, *A Brief History of Alexandria County, Virginia* (1907), p. 29.

40. Mr. Ernest W. Bowen and Mrs. Josephine Pollard Mitchell, interview by Elsie Smith, 1970, Hall's Hill Oral History Project, CLH.

41. Louise Gray, quoted in Oswald G. Smith, *Mount Zion Centennial, 1866–1966* (Virginia: Mount Zion Baptist Church Pamphlet, 1966), RG 6: Arlington County Churches, Box 3, File 1–18, CLH; Suburban Trust Company, *Suburban Trust Salutes: West Brothers Brick Company* (Virginia Suburban Trust Company Pamphlet), Vertical File: Brick Works, CLH.

42. Department of Defense measurements bring the towers to four hundred to six hundred feet, respectively, on their two-hundred-foot elevation on a hill.

43. Electromagnetic frequency information on radio waves courtesy of the Naval Facilities Engineering Command, Washington.

44. Statistics for the years 1900 to 1910. Donald B. Dodd, [comp.] *Historical statistics of the United States: Two centuries of the census* (1993).
45. Smith, "Cooper, Esther Georgina Irving."
46. The pair was married in September of 1913. Smith, "Cooper, Esther Georgina Irving."
47. The remaining twenty-five percent of federal workers were primarily made up of elected officials' constituents who lobbied for jobs. Yellin, *Racism in the Nation's Service.*
48. Federal Civil Service Act, 5 USC § 2101 (1871); Pendleton Civil Service Reform Act (1883), ch 27, 22 Stat. 403.
49. Masur, "Patronage and Protest in Kate Brown's Washington."
50. *US Census, 1910*, Leonard L. Gray, Employment (Washington, DC: Government Printing Office).
51. *US Census, 1910*, Solomon H. Thompson, Employment (Washington, DC: Government Printing Office).
52. *US Census, 1920. Heads of Families.* Arlington, Virginia. Neighbors to Solomon H. Thompson (Washington, DC: Government Printing Office).
53. Hadassah Backus, "Glencarlyn" (unpublished paper, 1952), RG 8: Glencarlyn, Box 2, CLH.
54. Statistics for 1907. Yellin, *Racism in the Nation's Service* (2013).
55. Other medical professionals include Hall's Hill residents Dr. Edward T. Morton and midwife Rebecca Williams. Arlington County Government, *High View Park Neighborhood Conservation Plan*, by Bell et al. (Virginia, January 1992).
56. National Register of Historic Places, *Harry W. Gray House*, by Jennifer Bunting Hallock, May 2003.
57. Arlington County Government, *High View Park Neighborhood Conservation Plan*, by Bell et al. (Virginia, January 1992).
58. *US Census, 1930, Arlington, Virginia*, Solomon H. Thompson: Employment Information (Washington, DC: Government Printing Office).
59. Gray worked for the US Government from 1872 to 1913. National Register of Historic Places, *Harry W. Gray House*, by Jennifer Bunting Hallock, May 2003.
60. Yellin, Racism in the Nation's Service.
61. Foltz, The Federal Service as Career; Yellin, Racism in the Nation's Service.
62. *US Census, 1930, Arlington, Virginia*, Neighbors to Solomon H. Thompson (Washington, DC: Government Printing Office).
63. Dittmer, Black Georgie in the Progressive Era, 1900–1920, 110–22.
64. Yellin, *Racism in the Nation's Service*, 102.
65. Virginia. Index of Acts of the General Assembly of the Commonwealth of Virginia [title varies] (Richmond, 1912–2000). KFV2440.A5.
66. *City Council of Alexandria v. Board of Supervisors* (Circuit Court of Arlington County, VA 1927); Rose Jr., "The 1929 Annexation from Arlington by Alexandria," 13–18; Arlington County Office of the County Manager, *Acts of Assembly*, ch. 167 (Virginia, 1930); Office of the County Manager, Arlington, "A History of the Boundaries of Arlington County, Virginia" (Virginia: 1955, 2011).
67. The City Council of Alexandria v. Alexandria County, et al., 117 Va. 230; Brief on Behalf of Arlington County, in the Circuit Court of Arlington County, City Council of Alexandria vs. Board of Supervisors of Arlington County; and the Common Law Order Books of the Arlington Circuit Court; Bunch-Lyone et al.,

"The Falls Church Colored Citizens Protective League and the Establishment of Virginia's First Rural Branch of the NAACP."

68. Alexandria County, *Deed Book* 165, 20.

69. *Buchanan v. Waverly*, 245 US 60 (1917).

70. Connerly, *The Most Segregated City in America*.

71. For more on how federal changes shaped residential segregation on the local level, see Lands, *The Culture of Property*.

72. Dieter, "Early Planning Progress in Arlington County, Virginia to 1945."

73. Arlington County Government, Acts of Assembly, "Special Act of 1927," 1927; Dieter, "Early Planning Progress in Arlington County, Virginia to 1945."

74. Wilson, *The City Beautiful Movement: Creating the North American Landscape*.

75. Radford, *Modern Housing for America*, 29–58.

76. Allen J. Saville, Inc., "Windsor Farms, a Residential Development on the James River at Richmond" (Richmond, VA: A. Hoen & Co, 1926).

77. Arlington County Government, *Zoning Ordinance Adopted by Board of Supervisors of Arlington County*, by Edward Duncan, et. al (Virginia, April 26, 1930), 1.

78. Arlington County Government, *Zoning Ordinance*, 12.

79. Arlington County, *Deed Book* 124, 14–16.

80. In 1962, the United States Commission on Civil Rights found that zoning and planning laws created in the northern Virginia suburbs of Washington, DC, throughout the previous decades were designed to "force Negroes out of established areas"; US Commission on Civil Rights, *Housing in Washington, D.C.*, 40–44.

81. Walter, *Barcroft: The Beginnings of a Suburban Neighborhood*.

82. Perry et al., "'We Didn't Have Any Other Place to Live.'"

83. Harry Gray Gillem, "The Arlington View Community—A Pillar for Arlington Neighborhood Conservation Program" (unpublished paper, 1985), RG 103: Freedman's Village, Box 1, File 2, CLH.

84. Thomas H. West, "US Census 1940," Sheet no. 64B.; Taylor, *Bridge Builders of Nauck/Green Valley*, 17.

85. O'Brien, "Historic Survey of Nauck Neighborhood, Arlington County, Virginia."

86. Arlington County Government, Neighborhood History Preservation Study of Hall's Hill, High View Park.

87. Benjamin "Benny" Robinson, interview by William Moris, Hall's Hill Oral History Project, November 6, 2003, CLH.

88. O'Brien, "Historic Survey of Nauck Neighborhood, Arlington County, Virginia."

89. "Row Houses Condemned," *The Arlington Courier*, August 11, 1938; Dieter, "Early Planning Progress in Arlington County, Virginia to 1945," 34.

90. For more on the use of racially restrictive zoning and planning laws used to side-step *Buchannan v. Waverly*, see Hanchett, *Sorting Out the New South City*; Wiese, *Places of Their Own*; Sugrue, *Sweet Land of Liberty*; Connerly, *The Most Segregated City in America*; Connolly, *A World More Concrete*.

91. Arlington County Government, *Zoning Ordinance Adopted by Board of Supervisors of Arlington* County, by Edward Duncan et al. (Virginia, April 26, 1930); Dieter, "Early Planning Progress in Arlington County, Virginia to 1945."

92. Pertinent Acts of Assembly affecting Arlington's representation in the General Assembly are: Ch. 162 /1870–71; Ch. 121/1877–78; Ch. 674 and Ch. 567 /1901–02; Ch. 140 and Ch. 271/ 1922; Ch. 387/1942; and Ch. 17 and Ch. 18/ 1952 X.

93. Arlington County Government, *Zoning Ordinance Adopted by Board of Supervisors of Arlington* County, by Edward Duncan et al. (Virginia, April 26, 1930), p. 1.

94. Arlington County Board, *Nauck Village Action Plan* (Virginia, July 10, 2004), p. 11.

95. Perry and Waters, "Southern Suburban/Northern City."

96. Perry and Waters, "Southern Suburban/Northern City," 664.

97. Perry and Waters, "Southern Suburban/Northern City," 664; James E. Taylor, interview by Chloe E. Muhammed, January 30, 2004, Hall's Hill Oral History Project, CLH.

98. Leonard L. Gray, "US Census, 1930," LV7G-DNP.

99. Arlington County Government, *Zoning Ordinance Adopted by Board of Supervisors of Arlington* County, by Edward Duncan et al. (Virginia, April 26, 1930).

100. Franklin Survey Co., "Atlas of Arlington County, Virginia" [1938], Plate Nos. 7, 22, Map Collection, CLH.; Arlington County Government, *Waycroft Woodlawn Neighborhood Conservation Plan*, by the Waycroft-Woodlawn Civic Association (Virginia, May 2012).

101. Arlington County Government, *High View Park Neighborhood Conservation Plan*, by Bell et al. (Virginia, January 1992).

102. Kast, "It's Getting Easier to Get to Hall's Hill," B-1.

103. Thompson's boarder was a middle-aged African American woman named Harriet H. Hopkins. *US Census, 1920*, Solomon B. Thompson (Washington, DC: Government Printing Office). Claude Richard took in a fellow bricklayer, John (age 18), and H. Hanson took in two boarders, M. Cooper (age 27, servant) and A. Cooper (age 67, farmhand). *US Census, 1900* (Washington, DC: Government Printing Office).

104. *US Census, 1910* (Washington, DC: Government Printing Office); "Platt of Queen City," *Alexandria County Deed Book* N-4, p. 265 (9 June 1892), CLH.

105. Testimony of John D. Normoyle, in City Legal Counsel *City Council of Alexandria v. Board of Supervisors* (Circuit Court of Arlington County, VA 1912).

106. By the 1920s, Arlington had approximately seven thousand homes countywide which were seventy-five percent owner occupied. A majority of Arlington's African American neighborhoods were consistent with these levels of home ownership.

107. *Evening Star* (Washington, DC), June 1, 1926.

108. Rose, "The Role of Frank Lyon and His Associates in the Early Development of Arlington County," 46–59.

109. John M. Johnson was testifying to the state of the county's water supply, arguing that the condition of groundwater is not an issue because all white neighborhoods have access to potable water beyond wells. There is no mention of the state of wells or water access in Black communities. Testimony of John M. Johnson, City Legal Counsel, Record No 773, *City Council of Alexandria v. Board of Supervisors* (Circuit Court of Arlington County, VA 1927).

110. Glencarlyn Citizens' Association, "GCA Meeting Minutes," RG 62: Glencarlyn, Box 3, File 7, CLH.

111. Arlington County Board, *Nauck Village Action Plan* (Virginia, July 10, 2004).

112. C. L. Kinnier, Directing Engineer, "Map of Road Improvements, Arlington Virginia" [1928–1931], Map Collection, CLH. Maps mark unpaved streets in Hall's Hill, for example, into the late 1950s. *Sanborn Fire Insurance Map from Arlington*

County, Arlington County, Virginia. Sanborn Map Company, Vol. 1 June 1950, Vol. 2 June 1959. Geography and Map Division, LOC.

113. William H. Pelham Sr., interview by Edmund D. Campbell and Cas Cocklin, November 21, 1986, 6–7, Arlington County Library Oral History Program, CLH.

114. "The Day a Yankee Gunboat Came: Memories Bind Him to Hill," 31.

115. "Towns Near the Capitol Where Negroes . . .," *The Washington Star,* January 26, 1908, Vertical File: Queen City, CLH.

116. Volin was born in 1903. *United States Census, 1930* (Washington, DC: Government Printing Office) index and images, *FamilySearch* (https://familysearch .org/), George E. Volin, Jefferson, Arlington, Virginia, United States; citing enumeration district (ED) 0015, sheet 7A, family 171, line 48, NARA microfilm publication T626 (Washington D.C.: National Archives and Records Administration, 2002), roll 2436; FHL microfilm 2,342,170.

117. Arlington County Government, "Candidates for County Board," November 1931; "Colored Physician Files In Arlington," *Washington Post,* July 31, 1931.

118. McDonnell. "U.S. Employees Dominate Arlington County Election."

119. Virginia House of Delegates, Voter Code, Chapter 14, Title 15, Section 15.1–669.

120. Anderson, "Arlington Adopts the County Manager form of Government," 64.

121. Virginia Legislature, "House Journal," 1930, p. 321; Arlington County Civic Federation, Petition to Judge Walter T. McCarthy of the Circuit Court on October 1, 1930.; "Arlington Votes for Manager Rule in County Offices," *The Evening Star,* November 5, 1930.

122. Virginia Legislature, Code of Virginia, Sec. 15.1–694 (1930).

123. County Engineer and Planning Engineer C. L. Kinnier headed the renaming of Arlington's streets. *The Arlington County Street System Guide* (Arlington County: Department of Public Works, 1984).

124. From 1932 to 1975, there were only four county managers: Roy S. Braden (1932–36), Frank C. Hanrahan (1936–47), A. T. Lundberg (1947–62), and Bert W. Johnson (1962–75).

125. MacLean, Behind the Mask of Chivalry; Wood, Lynching and Spectacle.

126. Ball, "Electric Railways of Arlington," 31–40.

127. George W. Keys testifies that Alexandria City saw two lynchings between 1900 and 1903. *City Council of Alexandria v. Alexandria County et. al.,* Record no. 773 (Virginia Supreme Court of Appeals, 1915); Rose, "Annexation of a Portion of Arlington County by the City of Alexandria in 1915," 31.

128. Pope, *Shotgun Justice;* McGerr, *A Fierce Discontent.*

129. Hopkins, "Atlas of Fifteen Miles Around Washington: 1878." For more on the life and times of Kate Brown, see Masur, "Patronage and Protest in Kate Brown's Washington," 1047–71.

130. "Kate Dodson," *Chicago Daily Tribune,* August 20, 1880.

131. 1868; US Congress, Senate, Committee on the District of Columbia, Report of the Committee on the District of Columbia, 40 Cong., 2 sess., 1868, S. Com. Rep. 131, p. 12. On ladies' cars and segregation, see, for example, Welke, "When All the Women Were White, and All the Blacks Were Men," 261–316; Coleman, "Black Women and Segregated Public Transportation: Ninety Years of Resistance," 295–302; Minter, "The Failure of Freedom," 993–1009; and Mack, "Law, Society, Identity, and the Making of the Jim Crow South," 377–74.

132. Meier and Rudwick, "Negro Boycotts of Segregated Streetcars in Virginia, 1904–1907," 479–87.

133. Editorial Writer, *The Planet*, Richmond, Virginia, April 6, 1904; Meier and Rudwick, "Negro Boycotts of Segregated Streetcars in Virginia, 1904–1907," 480.

134. Ball, "Electric Railways in Arlington."

135. "ALEXANDRIA'S 'JIM CROW' LAW: Lively Episode that Occurred on the Trolley One Day Last Week." *Washington Post*, February 21, 1904; Ball "Electric Railways of Arlington."

136. Ball, "Electric Railways in Arlington," 38.

137. Ball, "Electric Railways in Arlington," 38.

138. Bunch-Lyone et al., "The Falls Church Colored Citizens Protective League and the Establishment of Virginia's First Rural Branch of the NAACP."

139. Ball, "Electric Railways in Arlington."

140. The Hicks line began about 1924 but could not compete with multiple white businesses—including the R.L. May bus line; later, the Alexandria, Barcroft, and Washington (AB&W) line; and the Washington, Maryland and Virginia bus line. Hicks closed during the Depression years; Harwood, *Rails to the Blue Ridge*; *McGraw Electric Railway Manual*; McGraw, *Official Guide of the Railways*; Washington & Old Dominion Railway—Timetable, 1934 Arlington & Fairfax Railroad—Timetable, 1935 Washington & Old Dominion Railroad—Timetable, 1939.; Benjamin "Benny" Robinson, interview by William Moris, November 6, 2003, Hall's Hill Oral History Project, CLH.

141. Benjamin "Benny" Robinson, interview by William Moris, November 6, 2003, Hall's Hill Oral History Project, CLH.

142. MacLean, Behind the Mask of Chivalry.

143. *Washington Tribune*, November 11, 1927.

144. Robert Nickerson, interview by Stanford; Stanford, *Suburban Black Elderly* (1978).

145. Perry et al., "'We Didn't Have Any Other Place to Live.'"

146. *Washington Tribune*, November 11, 1927; Virginia Legislature, Code of Virginia, Sec. 15.1–694 (1930).

147. Washington, DC, had the highest urban Black population in 1910. "Census of Population and Housing from 1790–2000," US Census Bureau. Library of Virginia, Historical Census Browser; Taylor, *In Search of the Racial Frontier*, 193.

148. Manning "Inside Facts of the Washington Riots"; David F. Krugler, *1919, The Year of Racial Violence: How African Americans Fought Back*, 94.

149. Other growing tensions of the time regarding modernization, the Red Scare, and economic recession were also contributing factors to racial violence. Dittmer, *Black Georgia in the Progressive Era*, 203; MacLean, *Behind the Mask of Chivalry*; Wood, *Lynching and Spectacle*.

150. Krugler, *1919, The Year of Racial Violence*.

151. Krugler, *1919, The Year of Racial Violence*, 73.

152. Domeratzky, "Howard Fields Sheriff Since 1924," newspaper clipping, April 21, 1938, Vertical File: Black History 3, CLH; "Towns Near the Capitol Where Negroes . . . ," *The Washington Star*, January 26, 1908, Vertical File: Queen City, CLH.

153. Micale, "First Rural NAACP: A Response to Threat of Residential Segregation in Falls Church"; Perl, "Race Riot of 1919 Gave Glimpse of Future Struggles," A1.

154. Love, One Blood: The Death and Resurrections of Charles Drew.

155. National Register of Historic Places, *Charles Richard Drew House*, May 11, 1976; Love, *One Blood*.

156. US Census Bureau, "Households by Type and Size: 1900 to 2002," in *Statistical Abstracts of the United States* (2003), 19. https://www.census.gov

157. Mr. Ernest W. Bowen and Mrs. Josephine Pollard Mitchell, interview by Elsie Smith, 1970, Hall's Hill Oral History Project, CLH.

158. *US Census, 1900* (Washington, DC: Government Printing Office) database with images, *FamilySearch* (https://familysearch.org), John Chase, Arlington District, Alexandria, Virginia, United States; citing sheet 8B, family 173, NARA microfilm publication T623 (Washington, DC: National Archives and Records Administration, n.d.); FHL microfilm 1,241,698.

159. *US Census, 1900* (Washington, DC: Government Printing Office) database with images, *FamilySearch* (https://familysearch.org), Henry L. Holmes, Arlington District, Alexandria, Virginia, United States; citing sheet 8A, family 152, NARA microfilm publication T623 (Washington, DC: National Archives and Records Administration, n.d.); FHL microfilm 1,241,698.

160. John M. Langston Citizens Association formed in Hall's Hill in 1924. Arlington County Government, *High View Park Neighborhood Conservation Plan*, by Bell et al. (Virginia, January 1992).

161. *Bennett v. Garrett*, 132 VA 397 (Opinion June 15, 1922); *Cases Decided in the Supreme Court of Appeals of Virginia*, CXXXII (Richmond: David Bottom, Superintendent of Public Printing, 1922), 400.

162. "Population of Counties: Virginia. 1890–1990," in Forstall, US Bureau of the Census, *Population of States and Counties of the United States: 1790 to 1990 from the Twenty-one Decennial Census* (Washington, DC: 1996); O'Brien "Historic Survey of Nauck Neighborhood, Arlington County, Virginia," 175.

163. Rose, *Arlington County, Virginia*.

164. Gregory, *The Southern Diaspora*; Perry et al., "'We Didn't Have Any Other Place to Live.'"

Chapter 5: "Everybody Was Coming to Washington in Those Days"

1. Source for quotation used in chapter title: Margorie Downey, interview by Steve Vogel, February 11, 2004.

2. Rose, *Arlington County, Virginia: A History*, 247–48.

3. *US Census, 1970* (Washington, DC: Government Printing Office), Verlin W. Smith Collection, Box B-52, VHS; Perry, Reybold, and Waters, "'Everybody was Looking for a Good Government Job,'" 719–41.

4. Estabrook, "Washington & Old Dominion: Former Interurban in Northern Virginia," 42–46.

5. National Register of Historic Places, *Glebewood Village Historic District*, by Jana E. Riggle and Laura V. Trieschmann, August 2003.

6. Perry et al., "'Everybody Was Looking for a Good Government Job'"; *US Census, 1970* (Washington, DC: Government Printing Office), Verlin W. Smith Collection, Box B-52, VHS.

7. Hoover Airport (1926) became a federal installation in 1930 and was expanded to National Airport in 1938; Vogel, *The Pentagon: A History*, 39.

8. *US Census, 1930* (Washington, DC: Government Printing Office) and *US Census, 1940* (Washington, DC: Government Printing Office) NARA digital publication (Washington, DC: National Archives and Records Administration); Hill, "Census: More people moving to D.C."

9. Rose, *Arlington County, Virginia*.

10. Hofstadter, *The Age of Reform*.

11. Hofstadter, *The Age of Reform*; Schwarz, *The New Dealers*.
12. "Census of Population and Housing from 1790–2000," US Census Bureau. Library of Virginia, Historical Census Browser.
13. Smith, "Butler Holmes Subdivision" (unpublished paper, ca. 1940). RG 11: Papers of Edmund C. Fleet, Box 4, File 7, CLH.
14. Many African Americans employed by the federal government held custodial jobs; Perry et al., "'Everybody Was Looking for a Good Government Job.'"; Perry, "The Influence of Geography on the Lives of African American Residents of Arlington County."
15. Mary Gardner became Mary Scales and, eventually, Mary Koblitz. Mary P. Koblitz, interview by Shawna Helene Reed, December 3, 2003, Hall's Hill Oral History Project, CLH.
16. Perry et al., "'Everybody Was Looking for a Good Government Job.'"
17. African American pull was strong enough to make Washington, DC, among the major cities of the "Black metropolis," along with other destinations like New York and Chicago; Gregory, *The Southern Diaspora*, 11–43, 133–153.
18. Dennis Domer, "Escaping the City," 65–90.
19. Perry et al., "'Everybody was Looking for a Good Government Job.'"
20. Domer, "Escaping the City," 1–53.
21. Perry et al., "'Everybody was Looking for a Good Government Job.'"
22. In 1938, of African Americans employed in civil service jobs in Washington, DC, ninety percent were custodial, 9.5% were clerical, and 0.5% were subprofessional; Perry et al., "'Everybody Was Looking for a Good Government Job.'"
23. Vogel, *The Pentagon*, 313.
24. These were "general schedule" GS-2 or GS-3 positions. In the 1940s, federal employees at level GS-4 made sixteen hundred dollars annually; Vogel, *The Pentagon*; Reverend David T. Ray, "Integration of Church" (Unpublished Paper, July 1964), RG 6: Churches, Box 4, File: Our Lady Queen of Peace. CLH.
25. Mary Gardner worked at the Pentagon for about four years before postwar downsizing made her position redundant. Mary P. Koblitz, interview by Shawna Helene Reed, December 3, 2003, Hall's Hill Oral History Project, CLH.
26. Esther Irving Cooper taught stenography and shorthand at the National Training School for Women and Girls, and taught business at Arlington County Public Schools; Taylor, *Bridge Builders of Nauck/Green Valley*.
27. Ms. Dole previously lived in Clarksville, Virginia. Celestine Dole, interview by Steve Vogel, April 2004.
28. Reverend David T. Ray, "Integration of Church" (unpublished paper, July 1964), RG 6: Churches, Box 4, File: Our Lady Queen of Peace. Arlington Central Library, Center for Local History. Arlington, Virginia. For examples about how Arlington's middle-class population related to elite Black populations in other areas at the time, see Smith, II, *Racial Democracy and the Black Metropolis*.
29. Lula Mae Graham, interview by Eleanor Edwards, December 4, 2003, Hall's Hill Oral History Project, CLH.
30. This family recently moved from North Carolina for the husband's job in the government. Lula Mae Graham, interview by Eleanor Edwards, December 4, 2003, Hall's Hill Oral History Project, CLH.
31. Lula Mae Graham, interview by Eleanor Edwards, December 4, 2003, Hall's Hill Oral History Project, CLH.; *United States Census, 1940* (Washington, DC: Government Printing Office) database with images, *FamilySearch* (https://

familysearch.org/ark:/61903/1:1:VRY7-Y3F: accessed 31 May 2016), Lula M Graham in household of Linton Graham, Arlington County, Arlington, Virginia, United States; citing enumeration district (ED) 7–7, sheet 9B, family 161, NARA digital publication T627 (Washington, DC: National Archives and Records Administration, 2012), roll 4245.

32. Graham, interview by Edwards.

33. Wiese, *Places of their Own*, 34–66, 143–163.

34. Murphy and Ames Lumber, *Anniversary in Arlington*, 1948, brochure, RG 51: Murphy and Ames Business Files, CLH.

35. "Old Firm in New Quarters," *Northern Virginia Sun*, April 16, 1953, RG 51: Murphy and Ames Business Files, CLH.

36. Murphy and Ames provided upwards of seventy jobs to local residents, some positions were held by African American laborers. "Old Firm in New Quarters," *Northern Virginia Sun*, April 16, 1953, RG 51: Murphy and Ames Business Files, CLH; Friedman, *Covert Capital*, 33.

37. Vogel, *The Pentagon*, 79–104.

38. Arlington Forest Citizens' Association, "Arlington Forest Neighborhood Conservation Plan," 5–12. In the early 1940s, a skilled bricklayer was paid $1.75 per hour. This was about sixty cents an hour lower than the most skilled laborers in the area, such as an iron foreman, but it was still a good salary. Vogel, *The Pentagon*, 179.

39. Friedman, *Covert Capital*, 44.

40. Day laborers were paid only two dollars per hour into the 1950s and 1960s. Although $1.75 per hour marked a skilled labor position in the early 1940s, one to two decades later, this same pay scale could not match postwar inflation and cost of living rates. Friedman, *Covert Capital*, 33.

41. James "Jimmy" E. Taylor, interview by Chloe E. Muhammed, January 30, 2004, Hall's Hill Oral History Project, CLH.

42. Murphy and Ames Lumber, *Anniversary in Arlington*, 1948, brochure, RG 51: Murphy and Ames Business Files, CLH.

43. Arlington County Government, *Zoning Ordinance Adopted by Board of Supervisors of Arlington* County, by Edward Duncan et al. (Virginia, April 26, 1930).

44. In 1958, nearly two hundred homes and undeveloped land sold at public auction for suburban development. "Notice of Sale for Real Estate" (advertisement), November 5, 1958, Verlin W. Smith Collection, Box B-52, VHS; Arlington County Government, *Columbia Forest Neighborhood Conservation Plan*, by Columbia Forest Neighborhood Conservation Plan Committee (Virginia, November 2000), 13.

45. Lyon and Fitch, "The Book of Washington: Lyon Village," 1930, Vertical File: Lyon Park, CLH; "Home" (advertisement), ca. 1930–50, Vertical File: Lyon Park, CLH; Arlington County Government, *Arlington Forest Neighborhood Conservation Plan*, by Arlington Forest Citizen's Association (Virginia, November 14, 1990), 1.

46. Friedman, *Covert Capital*, 33.

47. Kennedy, "Arlington."

48. Cohen, *A Consumer's Republic*, 194–256.

49. National Capital Planning Commission, *Transportation Plan: National Capital Region* (Washington, DC, 1959), James J. McDonnell Transportation Collection, George Mason University: Special Collections and Archives, Fairfax, Virginia (hereinafter abbreviated as SC&A).

50. Regional Highway Planning Committee, *Washington Metropolitan Area Transportation Study: A Recommended Highway Improvement Program*, Volume 4 (Washington, DC: Department of Highways, 1952), James J. McDonnell Transportation Collection, SC&A.

51. The National Capital Region included Washington, DC; the counties of Loudon, Prince William, Fairfax and Arlington, and the cities Falls Church and Alexandria in Virginia; and Prince George's and Montgomery Counties in Maryland. National Capital Planning Commission, *Transportation Plan: National Capital Region* (Washington, DC, 1959), James J. McDonnell Transportation Collection, SC&A.

52. Regional Highway Planning Committee, *Washington Metropolitan Area Transportation Study: A Recommended Highway Improvement Program*, Volume 4 (Washington, DC: Department of Highways, 1952), James J. McDonnell Transportation Collection, SC&A.

53. Commonwealth of Virginia, Department of Highways, *Henry G. Shirley Memorial Highway Improvement* (Virginia, July 2, 1962), James J. McDonnell Transportation Collection, SC&A.

54. Allard, "Arlington, 50 Years Ago: Continuity and Change," Arlington Historical Society: 50th Anniversary Celebration (2006), CLH. Allard was a longtime member and former president of the Society.

55. Commonwealth of Virginia, Department of Highways, *Henry G. Shirley Memorial Highway Improvement* (Virginia, July 2, 1962), James J. McDonnell Transportation Collection, SC&A.

56. Allard, "Arlington, 50 Years Ago: Continuity and Change," Arlington Historical Society: 50th Anniversary Celebration (2006), CLH.

57. Commonwealth of Virginia, Department of Highways, *Henry G. Shirley Memorial Highway Improvement* (Virginia, July 2, 1962), James J. McDonnell Transportation Collection, SC&A.

58. Arlington County Government, *Dominion Hills Neighborhood Conservation Plan*, by Dominion Hills Civic Association (Virginia, December 11, 2004), 56; Arlington County Government, *Tara Leeway Heights Neighborhood Conservation Plan* (Virginia, April 2005), 8–12.

59. Netherton and Netherton, *Arlington County in Virginia*; Arlington County Government, *Arlington Forest Neighborhood Conservation Plan*, by Arlington Forest Citizen's Association (Virginia, November 14, 1990), 1. Arlington Forest is bordered by Carlin Springs Road and George Mason Drive to the north, North Henderson Road, Second Street North, North Pershing Drive, and Arlington Boulevard to the east, and Glencarlyn Park and the Washington and Old Dominion trail to the south and west.

60. Homes were advertised for fifty-nine hundred fifty dollars. "Home" (advertisement), ca. 1930–50, Vertical File: Lyon Park, CLH.

61. Arlington County Government, *Arlington Forest Neighborhood Conservation Plan*, by Arlington Forest Citizen's Association (Virginia, November 14, 1990), 14–17.

62. The main phases of construction are from 1939 to 1946, with all major neighborhood construction completed by 1951. Arlington County Government, *Arlington Forest Neighborhood Conservation Plan*.

63. Bellevue Forest Citizen's Association, "History," *Bellevue Forest Blog*, 2014. http://www.bellevueforest.org.

64. Kennedy, "Arlington."

65. "Rosslyn: Today-Tomorrow-Future," *Washington World* (November–December 1964). Verlin W. Smith Collection, VHS.

66. The Pomponio family concentrated on office buildings, constructing the Lyon Building, the Donata Building, and five other office buildings which were in planning or construction phases in the early 1960s. "Rosslyn: Today-Tomorrow-Future," *Washington World*.

67. The DeLashumutt family constructed the FHA-funded Barcroft Apartments. They were inspired by 1935's Colonial Village apartments, discussed below. Historic Preservation Committee, Arlington, Virginia, *The Barcroft Apartments: Arlington, VA*, by Marilyn M. Harper (April 25, 1986), Vertical File: Barcroft, CLH.

68. Basil served in these political offices from the late 1930s to late 1940s. Historic Preservation Committee, *The Barcroft Apartments*.

69. Radford, *Modern Housing for America*.

70. Early complexes include Radburn in New Jersey (1928), Sunnyside in Queens, New York (1924–1928), and Chatham Village in Pittsburgh (1931); Domer, "Escaping the City," 66.

71. National Register of Historic Places, *Colonial Village*, by Virginia Historic Landmarks Commission Survey, 1979; Domer, "Escaping the City."

72. Smith, "Gustave Ring, Noted Builder in Area, Dies."

73. Radford, *Modern Housing for America*.

74. "Interview with Gustave Ring," *Washington Post*; Smith, "Gustave Ring, Noted Builder in Area, Dies."

75. US Congress, House Committee on Banking and Currency, "National Housing Act: Hearings Before the Committee on Banking and Currency, House of Representatives, Seventy-third Congress, Second Session, HR 9620, a Bill to Improve Nation-wide Housing Standards, Provide Employment, and Stimulate Industry; to Improve Conditions with Respect to Home. . . ." (Washington, DC: US Government Printing Office, 1934).

76. National Register of Historic Places, *Colonial Village*, by Virginia Historic Landmarks Commission Survey, 1979; Domer, "Escaping the City."

77. Twelve buildings designed by DC Architect Harvey Warwick consisting of eighty-five apartments were added in the final phase of construction in the mid-1940s without FHA funding. National Register of Historic Places, *Colonial Village*, by Virginia Historic Landmarks Commission Survey, 1979.

78. "Building Money Series," *Architectural Forum* 71, no. 2 (August 1939): 135.

79. *Architectural Forum, Architectural Record, Insured Mortgage Portfolio*, and several other professional journals covered Colonial Villages. National Register of Historic Places, *Colonial Village*, by Virginia Historic Landmarks Commission Survey, 1979, 9.

80. Bestebreurtje, "Suburbanization and Segregation in Virginia."

81. Jackson, *Crabgrass Frontier*, 190–218.

82. US Federal Housing Administration, "Underwriting Manual, Underwriting and Valuation Procedure Under Title II of the National Housing Act" (Washington, DC, 1938).

83. US Federal Home Loan Corporation, *First Annual Report of the Federal Home Loan Bank Board* (Washington, DC: Government Printing Office, 1933); Jackson, *Crabgrass Frontier*; Woods, "The Federal Home Loan Bank Board,

Redlining, and the National Proliferation of Racial Lending Discrimination, 1921–1950," 1036–59.

84. Glotzer, "Exclusion in Arcadia," 479–94; Woods, "The Federal Home Loan Bank Board, Redlining, and the National Proliferation of Racial Lending Discrimination, 1921–1950."

85. Taylor, "City Growth and Real Estate Cycles," 24.

86. Colean, "An Early FHA Experiment," 86–88; National Register of Historic Places, *Colonial Village*, by Virginia Historic Landmarks Commission Survey, 1979.

87. Domer, "Escaping the City"; Netherton, *Arlington County in Virginia*; National Register of Historic Places, *Colonial Village*, by Virginia Historic Landmarks Commission Survey, 1979.

88. Domer, "Escaping the City."

89. "The Way to Record Breaking Rents," *Architectural Forum* 71 (August 1939): 135.

90. Domer, "Escaping the City"; Netherton, *Arlington County in Virginia*, 66; Bobeczko, "A Study in Decentralized Living," 1–19.

91. Jackson, "The Spatial Dimensions of Social Control," 79–129.

92. *Sun*, "Defense Housing Started Here Under F.H.A. Backing."

93. *Northern Virginia Sun*, Volume 25, Number 229, 2 July 1962.

94. Federal Housing Administration, *The FHA Story in Summary: 1934–1959* (Washington, DC: Office of Government Printing, 1959); National Register of Historic Places, *Garden Apartments, Apartment Houses and Apartment Complexes in Arlington County, Virginia: 1934–1954*, May 22, 2003.

95. Lyon Village Citizen's Association, *Lyon Village Bulletin* (Arlington, Virginia, September 12, 1960), RG 84: Lyon Village, CLH.

96. Lyon Village Citizens' Association, *Lyon Village Bulletin* (Arlington, Virginia, March 1963), RG 84: Lyon Village, CLH.

97. Mrs. Lillian Simms and Mrs. Sue Renfro, interview by Helen Blackwell, March 1983, Arlington County Library Oral History Program, CLH.

98. Today the area is called Aurora Highlands in honor of the three local communities that came together in the late twentieth century to form one larger community—Addison Heights (1896), Aurora Hills (1915), and Virginia Highlands (1930). Simms and Renfro, interview by Blackwell.

99. Aurora Hills is located very near Green Valley and bordering Queen City. Arlington County Government, *Aurora Highlands Neighborhood Conservation Plan: Update*, by Aurora Highlands Civic Association (Virginia, 2008), 4–10.

100. Mrs. Lillian Simms and Mrs. Sue Renfro, interview by Helen Blackwell, March 1983, Arlington County Library Oral History Program, CLH.

101. Lyon Village Citizens' Association, *Lyon Village Bulletin* (Arlington, Virginia, March 1963), RG 84: Lyon Village, CLH.

102. Mrs. Lillian Simms and Mrs. Sue Renfro, interview by Helen Blackwell, March 1983, Arlington County Library Oral History Program, CLH.

103. Lyon Park Citizens Association, *Lyon Park Directory* (Virginia, 1936), Vertical File: Lyon Park, CLH.

104. The Hay home is located at 917 North Danville Street in Arlington. Lyon Park Citizens Association, *Lyon Park Directory* (Virginia, 1936), Vertical File: Lyon Park, CLH; *United States Census, 1940* (Washington, DC: Government Print-

ing Office) database with images, FamilySearch (https://familysearch.org/ark :/61903/1:1:VRY4–6VL: accessed 24 May 2016), Harry E. Hay, Arlington County, Arlington, Virginia, United States; citing enumeration district (ED) 7–25, sheet 11A, family 196, NARA digital publication T627 (Washington, DC: National Archives and Records Administration, 2012), roll 4246.

105. Jeanne M. Holm, and Judith Bellafaire, *In Defense of a Nation*; Hartmann, *The Home Front and Beyond*.

106. Lyon Park Citizens Association, *Lyon Park Directory* (Virginia, 1936), Vertical File: Lyon Park, CLH; *United States Census, 1940* (Washington, DC: Government Printing Office) database with images, *FamilySearch* (https://familysearch .org/ark:/61903/1:1:VRY4-H85: accessed 7 June 2016), Miss Kate Ricker, Arlington County, Arlington, Virginia, United States; citing enumeration district (ED) 7–24, sheet 63B, family, NARA digital publication T627 (Washington, DC: National Archives and Records Administration, 2012), roll 4246.

107. Eleanor Lake, "Twenty Eight Acres of Girls," *The St. Louis Dispatch*, October 1, 1944, Vertical File: Arlington Farm, CLH; Lyon Park Citizens Association, *Lyon Park Directory* (Virginia, 1936), Vertical File: Lyon Park, CLH.

108. Lyon Park Citizens Association, *Lyon Park Directory* (Virginia, 1936), Vertical File: Lyon Park, CLH; *United States Census, 1940* (Washington, DC: Government Printing Office) database with images, *FamilySearch* (https://familysearch .org), Bessie M Blincoe, Arlington County, Arlington, Virginia, United States; citing enumeration district (ED) 7–24, sheet 4A, family 68, NARA digital publication T627 (Washington, DC: National Archives and Records Administration, 2012), roll 4246.; "United States Social Security Death Index," database, *FamilySearch* (https://familysearch.org), Emma Brown, Dec 1974; citing US Social Security Administration, *Death Master File*, database (Alexandria, Virginia: National Technical Information Service, ongoing).

109. *Washington Post*, "Room, Board to Cost Girls in U.S. Dorms Under $50," 20.

110. Lyon Park Citizens Association, "Lyon Park Directory" (1936). Vertical File: Lyon Park, CLH.; *United States Census, 1940* (Washington, DC: Government Printing Office) database with images, *FamilySearch* (https://familysearch.org), Kate Ricker, Arlington County, Arlington, Virginia, United States; citing enumeration district (ED) 7–24, sheet 63B, family , NARA digital publication T627 (Washington, DC: National Archives and Records Administration, 2012), roll 4246.

111. They owned their home at 407 North Bryan Street. Lyon Park Citizens Association, *Lyon Park Directory* (Virginia, 1936), Vertical File: Lyon Park, CLH; *United States Census, 1930* (Washington, DC: Government Printing Office) database with images, *FamilySearch* (https://familysearch.org), Maretta G. Hartshorn, 1930.

112. Vogel, "Oral History Interview of Marjorie Downey."

113. Brinkley, *Washington Goes to War*, 225–51.

114. Mundy, *Code Girls*.

115. Mundy, *Code Girls*, 208–9; Williams and Dickerson, NSA, "The Invisible Cryptologists."

116. Mundy, *Code Girls*; O'Connell, "Secret Weapons," *Arlington Magazine*.

117. NSA, "Organizational Chart, B-3-b," 15 November 1944, NARA; Williams and Dickerson, NSA, "The Invisible Cryptologists."

118. Center for Cryptologic History (CCH), Oral History Interview with Benson K. Buffham, 15 June 1999, NARA. https://ia601307.us.archive.org/view_archive .php?archive=/14/items/Oral-History-Interviews-nsa/Oral%20History %20Interviews.zip&file=Oral%20History%20Interviews%2Fnsa_oh_51_99 _buffham.pdf.

119. The grounds of the Experimental Farm became vacant after the farms relocated to Suitland, Maryland; *Washington Post*, "Planning Unit Picks Sites For Dormitories," 14.

120. Lake, "Twenty-Eight Acres of Girls," *The St. Louis Dispatch*, October 1, 1944, Vertical File: Arlington Farm, CLH.

121. Civilian employees stationed out of local Arlington Hall primarily worked at the Pentagon, Navy Annex, or the Army's Signal Intelligence Service; Lake, "Twenty-Eight Acres of Girls," *The St. Louis Dispatch*, October 1, 1944, Vertical File: Arlington Farm, CLH.

122. CCH, Oral History Interview with Carl Dodd, 14 July 1999, NARA.

123. "Title VI Rental Housing Projects," *Insured Mortgage Portfolio*, 6, no. 3 (First Quarter, 1942), 6.

124. McPherson, "A Large-Scale Community Development: Fairlington," 18–19. For more about federal housing and communities at this time, see Longstreth, "Housing Reform Meets the Marketplace"; Chamberlain, "Permanence in Time of War."

125. Rosenman, "Defense Housing—Are We Building Future Slums or Planned Communities?" 56.

126. Arlington County Government, *Columbia Forest Neighborhood Conservation Plan*, by Columbia Forest Neighborhood Conservation Plan Committee (Virginia, November 2000), 13.

127. "Arlington Sewer Project," *Evening Star* (Washington, DC), March 7, 1942. https://www.loc.gov/item/sn83045462/1942–03–07/ed-1/.

128. *Evening Star* (Washington, DC), August 15, 1940. https://www.loc.gov/item /sn83045462/1940–08–15/ed-1/; James E. Palmer Jr. *Carter Glass: Unreconstructed Rebel*. Roanoke, Virginia: Institute of American Biography, 1938.

129. This figure represents total land used by 1959. The largest of these were the War Department's Pentagon and the Navy Annex, built in 1941 to house overflow personnel from the Department of the Navy. *Trends, Office and Commercial Development for the Years 1960 through 1982* (Arlington: Department of Community Affairs, July 1982), 3.

130. U.S. Army Corps of Engineers, Office of History, "U.S. Army Corps of Engineers in the District of Columbia" (2014).

131. Palmer, "North Harvard Street: Recollections," 17–28.

132. For a comprehensive history of the building and planning process of the Pentagon, see Vogel, *The Pentagon*.

133. Freeland Chew, Arlington County Board Chairman, "Testimony to Senate Committee"; Vogel, *The Pentagon*, 112.

134. Princeton Simms, Evelyn B. Simms, and Vivian Bullock, interview by Judith Knudsen, December 3, 2007, Arlington County Library Oral History Project, CLH.

135. Commonwealth of Virginia, Department of Highways, *Henry G. Shirley Memorial Highway Improvement* (Virginia, July 2, 1962), James J. McDonnell Transportation Collection, SC&A.

136. Both East Arlington and Queen City formed after the closure of Freedman's Village. East Arlington remained a small area adjacent to the Queen City neighborhood (Pelham Town's relationship to Hall's Hill). Because Queen City was, by far, the larger development, relocation information focuses on that area.

137. Vogel, *The Pentagon*, 109.

138. William is the son of Howard Volin, one of George's children. *United States Census, 1940* (Washington, DC: Government Printing Office) database with images, *FamilySearch* (https://familysearch.org/ark:/61903/1:1:VRYH-S2W: 17 May 2014), Howard Volin, Arlington County, Arlington, Virginia, United States; citing enumeration district (ED) 7–39, sheet 7B, family 155, NARA digital publication T627 (Washington, DC: National Archives and Records Administration, 2012), roll 4246. *United States Census, 1930* (Washington, DC: Government Printing Office), database with images, *FamilySearch* (https://familysearch.org/ark:/61903/1:1:C8FJ-BT2: 8 December 2015), George E. Volin, 1930.

139. William Volin, interview by Susan Gilpin, in Gilpin, *Clarendon Metro Tour* (Arlington: January 17, 1985), 1, Vertical File: Clarendon Post 1959, CLH.

140. Jay Downer to Columbus Delano, September 2, 1941, RG 66, NARA; Vogel, *The Pentagon* (2007), 102.

141. Jay Downer, *National Capital Planning Commission Report* (Washington, DC: October 1941); Vogel, *The Pentagon*, 203.

142. Jay Downer to Columbus Delano, September 2, 1941, RG 66, NARA; Vogel, *The Pentagon* (2007), 102.

143. Gertrude Jeffress, interview by Steve Vogel, April 2004.

144. Vogel, *The Pentagon*, 202–05.

145. US Commission on Civil Rights, *Housing in Washington, D.C.* (Washington, DC: Government Printing Office, 1962), 40–44. https://www.law.umaryland.edu/marshall/usccr/documents/cr12h81.pdf; Perry, Crew, Waters, "'We Didn't Have Any Other Place to Live,'" 403–27.

146. Vogel, *The Pentagon*, 202–5.

147. Although some sold for less, the majority of homes in Hall's Hill sold for between five thousand and ten thousand dollars in 1950. According to the FHA, the average cost of a home in the suburbs of Washington, DC in 1950 was seventeen thousand dollars—eight times the amount awarded to Queen City residents. Homes in some of Arlington's nicest white communities, sold for up to thirty-nine thousand dollars in 1946. Arlington County Government, *Hall's Hill—Highview Park Proposed Community Conservation Program*, by James M. Langston Citizens' Association (Virginia, February 13, 1965); US Commission on Civil Rights, *Housing in Washington, D.C.* (Washington, DC: Government Printing Office, 1962), 14–18. https://www.law.umaryland.edu/marshall/usccr/documents/cr12h81.pdf; Colonial Realty County, "Homes" (advertisement), *Washington Post*, November 3, 1946, Verlin W. Smith Collection, Box B-52, VHS.; Stanley R. Rowland, "Home" (advertisement), 1946, Verlin W. Smith Collection, Box B-52, VHS; "Three Nearby Virginia Homes" (advertisement), *Evening Star*, 1946, Verlin W. Smith Collection, Box B-52, VHS.

148. For more on renters' rights and the use of eminent domain to remove African Americans, see Connolly, *A World More Concrete*.

149. Gertrude Jeffress, interview by Steve Vogel, April 2004.

150. Lt. Bob Furman. letter to Civil Aeronautics Administration, September 22, 1941; Vogel, *The Pentagon*, 131.

151. Jay Downer to Columbus Delano, September 2, 1941, RG 66, NARA; Vogel, *The Pentagon*, 202–05; Gertrude Jeffress, interview by Steve Vogel, April 2004.

152. Arlington County Government, *Columbia Heights Neighborhood Conservation Plan*, by Columbia Heights Civic Association (Virginia, November 30, 2004).

153. Ruth Shanklin, interview by Steve Vogel, April 2004.

154. Lamont Mackley, *Mt. Olive Baptist Church* (Arlington, VA: Centennial Souvenir Book, 1974), 4–7. RG 6: Arlington Churches, Box 3, CLH.

155. "Katherine Ross, Oral History Interview," by Cornelia Rose (ca. 1984). Vertical File: Black History—2, CLH.

156. July 1942, Clipped newspaper article describing community destruction, RG 6: Arlington Churches, CLH; Lamont Mackley, *Mt. Olive Baptist Church* (Arlington, VA: Centennial Souvenir Book, 1974), 4–7. RG 6: Arlington Churches, Box 3, CLH.

157. Celestine Dole, interview by Steve Vogel, April 2004.

158. Lt. Bob Furman, letter to Civil Aeronautics Administration, September 22, 1941; Vogel, *The Pentagon* (2007), 131.

159. Eunice, interview by Nancy Perry, October 3, 2012; Perry et al., "'We Didn't Have Any Other Place to Live.'"

160. Cornfield and Weber, "Housing of Federal Employees in the Washington (D.C.) Area in May, 1941"; Bobeczko, "A Study in Decentralized Living."

161. In southern cities like Atlanta, New Orleans, and Birmingham, African American residents experienced insufficient and subpar housing. By 1940, half of all African Americans living in northern cities lived in homes in need of repair; Smith, *The New Deal in the Urban South*, 168; Sterner, *The Negro's Share*, 186–87, 190; Weaver, *The Negro Ghetto*, 66–67. For more on local housing shortages, see Moon, "The African American Housing Crisis in Alexandria, Virginia, 1930s–1960s," 28–68; Perry et al., "'We Didn't Have Any Other Place to Live.'"

162. Celestine Dole, interview by Steve Vogel, April 2004.

163. John Henderson, quoted within Jessica Wallach, "The Loss of a Neighborhood, the Cost of Progress," *The Patch* (October 14, 2011).

164. Trailers went against Arlington' County zoning laws but were allowed in Alexandria City. Vogel, *The Pentagon*, 182.

165. Gertrude Jeffress, interview by Steve Vogel, April 2004.

166. Dunbar Homes was built on land that made up the homestead of community founders Levi and Sarah Jones; Rose, *Arlington County Virginia*; National Register of Historic Places, *George Washington Carver Cooperative Apartments*, by Laura V. Trieschmann and Gerald M. Maready, 2003, 1–23. For more on similar housing developments in Virginia, see Sipe, "Defying the Odds: An Analysis of the Newsome Park Community, Newport News, Virginia, 1943–1966" (lecture, Virginia Forum Conference Presentation, Williamsburg, Virginia, March 3, 2016); Carroll, "The Racial Politics of Place," 514–35.

167. Perry et al., "'We Didn't Have Any Other Place to Live,'" 420.

168. John Henderson, quoted in Jessica Wallach, "The Loss of a Neighborhood, the Cost of Progress" *The Patch*, October 14, 2011.

169. Maggie B. Speller, "Echoes of Alexandria," *The Virginia Arrow*, October 19, 1946, RG 11: Papers of Edmund C. Fleet, Box 4, Arlington Central Library, Center for Local History. Arlington, Virginia.

170. Lamont Mackley, *Mt. Olive Baptist Church* (Arlington, VA: Centennial Souvenir Book, 1974), RG 6: Arlington Churches, Box 3, CLH.

171. Taylor, *Bridge Builders of Nauck/Green Valley.*

172. Three construction companies in Hall's Hill and seven each in Johnson's Hill and Green Valley. All realtors were based out of Johnson's Hill by 1950; Perry and Waters, "Southern Suburban/Northern City," 664.

173. Isolde Weinberg, "New Church Center Spans Gulf Between Ways of Life," *Washington Post,* July 10, 1966, RG 6: Arlington Churches, Box 4, File: Our Lady Queen of Peace, CLH.

174. Arlington County Government, *Hall's Hill—Highview Park Proposed Community Conservation Program,* by James M. Langston Citizens' Association (Virginia, February 13, 1965).

175. National Capital Housing Authority, *Report: Shrinking Negro Neighborhoods* (Washington, DC, 1943); Brinkley, *Washington Goes to War,* 235–36.

176. Carroll, *Up on the Hill,* 15–16.

177. Marcia M. Miller, *St John's Baptist Church, Arlington, Virginia* (Virginia: Brochure, October 31, 1988), 8–12. RG 6: Arlington County Churches, Box 4, CLH.

178. Arlington County Government, *Hall's Hill—Highview Park Proposed Community Conservation Program,* by James M. Langston Citizen's Association (Virginia, February 13, 1965).

179. Perry et al., "'Everybody was Looking for a Good Government Job,'"; Perry et al., "'We Didn't Have Any Other Place to Live.'"

180. Arlington's 1950 total population as 135,449. *United States Census, 1970* (Washington, DC: Government Printing Office), Verlin W. Smith Collection, Box B-52, VHS.

181. In 1940, the entire county was ninety-five percent segregated. Individual neighborhood breakdowns are not possible before 1950 because the areas were not yet defined in individual census tracts. By 1970, Hall's Hill was eighty-four percent Black, and Green Valley and Johnson's Hill were one hundred percent Black; Perry et al., "'We Didn't Have Any Other Place to Live,'" 414–15.

182. Arlington County Government, *Hall's Hill—Highview Park Proposed Community Conservation Program,* by James M. Langston Citizen's Association (Virginia, February 13, 1965).

183. Arlington County Environmental Planning Divisions *Neighborhood Conservation Program, Arlington County Virginia, Nauck* (Virginia, May 1973).

184. Green Valley's population increased by 17.2%, or forty-four hundred sixty-seven people. During those same years, the County's overall population grew by 20.6%, or twenty-seven thousand nine hundred fifty-two people. Arlington County Government, *Report* (Arlington, ca. 1968), 39, RG 6: Arlington County Churches, Box 4, CLH.

185. The Truxton community is in Portsmouth, Virginia; Carroll, "The Racial Politics of Place," 518.

186. Marilyn Chase, "Dunbar Homes: Paying Their Own Way" *Green Valley News,* October 31, 1974. Vertical File: Nauck, CLH.; Thomas O'Brien, "Historic Survey of Nauck Neighborhood, Arlington County, Virginia" (unpublished paper, December 1987), CLH.

187. White developer James A. Hewitt helped secure a loan from a New York-based bank, and lawyers Preston H. Harris (Black) and Roy Halquist (white) helped

with the legal aspects of creating the Cooperative and bidding on the property. Marilyn Chase, "Dunbar Homes: Paying Their Own Way" *Green Valley News*, October 31, 1974. Vertical File: Nauck, CLH.

188. Susan Gilpin, *Clarendon Metro Tour* (Arlington: January 17, 1985), 1, Vertical File: Clarendon Post 1959, CLH.

189. Arlington County Department of Community Affairs, "Clarendon Sector Plan" (n.p., March 1984), 16; "Arlington County, Virginia Annual Report," 1952–1953, 24–25.

190. Longstreth, "The Neighborhood Shopping Center in Washington, D.C., 1930–1941," 5–34; George Kennedy, "Arlington," *Evening Star*, June 5, 1951, CLH.

191. To learn more about these changes in other local areas see Moon, "The African American Housing Crisis in Alexandria, Virginia, 1930s-1960s" 28–68; Cohen, *A Consumer's Republic*, 257–90.

192. National Register of Historic Places, *Colonial Village*, 1980; Arlington County Government, *Arlington Forest Neighborhood Conservation Plan*, by Arlington Forest Citizen's Association (Arlington, November 14, 1990), 5–12; Arlington County Government, *Williamsburg Neighborhood Conservation Plan* (Arlington, January 2001), 33–38; Arlington County Government, *Westover Neighborhood Conservation Plan*, by Westover Committee (Arlington, 1991), 3–6.

193. Seminary Rexall Drugs and Peoples Drugstore. *Hill's Alexandria City Directory* (Alexandria, VA: Hill Directory and Co., 1950), 84; "The Once Ubiquitous Peoples Drug Stores," *Streets of Washington Blog*, December 5, 2011. http://www.streetsofwashington.com/2011/11/once-ubiquitous-peoples-drug-stores.html; "History" *Good health to all from Rexall Blog*, June 14, 2011. http://capnrexall.blogspot.com/2011/06/rexall-history-short-version.html.

194. For more on segregated lunch counters and civil rights demonstrations challenging these accommodations, see the digital history site "Built By the People Themselves." http://lindseybestebreurtje.org/arlingtonhistory/.

195. Jenkins, "Balancing Nauck's Past and Future," Vertical File: Nauck, CLH; Perry et al., "'Everybody was Looking for a Good Government Job.'"

196. "Advertisements," *The Virginia Arrow*, RG 11: Papers of Edmund C. Fleet, Box 4, File 7, CLH.

197. Taylor, *Bridge Builders of Nauck/Green Valley*; Perry et al., "'Everybody Was Looking for a Good Government Job.'"

198. Princeton Simms, Evelyn B. Simms, and Vivian Bullock, interview by Judith Knudsen, December 3, 2007, Arlington County Library Oral History Project, CLH.

199. To avoid fines, Arlington's restaurants ended formal segregation policies in 1956. Simms, Simms, and Bullock, interview by Knudsen.

200. Oliver's husband worked for Buckingham housing complex and Navy Yard; Taylor, *Bridge Builders of Nauck/Green Valley*.

Chapter 6: "We Cannot Lose This Fight as We Lost Our Freedoms during Reconstruction Days"

1. Source for quotation used in chapter title: Morris, "A Chink in the Armor," 329.

2. US Commission on Civil Rights, *Housing in Washington, D.C.* (Washington, DC: Government Printing Office, 1962). https://www.law.umaryland.edu/marshall/usccr/documents/cr12h81.pdf.

3. Rose, *Arlington County Virginia: A History*, 207.

4. Morris, "A Chink in the Armor."

5. US Commission on Civil Rights, *Housing in Washington, D.C.* (Washington, DC: Government Printing Office, 1962). https://www.law.umaryland.edu/marshall/usccr/documents/cr12h81.pdf.

6. McKee, *The People Act*, 147.

7. Lassiter and Lewis, *The Moderate's Dilemma*, 1–21.

8. McKee, *The People Act*, 147.

9. Mrs. Lillian Simms and Mrs. Sue Renfro, interview by Helen Blackwell, March 1983, Arlington County Library Oral History Program, CLH.

10. James Franklin McCall, interview by Debra Murphy, 2001, Veterans History Project, American Folklife Center, LOC. https://memory.loc.gov/diglib/vhp/bib/29772.

11. Hawkins, Black American Military Leaders, 310–11.

12. James Franklin McCall, interview by Debra Murphy, 2001, Veterans History Project, American Folklife Center, LOC. https://memory.loc.gov/diglib/vhp/bib/29772.

13. For Lassiter, Lewis, and Hershman, see Lassiter and Lewis, *The Moderate's Dilemma*; Sugrue, *Sweet Land of Liberty*; Wiese, *Places of Their Own*; Theoharis, "Hidden in Plain Sight," 49–71.

14. In 1950, less than forty percent of US residents graduated high school, but in Arlington most residents had college degrees; McKee, *The People Act*, 148; *United States Census, 2000: Report* (Washington, DC: Government Printing Office), 158.

15. Mrs. Lillian Simms and Mrs. Sue Renfro, interview by Helen Blackwell, March 1983, Arlington County Library Oral History Program, CLH.

16. Mrs. Florence Cannon quoted within "Arlington Women Urged to Study Budget," *The Sun*, September 1948, RG 96, Box 2, Folder 7–2, CLH.

17. Virginia Code Chapter 14, Title 15, Section 15.1–664–9 allows for Counties of less than sixty square miles of highland with a minimum of five hundred inhabitants per square mile to hold special elections for a change in government representation type as long as a minimum of two hundred registered voters sign a petition.

18. Code of Virginia Acts of 1930, Ch. 167, 450 (Michie's Code of 1936, Sections 2773 (10)-2773 (23)).

19. The League of Women Voters, *Arlington Community Guide* (Arlington, Virginia: Pamphlet, 1979). VHS.

20. *Vollin v. Arlington Co. Electoral Bd.*, 216 Va. 674, 222 S.E.2d 793 (Va. 1976).

21. George Volin Jr. of Queen City ran for sheriff, and Mary B. Harris of Green Valley, Dr. Edward T. Morton of Hall's Hill, and C. H. Mosley of Hall's Hill ran for County Board. "Candidates for County Board," November 1931; "Colored Physician Files in Arlington," *Washington Post*, July 31, 1931. http://proquest.com.library.access.arlingtonva.us/docview/150124216?accountid=46215.

22. Harley M. Williams, Better Government League, "Letter to Members," September 1949, RG: 60: Eastman Fenwick Family Papers, CLH.

23. Allard, "Arlington, 50 Years Ago: Continuity and Change," Arlington Historical Society: 50th Anniversary Celebration (2006), CLH.

24. Harley M. Williams, Better Government League, to Members, September 1949, RG: 60: Eastman Fenwick Family Papers, CLH.

25. Williams, *Better Government League*.

26. McKee, *The People Act*, 147–69.

27. Conf. Rec. 76th Cong., 1st Sess., 1939, ch. 410. "The Hatch Activity Act"; Arlingtonians for a Better County, *ABCs of Good Government* (Arlington: Mailer, 1956), RG 60: Eastman Fenwick Papers, Box 71, CLH.

28. Smith, "'When Reason Collides with Prejudice,'" 22–50; Arlington County Civic Federation (ACCF), *Report of Local Government Committee* (Arlington, March 1, 1949), RG 84, Box 2, CLH.

29. Virginia General Assembly, *Virginia State Constitution*, Article II, Section 20 (1902). http://confinder.richmond.edu/admin/docs/Virginia_1902.pdf.

30. League of Women Voters of Arlington, *Voter's Guide: Facts for Voters in Arlington, Virginia* (Arlington: Pamphlet, 1956), RG 60: Eastman Fenwick Family Papers, Box 71, CLH.

31. Lyon Village Citizen's Association, *Lyon Village Bulletin* (Arlington, Virginia, April 1941), RG 84: Lyon Village, CLH.

32. League of Women Voters of Arlington, *Voter's Guide: Facts for Voters in Arlington, Virginia* (Arlington: Pamphlet, 1956), RG 60: Eastman Fenwick Family Papers, Box 71, CLH.

33. Citizens Committee for School Improvement (CCSI), "PTA County Council Stages Voter Drive," *School Improvement Newspaper*, 1 no. 1 (April 1955), RG 60: Eastman Fenwick Family Papers, Box 2, Arlington Central Library, Center for Local History. Arlington, Virginia.

34. Arlington County Civic Federation (ACCF), *Report of Local Government Committee* (Arlington, March 1, 1949), RG 84, Box 2, CLH.

35. Arlington County Government, Poll Tax Records, 1938, 1939, 1940, RG 60: Eastman Fenwick Family Papers, Box 71, Arlington Central Library, Center for Local History. Arlington, Virginia; *United States Census, 1940* (Washington, DC: Government Printing Office) Database with images. *FamilySearch*. http://FamilySearch.org: accessed 2016. Citing the Sixteenth Census of the United States, 1940, NARA digital publication T627. Records of the Bureau of the Census, 1790—2007, RG 29. Washington, DC: National Archives and Records Administration, 2012.

36. The community first grew around Rock Spring Road, which connects Falls Church to the Chain Bridge. In 1946, the home and land of original community founder George Nicholas Saegmuller were sold to make room for this suburban development. It is located in north Arlington and is bounded by Fairfax County on the west, Little Falls and Rock Spring roads on the South, and North Albermarle and Kensington streets to the north and east. Arlington County Government, *Rock Spring Neighborhood Conservation Plan*, by Rock Spring Civic Association (Virginia, March 2009), 5–9.

37. Born in Kootenai County, Idaho, Helmick traveled around the country and the world throughout his childhood, thanks to the military career of his father Major General Eli A. Helmick. Helmick was the Commander Fifth Corps Artillery of the First Army in France. Arlington County Government, *Rock Spring Neighborhood Conservation Plan*, by Rock Spring Civic Association (Virginia, March 2009), 5–9; William Sumner Junkin and Minnie Wyatt Junkin, *The Henckel Family Genealogy, 1500–1960* (Spokane, Washington: CW Hill Printing Company, 1964).

38. Arlington County Government, *Rock Spring Neighborhood Conservation Plan*, by Rock Spring Civic Association (Virginia, March 2009), 5–9.

39. League of Women Voters of Arlington, "History" (February 21, 2010); Mrs. Lillian Simms and Mrs. Sue Renfro, interview by Helen Blackwell, March 1983, Arlington County Library Oral History Program, CLH.

40. Mrs. Lillian Simms and Mrs. Sue Renfro, interview by Helen Blackwell, March 1983, Arlington County Library Oral History Program, CLH.

41. Dean C. Allard, "Arlington, 50 Years Ago: Continuity and Change," Arlington Historical Society: 50th Anniversary Celebration (2006), CLH.

42. Lyon Village Citizen's Association, *Lyon Village Bulletin* (Arlington, Virginia, March 1964), RG 84: Lyon Village, CLH.

43. Bunch-Lyone and Douglas, "The Falls Church Colored Citizens Protective League and the Establishment of Virginia's First Rural Branch of the NAACP."

44. Morris, "A Chink in the Armor."

45. Arlington, Alexandria, and Fairfax county branches made up the NAACP's Seventh District. Virginia was the NAACP's most active Southern state with twenty-two thousand members in 1955. The Seventh District branches were the largest in the state, with a combined total of one thousand fifty-four members. Morris, "A Chink in the Armor."

46. Korstad, "Civil Rights Unionism," 144–166.; Eskew, But for Birmingham.

47. *Butler v. Thompson* (E.D. VA. 1951) https://casetext.com/case/butler-v-thompson-2; Friedman, *Covert Capital*, 1–28.

48. Taylor Jr., *Bridge Builders of Nauck/Green Valley*, 7.

49. Payne, *I've Got The Light Of Freedom*, 265–83; Gilmore, *Gender and Jim Crow*.

50. *Butler v. Thompson* (E.D. VA. 1951) https://casetext.com/case/butler-v-thompson-2; Wallenstein, *Blue Laws and Black Codes*.

51. Princeton Simms, Evelyn B. Simms, and Vivian Bullock, interview by Judith Knudsen, December 3, 2007, Arlington County Library Oral History Project, CLH.

52. Princeton Simms, Evelyn B. Simms, and Vivian Bullock, interview by Judith Knudsen, December 3, 2007, Arlington County Library Oral History Project, CLH.

53. Citizens Committee for School Improvement (CCSI), *Vote for Progressive Democrats* (Arlington, VA: Mailer, August 5, 1947), RG 60: Eastman Fenwick Papers, Box 2, CLH.; Dean C. Allard, "Arlington, 50 Years Ago: Continuity and Change," Arlington Historical Society: 50th Anniversary Celebration (2006) CLH.

54. Harley M. Williams, Better Government League, to Members, September 1949, RG: 60: Eastman Fenwick Family Papers, CLH.

55. Arlington County Government, *History of County PTA Council, Arlington, Virginia, 1931–49*, by Belva Margaret Owens (Arlington, 1950); US Bureau of Education, "Report on the School Building Needs and School Finances of Arlington County, Virginia" (1930), Arlington Historical Society, Research Committee Files.

56. Arlington County Government, *Arlington Convention on School Board Candidates* (Arlington, VA: Flyer, September 1951), RG 60: Eastman Fenwick Family Papers, Box 2, CLH.

57. Dean C. Allard, "Arlington, 50 Years Ago: Continuity and Change," Arlington Historical Society: 50th Anniversary Celebration (2006) CLH.

58. McKee, *The People Act*, 148.
59. Arlington County Government, *History of County PTA Council, Arlington, Virginia, 1931–49*, by Belva Margaret Owens (Arlington, 1950); US Bureau of Education, "Report on the School Building Needs and School Finances of Arlington County, Virginia" (1930), Arlington Historical Society, Research Committee Files.
60. Paraphrase of Fletcher Kemp's statement by Fairlington resident Oscar LeBeau. McKee, *The People Act* (1955), 151.
61. Arlington County Government, *History of County PTA Council, Arlington, Virginia, 1931–49*, by Belva Margaret Owens (Arlington, 1950).; US Bureau of Education, "Report on the School Building Needs and School Finances of Arlington County, Virginia" (1930), Arlington Historical Society, Research Committee Files. Paraphrase of Fletcher Kemp's statement by Fairlington resident Oscar LeBeau. McKee, *The People Act* (1955), 151.
62. Morris, "A Chink in the Armor."
63. Citizens Committee for School Improvement (CCSI), *Objectives* (Arlington, VA: flyer, May 8, 1946), RG: 60: Eastman Fenwick Family Papers, File 2A, CLH.
64. Charles Fenwick, "The School Situation in Virginia" (Press Announcement, Arlington, VA, 24 June 1947). RG: 60: Eastman Fenwick Family Papers, CLH.
65. Arlington County Government, *Arlington Convention on School Board Candidates* (Arlington, VA: Flyer, September 1951), RG 60: Eastman Fenwick Family Papers, Box 2, CLH.
66. McKee, *The People Act*, 148.
67. Harley M. Williams, Better Government League, to Members, September 1949, RG: 60: Eastman Fenwick Family Papers, CLH.
68. McKee, *The People Act*, 147–69.
69. McKee, *The People Act*, 155.
70. Harley M. Williams, Better Government League, to Members, September 1949, RG: 60: Eastman Fenwick Family Papers, CLH.
71. McKee, *The People Act*, 156.
72. Joy worked for the Department of Agriculture, Stahl worked for the Federal Security Agency, Tuthill was a psychology professor at George Washington University, and Campbell was a teacher; McKee, *The People Act*.
73. Arlington County Government, *Arlington Convention on School Board Candidates* (Arlington, VA: Flyer, September 1951), RG 60: Eastman Fenwick Family Papers, Box 2, CLH.
74. Arlington County Civic Federation, *Report, Fiscal Year 1949–1950* (Arlington, 1950), RG 84: Lyon Village Civic Association, Box 3, CLH; McKee, *The People Act*.
75. The information about the NAACP's participation in the selection of candidates is found in the Papers of Barbara Marx, Local NAACP Activity Files, CLH.
76. See Chapter Three, "So That We May Occupy Our Rightful Place"; Taylor, *Bridge Builders of Nauck/Green Valley*.
77. Cooper taught English, shorthand, and typing in Arlington and DC. See Chapter Three, "So That We May Occupy Our Rightful Place"; Taylor, *Bridge Builders of Nauck/Green Valley*, 41.
78. Barbara Ann Mower, "The Vanishing Blacksmith," *The Washington Star*, January 31, 1960, Vertical File: Nauck, CLH.

79. Clarissa Thompson Sligh, *It Wasn't Little Rock* (Visual Studies Workshop Press, 2005), University of Virginia Special Collections and Archives, Charlottesville, Virginia (hereinafter abbreviated as UVA).

80. Stephen Thompson, interview by Clarissa T. Sligh. Sligh, *It Wasn't Little Rock* (2005), UVA.

81. Additionally, the economic realities of many of Arlington's Black families required older children to work. Hoffman Boston High School, *Memory Book 1959 Yearbook* (Arlington, VA: Graduating Class of 1959, 1959), RG 7-B: Records of Hoffman Boston School, Box 1, CLH.

82. Anderson, *The Education of Blacks in the South, 1860–1935*; Anderson, *Literacy and Education in the African American Experience*; Bullock, *A History of Negro Education in the South*; Butchart, *Northern Schools, Southern Blacks, and Reconstruction*; Du Bois, *The Conservation of Races*; DuBois, *Black Reconstruction in America*; Gutman, *The Black Family in Slavery and Freedom*; Jones, *Soldiers of Light and Love*; Leloudis, *Schooling the New South*; Heather Williams, *Self-Taught*.

83. Patterson, *Brown v. Board of Education*.

84. *Carter v. School Board of Arlington County*, 87 F. Supp. 745 (E.D. Va. 1949) (U.S. District Court for the Eastern District of Virginia 1949).

85. Sligh, *It Wasn't Little Rock*.

86. Arlington's population was five percent African American at this time. "Census of Population and Housing from 1790–2000," US Census Bureau. Library of Virginia, Historical Census Browser.

87. *Clarissa S. Thompson et al. v. the County School Board of Arlington*, 159 F. Supp. 567 (E.D. Va. 1957); William Korey, "Prejudice Knocked the Enemy's Sights Out of Focus in the Private War on Barbara Marx," *Midstream*, September 1, 1956. RG 11: Papers of Edmund C. Fleet, Box 4, File 3, CLH.

88. Arlington, Alexandria, and Fairfax Counties made up the NAACP's Seventh District. Virginia was the NAACP's most active Southern state, with twenty-two thousand members in 1955; and the Seventh District was the state's largest chapter, with one thousand fifty-four members. Morris, "A Chink in the Armor."

89. *Brown v. Board of Education of Topeka*, 347 U.S. 483 (1954). https://supreme.justia.com/cases/federal/us/347/483/; Hockett, *A Storm Over this Court*.

90. Muse, *Virginia's Massive Resistance*, 7; *Brown v. Board of Education of Topeka*, 347 US 483 (1954). https://supreme.justia.com/cases/federal/us/347/483/.

91. *Richmond Time-Leader*, November 15, 1954, p 4, Article describing Arlington's school integration process; Arlington County Public Schools, "Facts Concerning Segregation and Integration" (Arlington, VA: Flyer, November 1954).

92. Arlington County Public Schools, *Problems of Integration in Arlington Public Schools*, by Committee to Study Problems (Arlington, VA: Meeting Minutes, ca. 1956).

93. The measure was popular in southside Virginia voting districts at a rate of four to one; however, it lost in Arlington County. Lassiter, et al., *The Moderate's Dilemma*.

94. Morris, "A Chink in the Armor," 343.

95. Smith, "'When Reason Collides with Prejudice," 22–50.

96. Gates, *The Making of Massive Resistance*; Lassiter and Lewis, "Massive Resistance Revisited," 1–21.

97. US Congress. *Congressional Record*, 84th Cong., 2nd sess., 1956. 103, pt. 4; Lassiter, et al., "Massive Resistance Revisited," 1–21.

98. Alex Haley, "A Candid Conversation With The Fanatical Führer of The American Nazi Party," *Playboy Magazine* (April 1966).

99. Rockwell was born in Bloomington, Illinois, in 1918, educated at Brown University and the Pratt Institute of Art in Brooklyn, and served as a Navy pilot in World War II and Korea. He was assassinated in Arlington in 1967 by fellow Nazi party member John Patler over control of the organization. Baker and Gresham, "Nazi Rockwell Is Slain in Arlington"; Graham, "Rockwell's Murder Leaves Nazi Party Flagging for Dead"; Hildreth, "Patler Found Guilty, Jury Delivers 20-Year Sentence."

100. George Rockwell, "Rockwell Report," *The American Nazi Party Magazine*, 1962. RG 60: Eastman Fenwick Family Papers, Box 2, CLH.

101. Rockwell became famous for promoting the slogan "White Power"; Haley, "A Candid Conversation With The Fanatical Führer of The American Nazi Party."

102. Floyd Fleming lived in Washington, DC. Another local resident, Noel Arrowsmith Jr. from Baltimore, also donated property to the group; Kelly and Clifford, "Rockwell in Public, Rockwell in Private."

103. William Korey, "Prejudice Knocked the Enemy's Sights Out of Focus in the Private War on Barbara Marx," *Midstream*, September 1, 1956. RG 11: Papers of Edmund C. Fleet, Box 4, File 3, CLH.

104. Marx's neighbors, Mr. and Mrs. Jack Orndorff, originally filed for integration on behalf of their son Eugene, but they dropped out only days after news of the court case broke because of threats of violence. Korey, "Prejudice Knocked."

105. "Virginia at Crossroads," *Richmond Times Dispatch*, January 4, 1959. Governor J. Lindsay Almond Papers, Section 4, Box 28, VHS.

106. "Arlington, Va., May Defy State On Issue Of School Integration," *Courier Journal*, May 18, 1958. Almond Papers, VHS.

107. "Arlington Private Schools," George Herman, *CBS News*, aired August 21, 1958, on CBS. Civil Rights Digital Library, Digital Library of Georgia. http://crdl.usg .edu/do:ugabma_wsbn_39536.

108. *Clarissa S. Thompson et al. v. the County School Board of Arlington*, 159 F. Supp. 567 (E.D. Va. 1957). The Thompsons were one of four original families signed onto the case. They were joined by the Hamm and Stother (African American) families, and the Marx and Orndorff (white) families. The Orndorffs dropped out because of threats made before the trial.

109. Sligh, *It Wasn't Little Rock*.

110. Born in 1913, Ethel came to the area shortly after graduating from high school at the age of twenty-one; Sligh, *It Wasn't Little Rock*.

111. "Text of Judge Bryan's Ruling on Arlington" *The Evening Star*, September 17, 1958. J. Lindsay Almond Papers, Box 27, VHS.

112. "Arlington, Va., May Defy State On Issue Of School Integration," *Courier Journal*, May 18, 1958. Almond Papers, VHS.

113. Sligh, *It Wasn't Little Rock*.

114. School Board members were once again appointed by the County Board. Arlington County Government, *Arlington View Neighborhood Conservation Plan*, by Bert W. Johnson, County Manager (Arlington, 1965), 5.

115. Virginia General Assembly, *Pupil Placement Act* (Richmond, September 29, 1956), Records of the Virginia Pupil Placement Board, 1957–66, Library of Virginia, Richmond, Virginia.

116. "Text of Judge Bryan's Ruling on Arlington" *The Evening Star*, September 17, 1958. J. Lindsay Almond Papers, Box 27, VHS.

117. Student "A" was not admitted to a white school despite passing all but the "adaptability" test, because this student was an elementary schooler who would have attended the white Patrick Henry Elementary on their own. Judge Bryan ruled that having to attend on one's own would cause too much pressure. "Text of Judge Bryan's Ruling on Arlington" *The Evening Star*, September 17, 1958. J. Lindsay Almond Papers, Box 27, VHS.

118. Morris, "A Chink in the Armor."

119. Young Democrats Club of Arlington, *An Old Fashioned Candidates Rally* (Arlington, VA: pamphlet, June 12, 1965). RG 60: Eastman Fenwick Papers, CLH.

120. "Theda O. Henle, Obituary," *Washington Post*, April 2005.

121. Arlington Committee to Preserve Public Schools (ACCPS), "Mission Statement" (Arlington, VA: May 1958).

122. Peter B. Bart, "Vexed Virginians: Spreading Impacts of School Closings Worries Businessmen and Parents," *The Wall Street Journal*, September 28, 1958. Governor Lindsay J. Almond Papers, Section 4, Box 27, VHS.

123. "Biography," File: Joel T. Broyhill, Box C-34: Virginia (State of) Politics, Verlin W. Smith Collection. VHS.; Congressional Record, 84th Congress Second Session. 102, part 4. Washington, DC: Governmental Printing Office, 12 March 1956. 4459–60; "Broyhill's Net Worth Put at $3.89 Million" *The Washington Star*, August 26, 1974. Verlin W. Smith Collection, Box C-34: Virginia (State of) Politics, VHS.

124. "Broyhill's Net Worth Put at $3.89 Million" *The Washington Star*, August 26, 1974. Verlin W. Smith Collection. Box C-34: Virginia (State of) Politics, VHS.

125. Massive resistance effectively ended with the integration of Arlington and Norfolk public schools in February of 1959 and was formally found unconstitutional by the courts in April of 1959; Hershman Jr., "Massive Resistance Meets Its Match," 104–33.

126. "Text of Judge Bryan's Ruling on Arlington" *The Evening Star*, September 17, 1958. J. Lindsay Almond Papers, Box 27, VHS.

127. Krupsaw, "The Day Nothing Happened."

128. "Film Gathers Voices of Arlington's School Fight." RG 7-B: Records of Hoffman Boston High School, CLH.

129. Jones, "Four Enter School in Arlington" *Richmond Times Dispatch*, February 3, 1959. Governor J. Lindsay Almond Papers, Section 4, Box 28, VHS.

130. Jones, "Negroes to Enter Arlington School," *Richmond Times Dispatch*, February 2, 1959, Governor J. Lindsay Almond Papers, Section 4, Box 28, VHS.

131. "Film Gathers Voices of Arlington's School Fight." RG 7-B: Records of Hoffman Boston High School, CLH.

132. John Connors, "Violence ruled out in Arlington crisis" *Richmond News Leader*, July 31, 1958. Almond Papers, Box 25. VHS.

133. "School Group Has 'Chat' With Almond," *The Roanoke Times*, July 29, 1958; John Connors, "Violence Ruled Out In Arlington Crisis," *Richmond News Leader*, July 31, 1958. Almond Papers, Box 26. VHS.

134. *Invitation to ABC's 6th Annual Convention* (Arlington, VA: Mailer, May 1960). RG 60: Eastman Fenwick Papers, Box 71, CLH; "Theda O. Henle, Obituary," *Washington Post*, April 2005.

135. Edmund D. Campbell, "Oral History Interview of Theda Henle" (April 9, 1984), Oral History Collection, CLH.

136. Jones, "Four Enter School in Arlington, *Richmond Times Dispatch*, February 3, 1959. Governor J. Lindsay Almond Papers, Section 4, Box 28, VHS.

137. Sligh, *It Wasn't Little Rock*.

138. Jones, "Four Enter School in Arlington," *Richmond Times Dispatch*, February 3, 1959. Governor J. Lindsay Almond Papers, Section 4, Box 28, VHS.

139. In June 1960, Black students graduating from Stratford were asked not to attend prom by Principal Richmond; Morris, "A Chink in the Armor," 357.

140. Allan Jones, "Four Enter School in Arlington," *Richmond Times Dispatch*, February 3, 1959. Governor J. Lindsay Almond Papers, Section 4, Box 28, VHS.

141. Sligh, *It Wasn't Little Rock*.

142. Thomasina ("Tammy") was the daughter of Gloria Thompson, niece of Clarissa Thompson, and granddaughter of Ethel Thompson; Sligh, *It Wasn't Little Rock*.

143. Arlington County Government, *Hall's Hill—Highview Park Proposed Community Conservation Program*, by James M. Langston Citizen's Association (Virginia, February 13, 1965).

144. Residents with a high school degree increased from fifty people in 1950 to sixty people in 1960, and residents with a college degree increased from only seven people in 1950 to nineteen people in 1964; Arlington County Government, *Hall's Hill*.

145. For more on the development of this connection between homeowner rights and civil rights in the Black and white communities, see Connolly, *A World More Concrete*.

146. For more on the appeal of suburban environments to African Americans during the late twentieth century, see Wiese, "'The House I Live In,'" 99–119; Connolly, *A World More Concrete*; and Wiese, *Places of Their Own*.

147. Jenkins, "Balancing Nauck's Past and Future." Vertical File: Nauck, CLH.

148. Lyon Village Citizen's Association, *Lyon Village Bulletin* (Arlington, Virginia, June 1963), RG 84: Lyon Village, CLH.

149. Mr. E. L. Hamm and Mary H. Hicks to Arlington County Board, February 28, 1956; Arlington County Government, *Hall's Hill—Highview Park Proposed Community Conservation Program*, by James M. Langston Citizen's Association (Virginia, February 13, 1965).

150. Arlington County Government, *Hall's Hill—Highview Park Proposed Community Conservation Program*, by James M. Langston Citizen's Association (Virginia, February 13, 1965).

151. Arlington County Government, *Neighborhood Conservation Program, Arlington County, Virginia: Nauck*, by Department of Environmental Affairs Planning Division (Arlington, September 1973).

152. Arlington County Government, *Hall's Hill—Highview Park Proposed Community Conservation Program*, by James M. Langston Citizen's Association (Virginia, February 13, 1965).

153. Netherton and Netherton, *Arlington County in Virginia*; Regional Highway Planning Committee, "Washington Metropolitan Area Transportation Study: A Recommended Highway Improvement Program" Vol. 4 (Washington, DC:

Department of Highways, 1952) James J. McDonnell Transportation Collection, Box 8, SC&A.

154. Elen Anderson, "Planner Tom Moore Loves a Challenge" *Northern Virginia Sun*, May 27, 1959, Verlin W. Smith Collection, Box B-52, Folder: Arlington County VA (1959–1977), VHS.

155. "Urban Renewal Comparison," *Washington World Magazine*, Nov.-Dec. 1964. Verlin Smith Collection, Box B-52. File: Arlington County, VA (1959–1977), VHS.

156. Arlington County Planning Commission, *A Summary of the Master Plan of Arlington County, Virginia* (Arlington, 1961). RG 84: Records of the Lyon Village Civic Association, Box 9, CLH; Arlington County Government, *General Land Use Plan*, by Department of Community Planning, Housing and Development (Arlington, 1961).

157. Arlington County Government, *General Land Use Plan*, by Department of Community Planning, Housing and Development (Arlington, 1961).

158. Elen Anderson "Planner Tom Moore Loves a Challenge" *Northern Virginia Sun*, May 27, 1959, Verlin W. Smith Collection, Box B-52, Folder: Arlington County VA (1959–1977), VHS.

159. Eighty percent of the community's roads, curbs, and gutters were designated as needing improvements. Arlington County Government, *Conservation Program*, by Arlington View Civic Association (Arlington, 1965).

160. Thirty-six acres were single-family homes, and seven acres were multifamily homes. Arlington County Government, *General Land Use Plan*, by the Department of Community Planning, Housing and Development (Arlington, 1961); Arlington County Government, *Conservation Program*, by Arlington View Civic Association (Arlington, 1965).

161. Arlington County Government, *Conservation Program*, by Arlington View Civic Association (Arlington, 1965).

162. Arlington County Government, *Neighborhood Conservation Program, Arlington County, Virginia*: Nauck, by Department of Environmental Affairs Planning Division (Arlington, September 1973), 3.

163. Commission members were Dr. John Lohman, Sidney O. Dewberry, Preston C. Caruthers, H. Hall Gibson, Colonel J. Fuller Groom, Lutrelle F. Parker, Alice Sufit, Roy C. Wadlan, and Mrs. Elizabeth Wiehe. Lohman, Parker, and Sufit hailed from south Arlington. Sufit was the only individual not living in a single-family home, residing in the garden-apartment and town-home community of Fairlington. Arlington County Government, *The Planning Commission Report* (Arlington, 1961), RG 51: Murphy and Ames Business Papers, Box 1, Arlington Central Library, Center for Local History. Arlington, Virginia.

164. Local community preservation movements culminated in the national 1966 Historic Preservation Act. For more about historic preservation on the community level, see works including Bashir, "Looking at North Carolina's History Through Architecture," 297–311; Moon, "The African American Housing Crisis in Alexandria, Virginia, 1930s–1960s," 28–68; Richardson, *Built By Blacks*.

165. von Hoffman, "The Lost History of Urban Renewal," 281–301; King, *Cultural Resource*.

166. For more about how redevelopment at this time affected Black communities throughout the south, see Richardson, *Built By Blacks*; and Siskind, "Suburban Growth and its Discontents," 161–82.

167. Isolde Weinberg, "New Church Center Spans Gulf Between Ways of Life" *Washington Post* (10 July 1966). RG 6: Arlington Churches, Box 4, CLH.

168. Audrey Seleistad, "Determination of Friar Ray and Neighbors Makes Church Center of Community Life," *The Alexandria Gazette* (8 January 1972). RG 6: Arlington Churches, Box 4. Arlington Central Library, Center for Local History. Arlington, Virginia.

169. Arlington County Government, *Arlington View Conservation Program*, by Arlington View Civic Association (Virginia, 1965). https://arlingtonva.s3.dualstack.us-east-1.amazonaws.com/wp-content/uploads/sites/31/2014/02/NC_1965_ArlingtonViewPlan.pdf.

170. Arlington County Government, *Arlington View Conservation Program*, by Arlington View Civic Association (Virginia, 1965). https://arlingtonva.s3.dualstack.us-east-1.amazonaws.com/wp-content/uploads/sites/31/2014/02/NC_1965_ArlingtonViewPlan.pdf; Arlington County Government, *Maywood Neighborhood Plan*, by Parkway Citizen Association (Virginia, 1965).

171. Green Valley began in 1844, Hall's Hill began in 1865, and Johnson's Hill began in 1880. Arlington County Government, *Arlington View Conservation Program*, by Arlington View Civic Association (Virginia, 1965), 11. https://arlingtonva.s3.dualstack.us-east-1.amazonaws.com/wp-content/uploads/sites/31/2014/02/NC_1965_ArlingtonViewPlan.pdf.

172. Gambill "Housing Opportunities for the Black and the Poor in Arlington County, Virginia," 1–32.

173. Arlington County Government, *Hall's Hill—Highview Park Proposed Community Conservation Program*, by James M. Langston Citizen's Association (Virginia, February 13, 1965).

174. Arlington County Government, "Report" (ca. 1968) p 39. RG 6: Arlington County Churches, Box 4. Arlington Central Library, Center for Local History. Arlington, Virginia.

175. Arlington County Government, *Ashton Heights Neighborhood Conservation Plan* (Arlington, 1976), 31–32.

176. Schrag, *The Great Society Subway*, 32–64.

177. An eighty-nine-mile, sixty-five-station system with nineteen miles above ground; Schrag, *The Great Society Subway*, 52–53.

178. Clarendon Planning Commission, *Clarendon Planning: Rosslyn-Ballston Corridor Alternative Land Use Patterns* (Virginia: 1972) Vertical File—Clarendon, CLH; Woody J Merrell and Thomas M Young, "Rosslyn-Ballston Corridor: Struggling for Rezoning with Balance," *Washington Post*. Vertical File—Clarendon, CLH.

179. Arlington County Government, *Hall's Hill—Highview Park Proposed Community Conservation Program*, by James M. Langston Citizen's Association (Virginia, February 13, 1965); Helen E. Samuel, Pres. Board of Trustees, "Arlington Hospital Report on Expansion," James Hamilton Associates Report, 1965–1966.

180. Arlington County Government, *Hall's Hill—Highview Park Proposed Community Conservation Program*, by James M. Langston Citizen's Association (Virginia, February 13, 1965).

181. Arlington County Neighborhood Conservation Program, "Neighborhood Conservation's 50th Anniversary" (2014). https://projects.arlingtonva.us/neighborhood-conservation/50th-anniversary/.

182. In 1973, the Nauck, Arlington Ridge, and Lyon Park Neighborhood Conservation Plans were accepted in Arlington County. The Aurora Highlands Neigh-

borhood Conservation Plan was adopted between these two rounds of plans in 1970. Arlington County Government, *Neighborhood Conservation Plans*, by Arlington County Projects and Planning (1965–2016).

183. From 1960 to 1964, twenty-eight new homes were constructed in Maywood, bringing the total to two hundred fifty-six. Arlington County Government, *Maywood Neighborhood Plan*, by Parkway Citizen Association (Virginia, 1965); National Register of Historic Places, *Maywood Historic District*, by Carrie E. Albee and Laura V. Trieschmann, November 2002.

184. Mrs. Smith, President Maywood Community Development Committee, learned about the program in January of 1964 on hearing about Johnson's Hill's submission for funding. Arlington County Government, Maywood Neighborhood Plan, by Parkway Citizen Association (Virginia, 1965), 11.

185. Connerly, The Most Segregated City in America; Cobb, The South and America Since World War II; Sugrue, Sweet Land of Liberty; Wiese, Places of Their Own.

186. Similar programs led to the redevelopment of Foggy Bottom in Washington, DC and the end of the Black community there; Friedman, *Covert Capital*. Alexandria City was unanimously charged with using community improvement programs to demolish African American communities by the interracial Alexandria Citizens Advisory Committee on Minority Housing. US Commission on Civil Rights, *Housing in Washington, D.C.* (Washington, DC: Government Printing Office, 1962), 1–53. https://www.law.umaryland.edu/marshall/usccr /documents/cr12h81.pdf.

187. Alexandria City Government, *Finding The Fort*; Moon, "The African American Housing Crisis in Alexandria, Virginia, 1930s–1960s"; Richardson, *Built By Blacks*.

188. "Hall's Hill, High View Park" (advertisement), *The Washington Bee*, September 17, 1892; Arlington County Government, *A Guide to the African American Heritage of Arlington County, Virginia*, by Department of Community Planning, Housing and Development (Arlington, 2016).

189. Arlington View was not subdivided until the 1930s on an area in Johnson's Hill bounded by Thirteenth Road South, Fourteenth Road South, South Rolfe Street, and South Queen Street. For more on John Nauck and his subdivision, see Chapter One—"Where They Had Lived Undisturbed for Nearly a Quarter of a Century." "Hall's Hill, High View Park" (advertisement), *Washington Bee*, September 17, 1892; Arlington County Government, *A Guide to the African American Heritage of Arlington County, Virginia*, by Department of Community Planning, Housing and Development (Arlington, 2016).

190. Taylor, *Bridge Builders of Nauck/Green Valley*.

191. Mrs. Amanda Lewis, interview by Laura Annalora, November 26, 2003, Hall's Hill Oral History Project, CLH.

192. Arlington County Government, *High View Park Neighborhood Conservation Plan*, by Evelyn Bell, Darnell Carpenter, Daphine Ruffner, Inez Waynes, Frank Wilson, and Sherri Young (Virginia, January 1992).

193. Lula Mae Graham, interview by Eleanor Edwards, December 4, 2003, Hall's Hill Oral History Project, CLH.

194. Stephanie Voss, "Change comes with hesitation to Green Valley," *Washington Times*, July 24, 1983, Vertical File: Nauck, CLH.

195. Jenkins, "Balancing Nauck's Past and Future." Vertical File: Nauck, CLH.

196. For information on Arlington's school busing issues, see: "An Appeal to Reason Concerning the Largest Bond Issue Ever Submitted to Arlington County Tax

Payers," RG 60: Eastman Fenwick Family Papers, Box 71. CLH; Michelotti, "Arlington School Desegregation"; Vogel, "The Integration of Reed Elementary School," 33–42.

Conclusion: An End to Residential Segregation

1. US Commission on Civil Rights, *Housing in Washington, D.C.* (Washington, DC: Government Printing Office, 1962). https://www.law.umaryland.edu /marshall/usccr/documents/cr12h81.pdf.

2. Gambill, "Housing Opportunities for the Black and the Poor in Arlington County, Virginia" Special Report No. 2 (Metropolitan Washington Housing Opportunities Project, April 1971), SC&A.; Building Research Advisory Board, "Silver Anniversary," 20; Stowe, "An Integrative Force," 229–35.

3. Cleveland Gambill, "Housing Opportunities for the Black and the Poor in Arlington County, Virginia," Special Report No. 2 (Metropolitan Washington Housing Opportunities Project, April 1971) SC&A.

4. Gambill, "Housing Opportunities."

5. Domer, "Escaping the City," 65–90; William D. North, "Legal Up-Date," *Realtor Magazine* (September–October 1976), Verlin Smith Collection, VHS; Mrs. Chester H. Vosper, Chairman VAR Equal Opportunity Committee, "Equal Opportunity in Housing: It's the Law," *Realtor Magazine* (July–August 1975), Verlin Smith Collection, VHS.

6. James "Jimmy" E. Taylor, interview by Chloe E. Muhammed, January 30, 2004, Hall's Hill Oral History Project, CLH.

7. Allen, "A Feeling of Community." Vertical File: Nauck, CLH.

8. One son and one daughter moved to Maryland, and one moved to Massachusetts to find work. One daughter remained in Arlington, purchasing a town home in Johnson's Hill. Lula Mae Graham, interview by Eleanor Edwards, December 4, 2003, Hall's Hill Oral History Project, CLH.

9. Ms. Saundra Green, interview by Kevin Carney, November 20, 2003, Hall's Hill Oral History Project, CLH.

10. Jenkins, "Balancing Nauck's Past and Future." Vertical File: Nauck, CLH.

11. Cheek, "Arlington Board Cancels Meeting on Gang Rumble," Al.; Cheek, and Cronk," 11 Are Guilty in Parking Lot Rumble," Al; Cheek, "2 Arrested Buying Guns After Rumble," Al; Cheek, "County Asked for Its Story on Gang War," B1; Cheek, and Burchard, "Police Let Rival Gangs Clash So They Could Make Arrests," Al; Cronk and Winterble, "'Want to Take World Apart,' Blond Says of 'Pagan' Club"; Ericson, "Study Set on Gang War," A1; Ericson, "Hassan Plea Halts Talks on Shooting," Al; Gold and Walter, "Gangs Wage Arlington Gunfight," Al; Jones, "Car-Burning Ignited Feud, Avenger Says," 5; White, "Pagan, Companion Slain in Fairfax City Gun Battle," C1; *Washington Post*, "Gangs May Disarm, Reach Truce," C3; *Northern Virginia Sun*, "16 Jailed After Gang 'Shootout,'" A1.

12. Lillian Ambers, interview by Danielle Tope, February 3, 2004, Hall's Hill Oral History Project, CLH.

13. Mrs. Amanda Lewis, interview by Laura Annalora, November 26, 2003, Hall's Hill Oral History Project, CLH.

14. Lillian Ambers, interview by Danielle Tope, February 3, 2004, Hall's Hill Oral History Project, CLH.

15. Gail Baker, "Garden Apartments—Three Preservation Case Studies," 23–25.; Metropolitan Washington Council of Governments, "Growth Trends to the Year 2010: Forecasts for the Metropolitan Washington Region" (Virginia: Sept. 1986), Verlin Smith Collection, Box B-66, VHS.

16. von Hoffman, "The Lost History of Urban Renewal," 281–301; King, *Cultural Resource.*; Arlington County Government, *Ashton Heights Neighborhood Conservation Plan* (Arlington, 1976) p 31–32; Schrag, *The Great Society Subway: A History of the Washington Metro*, 32–64.

17. US Commission on Civil Rights, *Housing in Washington, D.C.* (Washington, DC: Government Printing Office, 1962). https://www.law.umaryland.edu/marshall/usccr/documents/cr12h81.pdf. For more on the process of "White flight," see Kruse, *White Flight.*

18. Lyon Village Citizen's Association, *Lyon Village Bulletin* (Arlington, VA: February 1977), RG 84: Lyon Village, CLH; Reed School, *Self-Study Report* (1975–76); *Northern Virginia Sun*, March 8, 1983.

19. Arlington County Government, *Economic Fact Book: Arlington, Virginia* (Arlington, August 1978), Verlin Smith Collection, Box B-52, VHS.

20. For more on similar changes in suburban demographics around the country see Jones-Correa, "Reshaping the American Dream," 183–204.

21. Morris, "A Chink in the Armor," 329–66.

22. Muzaffar Chishti, Faye Hipsman, and Isabel Ball, "Fifty Years On, the 1965 Immigration and Nationalist Act Continues to Reshape the United States," *The Immigration Policy Institute Policy Beat* (October 2015).

23. Friedman, *Covert Capital*, 163–219.

24. "The Barcroft Bible Church," Vertical File: Barcroft, CLH; Arlington County Government, *Barcroft Data of Community*, by Susan A. Ingraham, Planning Program, Arlington Division (Arlington, 2008), Vertical File: Barcroft, CLH.

25. Friedman, *Covert Capital*, 181–82.

26. *US Census, 1980* (Washington, DC: Government Printing Office); Netherton and Netherton, *Arlington County in Virginia.*

27. George Kennedy, "Arlington."

28. Arlington County Government, *Economic Fact Book: Arlington, Virginia* (Arlington, August 1978), Verlin Smith Collection, Box B-52, VHS.

29. Friedman, Covert Capital; Banham, The Fight for Fairfax.

30. Schrag, *The Great Society Subway*; *Washington Post*, "Clarendon; Happy With Its Identity as an Urban Village"; Arlington County Government, *Jefferson Davis Corridor* (Arlington, VA: planning booklet, ca. 1970) Verlin Smith Collection, Box B-52, File: Arlington County, Virginia (1959–1977), VHS.; Arlington County Government, *Rosslyn: Today-Tomorrow-Future* (Arlington, VA: planning booklet, 1964) Verlin Smith Collection, Box B-52, File: Arlington County, Virginia (1959–1977), VHS.

31. Arlington County Government, *Economic Fact Book: Arlington, Virginia* (Arlington, August 1978), Verlin Smith Collection, Box B-52, VHS.

32. Cleveland Gambill "Housing Opportunities for the Black and the Poor in Arlington County, Virginia," Special Report No. 2 (Metropolitan Washington Housing Opportunities Project, April 1971), SC&A.

33. Arlington County Government, *Economic Fact Book: Arlington, Virginia* (Arlington, August 1978), Verlin Smith Collection, Box B-52, VHS.; Cleveland Gambill "Housing Opportunities for the Black and the Poor in Arlington County,

Virginia" Special Report No 2 (Metropolitan Washington Housing Opportunities Project, April 1971), SC&A.

34. Cleveland Gambill, "Housing Opportunities for the Black and the Poor in Arlington County, Virginia," Special Report No. 2 (Metropolitan Washington Housing Opportunities Project, April, 1971), Special Collections and Archives. George Mason University.

35. Jenkins, "Balancing Nauck's Past and Future."

36. Lula Mae Graham, interview by Eleanor Edwards, December 4, 2003, Hall's Hill Oral History Project, CLH.

37. Ms. Saundra Green, interview by Kevin Carney, November 20, 2003, Hall's Hill Oral History Project, CLH.

38. Mount Zion Baptist Church, *Mt. Zion Centennial, 1866–1976* (Arlington: 1976) RG 6: Arlington Churches, Box 3. CLH.

39. Mrs. Amanda Lewis, interview by Laura Annalora, November 26, 2003, Hall's Hill Oral History Project, CLH.

40. The League of Women Voters, *Arlington Community Guide* (Arlington, Virginia: Pamphlet, 1979), VHS.

41. Arlington County Government, *A Guide to the African American Heritage of Arlington County, Virginia,* by Department of Community Planning, Housing and Development (Arlington, 2016) p. 34.

42. Lillian Ambers, interview by Danielle Tope, February 3, 2004, Hall's Hill Oral History Project, CLH.

43. Taylor, Bridge Builders of Nauck/Green Valley.

44. Mary Gardner became Mary Scales and, eventually, Mary Koblitz. Three aunts, her brother and his family, and cousins and their families all lived in Hall's Hill. In adulthood, children Gregory, Elle, and Tia stayed in Hall's Hill, Larry moved to Alexandria, and Charles lived in DC. Mary P. Koblitz, interview by Shawna Helene Reed, December 3, 2003, Hall's Hill Oral History Project, CLH.

45. Taylor, Bridge Builders of Nauck/Green Valley.

46. Mary P. Koblitz, interview by Shawna Helene Reed, December 3, 2003, Hall's Hill Oral History Project, CLH.

47. Allen, "A Feeling of Community."

48. Jenkins, "Balancing Nauck's Past and Future."

49. Varaday, "American Residential Segregation," 166–71.

50. Gowen, "Property Value Clouds Its Future."

51. Oswald G. Smith, *Mount Zion Centennial, 1866–1966* (Virginia: Mt. Zion Baptist Church Pamphlet, 1966), RG 6: Arlington County Churches, Box 3, File 1–18: Mount Zion Methodist Church, CLH.

52. Gowen, "Property Value Clouds Its Future."

53. Gowen, "Property Value Clouds Its Future"; In this circumstance, Northern Virginia is defined as Arlington, Fairfax, Loudoun, Prince William, Spotsylvania, Stafford, Fauquier, Clarke, and Warren Counties. Lisa A. Sturtevant, "The Northern Virginia Housing Market . . . Like No Other" (Presentation, George Mason University, Center for Regional Analysis, Fairfax, 2011). http://cra.gmu.edu/pdfs/studies_reports_presentations/The_Northern_Virginia_Housing_Market_Like_No_Other.pdf.

54. Jenkins, "Balancing Nauck's Past and Future."

55. Lillian Ambers, interview by Danielle Tope, February 3, 2004, Hall's Hill Oral History Project, CLH.

56. Jenkins, "Balancing Nauck's Past and Future."
57. Arlington County Government, *Nauck Neighborhood Comprehensive Action Plan*, by Nauck Neighborhood Planning Committee (Arlington, February 1998).
58. Jenkins, "Balancing Nauck's Past and Future."
59. Arlington County Government, *High View Park Neighborhood Conservation Plan*, by Evelyn Bell, Darnell Carpenter, Daphine Ruffner, Inez Waynes, Frank Wilson, and Sherri Young (Virginia, January 1992).
60. Arlington County Government, *Nauck Neighborhood Comprehensive Action Plan*, by Nauck Neighborhood Planning Committee (Arlington, February 1998).
61. Sullivan, "Arlington creates housing conservation district."
62. Sullivan and McCartney, "Arlington County Board"; Sullivan, "Waiting for Scrutiny."
63. Rothstein, "Second Washington Blvd. Bridge Opens Over Columbia Pike."
64. Ms. Saundra Green, interview by Kevin Carney, November 20, 2003, Hall's Hill Oral History Project, CLH.
65. Sullivan, "Arlington may swap Lee Highway name"; Sullivan, "Arlington can rename Jefferson Davis Highway."
66. Sullivan, "Arlington House."
67. Jenkins, "Balancing Nauck's Past and Future."
68. Jenkins, "Balancing Nauck's Past and Future."
69. Taylor, *Bridge Builders of Nauck/ Green Valley*, 44–45.
70. Clarissa T. Sligh, *It Wasn't Little Rock*.
71. Fadulu, "Arlington County."
72. National Register of Historic Places, *Colonial Village*, by Virginia Historic Landmarks Commission Survey, 1979, p. 2.

Bibliography

Abbreviations

CLH: Arlington Central Library, Center for Local History, Arlington, Virginia
LOC: Library of Congress, Washington, DC
LVA: Library of Virginia. Richmond, Virginia
NARA: National Archives, Washington, DC
SC&A: George Mason University: Special Collections and Archives, Fairfax, Virginia
UVA: University of Virginia Special Collections and Archives, Charlottesville, Virginia
VHS: Virginia Historical Society, Richmond, Virginia

Unpublished Primary Sources

Collections

Alcova Heights Neighborhood Photographs, PG 220, CLH
Almond James Lindsay Papers Collection, 1898–1986, Mss1 AL685 a FA2, Section 4, Boxes 23–28, VHS
Arlington County Churches, RG 6, Boxes 1–4, CLH
Arlington County Library Oral History Program, CLH
Arlington County Neighborhood Civic Associations Collected Records, RG 15, Box 22, CLH
Charles Lane Property Purchases, RG 103-C, Box 1, CLH
Clarissa Thompson Sligh, *It Wasn't Little Rock* (Visual Studies Workshop Press, 2005), University of Virginia Special Collections and Archives, Charlottesville, Virginia
Cruit Land Tract, Lyon Village Photographs, PG 800, CLH
David M. Rubenstein Rare Book and Manuscript Library, Duke University, Durham, North Carolina
Eastman-Fenwick Family Papers, RG 60, Boxes 2, 70–71, CLH
FitzGerald Bemiss Papers Collection, Mss1 B4252 a FA2, Boxes 1–2, 4–5, VHS
Freedman's Village and Reconstruction Collection, RG 103, Boxes 1–2, CLH
Glencarlyn Neighborhood, RG 8, Boxes 1–5, CLH
Glencarlyn Neighborhood History, RG 62, Boxes 1–3, CLH
Hall's Hill Oral History Project, CLH
Historic Neighborhood and Building Reports, RG 30, CLH
Historical Arlington Photographs, PG 208, CLH
James McDonnell Transportation Collection, Boxes 6–9, SC&A
Lyon Park Woman's Club Records, RG 96, Boxes 1–4, CLH
Mary Custis Lee Papers, Mss1 L5144 a 1397–1472, Section 26, VHS
Murphy and Ames Business Records, RG 51, Boxes 1–4, CLH
Northern Virginia Sun, Then and Now, PG 87, Boxes 1–2.2, CLH
Papers of Edmund C. Fleet, RG 11, Boxes 3–4, CLH
Papers of Frank L. Ball, RG 12, Boxes 1–2, CLH

Records of the Commission of Fine Arts, RG 66, Section 2, NARA
Records of Hoffman-Boston High School, RG 7-B, Box 1, CLH
Records of the Lyon Village Civic Association, RG 84, Boxes 14, 7, 9, CLH
Records of the Office of the Quartermaster General, RG 92, Box 7, Arlington Reservation, Arlington, Virginia, NARA
Verlin W. Smith Collection, Mss3 F2299a FA2, Section A, Boxes 2, 70; Section B, Boxes 52, 66; Section C, Boxes 2, 3, 7, 15, 21, 26, 34; Section D, Box 4, VHS

Vertical Files, CLH
Agricultural Farm
Alcova Heights
Amusement Park, Barcroft
Arlington House
Barcroft
Black History (1–3)
Brick Works
Cherrydale
Clarendon (pre-1959, post-1959)
Columbia Heights
Falls Church
Fort Myer Heights
Freedman's Village
Glencarlyn
Hall's Hill
Lyon Park
Lyon Village
Nauck
Potomac Yards
Sears Houses
Transportation
Williamsburg
Veterans History Project, American Folklife Center, LOC
William Mahone Papers, 1853–95, David M. Rubenstein Rare Book and Manuscript Library, Duke University, Durham, North Carolina
Zonta Oral History Program, CLH

Papers
Backus, Hadassah, "Glencarlyn" (unpublished paper, 1952), RG 8: Glencarlyn, Box 2, CLH.
Ballard, Amy, "Historical Analysis of Lyon Park" (unpublished paper, May 1988), Vertical File: Lyon Park, CLH.
Bendroth, Margaret L., "Church Architecture and Community in 20th Century Arlington" (unpublished paper, ca. 1990), RG 6: Arlington Churches, Box 4, CLH.
Fisher, Ann Marie, "Lyon Village" (unpublished paper, December 1987), Vertical File: Lyon Village, CLH.
Gillem, Harry Gray, "The Arlington View Community—A Pillar for Arlington Neighborhood Conservation Program" (unpublished paper, 1985), RG 103: Freedman's Village, Box 1, File 2: Copies of Articles about Freedman's Village, CLH.

Gilpin, Susan, "Queen City" (unpublished paper, 19 July 1984), Vertical File: Black History—2, CLH.

Harper, Marilyn M., "Arlington County, Virginia: Transportation through 1945" (unpublished paper, March 1985). Vertical File: Transportation, CLH.

O'Brien, Thomas, "Historic Survey of Nauck Neighborhood, Arlington County, Virginia" (unpublished paper, December 1987). Center for Local History, Arlington Central Library, Arlington, Virginia. Arlington County Cultural Affairs.

Ray, Reverend David T., "Integration of Church" (unpublished paper, July 1964), RG 6: Churches, Box 4, File: Our Lady Queen of Peace. CLH.

Smith, Virginia M., "Butler Holmes Subdivision" (unpublished paper, ca. 1940). RG 11: Papers of Edmund C. Fleet, Box 4, File 7, CLH.

Presentations

Bestebreurtje, Lindsey, "Suburbanization and Segregation in Virginia" (paper presented at Fifty Years of Reston Past and Future Conferences, Reston, Virginia, 2014).

Fenwick, Charles, "The School Situation in Virginia" (Press Announcement, Arlington, VA, 24 June 1947). RG: 60: Eastman Fenwick Family Papers, CLH.

Sipe, Richard, "Defying the Odds: An Analysis of the Newsome Park Community, Newport News, Virginia, 1943–1966" (lecture, Virginia Forum Conference Presentation, Williamsburg, Virginia, March 3, 2016).

Sturtevant, Lisa A., "The Northern Virginia Housing Market . . . Like No Other" (presentation, George Mason University, Center for Regional Analysis, Fairfax, 2011). http://cra.gmu.edu/pdfs/studies_reports_presentations/The_Northern _Virginia_Housing_Market_Like_No_Other.pdf.

Trust, Arthur W., "Clarendon Presbyterian Church: A Partial History through 1947" (Presentation Arlington, VA July 1, 1975), RG 6: Arlington Churches, Box 2. CLH.

Published Primary Sources

Maps

Franklin Survey Co., "Atlas of Arlington County, Virginia" [1938], Plate Nos. 7, 22. Map Collection, Arlington Central Library, Center for Local History, Arlington, Virginia.

Hopkins, G. M. "Atlas of Fifteen Miles Around Washington Including the Counties of Fairfax and Alexandria, Virginia," 1879. Map F232.A7.1878, VHS.

Howell and Taylor, "Map of Alexandria County, Virginia for the Virginia Title Co.," 1900. Map Division, LOC.

Kinnier, C. L., Directing Engineer, "Map of Road Improvements, Arlington Virginia," 1928–31. Map Collection, CLH.

"Map of Corbett," ca. 1886. Arlington Deed Book, C, no. 4. Arlington, Virginia.

US Army Quarter Master Department, "Map of Reservation: Arlington Va Fort Myer and Nat. Cemetery," 1883. NARA.

Virginia Title Company, "Map of Alexandria County Virginia," 1900. Map Division, LOC, Washington, DC. http://lccn.loc.gov/89692758.

Film and Photographs

"Arlington Private Schools," George Herman, *CBS News*, aired August 21, 1958, on CBS. Civil Rights Digital Library, Digital Library of Georgia. http://crdl.usg.edu /do:ugabma_wsbn_39536.

"J.E.B. Stuart Homes," ca. 1940, Arlington Central Library, Center for Local History. http://arlingtonvalibrary.s3.amazonaws.com/files/2007/05/230–1388.jpg.

Anonymous, *African American Integration Schools VA 1959*, February 2, 1959, *Associated Press*. http://www.apimages.com/metadata/Index/Watchf-AP-A-VA-USA-APHS355655-African American-/f994cbc86c674efa88d86f432330f0a7/63/0.

Collins, Marjorie, *General View*, 1942, Farm Security Administration Collection, Prints and Photographs Division, LOC. https://www.loc.gov/item/fsa2000056520/PP/.

Collins, Marjorie, *Project occupant tending his victory garden*, 1942, Farm Security Administration Collection, Prints and Photographs Division, LOC. https://www.loc.gov/item/fsa2000056518/PP/.

Gottscho-Schleisner, Inc, *Fairlington Houses, Arlington, Virginia. Exterior II*, 1943, Prints and Photographs Division, LOC. https://www.loc.gov/item/gsc1994020328/PP/.

Historic American Buildings Survey, *Colonial Village, Arlington, Arlington County, VA*, 1940, Theodor Horydczak Collection, Prints and Photographs Division, LOC.

J. R., *African American Integration Schools VA 1959*, February 2, 1959, Associated Press Photographer. http://www.apimages.com/metadata/Index/Watchf-AP-A-VA-USA-APHS355656-African American-/887315b149eb4a248dd855cc44b62b5b/64/0.

Advertisements

American Realty Exchange "Alcova Heights" (advertisement), ca. 1915, Vertical File: Alcova Heights, CLH.

Barbor, Williams & Company Real Estate Insurance, "Falls Church Virginia" (advertisement), ca. 1910.

Carlin Springs Syndicate, "Carlin Springs" (advertisement), 1887, RG 8: Glencarlyn, Box 1, File 1, CLH.

Clements, James E., "Lots" (advertisement), ca. 1900, in Mackey, *A Brief History of Alexandria County, Virginia* (Falls Church, VA: Newell Printing Co., 1907), p 42. https://archive.org/details/briefhistoryofal00alex.

Lyon & Fitch, Inc. "Lyon Village" (advertisement), ca. 1920, Vertical File: Lyon Park, Arlington Central Library, Center for Local History, Arlington, Virginia.

"Notice of Sale for Real Estate," (advertisement), November 5, 1958, Verlin W. Smith Collection, Box B-52, VHS.

Rowland, Stanley R., "Home" (advertisement), 1946, Verlin W. Smith Collection, Box B-52, VHS.

Simms, Charles I., "Simms Real Estate" (advertisement), ca. 1900, in Mackey, *A Brief History of Alexandria County, Virginia*, Falls Church, VA: Newell Printing Co., 1907, p 46. https://archive.org/details/briefhistoryofal00alex.

Washington-Virginia Railway, "Railway" (advertisement), 1910, Vertical File: Transportation, CLH.

Court Cases

Bennett v. Garrett, 132 VA 397 (Opinion June 15, 1922).

Brown v. Board of Education of Topeka, 347 US 483 (1954). https://supreme.justia.com/cases/federal/us/347/483/.

Buchanan v. Waverly, 245 US 60 (1917).

Butler v. Thompson (E.D. VA. 1951). https://casetext.com/case/butler-v-thompson-2.

Carter v. School Board of Arlington County, 87 F. Supp. 745 (E.D. Va. 1949), US District Court for the Eastern District of Virginia 1949.

Cases Decided in the Supreme Court of Appeals of Virginia, CXXXII (Richmond: David Bottom, Superintendent of Public Printing, 1922), p. 400.

City Council of Alexandria v. Alexandria County et al., Record no. 773 (Virginia Supreme Court of Appeals, 1915).

Clarissa S. Thompson et al. v. the County School Board of Arlington, 159 F. Supp. 567 (E.D. Va. 1957).

Government Documents and Records

Alexandria City Government. *Finding The Fort: A History of an African American Neighborhood in Northern Virginia, 1860s–1960s*, by Krystyn R. Moon (Virginia, September 2014).

Arlington County Civic Federation. Report, Fiscal Year 1949–50 (Arlington, 1950), RG 84: Lyon Village Civic Association, Box 3, CLH.

Arlington County Department of Community Planning, Housing and Development. *A Guide to African American Heritage of Arlington County* (Virginia, 2016).

Arlington County Government. *A History of the Boundaries of Arlington County, Virginia*, by Office of the County Manager (Virginia, 1955, 2011).

Arlington County Government, Arlington Convention on School Board Candidates (Arlington, VA: Flyer, September 1951), RG 60: Eastman Fenwick Family Papers, Box 2, CLH.

Arlington County Government, Arlington County Deed Book A, C, H–Z, L–P, XZ, Arlington County Office of Land Records, Arlington, VA.

Arlington County Government, Clarendon Planning: Rosslyn-Ballston Corridor Alternative Land Use Patterns, by Clarendon Planning Commission (Virginia, 1972). Vertical File: Clarendon. CLH.

Arlington County Government, *Community Voices: The Nauck Community Heritage Project*, by Arlington Cultural Affairs (Virginia, August 2008).

Arlington County Government, *Economic Fact Book: Arlington, Virginia* (Arlington, August 1978), Verlin Smith Collection, Box B-52, VHS.

Arlington County Government, General Land Use Plan, by Department of Community Planning, Housing and Development (Arlington, VA, 1961).

Arlington County Government, History of County PTA Council, Arlington, VA, 1931–49, by Belva Margaret Owens (Arlington, VA, 1949).

Arlington County Government, Jefferson Davis Corridor (Arlington, VA: planning booklet, ca. 1970), Verlin Smith Collection, Box B-52, File: Arlington County, A (1959–77), VHS.

Arlington County Government, Nauck Village Action Plan (Virginia, July 10, 2004).

Arlington County Government, The Planning Commission Report (Arlington, VA, 1961), RG 51: Murphy and Ames Business Papers, Box 1, CLH.

Arlington County Government, Poll Tax Records, 1938, 1939, 1940, RG 60: Eastman Fenwick Family Papers, Box 71, CLH.

Arlington County Government, Rosslyn: Today-Tomorrow-Future (Arlington, VA: planning booklet, 1964), Verlin Smith Collection, Box B-52, File: Arlington County, Virginia (1959–77), VHS.

Arlington County Government, Zoning Ordinance Adopted by Board of Supervisors of Arlington County, by Edward Duncan et al. (Virginia, April 26, 1930).

Arlington County Office of the County Manager. Acts of Assembly, Ch. 167 (Virginia, 1930).

Arlington County Office of the County Manager, Acts of Assembly, Special Act (Virginia, 1927).

Arlington County Planning Commission. A Summary of the Master Plan of Arlington County, Virginia (Arlington, 1961). RG 84: Records of the Lyon Village Civic Association, Box 9, CLH.

Arlington County Public Schools. "Facts Concerning Segregation and Integration" (Arlington, VA: Flyer, November 1954).

Arlington County Public Schools. Problems of Integration in Arlington Public Schools, by Committee to Study Problems (Arlington, VA: Meeting Minutes, ca. 1956).

Arlington County Public Schools. "Reed School: Self Study Report" (1975–76).

Arlington County Register of Historic Places. Reevesland, Torreyson Farm, by Beth Bolling (Arlington, VA: March 2002).

Arlington Department of Community Planning, Housing and Development. Virginian Foundation for the Humanities, "Community Voices: The Nauck Community Heritage Project" (Arlington, VA: August 2008).

Commonwealth of Virginia, Department of Highways, Henry G. Shirley Memorial Highway Improvement (Virginia, July 2, 1962), James J. McDonnell Transportation Collection, SC&A.

Congressional Record, 84th Congress Second Session. 102, part 4. Washington, D.C.: Governmental Printing Office, 12 March 1956, pp. 4459–60.

Delano, Columbus, et al. "Annual Reports of the Department of the Interior" (Washington, DC: Government Printing Office, 1875).

Downer, Jay. National Capital Planning Commission Report (Washington, DC: October 1941).

Federal Civil Service Act, 5 USC § 2101, (1871).

Historic Preservation Committee, Arlington, Virginia. *The Barcroft Apartments: Arlington, VA*, by Marilyn M. Harper (April 25, 1986), Vertical File: Barcroft. Arlington Central Library, Center for Local History, Arlington, VA.

Metropolitan Washington Council of Governments. "Growth Trends to the Year 2010: Forecasts for the Metropolitan Washington Region" (Virginia: Sept. 1986), Verlin Smith Collection, Box B-66, VHS.

Metropolitan Washington Housing Opportunities Project, Housing Opportunities for the Black and the Poor in Arlington County, Virginia, Special Report No. 2, by Cleveland Gambill (Washington, DC, April, 1971). Special Collections and Archives, George Mason University, Fairfax, Virginia.

National Capital Housing Authority. Report: Shrinking Negro Neighborhoods (Washington, DC, 1943).

National Capital Planning Commission. Transportation Plan: National Capital Region, (Washington, D.C., 1959), James J. McDonnell Transportation Collection, George Mason University: Special Collections and Archives, Fairfax, Virginia.

National Register of Historic Places, Ashton Heights Historic District, by Kristie Baynard et al., 2002.

National Register of Historic Places, Charles Richard Drew House, May 11, 1976. https://focus.nps.gov/GetAsset?assetID=629a0e70–3c05–4a1d-ae22 -d407653edb55.

National Register of Historic Places, Colonial Village, by Virginia Historic Landmarks Commission Survey, 1979.

National Register of Historic Places, Fairlington Historic District, 1998.

National Register of Historic Places, Garden Apartments, Apartment Houses and Apartment Complexes in Arlington County, Virginia: 1934–54, May 22, 2003.

National Register of Historic Places, George Washington Carver Cooperative Apartments, by Laura V. Trieschmann and Gerald M. Maready, 2003.

National Register of Historic Places, Glebewood Village Historic District, by Jana E. Riggle and Laura V. Trieschmann, August 2003. http://www.dhr.virginia.gov /registers/Counties/Arlington/000–9414_Glebewood_Village_Historic _District_2004_Final_Nomination.pdf.

National Register of Historic Places, Harry W. Gray House, by Jennifer Bunting Hallock, May 2003.

National Register of Historic Places, Lyon Park Historic District, Arlington County, Virginia.

National Register of Historic Places, Maywood Historic District, by Carrie E. Albee and Laura V. Trieschmann, November 2002.

Regional Highway Planning Committee, Washington Metropolitan Area Transportation Study: A Recommended Highway Improvement Program, Vol 4 (Washington, DC: Department of Highways, 1952), James J. McDonnell Transportation Collection, SC&A.

Senate Committee on the District of Columbia, The Improvement of the Park System of the District of Columbia, by Charles Moore, Clerk (Washington, DC: Government Printing Office, 1902).

US Census: 1840, 1850, 1860, 1870, 1880, 1900, 1910, 1920, 1930, 1940, 1970, 1980 (Washington, DC: Government Printing Office).

US Census Bureau, "Historic Census of Housing Tables," Home Ownership Rates, National and Virginia, 1900. http://www.census.gov/hhes/www/housing/census /historic/owner.html.

US Census Bureau, "Households by Type and Size: 1900 to 2002," in *Statistical Abstracts of the United States* (2003), p. 19. https://www.census.gov/statab/hist /HS-12.pdf.

US Census Bureau, Population of States and Counties of the United States: 1790 to 1990 from the Twenty-one Decennial Census, by Richard L. Forstall, (Washington, DC: 1996).

US Census. "Historic Census of Housing Tables," Home Ownership Rates, National and Virginia, 1900. http://www.census.gov/hhes/www/housing/census /historic/owner.html.

US Commission on Civil Rights. *Housing in Washington, D.C.* (Washington, DC: Government Printing Office, 1962). https://www.law.umaryland.edu/marshall /usccr/documents/cr12h81.pdf.

US Congress. Congressional Record, 48th Cong., 1883, Ch 27, 22 Stat. 403. "Pendleton Civil Service Reform Act."

US Congress, Congressional Record, 76th Cong., 1st Sess., 1939, Ch. 410. "The Hatch Activity Act."

US Congress, House Committee on Banking and Currency, "National Housing Act: Hearings Before the Committee on Banking and Currency, House of Representatives, Seventy-Third Congress, Second Session, H. R. 9620, a Bill to Improve Nation-wide Housing Standards, Provide Employment, and Stimulate Industry; to Improve Conditions with Respect to Home . . ." (Washington, DC: US Government Printing Office, 1934).

US Congress, House Committee on Banking and Currency, Congressional Record, 84th Cong., 2nd sess., 1956. 103, pt. 4.

US Federal Home Loan Corporation. First Annual Report of the Federal Home Loan Bank Board (Washington, DC: US Government Printing Office, 1933).

US Federal Housing Administration. "Underwriting Manual, Underwriting and Valuation Procedure Under Title II of the National Housing Act," (Washington, DC, 1938).

US Government. Valuation of Property in the Village, 1888, RG 92, CQMGF, MSS, NARA.

US Southern Claims Commission. "Bazil Hall no. 2422," Records of the Accounting Officers of the Department of the Treasury, Record Group 217, NARA.

US Southern Claims Commission, "Virginia, Alexandria, J. Jones, Levi" (ca. 1872-1877). Microfilm Publication M2062, 36 Rolls; NAI 55715 Records of the Accounting Officers of the Department of the Treasury, Record Group 217, NARA.

Virginia General Assembly. Pupil Placement Act (Richmond, September 29, 1956), Records of the Virginia Pupil Placement Board, 1957–66, Library of Virginia, Richmond, Virginia.

Virginia General Assembly, Acts of Assembly, 1920, chapter 241.

Virginia General Assembly, Virginia State Constitution, Article II, Sections 18–20 (1902). http://confinder.richmond.edu/admin/docs/Virginia_1902.pdf.

Virginia House of Delegates, Voter Code, Chapter 14, Title 15, Section 15.1–669.

Arlington County Government, Neighborhood Conservation Plans

Arlington Forest (1990)

Arlington Ridge (2013)

Arlington View (1965)

Ashton Heights (1976)

Aurora Highlands (1969, 2008)

Barcroft (2008)

Buckingham (2006)

Columbia Forest (2000)

Columbia Heights (2004)

Conservation Program Summary (1965)

Dominion Hills (2004)

High View Park, Hall's Hill (1965, 1987, 1992)

Maywood (1965)

Nauck (1973, 1998)

Neighborhood Conservation: 50th Anniversary (2014)

Rock Spring (2009)

Tara Leeway Heights (2005)

Waycroft (2012)

Westover (1991)

Williamsburg (2001)

Secondary Sources

Newspapers

Alexandria Gazette (Alexandria, VA)

Arlington Courier (Arlington, VA)

Arlington Journal (Arlington, VA)
Barcroft News (Arlington, VA)
Courier Journal (Louisville, IN)
Evening Star (Washington, DC)
Green Valley News (Arlington, VA)
Harpers Weekly (New York, NY)
The Monitor (Arlington, VA)
National Daily Intelligencer (Washington, DC)
New York Herald (New York)
New York Herald Tribune (New York, NY)
Northern Virginia Sun (Fairfax, VA)
The Planet (Richmond, VA)
Richmond News Leader (Richmond, VA)
Richmond Time-Ledger (Richmond, VA)
Richmond Times Dispatch (Richmond, VA)
Roanoke Times (Roanoke, VA)
School Improvement Newspaper (Arlington, VA)
St. Louis Dispatch (St. Louis, MO)
The Sun (Arlington, VA)
Sunday Chronicle (Washington, DC)
Washington Bee (Washington, DC)
Washington Post (Washington, DC)
Washington Star (Washington, DC)
Washington Times (Washington, DC)
Washington World (Washington, DC)

Unauthored Articles

"Biography," File: Joel T. Broyhill, Box C-34: Virginia (State of) Politics, Verlin W. Smith Collection. VHS.

"Biography of Charles Drew," The Charles R. Drew Papers [Profiles in Science Series], Bethesda, MD: National Library of Medicine. https://profiles.nlm.nih .gov/ps/retrieve/Narrative/BG/p-nid/336.

"Building Money," *Architectural Forum* 6. no. 3 (August 1935): 136–39.

"Building Money Series," *Architectural Forum* 71, no. 2 (August 1939).

"FHA Experience in Rental Housing," *Insured Mortgage* 4 (April 1940).

"Frank Lyon: Biographical Sketch," *History of Virginia: Virginia Biography* 6 (Chicago and New York: The American Historical Society, 1924): 123–25.

"The Once Ubiquitous Peoples Drug Stores," *Streets of Washington Blog*, December 5, 2011. http://www.streetsofwashington.com/2011/11/once-ubiquitous-peoples -drug-stores.html.

"Special Issue: Rosslyn—Arlington's New Potomac Landmark," *Washington World* (November–December 1964). Verlin W. Smith Collection, VHS.

"The Way to Record Breaking Rents," *Architectural Forum* 71 (August 1939) p 135.

"Title VI Rental Housing Projects," *Insured Mortgage Portfolio* 6, no. 3, (First Quarter, 1942): 6.

"Urban Renewal Comparison," *Washington World Magazine*, November–December 1964. Verlin Smith Collection, Box B-52. File: Arlington County, VA (1959–77), VHS.

Authored Articles

Abbott, Dorothea E., "The Land of Maria Syphax and the Abbey Mausoleum," *Arlington Historical Magazine* 7, no. 4 (October 1984): 64–80.

Allard, Dean C. "Arlington, 50 Years Ago: Continuity and Change." Arlington Historical Society: 50th Anniversary Celebration (2006), CLH.

Anderson, Robert Nelson. "Arlington Adopts the County Manager Form of Government" *Arlington Historical Magazine* 1, no. 2 (October 1958): 52–67.

Arlington County Archivist. "An Annotated Guide to Selected Maps of Arlington County 1600–1900," *Arlington Historical Magazine* 4, no. 2 (October 1970): 56–65.

Baker, Gail. "Garden Apartments—Three Preservation Case Studies," *Cultural Resource Management* 22, no. 5 (1999): 23–25.

Ball, Frank L. "Electric Railways in Arlington," *Arlington Historical Magazine*, 3, no. 2 (October 1966): 31–40.

Banham, Russ. *The Fight for Fairfax: A Struggle for a Great American County*. Fairfax, VA: GMU Press, 2009.

Bart, Peter B. "Vexed Virginians: Spreading Impacts of School Closings Worries Businessmen and Parents" *The Wall Street Journal*, September 28, 1958. Governor Lindsay J. Almond Papers, Section 4, Box 27, VHS.

Bashir, Catherine W., ed. "Looking at North Carolina's History Through Architecture," In *Southern Built: American Architecture, Regional Practice* (Virginia: University of Virginia Press, 2006), 297–311.

Bellevue Forest Citizens' Association. "History," *Bellevue Forest Blog*, 2014. http://www.bellevueforest.org/about/history/

Berlin, Ira, Barbara J. Fields, Steven F. Miller, Joseph P. Reidy, and Leslie S. Rowland, eds. "The Wartime Genesis of Free Labor, 1861–1865." In *Slaves No More: Three Essays on Emancipation and the Civil War* (Cambridge, United Kingdom: Cambridge University Press, 1992), 77–186.

Best, David, Vivian Bullock, Phyllis Costley, and Mignon Johnson. "Addendum to the Summary of Oral History Transcripts for High View Park (Hall's Hill)," August 9, 1995, Hall's Hill Oral History Project, CLH.

Bestebreurtje, Lindsey. "A View from Hall's Hill: African American Community Development in Arlington." *Arlington Historical Magazine* 15, no. 3 (Oct. 2015): 19–34.

Bestebreurtje, Lindsey. "Beyond the Plantation: Freedmen, Social Experimentation, and African American Community Development in Freedman's Village, 1863–1900." *The Virginia Magazine of History and Biography* 126, no. 3 (2018): 354.

Bird, Berry. "Building Community: Housing for Middle-Class African Americans in Washington, D.C., and Prince George's County, Maryland, 1900–1955." In *Housing Washington: Two Centuries of Residential Development and Planning in the National Capital Area*, edited by Richard Longstreth. Chicago: Center for American Places at Columbia College Chicago, 2010, 61-84.

Birge, Margaret Cooke, and C. B. Rose Jr. "Democratic Politics in the 8th District of Virginia, 1886." *Arlington Historical Magazine* 4, no. 2 (October 1970): 3–21.

Bly, Antonio T. "The Thunder during the Storm-School Desegregation in Norfolk, Virginia, 1957–1959: A Local History" *Journal of Negro Education* 67, no. 2 (Spring 1998): 106–14.

Bobeczko, Laura L. "A Study in Decentralized Living: Parkfairfax, Alexandria, Virginia" *Historic Alexandria Quarterly* 3, no. 6 (Spring 1997): 1–19.

Borchert, James. "Alley Landscapes of Washington, D.C." In *Common Places: Readings in American Vernacular Architecture*, edited by Dell Upon and John Michael Vlach, 281–314. Georgia: University of Georgia Press, 1986.

Brown, Elsa Barkley. "Constructing a Life and a Community: A Partial Story of Maggie Lena Walker" *OAH Magazine of History* 7, no. 4 (Summer 1993): 28–31.

Brown, Elsa Barkley. "Womanist Consciousness: Maggie Lena Walker and the Independent Order of Saint Luke" *Signs* 14, no. 3 (Spring 1989): 610–33.

Brown, Elsa Barkley, and Gregg Kimball. "Mapping the Terrain of Black Richmond," *Journal of Urban History* 21, no. 3 (March 1995): 296–346.

Building Research Advisory Board. "Silver Anniversary" *Journal of Building Research*, Vol. 1 No. 3 (1973): 131–37.

Bunch-Lyone, Beverly, and Nakeina Douglas. "The Falls Church Colored Citizens Protective League and the Establishment of Virginia's First Rural Branch of the NAACP." In *Long is the Way and Hard: One Hundred Years of the NAACP*, edited by Kevern Verney and Lee Sartain Arkansas: University of Arkansas Press, 2009: 89–104.

Burns, John F. "The History of the Washington and Old Dominion Railroad." *Arlington Historical Magazine* 1, no. 1 (October 1957): 32–35.

Campbell, Alison Bauer. "The Road to Integration: Arlington Public Schools 1959–1971." *Arlington Historical Magazine* 10, no. 4 (1996): 27–42.

Carnfield, Jerome, and Marjorie Weber. "Housing of Federal Employees in the Washington (D.C.) Area in May, 1941." *Labor Review* (November 1941): 1–21.

Carroll, Fred. "The Racial Politics of Place: Jim Crow, the New Deal, and Suburban Housing on the Virginia Peninsula." *Journal of Urban History* 40, no. 3 (May 2014): 514–35.

Chishti, Muzaffar, Faye Hipsman, and Isabel Ball. "Fifty Years On, the 1965 Immigration and Nationality Act Continues to Reshape the United States." *The Immigration Policy Institute Policy Beat* (October 2015): 18–28.

Clark, Charles S. "Arlington's Night of Gang Warfare." *Arlington Historical Magazine* 13, no. 4 (October 2008): 5–16.

Clark, Charles S. "The Assassination of an Arlington Nazi." *Arlington Historical Magazine* 13, no. 1 (October 2005): 5–18.

Colean, Miles L. "An Early FHA Experiment." *Mortgage Banker* 38 (May 1978): 86–88.

Covey, Paul. "Notes on Two Arlingtonians: Basil Hall; Robert S. Lacey." *Arlington Historical Magazine*, 2 no. 3 (October 1963): 22–23.

Deines, Ann. "A Survey of Development of Arlington County Virginia, 1940–1965." *Arlington Historical Magazine* 10, no. 3 (October 1995): 55–63.

Dieter, Frank L. "Early Planning Progress in Arlington County, Virginia to 1945." *Arlington Historical Magazine* 3, no. 3 (October 1967).

Domer, Dennis. "Escaping the City: New Deal Housing and Gustave Ring's Garden Apartment Villages [Arlington Village]." In *Urban Forms, Suburban Dreams*, edited by Malcolm Quantrill and Bruce Webb, 65–90. College Station: Texas A&M University Press, 1993.

Doyle, Evelyn R. "Rental Housing in Arlington in General and Colonial Village in Particular." *Arlington Historical Magazine* 6, no. 3 (October 1979): 15–19.

Estabrook, Robert H. "Washington & Old Dominion: Former Interurban in Northern Virginia." *Trains Magazine* (April 1948): 42–46.

Foster, Jack Hamilton. "Crandal Mackey, Crusading Commonwealth's Attorney." *Arlington Historical Magazine* 7, no. 4 (October 1984): 22–30.

Glotzer, Paige. "Exclusion in Arcadia: How Suburban Developers Circulated Ideas about Discrimination, 1890–1950." *Journal of Urban History* 41, no. 3 (May 2015): 479–94.

Guton, Joseph M. "Girl Town: Temporary World War II Housing at Arlington Farms." *Arlington Historical Magazine* 14, no. 3 (October 2011).

Hall, Jacquelyn Dowd. "The Long Civil Rights Movement and the Political Uses of the Past." *Journal of American History* 91, no. 4 (March 2005): 1233–63.

Hannabass, Darline. "Sears Roebuck Houses in Arlington." *Arlington Historical Magazine* 10, no. 1 (October 1993): 7–15.

Hershman, James H., Jr. "Massive Resistance Meets its Match: The Emergence of a Pro-Public School Majority," in *The Moderate's Dilemma: Massive Resistance to School Desegregation in Virginia* edited by Matthew Lassiter and Andrew B. Lewis, 104–33. Charlottesville: University of Virginia Press, 1998.

Holt, Wythe W. "The Virginia Constitutional Convention of 1901–1902: A Reform Movement Which Lacked Substance." *The Virginia Magazine of History and Biography* 76, no. 1 (January 1968): 67–102.

Hornsby, Anne R. "African American Entrepreneurship in Slavery and Freedom." In *A Companion to African American History*, edited by Alton Hornsby Jr., 325–31. Malden, MA: Blackwell Publishing, 2005.

Hurd, William B. "The City of Alexandria and Alexandria (Arlington) County." *Alexandria History* 5 (1983): 3–10.

Jackson, David H., Jr. "The Growth of African American Cultural and Social Institutions." In *A Companion to African American History*, edited by Alton Hornsby Jr., 312–24. Malden, MA: Blackwell Publishing, 2005.

Jackson, Kenneth T. "The Spatial Dimensions of Social Control: Race, Ethnicity, and Government Housing Policy in the United States, 1918–1968." In *Modern Industrial Cities: History, Policy, and Survival*, edited by Bruce M. Stave, 79–129. Beverly Hills, CA: Sage, 1981.

James, Felix. "The Establishment of Freedmen's Village in Arlington, Virginia." *Negro History Bulletin* 33, no. 4 (June 1970): 90–93.

Johnson, Ronald. "From Romantic Suburb to Racial Enclave: LeDroit Park, Washington, D.C., 1880–1920." *Phylon* 45 (1984): 264–70.

Kelley, Robin D. G. "'We Are Not What We Seem': Rethinking Black Working-Class Opposition in the Jim Crow South." *Journal of American History* 80, no. 1 (June 1993): 75–112.

Kinnier, C. L. "The Renaming of Arlington Streets," *Arlington Historical Magazine* 1 no. 3 (October 1959): 41–51.

Korye, William. "Prejudice Knocked the Enemy's Sights Out of Focus in the Private War on Barbara Marx," *Midstream*, September 1, 1956. RG 11: Papers of Edmund C. Fleet, Box 4, File 3, CLH.

Krupsaw, David L. "The Day Nothing Happened." *The Anti-Defamation League Magazine* (February 1959). https://projectdaps.org/exhibits/items/show/daps _exhibit/item/178.

Larman, Michael J. "Why Massive Resistance." In *Massive Resistance: Southern Opposition to the Second Reconstruction*, edited by Clive Webb, 21–38.(Oxford, United Kingdom: Oxford University Press, 2005.

Little, M. Ruth. "The Other Side of the Tracks: The Middle-Class Neighborhood that Jim Crow Built in Early Twentieth Century North Carolina" in *Everyday Landscapes: Perspectives in Vernacular Architecture VII*, edited by Annmarie Adams and Sally McMurry, 268–80. Knoxville: University of Tennessee Press, 1997.

Longstreth, Richard. "The Neighborhood Shopping Center in Washington, D.C., 1930–1941." *Journal of the Society of Architectural Historians* 51, no. 1 (March 1992): 5–34.

Marsh, Margaret. "Reconsidering the Suburbs: An Exploration of Suburban Historiography." *Pennsylvania Magazine of History and Biography* 112, no. 4 (October 1988): 579–605.

McClellan, Laurie. "Land of the Free." *Arlington Magazine* (November–December. 2013).

McClerking, Harwood K., and Eric L. McDaniel. "Belonging and Doing: Political Churches and Black Political Participation." *Political Psychology* 26, no. 5 (October 2005): 721–33.

McKinney, Charles W., Jr., and Rhonda Jones. "Jim Crowed—Emancipation Betrayed: African American Confront the Veil." In *A Companion to African American History*, edited by Alton Hornsby Jr. 271–82. Malden, MA: Blackwell Publishing, 2005.

Meier, August, and Elliott Rudwick. "Negro Boycotts of Segregated Streetcars in Virginia, 1904–1907." *Virginia Magazine of History and Biography* 81, no. 4 (October 1973): 479–87.

Micale, Barbara L. "First Rural NAACP: A Response to Threat of Residential Segregation in Falls Church." *Virginia Tech Research Magazine* (Winter 2009).

Michelotti, Cecilia. "Arlington School Desegregation." *Arlington Historical Magazine* 8, no. 4 (October 1988): 5–20.

Moon, Krystyn R. "The African American Housing Crisis in Alexandria, Virginia, 1930s–1960s." *Virginia Magazine of History and Biography* 124, no. 1 (2016): 28–68.

Morris, James McGrath. "A Chink in the Armor: The Black-Led Struggle for School Desegregation in Arlington, Virginia, and the End of Massive Resistance." *Journal of Policy History* 13, no. 3 (2001): 329–66.

Newman, Robert C. "Eighty Years in a Sears Mail-Order House: The Newmans of Cherrydale." *Arlington Historical Magazine* 8, no. 3 (October 1987): 6–13.

North, William D. "Legal Up-Date." *Realtor Magazine* (September–October 1976), Verlin Smith Collection, VHS.

O'Brien, John T. "Factory, Church, and Community: Blacks in Antebellum Richmond." *Journal of Southern History* 44, no. 4 (November 1978: 509–36.

Orser, Edward. "Secondhand Suburbs: Black Pioneers in Baltimore's Edmondson Village, 1955–1980." *Journal of Urban History* 10, no, 3 (1990): 226–62.

Palmer, Larry. "North Harvard Street: Recollections." *Arlington Historical Magazine* 13, no. 4 (October 2008): 17–28.

Parker, John L. *Henry Wilson's Regiment: History of the Twenty-Second Massachusetts Infantry, the Second Company Sharpshooters, and the Third Light Battery, in the*

War of the Rebellion. (Boston: Regimental Association Press of Rand Avery Co., 1887.

Payne, M. Louise. "Reminiscences of Bancroft's History," *Arlington Historical Magazine* 1, no. 3 (October 1959): 55–60.

Perry, Nancy, Spencer Crew, Nigel M. Waters, "'We didn't have any other place to live': Residential Patterns in Segregated Arlington County, Virginia." *Southern Geographer* 53, no. 4 (Winter 2013): 403–27.

Perry, Nancy, L. Earle Reybold, Nigel Waters. "'Everybody was Looking for a Good Government Job': Occupational Choice during Segregation in Arlington, Virginia." *Journal of Urban History* 40, no. 4 (March 2014): 719–41.

Perry, Nancy, and Nigel M. Waters. "Southern Suburban/Northern City: Black Entrepreneurship in Segregated Arlington County, Virginia." *Urban Geography* 33, no. 5 (2012): 655–74.

Place, Chelsea. "Remembering Freedman's Village." *United States Army: News* (February 28, 2012).

Pratt, Robert A. "New Directions in Virginia's Civil Rights History," *The Virginia Magazine of History and Biography* 104, no. 1 (Winter 1996): 149–56.

Pratt, Sherman. "Capital City and Arlington Boundaries." *Arlington Historical Magazine* 11, no. 2 (October 1998): 37–48.

Pratt, Sherman, "Arlington's At Large Electoral System: A Study of Its History, Strengths, and Weaknesses" *Arlington Historical Magazine* 10, no. 3 (October 1995): 19–36.

Rabinowitz, Howard N. "More Than the Woodward Thesis: Assessing the Strange Career of Jim Crow." *Journal of American History* 75, no. 3 (1988): 842–56.

Reidy, Joseph P. "Coming from the Shadow of the Past: The Transition from Slavery to Freedom at Freedmen's Village, 1863–1900," *Virginia Magazine of History and Biography* 95, no. 4 (October 1987): 403–28.

Research and Records Committee, Arlington Historical Society. "Community Efforts to Improve Schools in Arlington County" *Arlington Historical Magazine* 3, no. 2 (October 1966): 41–46.

Research and Records Committee, Arlington Historical Society. "County Officials in Arlington, 1870–1960." *Arlington Historical Magazine* 3, no. 3 (October 1967): 36–50.

Research and Records Committee, Arlington Historical Society, "Some Black History in Arlington County: A Preliminary Investigation." *Arlington Historical Magazine* 5, no. 1 (October 1973): 11–17.

Rockwell, George, "Rockwell Report," *American Nazi Party Magazine*, 1962. RG 60: Eastman Fenwick Family Papers, Box 2, CLH.

Rose, C. B., Jr. "The 1929 Annexation from Arlington by Alexandria." *Arlington Historical Magazine*, 3, no. 3 (October 1967): 12–18.

Rose, C. B., Jr., "Annexation of a Portion of Arlington County by the City of Alexandria in 1915." *Arlington Historical Magazine* 2, no. 4 (October 1964): 22–36.

Rose, C. B., Jr., "The Boundaries of Arlington" *Arlington Historical Magazine* 1, no. 1 (October 1957): 7–14.

Rose, C. B., Jr. "Civil War Forts in Arlington," *Arlington Historical Magazine* 1, no. 4 (Oct 1960).

Rose, C. B., Jr., "The Map of Arlington in 1878—Places and People." *Arlington Historical Magazine*, 2, no. 2 (October 1962): 17–33.

Rose, C. B., Jr., "Public Schools in Arlington District of Alexandria County Virginia, 1870–1905." *Arlington Historical Magazine* 3, no. 1 (October 1965): 17–39.

Rose, C. B., Jr., "Voting and Elections in Arlington" *Arlington Historical Magazine* 4, no. 4 (October 1972): 13–26.

Rose, Ruth P. "The Beginning of Arlington County's Public Water Supply," *Arlington Historical Magazine*, 6, no. 1 (October 1977):45–54.

Rose, Ruth P. "The Role of Frank Lyon and His Associates in the Early Development of Arlington County." *Arlington Historical Magazine*, 5, no. 4 (October 1976): 46–59.

Rothstein, Ethan. "Second Washington Blvd. Bridge Opens over Columbia Pike." *ARL Now* March 24, 2015. https://www.arlnow.com/2015/03/24/second-washington-blvd-bridge-opens-over-columbia-pike/.

Samuel, Helen E. "History and Development of Arlington Hospital—1934–1970." *Arlington Historical Magazine* 4, no. 2 (October 1970): 22–27.

Schildt, Bobbi. "Aladdin's Lamp: Education in Freedman's Village." *Arlington Historical Magazine* 10, no. 3 (October 1995): 7–18.

Schildt, Roberta. "Freedman's Village: Arlington Virginia 1863–1900." *Arlington Historical Magazine* 7, no. 4 (October 1984): 11–22.

Shafer, Mary Louise. "Recreation in Arlington, 1870–1920." *Arlington Historical Magazine* 6, no. 2 (October 1978): 62–68.

Shelton, Leslie L. "Fire Fighting in Arlington County." Arlington *Historical Magazine* 2, no. 1 (October 1961): 50–57.

Silberman, Barbara Warnick, and Gail H. Baker. "Maywood: Development of a Suburb, Birth of a Neighborhood." *Arlington Historical Magazine* 8, no. 3 (October 1987): 42–59.

Smith, J. Douglas. "'When Reason Collides with Prejudice': Armistead Lloyd Boothe and the Politics of Moderation." In *The Moderate's Dilemma: Massive Resistance to School Desegregation in Virginia*, edited by Matthew Lassiter and Andrew B. Lewis, 22–50. Charlottesville: University of Virginia Press, 1998.

Span, Christopher M., and James D. Anderson, "The Quest for 'Book Learning': African American Education." In *A Companion to African American History*, edited by Alton Hornsby Jr., 306. Malden, MA: Blackwell Publishing, 2005.

Still, Seymour B. "School Buildings in Arlington: 1922–1979." *Arlington Historical Magazine* 7, no. 3 (October 1979): 3–12.

Stowe, Mary E. "An Integrative Force: Arlington's Committee of 100." *National Civic Review* 65, no. 5 (May 1976): 229–35.

Syphax, Evelyn Reid. "William Syphax: Community Leader." *The Arlington Historical Magazine* 6, no. 1 (October 1977): 42–44.

Tasmussen, Wayne D., and Vivian Wiser. "Arlington—An Agricultural Experiment Farm in a Changing Era." *Arlington Historical Magazine* 3, no. 2 (October 1966): 24–30.

Taylor, James. "City Growth and Real Estate Cycles." *Insured Mortgage Portfolio* 2 (July 1937): 24.

Taylor, Scott S. "The View from Hall's Hill: Civil War Letters from Hall's Hill Virginia." *Arlington Historical Magazine* 12, no. 1 (October 1995): 49–60.

Templeman, Eleanor Lee. "Ballston's Beginnings." *Arlington Historical Magazine* 1, no. 3 (October 1959).

Theoharis, Jeanne. "Hidden in Plain Sight: The Civil Rights Movement Outside the South." In *The Myth of Southern Exceptionalism*, edited by Matthew Lassiter and Joseph Crespino, 49–71. Oxford, United Kingdom: Oxford University Press, 2009.

Varaday, David P. "American Residential Segregation: Five Books, Five Viewpoints." *Journal of Urban History* 43, no. 1 (December 2016): 166–71.

Vogel, Sophie B. "Arlington School Closings, 1970–1984 and the Aftermath." *Arlington Historical Magazine* 11, no. 3 (October 1999): 27–42.

Vogel, Sophie B. "The Integration of Reed Elementary School." *Arlington Historical Magazine* 11, no. 1 (October 1997): 33–42.

von Hoffman, Alexander. "The Lost History of Urban Renewal." *Journal of Urbanism: International Research on Placemaking and Urban Sustainability* 1, no. 3 (November 1, 2008): 281–301.

Vosper, Chester H. "Equal Opportunity in Housing: It's the Law." *Realtor Magazine* (July–August 1975), Verlin Smith Collection, VHS.

Walker, Cam. "Corinth: The Story of a Contraband Camp." *Civil War History* 20, no. 1 (March 1974): 5–22.

Wallace, Jerry L. "The Ku Klux Klan in Calvin Coolidge's America." *Calvin Coolidge Memorial Foundation Blog*, July 14, 2014. https://coolidgefoundation.org/blog/the-ku-klux-klan-in-calvin-coolidges-america/.

Wallach, Jessica. "The Loss of a Neighborhood, the Cost of Progress." *The Patch*, October 14, 2011.

Walter, Elizabeth. "The Original Developers of Barcroft." *Arlington Historical Magazine* 12, no. 3 (October 2003): 5–20.

Wamsley, Janet. "The KKK in Arlington in the 1920s." *Arlington Historical Magazine* 10, no. 1 (October 1993): 55–59.

Wise, Donald A. "Bazil Hall of Hall's Hill." *Arlington Historical Magazine* 6, no. 3, (October 1979): 20.

Woods, Louis Lee. "The Federal Home Loan Bank Board, Redlining, and the National Proliferation of Racial Lending Discrimination, 1921–1950." *Journal of Urban History* 38, no. 6 (November 2012): 1036–59.

Books

Allen, James. *Without Sanctuary: Lynching Photography in America*. Santa Fe, NM: Twin Palms Publishers, 2000.

Anderson, James D. *The Education of Blacks in the South, 1860–1935*. Chapel Hill: University of North Carolina Press, 1988.

Anderson, James D. *Literacy and Education in the African American Experience*. Cresskill, NJ: Hampton Press, 1995.

Arlington Historical Society. *Images of America: Arlington*. Arlington, Virginia: Arcadia Publishing, 2000.

Ashmore, Susan Youngblood. *Carry It On: The War on Poverty and the Civil Rights Movement in Alabama, 1964–1972*. Athens: The University of Georgia Press, 2008.

Ball, Frank L. *Mt. Olivet Methodist: Arlington's Pioneer Church*. Arlington, VA: Southern Printing and Lithograph, Inc., 1965.

Berlin, Ira, Joseph P. Reidy, and Leslie S. Rowland. *Freedom: A Documentary History of Emancipation, 1861–1867*. New York: Cambridge University Press, 1982.

Bethel, Elizabeth Rauh. *Promisedland: A Century of Life in a Negro Community*. Philadelphia: Temple University Press, 1981.

Bleser, Carol. *The Promised Land: The History of South Carolina's Land Commission, 1869–1890*. New York: Columbia University Press, 1969.

Blight, David W. *Race and Reunion: The Civil War in American Memory*. Cambridge, MA: Harvard University Press, 2001.

Boston, Thomas D. *Affirmative Action and Black Entrepreneurship*. New York: Routledge, 1999.

Brinkley, David. *Washington Goes to War*. University Park: Pennsylvania State University Press, 1988.

Brown, Canter. *Florida's Black Public Officials, 1867–1924*. Tuscaloosa: University of Alabama Press, 1998.

Brown, Leslie. *Upbuilding Black Durham: Gender, Class and Black Community Development in the Jim Crow South*. Chapel Hill: University of North Carolina Press, 2008.

Brundage, W. Fitzhugh. *Lynching in the New South: Georgia and Virginia: 1880–1930*. Chicago: University of Illinois Press, 1993.

Bullock, Henry. *A History of Negro Education in the South: From 1619 to the Present*. Cambridge, MA: Harvard University Press, 1967.

Butchart, Ronald. *Northern Schools, Southern Blacks, and Reconstruction: Freedmen's Education, 1862–1875*. Westport, CT: Greenwood Press, 1980.

Carroll, Thomas D. *Up on the Hill: An Oral History of the Hall's Hill Neighborhood in Arlington County, Virginia*. Arlington, VA: Arlington County Public Library, 2002.

Chafe, William H. *Civilities and Civil Rights: Greensboro, North Carolina, and the Black Struggle for Freedom*. Oxford, United Kingdom: Oxford University Press, 1980.

Chataigne, J. H. *Chataigne's Alexandria City Directory, 1876–77*. Alexandria, VA: Geo. E. French, J. T. Cox, Booksellers, Stationers, and New Dealers, 1876.

Cimbala, Paul. *Under the Guardianship of the Nation: The Freedmen's Bureau and the Reconstruction of Georgia, 1865–1870*. Athens: University of Georgia Press, 1997.

Clark, Clifford Edward, Jr. *The American Family Home, 1800–1960*. Chapel Hill: University of North Carolina Press, 1986.

Cobb, James Cobb. *The South and America Since World War II*. Oxford, United Kingdom: Oxford University Press, 2010.

Cohen, Lizabeth. *A Consumer's Republic: The Politics of Mass Consumption in Postwar America*. New York: Knopf Doubleday Publishing, 2008.

Collins, Sara, George W. Dodge, Mary Mallen, Deborah L. Powers, William C. Thomas, Joan M. White, *Freedman's Village: Arlington's First Free Neighborhood*. Arlington, VA: The Black Heritage Museum of Arlington County, 2002.

Connerly, Charles E. *The Most Segregated City in America: City Planning and Civil Rights in Birmingham, 1920–1980*. Charlottesville: The University of Virginia Press, 2006.

Connolly, N. D. B. *A World More Concrete: Real Estate and The Remaking of Jim Crow South Florida*. Chicago: University of Chicago Press, 2016.

Cooling, Benjamin Franklin. *Symbol, Sword, and Shield: Defending Washington, D.C. During the Civil War*. Hamden, CT: Archon Books, 1975.

R. Shoppell, *Selected Designs from Shoppell's Modern Houses*. New York: The Cooperative Building Plan Association, Architects, 1890.

Dabney, Virginius. *Virginia: The New Dominion*. Garden City, NJ: Doubleday and Company, Inc., 1971.

Dailey, Jane. *Before Jim Crow: The Politics of Race in Post-Emancipation Virginia.* Chapel Hill: University of North Carolina Press, 2000.

Dittmer, John. *Black Georgia in the Progressive Era, 1900–1920.* Chicago: University of Illinois Press, 1977.

Du Bois, W. E. B. *Black Reconstruction in America.* New York: Oxford University Press, 2014.

Du Bois, W. E. B. "The Conservation of Races." In *The Idea of Race,* edited by Robert Bernasconi and Tommy Lee Lott, 108–17. New York: Hackett, 2000.

Escott, Paul D. *"What Shall We Do with The Negro?": Lincoln, White Racism, and Civil War America.* Charlottesville: University of Virginia Press, 2009.

Eskew, Glenn T. *But for Birmingham: The Local and National Movements in the Civil Rights Struggle.* Chapel Hill: University of North Carolina Press, 1997.

Foltz, El Bie. *The Federal Service as Career.* Los Angeles: Hard Press Publishing, 1909, 2014.

Foner, Eric. *A Short History of Reconstruction, 1863–1877.* New York: Harper and Row, 1990.

Ford, Brian H., ed. *Colonial Village: The Cultural and Architectural Heritage.* Arlington, VA: Colonial Village Preservation Committee, 1978.

Ford, Lacy K. *Deliver Us from Evil: The Slavery Question in the Old South.* Oxford, United Kingdom: Oxford University Press, 2009.

Frazier, E. Franklin. *The Negro Church in America.* New York: Schocken Books, 1974.

Friedman, Andrew Friedman. *Covert Capital: Landscapes of Denial and the Making of the US Empire in the Suburbs of Northern Virginia.* Berkeley: University of California Press, 2013.

Gates, Robbins. *The Making of Massive Resistance: Virginia's Politics of Public School Desegregation, 1954–1956.* Chapel Hill: University of North Carolina Press, 1962).

Gatewood, Willard. *Aristocrats of Color: The Black Elite, 1880–1920.* Fayetteville: University of Arkansas Press, 1990.

Genovese, Eugene D. *Roll, Jordan, Roll: The World the Slaves Made.* New York: Vintage Press, 1976.

Gillette, William. *Retreat from Reconstruction, 1869–1879.* Baton Rouge: Louisiana State University Press, 1979.

Gilmore, Glenda Elizabeth. *Gender and Jim Crow: Women and the Politics of White Supremacy in North Carolina, 1896–1920.* Chapel Hill: University of North Carolina Press, 1996.

Gilmore, Matthew. *Historic Photos of Arlington County.* Nashville, Tennessee: Turner Publishing Company, 2007.

Green, Constance McLaughlin. *Washington: Village and Capital, 1800–1878.* Princeton, NJ: Princeton University Press, 1962.

Gregory, James N. *The Southern Diaspora: How the Great Migrations of Black and White Southerners Transformed America.* Chapel Hill: University of North Carolina Press, 2005.

Gutman, Herbert. *The Black Family in Slavery and Freedom, 1750–1925.* New York: Pantheon Books, 1976.

Hahn, Stephen. *A Nation Under Our Feet: Black Political Struggles in the Rural South from Slavery to the Great Migration.* Cambridge, MA: Harvard University Press, 2003.

Hanchett, Thomas. *Sorting Out the New South City: Race, Class, and Urban Development in Charlotte, 1875–1975*. Chapel Hill: University of North Carolina Press, 1998.

Hartmann, Susan M. *The Home Front and Beyond: American Women in the 1940s*. Boston: Twayne Publishers, 1982.

Hawkins, Walter L. *Black American Military Leaders: A Biographical Dictionary*. Jefferson, NC: McFarland & Co., Inc, 2007.

Higginbotham, Evelyn Brooks. *Righteous Discontent*. Cambridge, MA: Harvard University Press, 1993.

Hine, Darlene Clark, William C. Hine, Stanley C. Harrold. *The African American Odyssey*, 6th ed. London: Pearson, 2000.

Hockett, Jeffrey D. *A Storm Over This Court: Law, Politics, and Supreme Court Decision Making in* Brown v. Board of Education. Charlottesville: University of Virginia Press, 2013.

Hofstadter, Richard. *The Age of Reform*. New York: Vintage Books, 1955.

Holm, Jeanne M., and Judith Bellafaire. *In Defense of a Nation: Servicewomen in World War II*. Arlington, Virginia: Vandamere Press, 1998.

Hunt, Martin K., and Jacqueline E. Hunt. *The History of Black Business: The Coming of America's Largest African American Owned Businesses*. Chicago: Knowledge Express Company, 1999.

Hunter, Tera W. *To 'Joy My Freedom: Southern Black Women's Lives and Labors After the Civil War*. Cambridge, MA: Harvard University Press, 1997.

Jackson, David. *A Chief Lieutenant of the Tuskegee Machine: Charles Banks of Mississippi*. Gainesville: University Press of Florida, 2002.

Jackson, Kenneth T. *Crabgrass Frontier: The Suburbanization of the United States*. Oxford, United Kingdom: Oxford University Press, 1985.

Jalloh, Alusine, and Toyin Falola. *Black Business and Economic Power*. New York: University of Rochester Press, 2002.

John R. Neff. *Honoring the Civil War Dead: Commemoration and the Problem of Reconciliation*. Lawrence: University Press of Kansas, 2005.

Jones, Jacqueline. *Labor of Love, Labor of Sorrow: Black Women, Work, and the Family, from Slavery to Present*. New York: Basic Books, 1995.

Jones, Jacqueline. *Soldiers of Light and Love: Northern Teachers and Georgia Blacks*. Athens: University of Georgia Press, 1992.

Junkin, William Sumner, and Minnie Wyatt Junkin. *The Henckel Family Genealogy, 1500–1960*. Spokane, Washington: CW Hill Printing Co., 1964.

Kaye, Anthony E. *Joining Places: Slave Neighborhoods in the Old South*. Chapel Hill: University of North Carolina Press, 2009.

Kelley, Robin. *Hammer and Hoe: Alabama Communists During the Great Depression*. Chapel Hill: University of North Carolina Press, 1990.

Kelley, Robin. *Race Rebels: Culture, Politics, and the Black Working-Class*. New York: Free Press, 1996.

King, Thomas F. *Cultural Resource: Law and Practice*, 2nd ed. New York: Altamira Press, 2004.

Korstad, Robert. *Civil Rights Unionism: Tobacco Workers and the Struggle for Democracy in the Mid-20th Century South*. Chapel Hill: University of North Carolina Press, 2003.

Krugler, David F. *1919, The Year of Racial Violence: How African Americans Fought Back*. Cambridge, United Kingdom: Cambridge University Press, 2014.

Kruse, Kevin M. *White Flight: Atlanta and the Making of Modern Conservatism.* Princeton, NJ: Princeton University Press, 2005.

Kruse, Kevin M., and Thomas J. Sugrue, editors. *The New Suburban History.* Chicago: University of Chicago Press, 2006.

Lands, LeeAnn. *The Culture of Property: Race, Class, and Housing Landscapes in Atlanta, 1880–1950.* Athens: University of Georgia Press, 2009.

Lassiter, Matthew, and Andrew B. Lewis. *The Moderate's Dilemma: Massive Resistance to School Desegregation in Virginia.* Charlottesville: University of Virginia Press, 1998.

Lee, Dorothy Ellis. *A History of Arlington County, Virginia.* Richmond, Virginia: The Dietz Press, Inc., 1946.

Leloudis, James L. *Schooling the New South: Pedagogy, Self, and Society in North Carolina 1880–1920.* Chapel Hill: University of North Carolina Press, 1996.

Lincoln, C. Eric, and Lawrence H. Mamiya. *The Black Church in the African American Experience.* Durham, NC: Duke University Press, 1990.

Link, William A. *The Paradox of Southern Progressivism, 1880–1930.* Chapel Hill: University of North Carolina Press, 1997.

Litwack, Leon. *Trouble in Mind.* New York: Vintage Press, 1998.

Longstreth, Richard, editor. *Housing Washington: Two Centuries of Residential Development and Planning in the National Capital Area.* Chicago: Center for American Places at Columbia College Chicago, 2010.

Love, Spencie. *One Blood: The Death and Resurrections of Charles Drew.* Chapel Hill: University of North Carolina Press, 1996.

Mackey, Crandal. *A Brief History of Alexandria County, Virginia.* Falls Church, VA: Newell Printing Co., 1907. https://archive.org/details/briefhistoryofal00alex.

MacLean, Nancy. *Behind the Mask of Chivalry: The Making of the Second Ku Klux Klan.* New York: Oxford University Press, 1994.

Masur, Kate. *An Example for All the Land: Emancipation and Struggle Over Equality in Washington, D.C.* Chapel Hill: University of North Carolina Press, 2010.

McGerr, Michael. *A Fierce Discontent: The Rise and Fall of the Progressive Movement in American, 1870–1920.* Oxford, United Kingdom: Oxford University Press, 2003.

McKee, Elmore M. The People Act: Stories of How Americans Are Coming Together to Deal With Their Community Problems. New York: Harper and Brothers, 1955.

Merriken, John E. *Old Dominion Trolley Too: A History of the Mount Vernon Line.* Dallas, TX: Taylor Publishing Company, 1987.

Morris, Robert Charles. *The Freedman Record, Vol. 1.* New York: AMS Press, 1980.

Mundy, Liza. *Code Girls: The Untold Story of the American Women Code Breakers of World War II.* New York: Hachette Books, 2017.

Muse, Benjamin. *Virginia's Massive Resistance.* Bloomington: Indiana University Press, 1961.

Netherton, Nan, and Ross Netherton. *Arlington County in Virginia: A Pictorial History.* Norfolk, Virginia: Donning Company Publishers, 1987.

Painter, Nell Irvin. *The Narrative of Hosea Hudson: His Life as a Negro Communist in the South.* Cambridge, MA: Harvard University Press, 1979.

Patterson, James T. Brown v. Board of Education: *A Civil Rights Milestone and Its Troubled Legacy.* London: Oxford University Press, 2002.

Payne, Charles M. "A Women's War." In *I've Got The Light Of Freedom: The Organizing Tradition And The Mississippi Freedom Struggle*, 265–83. Los Angeles: University of California Press, 2007.

Poole, Robert M. *On Hallowed Ground: The Story of Arlington National Cemetery.* New York: Walker Publishing Company, 2009.

Pope, Michael Lee. *Shotgun Justice: One Prosecutor's Crusade Against Crime and Corruption in Alexandria and Arlington.* Charleston, SC: The History Press, 2012.

Provine, Dorothy S. *Alexandria County, Virginia Free Negro Registers 1797–1861.* Bowie, MD: Heritage Books, 1990.

Rabinowitz, Howard N. *Race Relations in the Urban South, 1865–1890.* Athens: University of Georgia Press, 1978.

Radford, Gail. *Modern Housing for America: Policy Struggles in the New Deal Era.* Chicago: University of Chicago Press, 1996.

Richardson, Selden. *Built by Blacks: African American Architecture and Neighborhoods in Richmond, Virginia.* Richmond, Virginia: The Deitz Press, 2007.

Rose, C. B. *Arlington County Virginia: A History.* (Arlington, VA: The Arlington Historical Society, 1976.

Rose, Willie Lee. *Rehearsal for Reconstruction: The Port Royal Experiment.* Athens: University of Georgia Press, 1964.

Rosengarten, Theodore. *All God's Dangers: The Life of Nate Shaw.* Chicago: University of Chicago Press, 1974.

Schrag, Zachary M. *The Great Society Subway: A History of the Washington Metro.* Baltimore: Johns Hopkins University Press, 2006.

Schwarz, Jordan A. *The New Dealers: Power Politics in the Age of Roosevelt.* New York: Vintage Books, 1993.

Sears, Roebuck & Co. *Book of Modern Homes.* Chicago: Skyhorse Publishing, 1908.

Self, Robert O. *American Babylon: Race and Struggle for Postwar Oakland.* Princeton, NJ: Princeton University Press, 2003.

Sharpless, Rebecca. *Cooking in Other Women's Kitchens: Domestic Workers in the South, 1865–1960.* Chapel Hill: University of North Carolina Press, 2010.

Sides, Josh. *LA City Limits: African American Los Angeles from the Great Depression to the Present.* Los Angeles: University of California Press, 2003.

Smith, Douglas L. *The New Deal in the Urban South.* Baton Rouge: Louisiana State University Press, 1988.

Smith, Preston H. II. *Racial Democracy and the Black Metropolis: Housing Policy in Postwar Chicago.* Minneapolis: University of Minnesota Press, 2012.

Stanford, E. Peril, Suburban Black Elderly. (California: Hong, 1978).

Stephenson, Katherine Cole, and H. Ward Jaindl. *Houses by Mail: A Guide to Houses from Sears, Roebuck, and Company.* New York: John Wiley & Sons. 1986.

Stephenson, Richard W. The Cartography of Northern Virginia: Facsimile Reproductions of Maps Dating From 1608 to 1915. Fairfax, VA: History and Archaeology Section, Office of Comprehensive Planning, 1981.

Sterner, Richard. *The Negro's Share: A Study of Income, Consumption, Housing and Public Assistance.* Westport, CT: Negro Universities Press, 1971.

Stile, John R. *Borderland: Origins of the American Suburb, 1820–1939.* New Haven, CT: Yale University Press, 1988.

Sugrue, Thomas J. *Sweet Land of Liberty.* New York: Random House, 2008.

Sweig, Donald. *Registrations of Free Negroes, Book 2.* Fairfax, VA: Fairfax Historical Commission, 1977.

Taylor, Alfred O., Jr. *Bridge Builders of Nauck/Green Valley: Past and Present.* Pittsburgh, PA: Dorrance Publishing, 2015.

Taylor, Quintard. *In Search of the Racial Frontier: African Americans in the American West 1528–1990.* New York: W. W. Norton & Co., 1998.

Templeman, Eleanor Lee. *Arlington Heritage: Vignettes of a Virginia County.* Self-published: 1959. https://arlingtonhistoricalsociety.org/product/arlington-heritage-vignettes-of-a-virginia-county/.

Todd, Gwendolyn P. *Innovation and Growth in an African American Owned Business.* London: Routledge, 1996.

US Pharmacopoeia Convention. *Pharmacopeia of the United States.* Philadelphia: Author, 1905.

Vogel, Steve. *The Pentagon: A History—The Untold Story of the Wartime Race to Build the Pentagon, and to Restore It Sixty Years Later.* New York: Random House, 2007.

Walker, Julie. *The History of Black Business In America: Capitalism, Race, and Entrepreneurship.* Chapel Hill: University of North Carolina, 1998.

Wallenstein, Peter. *Blue Laws and Black Codes: Conflict, Courts, and Change in Twentieth Century Virginia.* Charlottesville: University of Virginia Press, 2004.

Walter, Elizabeth J. *Barcroft: The Beginnings of a Suburban Neighborhood.* Fairfax, VA: George Mason University Press, 2002.

Weaver, Robert C. *The Negro Ghetto.* New York: Harcourt, Brace, 1948.

Welke, Barbara Young. *Recasting American Liberty: Gender, Race, Law, and the Railroad Revolution, 1865–1920.* Cambridge, United Kingdom: Cambridge University Press, 2001. p 33.

White, Deborah Gray. *Too Heavy a Load: Black Women in Defense of Themselves, 1894–1994.* New York: W.W. Norton and Company, 1999.

Wiese, Andrew. *Places of Their Own: African American Suburbanization in the Twentieth Century.* Chicago: University of Chicago Press, 2004.

Williams, Heather. *Self-Taught: African American Education in Slavery and Freedom.* Chapel Hill: University of North Carolina Press, 2005.

Wilson, William H. *The City Beautiful Movement: Creating the North American Landscape.* Baltimore: Johns Hopkins University Press, 1994.

Wood, Amy Louise. *Lynching and Spectacle: Witnessing Racial Violence in America 1890–1940.* Chapel Hill: University of North Carolina Press, 2009.

Woodward, C. Vann. *The Origins of the New South, 1877–1913.* Baton Rouge: Louisiana State University Press, 1972.

Woodward, C. Vann. *The Strange Career of Jim Crow.* Oxford: Oxford University Press, 1955.

Yellin, Eric S. *Racism in the Nation's Service: Government Workers and the Color Line in Woodrow Wilson's America.* Chapel Hill: University of North Carolina Press, 2013.

Dissertations and Theses

James, Felix. "Freedman's Village, Arlington, Virginia: A History." Master's thesis, Howard University, 1967.

Perry, Nancy. "The Influence of Geography on the Lives of African American Residents of Arlington County, Virginia During Segregation." Doctoral dissertation, George Mason University, 2013.

Index